All Things in the

Bible

An Encyclopedia of the Biblical World

Volume 1

A–L

Nancy M. Tischler

Ellen Johnston McHenry, Illustrator

Greenwood Press
Westport, Connecticut • London

Library of Congress Cataloging-in-Publication Data

Tischler, Nancy Marie Patterson.
　　All things in the Bible / by Nancy M. Tischler ; Ellen Johnston McHenry, illustrator.
　　　p.　cm.
　　Includes bibliographical references and index.
　　ISBN: 0–313–33082–4 (set: alk. paper)—ISBN 0–313–33083–2 (Vol. 1: alk. paper)—
　ISBN 0–313–33084–0 (Vol. 2: alk. paper)
　　1. Bible—Encyclopedias.　I. Title.
　BS440.T57　2006
　220.3—dc22　　　2005034355

British Library Cataloguing in Publication Data is available.

Library of Congress Catalog Card Number: 2005034355
ISBN: 0–313–33082–4 (set)
　　　　0–313–33083–2 (Vol. 1)
　　　　0–313–33084–0 (Vol. 2)
ISSN:

First published in 2006

Greenwood Press, 88 Post Road West, Westport, CT 06881
An imprint of Greenwood Publishing Group, Inc.
www.greenwood.com

Printed in the United States of America

The paper used in this book complies with the
Permanent Paper Standard issued by the National
Information Standards Organization (Z39.48–1984).

10　9　8　7　6　5　4　3　2　1

For Merle

Contents

Preface

The Holy Bible is rooted in fact, in the common life of the people. The words of Scripture are thick with imagery drawn from everyday life: the voice of the turtledove in spring, the wondrous flight of the eagle in the air, the sturdy industry of the ant. Although the Bible reaches through time into eternity, from life on earth to mansions in Heaven, yet it is firmly rooted in things, people, and places. The Hebrews were a people whose way of thinking was concrete and vivid, filled with insights from the world around them. They were also a people with a genius for metaphor, seeing transcendent meanings behind simple things.

Their history, that great drama of God's love of his creation, their disobedience and suffering, their redemption and eternal hope, is narrated through a series of "books." The Bible is this collection of poetry, stories, chronicles, proverbs, and prophesies that form their grand epic. To visualize the context in which the stories unfold and to understand the nuances of the prophetic words in Scripture, the reader must have a wide and deep knowledge of the "things" that were the everyday stuff of the ancient world.

"Things"(as defined for the purposes of this study) need not be inanimate objects: they can be animals, concepts, titles, or historical events. The term *things* is used here to refer to groups of people (such as professions, nationalities), commonly referenced cultures and places (such as Egypt, Galilee), theological constructs (such as the Fall of Man, the Resurrection), events and activities (festivals, the Great Flood), and pagan gods (Dagon, Asherah). They are the common reference points among the people who walk through the pages of Scripture.

This journey included the tending of sheep, the mending of coats, the selling of grain, and the swaddling of newborn babes. The Jews and Christians were also intensely aware of the neighboring peoples who threatened Israel's existence or martyred the early Christians. The life presented in Scripture is full of kings and judges, priests and prophets, whose roles were fully understood by the community around them. The Jews believed that their history was the story of God's covenant with them involving the call of the Patriarchs, the Egyptian captivity, the miraculous Exodus, the battles with the indigenous people of Canaan and with the Philistines, the many invaders, the Exile, the return—all watershed events in Israel's history. It is clearly impossible to chronicle every thing, every group, every event, but this study is an effort to capture those that appear most frequently in Scripture in both the Old and New Testaments.

This book, which is a compilation of ideas and facts from hundreds of sources, is designed as a reference tool for the lay reader of Scripture. It has little of the scholarly detail and debate that advanced theological students would demand, nor the discussions of derivations from original languages that they would expect in their research. It is for those "common readers" who know something of Scripture, wonder about details and ideas, and are searching for fuller understanding.

The book is organized alphabetically, with considerable cross-referencing. If items are not in the Contents, the reader should search the Index at the back of the second volume. Each entry has selected Bible sources, etymology (if possible and helpful), scholarly commentary, archaeological detail (when relevant), and occasional references regarding later influences on intellectual, artistic, or religious history. If the item has symbolic implications, those also appear in the entry. The cross-references are in bold type and are also listed after the entry. The bibliographical references are included in the text and in the concluding section of the entry. There is also a selected bibliography at the end of the second volume. These are by no means exhaustive. Scholarly studies of almost every one of these 200 plus entries are available in theological libraries and often on the Internet.

In a few cases, the listings are clustered. Under *Law* or *Cloth* or *Clothing,* the related items appear one after another for more efficient use of the material. In some cases, a drawing appeared necessary for better explanation of the process or the object.

I owe my deepest thanks to Ellen McHenry and her assistants—Andrew McHenry, Hannah McHenry, Levi Staver, and Monica Houston—who supplied these beautifully drawn and carefully researched illustrations and maps that are scattered through both volumes. I also owe Jean Sherman a debt of gratitude for her careful, thoughtful, and tireless proofreading of these two volumes to ensure that they are coherent and clear.

We all hope that this proves a handy resource for readers of Scripture, who will gain a richer understanding of vineyards and funerals, weddings and hospitality, Pharisees and Sadducees, kings and shepherds as a result of using these volumes.

Nancy Tischler

Alphabetical List of Entries

Guide to Related Topics

Agriculture

Agriculture
Chaff
Goad
Grains
Insects
Olives, Olive Oil, Olive Trees
Olive Press
Ox, Oxen
Plagues
Plants
Plow
Sheepfold
Threshing, Threshing Floor
Trees
Vineyards
Watchtower
Winepress, Wine-making
Yoke

Animals

Animals
Behemoth, Leviathan
Birds
Blood
Camel
Dogs
Donkey, Ass
Fish
Goats
Horse
Hunting
Ox, oxen
Serpent
Sheep
Swine, Pigs

Arts and Crafts

Art: Christian
Art: Jewish
Cosmetics, Ornamentation
Dance
Gemstones
Ivory
Jewelry
Leather
Metal and Mines
Metal: Copper and Bronze
Metal: Gold
Metal: Iron
Metal: Silver
Music

Blessing
Candle, Candlestick
Circumcision
Divorce
Education
Family
Husband and Wife
King's Household
Marriage
Meals
Weddings
Women
Work: Men's
Work: Women's

Food

Bees, Honey
Bread
Clean, Unclean
Cooking, Cooking Utensils
Fast, Fasting
Festivals
Fish
Food
Grain
Meals
Wine

Governance

Court Officials
Covenant
Government, Civil
  Authority
Kings
Taxes, Tithes, Tributes

Health

Clean, Unclean
Disease
Illness
Physicians
Plagues

Housing, Furnishings, Supplies—Sacred and Profane

Bricks, Bricklayers
Candle, Candlestick
Carpenters, Carpentry
Caves
Cistern
Fortifications, Fortified
  Cities, Fortresses
Furnishings, Household
Gardens
Gate
Houses
Inns
Lamp
Palaces
Synagogue
Tabernacle
Temple
Tents
Throne

Insects

Bees, Honey
Insects
Locusts

Law

Adoption
Betrothal
Birth
Birthright
Blasphemy
Cities of Refuge
Clean, Unclean
Court Officials
Covenant
Crucifixion, Cross
Divorce
Inheritance
Judges

Law
Law: Civil and Criminal
Law: Dietary
Law: Property
Punishments
Trial by Ordeal
Trials, Courts

Literary Forms
Epistles
Gospel, Gospels
Lamentations
Parable
Poetry
Prayer
Proverbs
Psalms
Song
Writing and Reading
Writing Materials

Neighboring Peoples
Ammon, Ammonites
Amorites
Assyria, Assyrians
Babylon, Babylonia
Canaan, Canaanites
Edom, Edomites
Egypt, Egyptians
Enemies
Hittites
Kenites
Midian, Midianites
Moab, Moabites
Philistines
Rome, Romans

Palestine
Canaan, Canaanites
Climate
Geography

Philistines
Weather
Wells

Professions
Bricks, Bricklayers
Carpenters, Carpentry
Fishermen, Fishing
Hunting
Metalsmiths
Judges
Leather
Money Changers
Physicians
Potters and
  Pottery-Making
Prophet
Shepherds
Stonemasons
Tax Collector
Work: Men's
Work: Women's

Religion of Jews and Christians
Aaron's Rod
Abomination
Alms, Almsgiving
Alpha and Omega
Altar
Amen
Anathema
Angels
Annunciation
Anointing
Antichrist
Apocalypse, Apocalyptic
  Literature
Apocrypha
Ark of the Covenant
Atonement, Day of
Baptism
Beatitudes

Birthright
Blasphemy
Blessing
Blood
Bread
Candle, Candlestick
Cherub, Cherubim
Circumcision
Covenant
Crucifixion, Cross
Curse
Day of Atonement
Day of Judgment, Day of
  the Lord
Demons
Fast, Fasting
Festivals
Holy Spirit, Holy Ghost
Hypocrite
Incarnation
Incense
Lamp
Lord's Prayer
Lord's Supper, Mass,
  Eucharist, Communion
Messiah
New Moon, Festival of the
Oaths
Offerings
Ointment
Passover, or the Feast of
  Unleavened Bread
Pentecost or the Day of
  the First Fruits
Prayer
Purim
Resurrection
Sabbath
Sabbatical
Sacrifice
Sanctuary
Sin
Urim and Thummim,
  Casting of Lots

Religions of Others

Asherah, Ashtoreth,
  Ashtaroth
Baal, Baalim
Babel, Tower of
Chemosh
Cherub, Cherubim
Dagon
Idols, Idolatry
Moloch

Religious People, Groups

Apostle
Christian
Church
Disciples
Essenes
Evangelists
Gnostics
Nazarites
Pharisees
Priest, High Priest
Rabbi
Sadducees
Sanhedrin
Scribes
Slavery, laws
Tribes of Israel
Zealots

Trade

Measures
Seals
Trade

Travel

Ark
Boats and Ships
Camel

Abbreviations

Translations of the Bible
English Standard Version—ESV
King James Version—KJV
New International Version—NIV
New Revised Standard Version—NRSV
Revised Standard Version—RSV

Books of the Bible—Old Testament
Genesis	Gen.
Exodus	Exod.
Leviticus	Lev.
Numbers	Num.
Deuteronomy	Deut.
Joshua	Josh.
Judges	Judg.
Ruth	Ruth
1 Samuel	1 Sam.
2 Samuel	2 Sam.
1 Kings	1 Kings
2 Kings	2 Kings
1 Chronicles	1 Chron.

2 Chronicles	2 Chron.
Ezra	Ezra
Nehemiah	Neh.
Esther	Esther
Job	Job
Psalms	Ps. (*pl.* Pss.)
Proverbs	Prov.
Ecclesiastes	Eccles.
Song of Solomon	Song of Sol.
Isaiah	Isa.
Jeremiah	Jer.
Lamentations	Lam.
Ezekiel	Ezek.
Daniel	Dan.
Hosea	Hos.
Joel	Joel
Amos	Amos
Obadiah	Obad.
Jonah	Jon.
Micah	Mic.
Nahum	Nah.
Habakkuk	Hab.
Zephaniah	Zeph.
Haggai	Hag.
Zechariah	Zech.
Malachi	Mal.

New Testament

Matthew	Matt.
Mark	Mark
Luke	Luke
John	John
Acts of the Apostles	Acts
Romans	Rom.
1 Corinthians	1 Cor.
2 Corinthians	2 Cor.
Galatians	Gal.

Ephesians	Eph.
Philippians	Phil.
Colossians	Col.
1 Thessalonians	1 Thess.
2 Thessalonians	2 Thess.
1 Timothy	1 Tim.
2 Timothy	2 Tim.
Titus	Titus
Philemon	Philem.
Hebrews	Heb.
James	James
1 Peter	1 Pet.
2 Peter	2 Pet.
1 John	1 John
2 John	2 John
3 John	3 John
Jude	Jude
Revelation	Rev.
or Apocalypse	Apoc.

Apocrypha

1 Esdras	1 Esd.
2 Esdras	2 Esd.
Tobit	Tob.
Judith	Jth.
The Rest of Esther	Rest of Esther
The Wisdom of Solomon	Wisd of Sol.
Ecclesiasticus	Ecclus.
Baruch	Bar.
The Song of the Three Holy Children	Song of Three Children
Susanna	Sus.
Bel and the Dragon	Bel and Dragon
Prayer of Manasses *or* Manasseh	Pr. of Man.
1 Maccabees	1 Macc.
2 Maccabees	2 Macc.

A

Aaron's Rod

(Exod. 4:14; Num. 17:1.) Aaron, the older brother of Moses, became the first high priest of the Israelites. Each tribal leader carried a rod as a **scepter**, marking his authority. When Aaron was confronted with the rebellion of Korah and his associates, who challenged the tribe of Levi's right to the priestly function, the leader of each of the **Tribes of Israel** had his name written on his rod. The 12 rods were then placed in the Tent of Meeting (the **Tabernacle**) in front of the **Ark of the Covenant**. The next morning, Aaron's rod had flowered, putting forth buds, blossoms, and ripe almonds. This was interpreted as evidence that God had chosen Aaron for his priestly office and that God was present in their midst. Hebrews 9:4 indicates that this rod was kept with the Tablets of the Covenant inside the Ark.

The budding almond became a rich symbol for the Jews. During the brief time they had their own coinage, it was stamped on Jewish coins. It was interpreted by later commentators as a sign of God's election. It was also used to fortify the concept of the divine right of **kings**. *See also* Kings; Priest, High Priest; Shepherds; Scepter; Tabernacle.

Further Reading

Figgis, John. *The Divine Right of Kings.* Gloucester, Mass.: P. Smith, 1970. Gillespie, George. *Aaron's Rod Blossoming.* London: Richard Whitaker, 1670. Lawrence, David H. *Aaron's Rod.* New York: Thomas Selzer, 1922. Wiesel, Elie. "Aaron: The Teflon Kid," in *Biblical Archaeology,* August 1998.

Ablution. *See* Bath, Bathing

Abomination

(Lev. 11; 1 Kings 11:5; Dan. 9:27, 11:31, 12:11; Matt. 24:15; Mark 13:14; Rev. 17:5) Anyone or anything that is offensive to God and his plan for the righteous way of life, including eating **unclean** foods, engaging in forbidden sexual activities, or the worship of **idols**, was considered *abominable.* It was a term frequently used in connection with Israel's enemies and their pagan worship practices, and it was also used for any Israelite who approached the worship of God with the wrong spirit. For example, the writer of Proverbs (26:25) noted that the fool has "seven abominations in his heart."

Daniel used the term *abomination of desolation*, perhaps referring to the profanation of the **Temple** by Antiochus Epiphanes, who set up an **altar** to Zeus there and sacrificed unclean animals, including a pig. Jesus used the term to signal the beginning of the Messianic Age. In Revelation, John saw printed on the forehead of the great whore of **Babylon**: "Mystery, Babylon the Great, the mother of harlots and abominations of the earth." *See also* Altar; Clean, Unclean; Food; Sacrifice.

Further Reading

Miller, Madeleine S. and J. Lane Miller. "Abomination," in *Harper's Bible Dictionary*. New York: Harper and Row, 1961.

Abraham's Bosom

(Luke 16:22) *Abraham's bosom* was another term for death and the life thereafter. Jesus used the term *Abraham's bosom* in his **parable** of the Rich Man and Lazarus. After his death, Lazarus was carried by **angels** to Abraham's bosom, that is, to be with Abraham in **Heaven**. Considering the manner in which guests were seated at feasts in New Testament times, this may refer to sitting or reclining next to Abraham at the heavenly feast. The same term—"leaning on Jesus's bosom"—was used in reference to the place at the **Last Supper** of the beloved Disciple John.

In Renaissance literature, the term became a poetic means of describing death and was used by Shakespeare and others. Among African Americans, the term became popular as a comforting concept of the **afterlife**. Paul Green's famous play, *In Abraham's Bosom*, is one of the fullest uses of the image in American literature. *See also* Afterlife; Meals.

Further Reading

Green, Paul. *In Abraham's Bosom*. New York: R. M. McBride, 1927.

Abyss

(Rom. 10:7; Rev. 9:11, 17:8, 20:1–3) Also called the "bottomless pit" or "the deep," *abyss* sometimes refers to the primordial **waters** at the **Creation**, particularly the waters under the earth. More specifically, it seems to represent the realm of the dead in the underworld, the dwelling place of evil spirits under Satan or Apollyon. *See also* Afterlife; Creation.

Further Reading

Pleins, David J. *When the Great Abyss Opened: Classic and Contemporary Readings of Noah's Flood*. New York: Oxford University Press, 2003. Stoops, Robert.

"Abyss," in *The Oxford Companion to the Bible*. New York: Oxford University Press, 1993.

Adoption

(Gen. 15:3, 16:1–4, 30:1–13; Ruth 4:16; Esther 2:7; 1 Kings 19:19–21; Rom. 8:15, 9:4; Eph. 1:5) Although the Hebrews had no technical term for adoption, the practice of taking a person who was not a blood descendant as a legal heir undoubtedly existed from earliest times, apparently appropriating the custom current in much of the Middle East. For example, Abraham considered his servant Eliezer to be his heir if he should die without having a natural son. Some believe that Laban considered Jacob his adopted son and heir because of his long years of work on his land and his **marriage** to Laban's daughters. The theft of the household gods, which usually signified rights to the legacy, seems to reinforce this supposition. When Jacob traveled to **Egypt** and met Joseph's two sons for the first time, he adopted them as his own, dividing Joseph's portion of his land to Ephraim and Manasseh. Moses was probably adopted by the Pharaoh's daughter, following Egyptian legal practices.

Practices such as polygamy and levirate marriage provided for the orderly distribution of property within the tribe. Other terms seem to imply a form of adoption or at least protection. For example, Ruth placed her child on Naomi's breast, apparently allowing her to be the child's nurse. Some believe that, because Ruth was a Moabite, her effort to seek refuge under the wings of the Lord was a desire to be adopted into the Israelite community. In the case of Elijah and Elisha, the casting of the mantle on the younger prophet appears to designate him as Elijah's spiritual heir.

Theologically, the formula for adoption in Psalm 2:7, "You are my son," reappears in the New Testament. Paul used it to signify God's election of his chosen people: The natural or physical sonship might belong to the descendants of Abraham, but God chose to bless the gentiles as well through their faith in his Son, redeeming them from "slavery to sonship." *See also* Law.

Adultery. *See Law*

Afterlife

(Gen. 3:22; Exod. 20:12; Ps. 72:16; Job 19:25–26; Eccles. 9:5; John 11:17, 25) For most of the Old Testament period, the Hebrews believed that humankind was created to be immortal, but lost eternal life through sin. Although, when a person had reached a ripe old age, death itself was regarded as a sleep, a rest, and a blessing, early death was seen as a dreadful misfortune. Without any sense of a beatific notion of the afterlife for anyone, the Hebrews thought of death as a "huge silence." The dead could "neither help nor be helped" (Alan F. Segal 2004, 121–123, 129).

Some believed that a long life was ensured by proper concern for one's parents. The custom of burying family members in a shared tomb suggests the continuing relationship of families with their ancestors, perhaps even a "cult of the dead." The commandment to "honor" father and mother was taken to mean that the parents were to be buried properly so that the next generation would "long endure on the land" that God had given them.

A certain kind of afterlife might be implied by some of the **grave** sites—like the one at Dothan, north of Shechem, in which the remains of 288 individuals have been found in a rock-cut family tomb. The corpses were placed in an extended position on the floor along with some 3,000 artifacts. These bits of everyday life were probably intended to serve the needs of the deceased in the next world, suggesting a continued existence. These artifacts include pots, lamps, bowls, vessels, clothes, **jewelry**, daggers, and household supplies. Even combs and mirrors have survived, indicating that they thought the dead continued to be concerned with their appearance. The **lamps** were thought to be particularly useful in the dark world of death as the lost souls sought their way to their final home. Scraps of food offerings, including **animals** for slaughter—**sheep, goats** and **birds**—may reveal that the living assumed that the dead also continued in their daily appetites.

The dead were thought to be able to communicate with the living—at least for a time. The witch of Endor's ability to raise Samuel's spirit to speak to Saul suggests that people continued to exist in some kind of half-life well after their physical death—at least until the body was entirely consumed in the grave. In Jewish lore, many allegorical tales relate to the communication of the dead with the living, but the more common view is the one in Ecclesiastes (9:5): "The dead know not anything." Nonetheless, the practice of praying for the intercession of the dead reaches back as far as stories of Caleb, who was thought to have visited the cave of Machpelah and prayed to Abraham to save him from Moses's scouts.

Even today, Jewish thought is conflicted with regard to a belief in the immortality of the soul. In fact, the belief in a continuous life of the soul, which "underlies primitive Ancestor Worship and the rites of necromancy, practiced also in ancient Israel" was discouraged by **prophets** and lawgivers, who thought of God as the ruler of Heaven and Earth—but not Sheol—at least not according to post-exilic thought (Kaufmann Kohler 2004, "Immortality of the Soul").

In later days, some of the Jews did come to believe in a **resurrection** of the dead, a time when the souls—at least the souls of the righteous—would return to the bodies and the person would return to the Holy Land. This is one reason so many are buried near Jerusalem, in preparation for the Resurrection Day. The positioning of the body also signals such a belief: a number of corpses were buried with the thumb bent so that the hand resembled the word "Shaddai" and a shard was placed in the eyes, a little stick in the hands, a piece of metal on the body, a little bag with earth from the Holy Land under the head, and a three-toothed wooden fork in the hands to help with the digging on the day of resurrection. A towel was hung up and a glass of water placed beside it so that the body might be bathed when the soul returns . As one historian notes, "Jerusalem alone is the city of which the dead shall blossom forth like graves. . . . Those that are buried elsewhere will therefore be compelled to creep through cavities in the earth until they reach the Holy Land." (See Ps. 72:16 and Ezek. 37:13; George Barton and Kaufmann Kohler 2004, "Resurrection.")

Job is one of the earliest examples of this longing for resurrection (Job 19:25–26). Under the influence of Greek thought, especially Plato, the **Pharisees** and **Essenes** came to believe in the resurrection of the dead, whereas the **Sadducees** denied both the immortality of the soul and the resurrection of the dead. Eventually, resurrection became a dogma of Judaism, fixed in the Mishnah and the liturgy. It was firmly established as a part of the Messianic hope— largely tied to the resurrection of the righteous—as spirits only.

Their ideas changed somewhat with the Exile and the Diaspora. The prophets preached of a new day, when the Heavenly Jerusalem would be the home of God's chosen. At the **Day of Judgment**, the Jews expected a trumpet to be blown to gather together the Tribes of Israel (Isa. 27:13). This event would also raise the dead. The evil—all except for the pious Jews—would be cast into Gehenna, but Israel (or at least the true Israel) would be saved by its God (Isa. 66:14; Ps. 23:4; Micah 4:5). Gradually, the resurrection and the Last Judgment were envisioned as acts of God completing the pattern of human history

This tradition was the heritage of the early Christians, who knew about the "dark land of death" (Matt. 4:16). They believed that the Creator had power over death (Mark 5:38–42), as was demonstrated in various miracles. John's **gospel** has numerous references to death and resurrection, including the miracle of Lazarus's being called back from the dead (John 11:17). At that point, Jesus told Martha, "I am the resurrection, and the life: he that believeth in me, though he were dead, yet shall he live" (John 11:25). Christ himself spoke of the Last Judgment, the resurrection of the dead, of his own resurrection, and finally he appeared in his resurrected body to his disciples and others. It therefore became an essential of Christian thought. As Paul proclaimed, "Death is swallowed up in victory" (1 Cor. 15:54). He wrote to his beloved Timothy, "Christ . . . hath abolished death, and hath brought life and immortality to light through the gospel (2 Tim. 1:10). His writings are saturated with a delight in the knowledge of the life to come, believing that death was truly a victory for the Christian.

The celebration of Easter and the change of worship practices from the Sabbath to the Lord's Day (Sunday), in memory of the Resurrection, testify to its centrality for Christians—as does the Apostle's Creed, which ends,

"I believe ... in the Resurrection of the Dead and the Life Everlasting. Amen" *See also* Graves; Heaven, New Jerusalem, Paradise; Hell, Sheol; Mourning; Resurrection; Witchcraft, Witches.

Further Reading

Barton, George A., Kaufmann Kohler, and the Editorial Board. "Resurrection," http://www.encyclopedia.com (accessed December 20, 2004). DeVaux, Roland. *Ancient Israel: Its Life and Institutions.* Grand Rapids, Mich.: William B. Eerdmans Publishing Company, 1997. Kohler, Kaufmann. "Immortality of the Soul," http://www. jewishencyclopedia.com (accessed December 20, 2004). Segal, Alan F. *Life after Death: A History of the Afterlife in Western Religion.* New York: Doubleday, 2004.

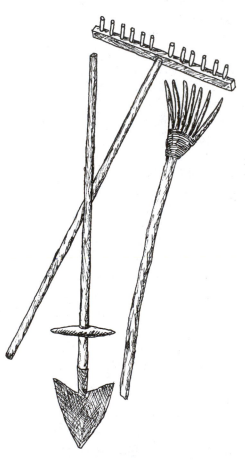

Tools used by the farmers in ancient Israel: a "broom rake," which could also serve as a winnowing fork for tossing the grain and separating the wheat from the chaff; a "comb rake," which could serve as a harrow, used to break up clods of earth after plowing; and a shovel with a sharp point.

Agriculture

References to agriculture occur in almost every book of Scripture. Seedtime and harvest marked the great divisions of the Hebrew calendar. The major **festivals** were in celebration of God's gift of rains and crops—the barley, wheat, figs, and **olives**—the fruitfulness of the land. From the time of Creation, humans were given the task of tending the **Garden**. After the Expulsion and the birth of the first children, Cain became a **farmer** and Abel a herdsman whose **blood** sacrifice was honored by God over Cain's grain sacrifice. After the Great **Flood**, Noah harvested grapes and drank too much of the fruit of the vine. Although a nomad much of his life, Abram was concerned with locating land that would produce **grains** to feed his growing tribe and flocks. His division of territory with the greedy Lot indicates his concern with **food** for his people and animals.

Mesopotamia, the land from which Abram came, produced the Gerzer Calendar with these seasons delineated:

His two months are (olive) harvest;
his two months are planting (grain);
his two months are late planting;

8

his month is hoeing up of flax;
his month is harvest of barley;
his month is harvest and festivity;
his two months are vine-tending;
his month is summer-fruit. (Fred Heaton 1956, 98)

Agriculture is a mark of the settled life, arguing against the assumption that the early Israelites were totally migratory in their habits. Although they were **tent**-dwellers until (and even after) they settled in **Canaan**, they apparently stayed long enough in one place to grow crops for themselves and their animals. They seem to have had a pattern of annual or seasonal migration, returning to grazing grounds they found appealing. Among the things that delighted Abram and his **tribe** on entrance to the Promised Land was the abundance of foods already growing.

During their prolonged stay in Egypt, when the Israelites were transformed from welcome guests into despised **slaves**, they were limited to one area (Goshen), largely because the Egyptians were hostile to herdsmen. After the **Exodus**, when the Israelites settled the Promised Land, they divided it up among the tribes, transforming themselves into settled farmers. As they grew wealthier and their lives were more abundant, social classes developed, kings were anointed, and the powerful might either buy out the small landowner or take the land by force. The most famous example of this was Jezebel's insistence that her husband take Naboth's **vineyard** for her pleasure (1 Kings 21:1–16). Carefully cultivated vineyards and gardens were cherished by their owners and coveted by their neighbors.

Jesus lived in farm country, passing through fields as he walked through the countryside, picking bits of grain to nibble, even on the **Sabbath**. His parables describe tilling the soil, dealing with rocky ground and weeds, and cutting down the unproductive fig tree. He knew about tares that grew up along with the wheat, and about times for planting and times of harvest, as well as the perennial need for harvesters. He knew the tiny size of the mustard seed and the amazing grandeur of the full-grown tree. His home was in Nazareth, a small town adjacent to farms, vineyards, and pastures. Throughout his ministry, he walked to other cities and towns, an activity that provided him with plenty of opportunity to watch farmers at work and to contemplate their use of the very tools he had often crafted in his father's carpentry shop, which probably became his own after his father died.

Much of Palestine is uneven and rocky land, unsuitable for agriculture. Some regions, such as the Jordan Valley, which has abundant water, are very productive. Others demand terracing and irrigation if tender plants are to thrive. "The best grain lands were the benches of the Jordan valley that could be irrigated by the tributaries of the Jordan, the Philistine plain, Esdraelon (although part of it was then marshy), Bashan and **Moab**.... Narrow stair-like terraces were erected on the mountainside.... The lower hills, such as the Shephelah, gave a wider distribution to crops, adding the vine and the olive to the grains, making a famous trio of crops often referred to in OT. The better sections of the higher land were farmed, but much was left for grazing or forestry" (F. N. Hepper 1980, 22).

The seasons of heavy rains followed by drought made the year predictable, but difficult. The heavy summer dews helped certain regions produce grapes, cucumbers, and melons. Generally, wheat and barley were the best grain crops, figs and dates grew abundantly, olive trees could thrive in the rocky soil, and vineyards produced rich harvests of grapes.

In smaller gardens, the farmer might grow his herbs and spices, melons and those vegetables that demand more water. These kitchen gardens provided lentils and beans, which the poor folks used in their stews, as well as cucumbers, leeks, onions, and garlic.

The land was generally not fenced or walled in, and much of the agricultural activity was a community effort. People who lived in villages went out to the fields each day to work the land, with little separation between town and country. There were few agricultural implements—the wooden **plow**, the wood-and-flint sickle, and the **yoke**. Farmers also used the **goad** to keep the **oxen** moving, and they must have had some kind of shovels and **rods** for leveraging rocks out of the soil, not to mention primitive wheelbarrows to move soil, manure, and rock from place to place.

Their main animal helpers were their **donkeys** and oxen, which could plow the stony soil and haul the loads from the fields. Their **enemies**—aside from the humans who liked to invade during harvest time—were the **locusts**, mildew, various plant **diseases**, and the hot sirocco winds.

The **Law** of Moses touched the soil, just as it did virtually every element of human life. According to the law, the land, too, was to have **sabbaticals**, times when it lay dormant (Lev. 25), and land that had been sold out of the tribe was to be returned in the Year of the Jubilee. *See also* Animals; Gardens; Geography; Goad; Law; Vineyards; Weather; Yoke.

Further Reading

Heaton, E. W. *Everyday Life in Old Testament Times.* New York: Charles Scribner's Sons, 1956. Hepper, F. N. "Agriculture," in *The Illustrated Bible Dictionary.* Sydney, Australia: Tyndale House Publishers, 1980. King, Philip J. and Lawrence E. Stager. *Life in Biblical Israel.* Louisville, Ky.: Westminster John Knox Press, 2001.

Alms, Almsgiving

(Deut. 15:11; Prov. 21:21, 25:21; Dan. 4:24; Matt. 6:1–4) The word *alms* derives from the Greek word for "mercifulness," charity to the needy

(Kaufmann Kohler 2004). Jesus's warning that true believers should not be ostentatious in their charitable giving is the only explicit mention of alms in Scripture, but the concept is implied in the Law of Moses. "After the cessation of **sacrifice**, almsgiving seems to have ranked among the Jews as the first of religious duties. In every city there were collectors who distributed alms of two kinds, *i.e.,* money collected in the **synagogue** chest every sabbath for the poor of the city, and food and money received in a dish" (J. D. Douglas 1980, 33).

This clearly derives from the law's emphasis on compassion. The prophets had also encouraged charity, and the Psalmist applauded the practice: "Blessed is he that considers the needy and the poor" (Ps. 40:2). The Jews saw wealth as a loan from God, on which the poor have a claim. Along with **fasting** and **prayer**, almsgiving was a central expectation of the pious Jew. The **apocryphal** story of Tobit is a lesson in almsgiving and the benefits derived from generosity of the spirit.

Although few beggars are mentioned in the Bible, the disabled who languished around the Pool of Bethesda or near the city gates or the Temple were probably beggars who appealed to Jesus for healing as they had appealed to others for money. The rich young ruler, who came to Jesus asking what he must do to inherit eternal life, balked when told, "Sell whatever thou hast, and give to the poor, and thou shalt have treasure in heaven." (Mark 10:21). The giving of alms was considered all through Scripture as a sign of a righteous man.

In the early **Christian** community, the distribution of alms was specifically assigned to the deacons (Acts 4:32, 34). Widows and orphans were among those most often mentioned as having special needs for such attention. Among the members of the young Christian **Church**, as pictured in Acts, members of one congregation gave free-will offerings to other churches that were facing troubles (1 Cor. 16:1–3; 2 Cor. 8–9). Paul admonishes them to be "cheerful givers" out of their abundance.

The Christian concept of charity—giving for Jesus's sake and in his name—has continued into modern time. The outpouring of gifts to victims of disasters, such as a flood, tsunami, or an earthquake, which leaves many homeless and in distress, is evidence of the continuing power of this ancient ethical imperative.

Further Reading

Douglas, J. D. "Alms, Almsgiving," in *The Illustrated Bible Dictionary*. Sydney, Australia: Tyndale House Publishers, 1980. Kohler, Kaufmann. "Alms," http://www.jewishencyclopedia.com (accessed February 22, 2005). O'Neill, James David. "Alms and Almsgiving," http://www.newadvent.org (accessed February 22, 2005).

Alpha and Omega, "the beginning and the end," in Greek script common in Jesus's lifetime.

Alpha and Omega

(Rev. 1:8, 21:6) Alpha and omega are the first and last letters of the Greek alphabet. When used, as in Revelation, as a name for God, they indicate that he is the beginning and the end, the first and the last. This is reinforced by the pattern of the entire Scripture, which begins in Genesis with, "In the beginning, God" and concludes in Revelation with, "Even so, come Lord Jesus," followed by the **blessing**: "The grace of our Lord Jesus Christ be with you all. Amen." For Christians, this means that God was the Creator of the Universe and will be the Judge at the Last Judgment. *See also* Creation.

Altar

(Exod. 27:2, 30:1; Heb. 13:10) An altar in the ancient world was simply a place where the slaughtering or sacrificing was done, usually by a **priest**. The word occurs 400 times in the Bible. We find altars marking places of theophany—where God and humans had met face to face—or where people came to worship and to make sacrifices in hopes of having direct access to the deity. "An altar of earth thou shalt make unto me, and shalt **sacrifice** thereon thy burnt **offerings**, and thy peace offerings, thy sheep, and thine oxen. . . . And if thou wilt make me an altar of stone, thou shalt not build it of hewn stone: for if thou lift up thy tool upon it, thou has polluted it. Neither shalt thou go up by steps unto mine altar, that thy nakedness be not discovered theron" (Exod. 20:24–26).

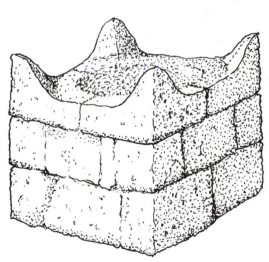

Altar with "horns" made of stone. Supplicants sometimes grasped the horns of the altar to seek asylum, or the protection of God (1 Kings 1:50), believing these raised corners to be particularly sacred portions of the altar, as this was where the priest smeared the blood of the animals (Exod. 29:12; Lev. 4:7) during the sacrificial ritual.

Physically, an altar was a flat or concave space on which the **animals** might be placed for the slaughter. Altars often had troughs to carry off the **blood**. The priest burned the sacrificial offering of **grain** or flesh, or poured the libations of **wine** and blood onto the altar. Although often made of stone, the altar was a built structure, which was not thought to be inhabited by any supernatural force: it was not a sacred stone (Philip C. Hammond 1993, 21). The altar later became a place of asylum or sanctuary (1 Kings 1:50–53, 2:28–34). Refugees from the **law** might claim divine protection by holding onto the "horns" at the corners of the altar.

We see altars all through Scripture—from the altar of promise built by Noah after the Great **Flood** (Gen. 8:20) to the carefully specified altars of the **Tabernacle** and the **Temple**. In these designs, both the altars of holocaust and of **incense** are included, the latter being a tiny copy of the massive design of the great bronze altar. The bronze altar of the Tabernacle, described in Exodus 27, was to be made of "shittim wood, five cubits long, and five cubits broad" with "horns of it upon the four corners" and the whole thing "overlay with brass."

An example of an altar with the horns has been discovered at Beer-sheba, dating to the eighth century B.C. A version of this "built altar" was also included in the design for the Temple of Solomon (2 Sam. 24:25). Such bronze altars as these probably enclosed piles of earth and rubble with the altar itself made of brick for burnt offerings (T. C. Mitchell 1980, 36).

After the destruction of the Temple, the **prophets** condemned the "false altars" or unlawful ones (Amos 3:14; Hos. 8:11). Ezekiel had a vision of the restoration of Israel and of the Temple (Ezek. 40–44) that describes the three stages of the altar of burnt offering (43:13–17), a design that echoes the pattern of the **Babylonian** ziggurat, including a flight of steps that the priests must climb. It is assumed that the Second Temple had the altars Josephus described as being in Solomon's Temple. This "golden altar" was the one that Antiochus Epiphanes carried off (1 Macc. 1:21) and the altar of burnt offerings was the one he desecrated (1 Macc. 1:54). These were restored by the Maccabees and probably were in use at the time that Herod enlarged the Temple. By this time, "the altar of burnt offering was a great pile of unhewn stones, approached by a ramp" (T. C. Mitchell 1980, 37).

The New Testament has numerous references to the altar (Matt. 5:23–24. 23:18–20, 35; Luke 11:51; 1 Cor. 9:13, 10:18; Heb. 7:13; Rev. 11:1). A fundamental Christian belief is that the sacrifice of Christ was the once-and-for-all offering, so the altar became either an image of Christ's sacrificial death or a symbol of unnecessary and repetitive sacrifices. With the destruction of the Temple in 70 A.D., the great altar was destroyed and its sacrifices ended. Modern **synagogues** therefore do not have altars.

Archaeologists have found altars of earth and stone, as well as bronze. The prohibition against steps was apparently frequently broken, because the usual shape of the altar included steps to allow the priests to stand above the community to make the offering. In later days, when invaders had polluted the traditional places of worship, offerings might have been made on rooftops. Josiah required that these worship sites be destroyed (2 Kings 23:12), probably because they were frequently associated with local **Canaanite** deities. The **Philistines**, for example, apparently made a habit of offering incense on rooftop altars (Philip King and Lawrence Stager 2001, 339).

In modern churches, especially Roman Catholic, the altar is seen as "the meeting point between God and mankind, the true centre of all religious buildings" (Dom Robert LeGall 2000, 90). It is usually situated in a high place, above the congregation. At the dedication of churches, relics of the saints are placed inside the altar to mark the continuity between the sacrifice of Christ and of his faithful. It is the designated place for the mass, the reenactment of Christ's sacrifice of his blood and flesh for the sins of humankind.

On the other hand, most Protestants, believing that the communion is a symbolic rather than literal act, do not have altars in their churches. The communion table replaces the altar for those who see the celebration of the **Last Supper** as a means to remember Christ's sacrifice, but not the occasion for a miracle transforming the bread into flesh and the wine into blood. The theological debate that underlies this difference was a significant factor in the Reformation, with Luther admitting the "real presence" but repudiating transubstantiation, and Calvin insisting instead on the "virtual presence" of the blood and flesh and repudiating Luther's concept of consubstantiation (Dominic Manganiello 1992, 775–7). *See also* Incense; Last Supper; Sacrifice; Temple.

Further Reading

Hammond, Philip C. "Altars," in *The Oxford Companion to the Bible*. New York: Oxford University Press, 1993. Josephus, Flavius. *The Works of Josephus*. Peabody, Mass.: Hendrickson Publishers, 2001. King, Philip J., and Lawrence E. Stager. *Life in Biblical Israel*. Louisville, Ky.: Westminster John Knox Press, 2001. LeGall, Dom Robert. *Symbols of Catholicism*. New York: Assouline Publishing, 2000. Manganiello, Dominic. "Transubstantiation," in *A Dictionary of Biblical Tradition in English Literature*. Grand Rapids, Mich.: William B. Eerdmans Publishing Company, 1992. Mitchell, T. C. "Altars," in *The Illustrated Bible Dictionary*. Sydney, Australia: Tyndale House Publishers, 1980.

Amen

(**Mark 3:28; John 21:18**) The word *amen,* meaning "May it be so," "surely," or "truly," was used in the Old Testament as a liturgical formula by the congregation to assert the validity of an **oath** or **curse**. It also served to underscore a benediction or a doxology. It might occur at either the beginning or the end of a statement.

In the recorded statements of Jesus, it is usually translated as, "truly, truly," indicating that the words that follow are authoritative. In the New Testament **Church**, following the pattern of the **Lord's Prayer**, it was regularly used to conclude the **prayer**—as a confirmation, by either the person praying or the congregation.

The title "the Amen" was attributed to God, who has the authority to fulfill his promises (Rev. 3:14; 2 Cor. 1:20). Thus, Jesus's use of "Amen" as the opening of his statements indicates his claim to divine authority. In Revelation 3:4, it is used as a name for Christ. *See also* Blessing; Curse; Prayer.

Further Reading

Miller, Madeleine S. and J. Lane Miller. "Amen," in *Harper's Bible Dictionary*. New York: Harper and Row, 1961.

Ammon, Ammonites

(Gen. 19:38; Deut. 2:19; Ezek. 25:1) The Ammonites were akin to the **Moabites**, both thought to have descended from illicit relations between Lot and his daughters after the fall of Sodom and Gomorrah. (Some believe this story to be satirical, intended to cast aspersions on the people and their ancestry.) The Ammonites lived on a narrow strip of land west of the Jordan, the boundaries of which are still in dispute among scholars. In Judges 11:13, the **king** of Ammon claimed that the land "from Arnon even unto Jabbok and unto Jordan" rightfully belonged to him and his countrymen, but the claim is cited as illegitimate in Scripture. Ammon does appear to have bordered on **Israel** on the one side and Moab on the other. There are references to 20 cities in their territory and comments that their territory previously was in the possession "of a mysterious nation, the Zamzummim (also called Zuzim) (Gen.14:5). "When the Israelites invaded **Canaan**, they passed by the frontier of the Ammonites" (W. Max Muller and Kaufmann Kohler 2004; Num. 21:24; Deut. 2:19, 37; Josh. 13:25).

The Ammonites and the Moabites are frequently mentioned together, as in the case of the hiring of Balaam to **curse** the Israelites (Deut. 23:4, 5). Scholars suspect that Ammon was such a tiny country that it could face Israel only if in alliance with another power. When King Nahash attacked Jabesh in Gilead, for example, he was easily defeated by Saul (1 Sam.11:14:47).

The Ammonites also became involved from time to time in Israel's affairs, battling the Hebrews, helping them, and becoming enslaved to them. Nahash assisted David, perhaps out of hatred for Saul. But his son infuriated David by mistreating his ambassadors, provoking David to attack their capital on its strong acropolis, Rabbath-Ammon (modern-day Ammon, Jordan) and to enslave the "cities of the children of Ammon" (2 Sam. 10:2). David used the captives in public works and enlisted a number of them in his army (2 Sam. 17:27). He appointed Shobi as his vassal king over the Ammonites to keep peace.

Later, Solomon married an Ammonitess, probably King Shobi's daughter, who became the mother of his heir, Rehoboam. Still later, hostilities broke out under Jehosaphat (2 Chron. 20) Jereboam II (Amos 1:13), and Jotham, who forced them into subjection (2 Chron. 27:5).

The Ammonites are mentioned briefly in the records of the various conquerors of the region: the Assyrians demanded tribute from them. This seems to have been a prosperous period (late eighth to late seventh century B.C.), when the Assyrians guaranteed the Ammonites' position on international trade routes and helped protect them from various nomadic groups who threatened the routes. "Excavations and Assyrian texts indicate that Ammon extended its boundaries during this period, westward to the Jordan River, northward into Gilead, and southward toward Heshbon. The most substantial ruins of the Iron Age date to this period, and **seals**, inscriptions, and statuary indicate the kingdom's wealth" (Wayne T. Pitard 1993, 23). The Ammonites assisted Nebuchadnezzar against the Jews (2 King 24:2), and then they rebelled against the Babylonians, even helping Jews who were fleeing from the Babylonians and arranging the murder of the first Babylonian governor (Jer. 40:11–15). Because of their role in the great rebellion (589–586 B.C.), they were annexed into the Babylonian provincial system. When the Jews began the rebuilding of Jerusalem, the Ammonites sought to hinder the work (Ezra 9:1).

By the Persian period, only the name of the Ammonites survived, more as a description of a region than of a political or ethnic group. Judas Maccabeus was said to have defeated them, although by this time "Ammonite" meant all Arabs living in the former country of Ammon. This defeat resulted in Jewish **warriors**' taking Ammonite women as captives and as wives. The sons from these intermarriages claimed recognition as Jews, in spite of the **law** of Moses, which ruled that "Ammonite and Moabite men are excluded from the Jewish community for all time." The adjusted ruling added, "their women are admissible."

Scripture records nothing of their customs, mentioning only that their chief deity was Milcom, probably another name for **Moloch** (1 Kings 11:5). They were characterized in Scripture as "inveterate enemies of **Israel** and a force for spiritual corruption" (Madeleine S. Miller and J. Lane Miller 1961, 16).

The Jews despised the Ammonites because they rejoiced in the misfortunes of Israel and spread their "abominations" through intermarriage—corrupting the faith of King Solomon among others (1 Kings 11:5, 7). Ezra and Nehemiah, leaders who were especially aware of the perils of intermarriage with this group, were contemptuous of them. Ezekiel foretold an era when their great city Rabbath would become "a stable for **camels**, and the Ammonites a couching place for flocks" (Ezek. 25:5). This is the same city that was the legendary burial place of Og, king of Bashan, whose ironstone sarcophagus was called a "bedstead of iron" (Deut. 3:11).

The city was "rebuilt by Ptolemy Philadelphus in the third century B.C., and named Philadelphia"; today Ammon is a "busy trading center of Arabs and goal of travellers, who delight in its Roman hillside theatre and other marks of ancient occupation of the city" (Madeleine S. Miller and J. Lane Miller 1961, 16). *See also* War, Warfare: General.

Further Reading

Miller, Madeleine S. and J. Lane Miller. "Ammonites," in *Harper's Bible Dictionary*. New York: Harper and Row, 1961. Muller, W. Max and Kaufmann Kohler, "Ammon, Ammonites," http://www. jewishencyclopedia.com (accessed December 20, 2004). Pitard, Wayne T. "Ammon," in *The Oxford Companion to the Bible*. New York: Oxford University Press, 1993.

Amorites

(Gen. 10:16; Exod. 33:2; Num. 13:29; Josh. 24:15; Ezek. 16:3) The Amorites, like the **Hittites**, were among the original inhabitants of **Canaan**, remnants of ancient cultures, once dominant in the region (Gen. 15:16, 48:22; Joshua, 5:1, 24:15, 18; Judg., 10:11; 1 Sam. 7:14; 1 Kings 21:26; 2 Kings 21:11; Amos 2:9, and so forth) At times, the whole "aboriginal population of Canaan is also called 'Amorite' (Gen. 15:13–16)," making it difficult to determine the specific peoples designated by the term (Joseph A. Greene 1993, 24). The Hebrews traced the Amorites' lineage back to Canaan, a descendant of Ham, the cursed son of Noah, doomed for his iniquities to perpetual servitude (Gen. 9:25, 10:16; 1 Chron. 1:14).

Around 2000 B.C., there were "barbarian" invasions throughout the Near East, especially in Northern Syria and Mesopotamia. The Babylonians called these semi-nomadic Semites, "Westerners," or "Amorites" (G. Ernest Wright 1957, 41–42). The Amorite movement was one of the first of the great Semitic invasions. Amorite **kings** appeared all over the area, including in Haran, Paddan-Aram, and even **Babylon**, which was considered the capital of the Amorite state, where they ruled for about 300 years. The greatest of their kings was the renowned **law**-giver, Hammurabi. This culture was a strong influence on the Hebrews, who migrated from this region to Canaan.

The Amorites, known as "Amurru" in Akkadian, gradually moved to the regions of Syria and Palestine, settling numerous cities there. Joshua 10:5 mentions the kings of five Amorite cities: Jerusalem, Hebron, Jarmuth, Lachish, and Eglon. We know nothing of their life there, but remnants of their general culture have been uncovered by archaeologists, especially in Mari, an eighteenth century B.C. Syrian city on the Euphrates, considered an Amorite town. G. Ernest Wright notes that they were considered "giants" in comparison with the smaller Israelites (Wright 1957, 37).

Among the discoveries at Mari were more than 20,000 clay tablets. The king's palace, with its nearly 300 rooms, covered more than 15 acres. The

Amorites had a system of **writing** and a system of law that drew from the peoples around them. These early developments were probably enhanced by their regular trading with other cultures. Like the others who invaded Babylon, the Amorites came to accept the patron deity of that country, Marduk. They also apparently developed a system of divination. Memories of Amorite **witchcraft** appear in later stories among the Jews.

Canaanites, who are frequently spoken of as "Amorites" in post-biblical literature, were characterized as heathen idolaters and practitioners of black arts and witchcraft—"impure mysteries, by which they contaminated Israel in the time of the **Judges**" (W. Max Muller and Kaufmann Kohler 2004).

Certain groups within the Amorites seem to bear the same name as the later Hebrew tribe, *Benjamin,* or "children of the right hand," that is, people from the south (G. Ernest Wright 1957, 37). In fact, although Amoritish names such as *Adonizedek* (Josh. 10:3) appear in Scripture, the actual people and their relationship to the Hebrews remain cloudy. It may well be that the various groups among the Canaanites were clustered together under the single name of "Amorite" for convenience. *See also* Babylon, Babylonia; Canaan, Canaanite; Law; Witchcraft, Witches; Writing and Reading.

Further Reading

Greene, Joseph A. "Amorites," in *The Oxford Companion to the Bible*. New York: Oxford University Press, 1993. Keller, Werner. *The Bible as History*. New York: Bantam Books, 1982. Muller, W. Max and Kaufmann Kohler, "Amorites," http://www.jewishencyclopedia.com (accessed December 20, 2004). Wright, G. Ernest. *Biblical Archaeology*. Philadelphia: The Westminster Press, 1957.

Anathema

(Lev. 27:28; Luke 21:5;1 Cor. 16:20) The word *anathema* is derived from a Greek word akin to the Hebrew word for "ban" or "**curse**." The original concept was the designation of "something set up" in a **temple**, like an **offering**. Later it came to mean a cursed person or thing. The idea was to hand over to God a despised person or thing for complete destruction. According to Leviticus, a person who had been so cursed could not be ransomed. Paul pronounces anathema on those who preach a deviant gospel (Gal. 1:8, 9). Christians were sometimes challenged to "anathema Jesus" or to curse him, as an act of blasphemy. *Anathema* came to be a synonym for excommunication. Because the person or item had once been consecrated, the anathema is a verdict requiring obliteration.

The anathema was a common element in an **oath**, invoked by the oath-takers on themselves in the event that they failed to perform the promises made in the oath. *See also* Curse; Oaths.

Angels

(Gen. 16:7; Ps. 8; Rev. 22:16; and so forth) Angels are God-created beings that exist somewhere between God and humans. The word *angel* means "messenger," but Biblical angels also acted as rescuers, guardians, guides, admonishers, encouragers, interpreters of visions, **warriors**, destroyers, and worshipers. References all through the Old and New Testaments indicate that these emissaries of God have appeared at frequent intervals in human history, most prominently in biblical visions. Psalm 8 indicates that they, like humans, are creatures; that is, they were created by God, but they are of a higher order than humans. Nevertheless, the author of Hebrews makes clear that they are of a lower status than Christ (chapter 2).

Angels through Scripture

Angels were apparently present at the **Creation**, mentioned by Job as "the morning stars" that sang together in joyful participation of the great event (Job 38:7). They were also celebrants of the birth of Christ, appearing to the **shepherds** in the field and singing, "Glory to God in the highest, and on earth, peace, good will toward men" Luke 2:14).

On some occasions, they looked like men, recognized only by special people chosen by God to receive specific messages—sometimes to encourage, sometimes to warn. Abram did not immediately recognize his angelic visitors as supernatural (Gen. 18). Lot served as host to these same visitors and thereby saved himself and part of his family from the destruction of Sodom and Gomorrah (Gen. 19). The angels then slaughtered the townspeople who had failed to recognize them or treat them with the proper **hospitality** due guests.

Hagar and Ishmael were comforted and advised by an angel in the wilderness (Gen. 21:17–19). An angel interrupted the **sacrifice** of Isaac (Gen. 22:10–12). Jacob saw angels on the ladder between Earth and **Heaven**, descending and ascending. He also wrestled with one, who left him wounded in the thigh (Gen. 28:12). Moses saw an angel in the burning bush (Exod. 3:2), although it is not always clear whether Moses (or Jacob) was confronting God himself or one of his messengers. In the lions' den with Daniel, the angelic protector appeared as a man who subdued the beasts (Dan. 6:22). It was also a "man" (i.e., an angel who appeared in the form of a man) who guided Ezekiel through the ideal **Temple** (Ezek. 40).

Earlier, the **prophet** Ezekiel had a different set of guides: the "four living creatures" each with four faces and four wings, "as for the likeness of their faces, they four had the face of a man, and the face of a lion, on the right side: and they four had the face of an ox on the left side; they four also had the face of an eagle" (Ezek 1:10). These are usually interpreted as **cherubim**, creatures who sometimes served as a divine chariot on which God rode, and at other times guarded the entrance to the **Garden of Eden**—keeping humankind from reentering (1 Sam. 4:4; Gen. 3:24). Later, images of these creatures were situated on either side of the **Ark of the Covenant**; the carved cherubim's' outstretched wings came together above, forming the **throne** on which the glory of God appeared.

Angelic Nature and Appearance

Angels are referred to on occasion as the "host" of Heaven, as if they are God's army, or perhaps his court—thus his title "Lord God of Hosts." They are immortal, holy, and invisible much of the time, and made of a substance that allows them to move through space and to appear and disappear. They do have free will, allowing one of their members, Satan, to fall into sin, and leading others to follow his tragic example. This rebellion in Heaven, often called the Battle of Angels, where the good and evil angels engaged in **warfare**, is chronicled only indirectly by certain hints in Scripture and in even more extensive legends outside of the canon of Scripture. (Job 4:18; Isa. 14:12–15; Ezek. 28:12–19). Such fallen angels subsequently were thought to have become **demons**.

In Job, angels at the Creation are referred to as "sons of God." Jesus seems to confirm the asexual nature of the angels when he speaks of the **afterlife** as a time and place when there is no marriage, when we become "like angels" (Mark 12:25). (This may explain the frequent presentation of the afterlife as a time when we all look like the nineteenth-century angels, with wings, white robes, and harps.)

When they do appear to selected individuals, their countenance is beautiful or awe inspiring. In the story of Baalam's ass, the animal can see the angel before Baalam can, suggesting that angels may allow certain people (or **animals**) to recognize them while remaining invisible to others (Num. 22:23 28). They sometimes appear suddenly as "shining ones," as at the **Resurrection**. Matthew tells us that the women went to the tomb, "And behold, there was a great earthquake: for the angel of the Lord descended from heaven, and came and rolled back the stone from the door, and sat upon it. His countenance was like lightning, and his raiment white as snow" (Matt. 28:2–3).

Guardian angels watch over individuals, protecting and helping them. The angels of the **churches** in Revelation, or the "seven stars" (Rev. 1:20), to whom the book is addressed, are considered guardian angels. Some believe that the term may refer to a personification of the churches, a heavenly counterpart to the earthly churches (C.J. Hemer 1960,151–152). Angels were frequently present in visions or in **apocalyptic** literature, thus appearing in Daniel, Ezekiel, and Revelation with greater frequency than elsewhere.

Names and Ranks of Angels

The term *Angel of the Lord*, which appears in the story of Abram, is used several times in Scripture, indicating a heavenly being sent by God as his personal spokesman to humans. It is not clear whether this refers to a single angel or whether it is simply a function assumed by a selected angel for these particular occasions. Examples of this usage would include the sacrifice of Isaac (Gen. 22:11) and the theophanies of Hagar (Gen. 16:7), Jacob (Gen. 31:13), Moses at the burning bush (Exod. 3:2), Gideon (Judg. 6:11), and others.

Early Scripture shows angels refusing to provide their names, but in later biblical literature, the angels are named. Michael and Gabriel are both named in Daniel. Gabriel is sometimes characterized as the agent of destruction and judgment, sometimes of protection and deliverance, and sometimes the means for providing instructions. He gave selected mothers the foreknowledge of their children, as in the birth of Samson, John the Baptist, and Jesus. In the New Testament, Gabriel (Luke 1:19) seems to have been the specific agent of God to Mary at the moment of the **Annunciation**. Although not always immediately recognized as an angel because of his human form, he was clearly different from humans. He was not God, yet he was nonetheless addressed as God (Gen. 16:13) and used the first-person singular in speaking for God, as in: "I am the god of Bethel" (Exod. 3:2). Michael had a somewhat more combative role. In Daniel, Jude, and Revelation, he was presented as the defender against the forces of evil (Dan. 10:12; Jude 9:1; Rev. 12:7).

There is apparently some kind of hierarchy among the angels. Raphael, for example, is "one of seven angels who stand ready and enter before the glory of the Lord" (Rev. 8:2), leading scholars to identify this grouping as "archangels." In the period of the Exile and thereafter, the Jews were influenced by foreign religions, leading them to elaborate a system of *angelology*—or the study of angels. Much of this fresh speculation on angels relied on an extra-biblical book that was never considered a part of inspired Scripture—Enoch. In it, Enoch described his trip to Heaven and the angelic hosts he saw there. In Enoch 20, the writer listed the archangels: Uriel, Raphael, Raguel, Michael, Sariel, Gabriel, and Remiel—or Jeremiel.

This visionary writing encouraged the Jewish scholars to embellish their own understanding, ranking the angels into seven categories, naming many of them, and generally expanding on the hints given in Scripture. Cherubim (noted in Ezekiel's visions) had also been mentioned in connection with the Holy of Holies and seraphim by Isaiah (chapter 6). These angels were thought to guard the **throne** of God. Paul later mentioned thrones, dominions, principalities, and powers (Rom. 8:38; Eph. 1:21; Col. 1:16), which are thought to be ranks among the fallen angels.

In the fifth century A.D., Dionysus the Aereopagite enumerated nine orders of heavenly beings, dividing them into three groups of three: (1) Seraphim, Cherubim, and Thrones; (2) Dominations, Virtues, and Powers; (3) Principalities, Archangels, and Angels. Dante, in his *Paradiso,* placed the different angelic ranks, connected with the different planets, in different heavenly realms. Milton, of course, expanded the battle of angels into *Paradise Lost,* an epic of the Creation and the **Fall**. To portray the angels, he was forced to give them names and appearances that went well beyond Scripture, often drawing from classical mythology. (He used the warring gods on Olympus as his models, basing this on Homer's *Iliad* and *Odyssey.*)

Belief in Angels

The Jews of Jesus's time were split on their faith in angels: the **Essenes** not only believed in them, but elaborated their roles and categories. On the other hand, the **Sadducees** denied their existence. Jesus, whose ideas were closer to those of the **Pharisees** on this subject, made frequent mention of angels. From the moment of the **Incarnation** until after Jesus's death and Resurrection, the **Gospels** indicate the presence of angels.

In fact, the New Testament period is full of references to both angels and **demons**, indicating a general belief in them and their activities among humankind. Apparently, the liveliness of the belief in the spirit world became a threat to the young church, where some of its members turned to angel-worship. The New Testament specifically prohibits the worship of angels (Rev. 19:10, 22:9). In fact, demons may sometimes masquerade as angels (2 Cor. 11:14–15).

Angels in Art and Culture

In both Hebrew and **Christian art**, angels were among the first religious images allowed. As noted, the cherubim were carved on either side of the throne of God, signifying that God had spoken to Moses from between two cherubim. They were also embroidered on the tapestries of both the **Tabernacle** and the Temple. Some portrayals of these creatures were like **Egyptian** and **Assyrian** art: huge eagle-winged, human faced, bull-lion hybrids. These cherubim were a far cry from the later artistic concept of baby-faced cherubs floating among the puffy clouds. By the sixth century, there were examples of cherubs with a human head and six wings; by the fifteenth century, they appeared as winged children, derived from the *putti* of classical art, particularly from images of Eros. Gradually they reverted to adult effeminate forms and accumulated the long hair and splendid flowing robes of the classical Victory, and finally even gained **musical instruments**.

(Harold Osborne 1970, 45–46). They were pictured in white linen garments, barefoot, and shining. Although wings were not always mentioned in scriptural descriptions, artists settled on the idea that wings were symbols of the angels' divine missions, picturing them as birdlike, while devils might have wings more like bats, along with tails, horns, and pitchforks they used to torment the wicked.

In recent years, angels have become very popular, but divorced from the usual theological doctrines. Television shows such as *Touched by an Angel* have made colorful drama out of very human angelic helpers. In a peculiar reversal of traditional theology, *Angels in America,* which was both a hit play and a television special, used angels to bless homosexuals, especially those afflicted with AIDS. These works suggest a gentler, less judgmental view of extraterrestrial helpers, who seem to be vaguely supernatural spirits unrelated to any particular religious dogmas. *See also* Apocalypse, Apocalyptic Literature; Art: Christian; Art: Jewish; Cherub, Cherubim; Essenes; Pharisees; Sadducees; Tabernacle; Temple.

The cherubim or "living creatures," guarded the tree of life in Eden (Gen. 3:24), were regularly listed among the angelic beings and portrayed at either end of the Mercy Seat on the Ark of the Covenant. They were described in Ezekiel 10 and elsewhere as having a human face, a lion's body, and powerful wings, contrasting with the human-appearing figures with wings pictured in other sections of Scripture and in most Christian art. In fact, most angels who appeared to Abraham and others seem to have been mistaken for men and thus must have been without wings.

Further Reading

Cohn-Sherbok, Dan. *The Vision of Judaism: Wrestling with God.* St. Paul, Minn.: Paragon House, 2004. Davidson, Gustav. *A Dictionary of Angels, including the Fallen Angels.* New York: The Free Press, 1967. Hemer, C. J. "Angels of the Churches," in *The Illustrated Bible Encyclopedia.* Sydney, Australia: Tyndale House Publishers, 1960. Osborne, Harold. "Angel," in *The Oxford Companion to Art.* Oxford: The Oxford Press, 1970.

Animals

(Gen. 1 and 2; Exod. 20–21; Deut. 22) On the fourth day of **creation**, God created the animals—first the "swarms of living creatures" in the **waters**, then the **birds** flying "above the earth across the firmament of the **heavens**." He created the "great whales, and every living creature" that moves, and then "every winged fowl" (Gen. 1:20–21, RSV and KJV).

Then, on the fifth day of creation, "God said, Let the earth bring forth the living creature after his kind, **cattle**, and creeping thing, and the beast of the earth after his kind" (v. 24). Finally, on the sixth day, God created man and woman directly and gave them dominion over "the **fish** of the sea, and over the fowl of the air, and over the cattle, and over all the earth, and over every creeping thing that creepeth upon the earth" (v. 26). Settled among the animals in the **Garden of Eden**, Adam named the creatures (Gen. 2:20), and yet found none of them "fit" to serve as his "helper." These verses clearly establish a hierarchy with man above the animals, created in a different manner, with the gift of speech, and holding dominion over the creatures of the earth, sea, and heavens, although in harmony with them.

The great divide between human and animal came in the **Temptation** and **Fall**, when the **serpent**, "more subtil than any beast of the field" convinced Eve to eat of the forbidden fruit in defiance of God's express command. In her appetite to become more than human, she actually became less than the God-created human. She became "natural"—more like the animals that act on impulse and appetite. God subsequently cursed the serpent: "Because thou hast done this, thou art cursed above all cattle, and above every beast of the field; upon thy belly shalt thou go, and dust shalt thou eat all the days of thy life; And I will put enmity between thee and the woman, and between thy seed and her seed" (Gen. 3: 14–15).

The expulsion from Eden marks the end of harmony between humans and animals: for the first time, recognizing their nakedness, the first couple used animal skins to clothe themselves (v. 21), suggesting that they killed animals for their pelts. Abel, the second son of Adam and Eve became "keeper of **sheep**," implying that the first family had domesticated certain animals for their own use, including for use as **sacrifice**. The murderous Cain, sent away to become a wanderer over the earth, produced a family, which in later generations included Jabal, "the father of such as dwell in tents and of such as have cattle" (Gen. 4:20). The close association between **worship** and animal sacrifice, and the constant references in the **law** to regulations for selecting and eating meat, indicate that humans slaughtered, cooked, and ate animals from early times.

Animals in Scripture

Scripture teems with animal life. Their flesh was used for food, their skins and hair for clothing and shelter. God's love for them was marked by his specific admonition to Noah to preserve them (Gen. 7:2–3) and to lead them into the **ark** two by two. Birds served as Noah's spies: Noah first sent out a raven to look for dry land, but the dove was the one that returned with the "freshly plucked **olive** leaf" (Gen. 8:11). The final dove did not return. To celebrate the salvation from the flood over all the earth, Noah built an **altar** and offered up a burnt offering of "every **clean** animal and every clean bird" (Gen. 8:20), indicating that humankind had already selected "clean" creatures as suitable for food, probably based on the experience of the animals' eating habits (scavengers were particularly dangerous), as was their effect on humans.

From the days of Abraham until the Hebrews were forced from their land, taken captive to the great cities of the Babylonians and the Assyrians, they had animals in their households. At first, the Chosen People were nomadic herders of sheep and **goats**, and later **farmers** and **fishermen**. They had animals near their **tents** and in their homes; they rode them, worked them, sheared them, tended them, and sacrificed every tenth one of the newborn sheep, cattle, and goats to the Lord.

They drew clear distinctions among animals, especially the threatening wild animals and the useful domesticated ones. Some of the wild creatures, such as the ox, the camel, the donkey, the goat, or the horse, could be domesticated. The goats and cattle provided milk and the oxen helped plow the fields and thresh the **grain**. The goats and sheep provided hair and wool for their looms, and the donkeys and camels carried the loads during their frequent journeys. Later, the **horses** would pull their **chariots**, and the warriors would ride them to **war**.

Other animals remained wild and threatening: the snake, the lion, the jackal, and so forth. Certain animals' enmity to humans is clear in much of Scripture. Not only the serpent, which became an early symbol of Satanic forces, but also the many creatures of the **plagues** in **Egypt**, such as the frogs and the **insects**, were recognized adversaries. Human-eating wild beasts—the **lion** and the wolf—were enemies of both humans and domesticated animals. Nature, like humanity, was set off kilter by the sin in the Garden of Eden.

Natural history studies of the Bible testify to the extensive range of animal life that once flourished in the region. George Cansdale (p.14), in his encyclopedic study of biblical animals, places them in four classes:

1. Domestic stock, both working and edible, and those wild animals considered suitable for food, ranging from mammals to insects, and fish
2. Dangerous animals and insects, such as the wolf, lion, flea, and moth, that were a peril to human life, stock, crops, and other possessions
3. Familiar wild animals, birds, and insects that Hebrews would have seen along the sides of roads or around their homes, including the swallow, sparrow, harvester ant, and others

Sheep were a favorite of the ancient Israelites.

25

4. Unclean animals, specifically forbidden as food to the **Hebrews**, such as, birds of prey, those animals without the cloven hoof, and shellfish

The animals in the Bible, whether wild or domesticated, threatening or useful, are carefully observed, and provide a rich source of imagery. The Psalmist portrays himself thirsting for God as a deer "pants for streams of water" (Ps. 42). Jeremiah compares the people's rebellion to a "wild ass used to the wilderness, that snuffeth up the wind at her pleasure"—uncontrollable and full of lust (Jer. 2:23); he hears the threat of war in the "snorting" of the horses (Jer. 8:16); he charges that they have treated their **prophets** "like a destroying lion" (Jer. 2:30). He warns that these oxlike people have broken their **yoke** and that they will now fall prey to a "lion out of the forest … and a wolf of the evenings … a leopard shall watch over their cities: every one that goeth out thence shall be torn in pieces" (Jer. 5:6).

Job had spoken of venomous serpents (20:16); he complained he had become "a brother of jackals and a companion of owls" (30:29). The book of Job has a splendid catalogue of animals God created when "the morning stars sang together and all the **angels** shouted with joy" (Job 38:7–41:34): the lions and mountain goats, the doe and her fawn, the wild **donkey** and the wild ox, the ostrich, the stork, the horse, the hawk and the eagle, the **behemoth**, and the **leviathan**.

A sand lizard (listed as "unclean" in Lev. 11:29). Palestine has 40 recognized species of lizard, including the green lizard, the crocodile, and the chameleon.

Isaiah also loved animal imagery—the ox that "knows his master" and the "donkey his owner's manger" (Isa. 1:2); the fruitless sacrifice of rams, the blood of bulls and lambs and goats (1:11); the **idols** that men will throw away "to the rodents and bats" (2:20).

Jesus also found many of his images among the animals. He spoke of **dogs** being given the crumbs dropped from the table, the Prodigal Son feeding the **pigs**, and the foxes that had their holes and the birds their nests (Matt. 8:20). When confronted with a question of human worth in God's eyes, Jesus noted that two sparrows are "sold for a farthing," yet "one of them shall not fall on the ground" without the Father's knowledge (Matt. 10:29).

Among the vast array of animals included in Scripture, besides those already mentioned, are adders, antelopes, apes, badgers, bears, chameleons, coneys, badgers, gazelles, hares, hyenas,

A fox, which is mentioned in the Song of Solomon 2:15. Palestine had two varieties of fox that loved holes (Matt. 8:20) and deserted ruins (Lam. 5:18).

ibexes, elephants, jackals, leopards, lizards, mice, wild boars, wolves, and "whatever has many feet" (Lev. 11:41–42).

Animals in the Law of Moses

The concern that God shows for even the sparrow is mirrored in the law given to Moses. In the great chain of being, animals fall awkwardly between humans and property. They have feelings, need rest, display willfulness, can be overburdened, and respond to punishment. They are not simply "things." On the other hand, they have monetary value and can be bought and sold, stolen, lost, hurt, or coveted. Exodus 20–21 and Deuteronomy 22 note a number of issues concerning the treatment of animals. In addition, animals are included among those of God's creatures that need **Sabbath** rest.

A man who violated an animal sexually was to be put to death (Exod. 35:19). The Hebrews also believed that it was unlawful to cross-breed animals, thereby forbidding the breeding of mules (a blend of donkey and horse). One who fails to restrain a dangerous animal can be punished according to the damage the animal has done, even to the point of death. An ox that gores a man or woman to death is to be stoned to death and his flesh not eaten (Exod. 27:8). There are further rules that treat these creatures as property, with appropriate **punishments** for those who steal, fail to return, or damage their neighbor's beasts. Their helplessness is also noted in the requirement that the passerby must help the fallen animal out of a ditch and avoid taking eggs from a mother bird (Lev. 22:6).

All of these regulations and many others developed over time suggest the special relationship of people and animals—particularly those in their own households. Humans were originally granted dominion over the animals. After the fall, this was hard to maintain, but many creatures became

A gazelle (*Gazella gazella*), or an antelope, sometimes called a "roe" or a "buck," was an animal considered "clean" in Jewish law.

friends and helpers of men and women. *See also* Behemoth, Leviathan; Birds; Creation; Dogs; Food; Sacrifice; Serpent; Sheep.

Further Reading

Cansdale, George. *All the Animals of the Bible Lands*. Grand Rapids, Mich.: Zondervan Publishing House, 1970. Darom, David. *Animals of the Bible*. Herzliam, Israel: Palphot Ltd., n.d. Falk, Ze'ev W. *Hebrew Law in Biblical Times*. Provo, Utah: Brigham Young University Press, 2001.

Annunciation

(**Luke 1:28–32**) *Annunciation* is the term used to describe the moment when the **angel** Gabriel came to Mary to announce to her that she was to bear a child, whose name was Jesus, that he was to be the **Messiah**, and that God would give him the **throne** of David. The theological concept of the Incarnation—when God became man, a flesh and blood human—is essential in most Christian churches, and is enshrined in the Apostles' Creed: "I believe in ... Jesus Christ, his only son, our Lord, who was born of the Virgin Mary."

As the medieval church celebrated the events of her life and came to venerate the Virgin Mary, artists such as Fra Angelico painted famous portrayals of this event. In time, the doctrine of the Immaculate Conception, the idea that Mary herself, by the grace of God, was preserved free from original sin, became a dogma of the Roman Catholic Church. *See also* Angels; Messiah.

Anointing

(**Exod. 29:36; Lev. 8:11, 30; 1 Sam. 10:1, 16:13; 24:1-7; 26:7–11; 1 Kings 1:39; 2 Kings 9:3; Is. 6:1:1; Dan. 9:24; Luke 4:18, 9:1-6; Acts 4:27; Mark 6:13**) Pouring or sprinkling a few drops of olive oil or other pungent balm on a man's head, especially the face, was a custom in much of Hebrew history and continued into the Christian era. Anointing came to be a sign of **hospitality** and a means of personal enhancement; it was also used for healing and for sacred ceremonies.

With women, the anointing appears to have been part of the process of bathing, involving the entire body rather than the head alone. In private, informal usage, men and women "anointed" their whole body in preparation for a **feast**, making the hair and skin glisten. With royalty—like Esther—the anointing would have followed the **bath**, when servants prepared the queen for her elaborate **clothing**. It was refreshing—serving as a soothing balm against the fierce heat and wind of Palestine. Earlier, when Ruth took her bath, preparing to meet Boaz, she too completed it by anointing her body with oils and perfumes, as did Susanna and Judith at later times. They probably used aromatic ointments to enhance their sex appeal.

There are numerous references to "dabbing" or "smearing" the **olive oil** or ointment on the skin and hair. In many cases, the oil was lavishly applied. The Psalmist tells us: brotherhood "is like the precious **ointment** upon the head, that ran down upon the **beard,** even Aaron's beard: that went down to the skirts of his garments" (Ps. 133:2). This is clearly a sacramental description of anointing for **priests** or for **kings**.

The **Greek** athletes later found that pouring larger quantities over the entire body after a bath and scraping it off left them clean and smooth—emphasizing the beauty of the skin and muscles. The aesthetic purpose here of enhancing the physical beauty of the male body reveals a different cultural attitude, reflecting the Greek celebration of physical splendor.

In its sacramental usage, things as well as people were sometimes anointed. Jacob anointed the **stone** of Bethel by pouring oil on it. In ceremonies, anointing became especially important: Moses prepared ointment in the wilderness, according to an ancient legend, that was sufficient to anoint all the kings and high priests of Israel throughout history and was to be used until the anointing of the **Messiah** (George Barton and Kaufmann Kohler 2004).

For the Hebrews, the anointing was often associated with sacred persons, especially the high priest and the king. Every priest had to be anointed according to established rules. From the time of Samuel, the king of Israel was anointed by a **prophet** or priest, signaling his divine selection and placing his life in a special category. The oil was dropped on his head, tracing the shape of a **crown** all around the head. This ensured God's protection of his chosen leader and promised harm to anyone who attacked the king. Even after he himself had been anointed king by Samuel, and even though Saul was seeking his death, David was fearful of harming Saul. He was "the Lord's anointed."

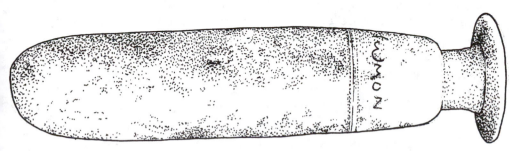

An Egyptian alabaster vase from the Hellenistic period. Unguents, used for anointing, were preserved best in alabaster containers where they improved with age. (See references to a "box" of ointment in Matt. 26:7; Mark 14:3; and Luke 7:37 as well as other paraphernalia for holding cosmetics.)

This tradition of the divine protection and right of anointed kings figures in much of history. The Europeans accepted this concept, as we see in the *Tragedy of Macbeth* and many other of Shakespeare's plays. Even an evil king had God's protection ringing him about. In the seventeenth century, with the execution of Charles I, the English engaged in explosive controversies over the violation of this anointed king. This was also a central issue in the beheading of Louis XVI during the French Revolution.

The anointing ceremony usually appears to have been a private one, but it was clearly public on certain occasions: At Solomon's coronation, "Zadok the priest took the horn of oil from the sacred tent and anointed Solomon. Then they sounded the trumpet and all the people shouted, 'Long live King Solomon!'" (1 Kings 1:39).

Anointing came to signify the blessing of God poured out on the chosen one, often referring to the Messiah. In the early **Christian Church**, it was also used to signify the blessing of the **Holy Spirit**, poured out on believers. The anointed person was considered holy and was fully equipped with authority from God for service. *See also* Bath, Bathing; Priest, High Priest; Hospitality; Kings; Olives, Olive Oil, Olive Trees.

Further Reading

Barton, George A. and Kaufmann Kohler, "Anointing," http://jewishencyclopedia. com (accessed December 20, 2004). Motyer, J. A. "Anointing, Anointed," in *The Illustrated Bible Dictionary*. Sydney, Australia: Tyndale House Publishers, 1980.

Antichrist

(1 John 2:18, 22, 4:3; 2 John 7; 2 Thess. 2:1–12; Rev. 13, 17) Literally, *antichrist* means "instead of Christ," or an antagonist of Christ. Although the term appears mainly in John's **epistles**, the basic idea was widespread. It means a person who deliberately opposes Christ, not just a false **prophet** who claims to be Christ. Thus, it refers to the strong opposition by forces of evil, such as those mentioned in Daniel 7:7 and is usually associated with the Last Days, appearing in references to the **Apocalypse**. The Antichrist is one who, according to John, "denies the Father and the Son" (1 John 2:22). Such a person is doing the work of Satan, opposing the things of God. The reference in Thessalonians is to the "man of lawlessness" (2 Thess. 2:3), a man who "opposes and exalts himself against every so-called god or object of **worship**," exalting himself to be God. Although the Antichrist is not Satan, his coming is a foreshadowing of Satan himself. In other scripture, he is called the "man of sin," the "son of perdition," the "wicked one," or the "beast." In the great apocalyptic battle of good and evil at the end of time, the Antichrist will make his final challenge to God. This explains the use of the image of the "beast" in Revelation. Here the great battle of **Armageddon** pits the final surge of evil forces against the forces of good.

Because of the strong belief in the early Church that the Second Coming was imminent, many sought to identify the Antichrist with contemporary figures, just as many do in modern times. During the Protestant Reformation, the references to the *Antichrist* in polemical and popular literature refer to the Pope. The term has also been used against numerous political leaders from Nero to Cromwell. In the twentieth century, Hitler, Mussolini, and others earned the title. In contemporary apocalyptic literature, efforts continue to identify the Antichrist. *See also* Apocalypse, Apocalyptic Literature; Armageddon.

Further Reading

Bousset, W. *The Antichrist Legend: A Chapter in Christian and Jewish Folklore.* London: Hutchinson, 1896. Morris, L. L. "Antichrist," in *The Illustrated Bible Dictionary.* Sydney, Australia: Tyndale House Publishers, 1980. Williams, W. Roger. "Antichrist," in *A Dictionary of Biblical Tradition in English Literature.* Grand Rapids, Mich.: William B. Eerdmans Publishing Company, 1992.

Apocalypse, Apocalyptic Literature

(Ezek. 38–39; Isa. 24–27; Zech. 12–14; Joel 3; Daniel; Revelation)
The terms *apocalypse* and *apocalyptic* come from the Greek root meaning "to uncover" or "to reveal." They are used to describe a written account of a **vision** that reveals the hidden things of God, given to one of his chosen saints. The Book of Revelation was originally called "The Apocalypse of John," thereby leading Bible scholars from the second century A.D. to use this as a term describing Jewish and Christian literature of the same general pattern.

The following elements are usually present:

1. It is a revelation of mysteries, the secrets of **heaven**, the purposes of God, impending events, the future of humankind, the end of the world, and the Last Judgment.
2. The disclosure comes by means of a vision or a **dream**, usually involving difficult symbolism and numerology that require interpretation.
3. **Angels** are usually the bearers or interpreters of the revelation.
4. The major topic is the future, often going beyond prophesy to the future of humankind at the end of time, when the **Day of the Lord** comes. Contemporary events and people may also be included, usually in veiled imagery. The great final battle is often

prophesied, as is the following reign of God and the judgment of all of the peoples of the earth (Charles C. Torrey 2004).

5. Standard imagery includes beasts and monsters of epic nature, visions of Heavenly Jerusalem and the **Temple**, angelic hosts singing around the **throne** of God.

6. The language tends to be ecstatic and disconnected, in the mode of **poetry** and mystical writing.

The earliest biblical examples that appear in the Old Testament are **prophets** such as Ezekiel, Isaiah, Zechariah, and Joel—all of whom speak of the end of days and the final accomplishment of God's purpose. The Book of Daniel is also filled with elements of apocalyptic power. The Revelation of John follows the form of an epistle to the seven churches, describing **Armageddon** in great detail. It is full of rich symbolism and ecstatic moments of vision, often captured in dramatic poetic form.

A number of extra-biblical books, such as Enoch and the Apocalypse of Baruch, were also written during the Greco-**Roman** period, prophesying the eventual triumph of God's people. The **Essenes** of the Qumran community appear to have been deeply committed to an apocalyptic vision of the end times and secret knowledge—as in the "War Scroll," "Hymns," their "Book of Mysteries," their "Genesis Apocryphon," and the "Description of the New Jerusalem" (Robert C. Dentan 1993, 37). In recent times, with the revived interest in the Gnostics and the Essenes, these have received considerable scholarly and popular attention.

Apocalyptic form—especially the poetic use of visions—has appealed to writers through the centuries, influencing many of the medieval and Renaissance writers, most notably Dante and the English romantic poets (William Kinsley 1992, 47). It has also become a part of modern secular literature, which uses the form without the underlying experience. *See also* Armageddon; Day of Judgment, Day of the Lord; Essenes.

Further Reading

Dentan, Robert C. "Apocalyptic Literature," in *The Oxford Companion to the Bible*. New York: Oxford University Press, 1993. Kinsley, William. "Apocalypse," in *A Dictionary of Biblical Tradition in English Literature*. Grand Rapids, Mich.: William B. Eerdmans Publishing Company, 1992. Torry, Charles C. "Apocalypse." http://www.jewishencyclopedia.com (accessed December 20, 2004).

Apocrypha

The term *apocrypha* means "hidden." It was used to describe writings that were accepted as part of the Old Testament canon by some groups, but not by others. Some of the apocryphal books are additions to existing books, such as Ezra, Esther, and Daniel. Some are completely independent stories and histories, such as the books of the Maccabees, Tobit, Susanna, and Judith. Because they were included in the Septuagint, the Greek translation of the Scriptures, the early **Christian Church** included them in their transcriptions of the Old Testament. After the destruction of the **Temple** in 70 A.D., Jewish scholars became concerned with identifying themselves as Jews and did not approve of books not written in Hebrew. They chose to exclude those books that appeared only in the Greek translation, using them only for edification, but not considering them authoritative.

Among Christians who accept the Septuagint as authoritative, these books have continued to be included between the Old Testament and the New Testament in copies of the Bible. Leaders of the Protestant Reformation and Calvin in particular objected to their inclusion; Luther and the Anglicans admitted them only for private edification. The Eastern Orthodox Churches have continued to include and refer to them.

The New Testament also had apocryphal writings. There were a number of late **Gospels** and stories of the **Disciples** that the early church considered less reliable than those they included in the canon. Among the primary apocryphal writings in this group are the Gospels of Mary Magdalene, Thomas, Nicodemus, and James; and the Acts of Peter, John, Andrew, Thomas, and Paul.

The discoveries in 1945 of the library at Nag Hammadi have enlivened this controversy on the authenticity of many of these extra-biblical gospels and stirred considerable theological debate. In recent years, the so-called "Gnostic gospels" have received considerable attention from scholars, some of whom insist that they provide contemporary insights into the life and sayings of Jesus and those around him. It is, for instance, in the Acts of Paul that we are told that Paul was "little in stature with a bald head and crooked legs . . . eyebrows meeting , and a nose somewhat hooked" (Bruce Metzger 1993, 40). Stories of Jesus's childhood and additional of his sayings and actions often seem out of character with the Jesus presented in the four traditional Gospels.

With the discoveries of a growing list of Gnostic works, "hidden" books, and "secret" narratives, the rage for these apocryphal writings continues. They feed the natural human appetite for clear answers to questions left open by the canon of Scripture. *See also* Disciples; Gospel, Gospels.

Further Reading

Birdsall, J. N. "Apocrypha," in *The Illustrated Bible Dictionary.* Sydney, Australia: Tyndale House Publishers, 1980. Jenkins, Philip. *Hidden Gospels: How the Search for Jesus Lost Its Way.* New York: Oxford University Press, 2001. Metzger, Bruce. "Aprypha," in *The Oxford Companion to the Bible.* New York: Oxford University Press, 1993. Miller, Robert J., ed. *The Complete Gospels.* San Francisco: Harper Collins Publisher, 1992.

Apostle

(**Matt. 28:19–20, 10:1–4; Mark 3:13–19; Luke 6:12–16; Acts 1:8, 21–22; 1 Cor. 9:1, 12:29; Eph. 4:11**) An apostle is an ambassador, "someone who has been sent," or a person delegated by Jesus to be a "messenger" of the **Gospel**. The word derives from the Greek word *apostello,* meaning "to send forth," indicating someone who is entrusted with a mission, that is, a delegate.

The first apostles were the **Disciples**, selected, instructed, and sent out by Jesus to proclaim the kingdom and heal the sick. After the **Resurrection**, Christ instructed his disciples to go into all the world, make disciples, and baptize in his name (Matt. 28:19–20). The term *apostle* encompasses these first 12 (except for the traitor Judas) and extends to others who were also specially called by Christ to do his work. The listing of the apostles appears in 1 Corinthians and Ephesians.

Paul, who did not see Jesus "in the flesh" or follow him as a disciple, often defended his own designation as apostle by citing his Damascus Road experience, when he was called directly by Christ to take his message to the world. Luke believed that a true apostle must have been a companion of Jesus and a witness to the Resurrection (Acts 1:21–22). For Paul, the role of the apostles was much like that of the Old Testament **prophets**, who were servants of the Lord, bringing his message to his people.

The early Church, which venerated the apostles in their lifetimes and after their deaths, instituted feasts for various of the more beloved and remarkable saints such as John, Peter, Paul, and Andrew, which are still celebrated by Eastern Orthodox and Roman Catholic Churches. *See also* Disciples; Prophet; Resurrection.

Further Reading

Betz, Otto. "Apostle," in *The Oxford Companion to the Bible*. New York: Oxford University Press, 1993. Coppieters, Honoré. "Apostles, The," http://www.newadvent.org (accessed February 28, 2005).

Appeal to Caesar. *See Law*

Ark

(**Gen. 6:14–16; Exod. 2:3**) An ark is a "chest" or "box." In the case of Noah's ark, which is described fully in Genesis, it was designed to be seaworthy so as to withstand the **Great Flood**. It was made of gopher wood and caulked with pitch, typical of Mesopotamian construction. Noah's ark was large enough to contain a pair of every living species of animal. It had three decks and an opening all around just below the roof to allow light and air inside. It also had a door and windows that allowed access. Werner Keller notes the extensive work of the missionary Dr. Aaron Smith, who spent years collecting 80,000 works in 72 languages about the Flood, of which 70,000 works refer to the wreckage of the Ark, which is thought to have finally landed on Mt. Arat (Werner Keller 1982, 38).

By contrast, the tiny ark in which the baby Moses was set afloat was a basket made of bulrushes or papyrus smeared with mud and pitch. It held the child until he was discovered in the Nile by Pharaoh's daughter.

The **Ark of the Covenant** was a chest that held relics of Israel's history as God's Chosen People. It was placed in the Holy of Holies, first in the **Tabernacle** and later in the **Temple**. *See also* Ark of the Covenant; Flood, the Great.

Further Reading

Keller, Werner. *The Bible as History*. New York: Bantam Books, 1982. Knight, George A. F., "Ark," in *The Oxford Companion to the Bible*. New York: Oxford University Press, 1993. Miller, Madeleine S. and J. Lane Miller. "Ark," in *Harper's Bible Dictionary*. New York: Harper and Row, 1961.

Ark of the Covenant

(Exod. 26:31–33; Heb. 9:4) The Ark of the Covenant was a rectangular box holding the **stone** tablets inscribed with the **Ten Commandments** (Exod. 31:18; 32:15–16), the golden jar of **manna** (Exod. 16:32–34), and Aaron's staff (Num. 17:8–10). The Ark was placed behind a veil in the Holy of Holies and was approached once a year by the **High Priest**. God provided Moses with a detailed description of the Ark, including the wood from which it was constructed and the gold leaf covering, the **cherubim** on either side of the "mercy seat," which formed a lid for it. The gold rings through which poles were pushed allowed the ark to be portable, moving with the **Tabernacle** and the people of Israel. Even the two men involved in making it, Bezaleel and Ahoiliab, were specifically designated by God.

In the march from Sinai and at the crossing of the Jordan River, the Ark of the Covenant was carried before the people and signaled their advance. **Miracles—blessings** and **curses**—followed its movement, with the Jordan growing dry when the feet of the **priests** who were carrying it touched the waters. When the Ark was carried around Jericho and horns were blown, the walls of the city fell. The Ark itself was considered the potent force for the victory over the city. Later Joshua read his people the **law** as they stood

Ark of the Covenant, with cherubim sheltering the sacred throne, based on description in Exod. 25:10–22. (No drawings or carvings have survived depicting the Ark, and these cherubim are more human in appearance than others in Scripture.)

on either side of the Ark (Josh. 8:33) and then set it up at the **sanctuary** at Shiloh (Josh. 18:1).

The Ark served as a symbol of God's presence, guiding his people. The Israelites frequently carried the Ark with them into battle, perhaps explaining the Philistines' determination to capture it (1 Sam. 3:3). When the messenger carried the news of this catastrophe to his people, he rent his clothes and poured dirt on his head. The old priest Eli fell dead when he heard the news, and his daughter-in-law, who was bearing a son at the time, named the baby "Ichabod"—meaning "Where is the glory"—referring to the departed Ark (1 Sam. 4:12–220).

The Philistines found that the Ark was no blessing for them. During the seven months the Ark remained with them, the **temple** of Dagon at Ashdod saw miraculous events, with the pagan god prostrate and broken before the Ark, and a **plague** of boils (perhaps hemorrhoids) and of mice sent over the land (1 Sam. 6:5). In an effort to placate this alien deity, the Philistines formed golden images of the boils and mice, placed the Ark in the field of Joshua the Beth-shemite, and offered **sacrifices** and burnt offerings to it. Out of curiosity, the men of Beth-shemesh gazed at it and 50,000 of them were "smitten by the Lord." They were so frightened and alarmed that they begged to have it removed, resulting in its return to the house of Abinadab and the sanctification by Eleazer (1 Sam. 6–7). The Ark remained in this location for 20 years.

Apparently, kings and other military leaders came to see the Ark as essential to victory in battle, praying before it before battles. King Saul, however, was too impatient to pay proper homage to the Ark before going into battle and suffered the consequences. David, understanding the Ark's importance, had it moved to Zion, amid great rejoicing. Along the way a cart-driver who tried to steady it was slain, causing a delay of three months and reminding all concerned that this was a sacred relic to be handled with awe. The final stage of the journey was managed by Levites, whose task it was to care for the Ark. David danced and sang along the way, dressed in a linen ephod, proclaiming his delight that the Ark was to be at home in his city. He had it placed in the Tabernacle, and Solomon later had it housed in the Holy of Holies—the most sacred portion of his Temple. The Ark was the Jews' holiest object, considered the seat of God, the place where man and God could meet when the High Priest entered the Holy of Holies on the **Day of Atonement**. The city of Jerusalem was itself considered holy largely because the Ark of the Covenant was located there (Morris Jastrow, Jr., Charles Mendelshon et al. 2004).

No one is sure of the eventual fate of the Ark after the destruction of Solomon's Temple. Some believe it was taken to **Babylonia**. Some think that King Josiah hid the Ark and other sacred vessels and perhaps buried them. Some believe that God took the Ark to **Heaven**, and the **angels** brought it down again to **Earth** from time to time. Jeremiah 3:16 anticipated a time when the Ark would no longer be required, a view echoed in Hebrews 9:4, with Christ as the High Priest, residing eternally in the presence of God. *See also* Ark; Priest, High Priest; Tabernacle; Temple; War, Warfare: General.

Further Reading

Jastrow, Morris, Jr., Charles J. Mendelshon, Marcus Jastrow, Isaac Husik, Duncan B. McDonald, and George A. Barton, "Ark of the Covenant," http://www.jewishencyclopedia.com (accessed December 20, 2004). Kitchen, K. A. "Ark of the Covenant," in *The Illustrated Bible Dictionary*. Sydney, Australia: Tyndale House Publishers, 1980.

Armageddon

(**Rev. 16:16**) The name *Armageddon* appears to be derived from "Megiddon," or "Mountain of Megiddo." In Revelation, it designates the final contest, the great war between good and evil, also referred to as the **Day of the Lord**. Ezekiel seemed to be referring to this final epic battle when he spoke of the "mountains of Israel" witnessing Gog's defeat (Ezek. 39:1–4).

The Plain of Megiddo had already seen numerous conflicts, such as those recorded in Judges 5:19 and 2 Kings 9:27, 23:29. In more recent times, it was the scene of a major battle in World War I, when Lord Allenby used the same strategy that Deborah had used to defeat the enemy: he calculated the time that the rivers would flood the plain and cause the enemy's heavy equipment to bog down. This gives the advantage to the army that has the high ground and is on foot.

Megiddo is strategically located at the intersection of trade routes, an appropriate place for the end-of-time battle of "the kings of the east." The actual location of this battle is less important than its symbolic meaning as the **apocalyptic** climax of antagonistic forces on earth. In modern times, the word *Armageddon* has been used repeatedly for almost any large-scale battle that may have disastrous results. Even a film about Viet Nam and Cambodia was given that name. *See also* Apocalypse, Apocalyptic Literature; Day of Judgment, Day of the Lord; War, Warfare: General.

Armor, Arms. *See* Warfare

Army. *See* Warfare

Art: Christian

(**Exod. 20:4; John 1:1–2**) Unlike the Jews, the early Christians believed themselves to be set free of the old **law** that forbade graven images, and empowered by the **Incarnation** to portray God's **creation**. In the early **Christian Church**, the influx of gentile members from Greco-Roman and other cultures, which had long artistic traditions, overwhelmed the Jewish Christians. Pagans were all too eager to form images of their deities, but the recently Christianized Jews still retained strict limitations. This tension between the supporters and prohibitors of artistic expression has continued in the Christian community to modern times.

In the early Church, there was little occasion for art. At first, Christians used only such simple symbolic representations as the **fish** for Christ, the anchor for hope, or the dove for the soul. Then the image of the Good Shepherd, with Christ carrying a lamb around his shoulders, opened the door for more representational art, including narratives based on Scripture. Because Jesus lived a very human life, his followers felt free to portray his remembered and imagined image in paint, plaster, stone, and metal.

Early Christians decorated their meeting places, the catacombs, those subterranean burial galleries cut out of the ground. Frescoes, paint in wet plaster, depicted scenes of Christ's miracles or scenes from his life. He was usually represented without a beard in the style of classical art (Harold Osborne 1970, 352–355).

Some theologians objected to the representation of either Christ or God; others argued against any depiction of the **Crucifixion**. The argument has raged over the centuries, involving such profound thinkers as Eusebius and Augustine. This debate led eventually to the iconoclastic controversy in the Eastern Orthodox Church and centuries later to the Puritans' rejection of images in their churches at the time of the Reformation.

For the most part, these images were not designed to provide aesthetic pleasure for its own sake, but to call the worshippers to prayer and contemplation. In the absence of a literate congregation who could read Scripture for themselves, the art developed into an elaborate system of symbols that grew into medieval iconography. It was only after the Christian Church became the official religion of the Roman Empire under Constantine (313 A.D.) that Christian art and architecture blossomed, with increasingly ornate churches and cathedrals, decorated with glorious stained glass windows, elaborately wrought doorways, and finely carved or cast statuary .

These splendid creations seemed to be a human effort to make the vision of the heavenly Jerusalem a reality on earth. The vision of John in Revelation became the key to much of Christian art. Mont St. Michel and Chartres, with their luminous windows, Canterbury Cathedral, Westminster Abbey, and Notre Dame, are elegant monuments to a time when religion was the main subject matter of art and the church was the main patron of the arts. *See also* Art: Jewish; Incarnation.

Further Reading

Morey, Charles Rufus. *Christian Art*. New York: Longmans, Green, 1935. Osborne, Harold. *The Oxford Companion to Art*. Oxford: Oxford University Press, 1970. Volbach, Wolfgang F. and Max Hirmer. *Early Christian Art*. New York: Abrams, 1961.

Art: Jewish

(**Exod. 20:4; Deut. 4:16–18**) Because of the strict prohibition in the Ten Commandments against the making of graven images, the Jews considered the creation of art to be sacrilegious. In fact, the first evidence of crafting a statue—the image of the golden calf—led to Moses's breaking the tablets of the **law** and the Lord commanding Moses that he burn the gold object and grind it into the water and force the people to drink it (Exod. 32:1–24).

The very use of the term *Jewish art* is incorrect inasmuch as many artifacts discovered in ancient Hebrew digs have been influenced if not actually produced by non-Jewish artisans (Joseph Jacobs, Kaufmann Kohler et al. 2004). Having seen beautiful art in **Egypt**, the Hebrews contributed their most cherished items to the Lord, especially in the creation of the **Tabernacle**. This provided the opportunity for lavish ornamentation.

It is in the construction and decoration of the Tabernacle and later of the **Temple** that God permitted a limited number of images—the **cherubim**, the decorative curtains, the figures on the doorway, and so forth. The elaborate descriptions of both of these places of worship include the names of the master craftsmen involved. Bezalel, who was chosen to design the decorations for the Tabernacle, seems to have had skill in working in wood, **metal,** and embroidery (Exod. 35:30–33). In the case of the Temple, Solomon imported Phoenician craftsmen, suggesting the Israelites did not have the workers for either the construction or the decorations for the magnificent buildings he envisioned.

In later times, the **prophets** lamented the excessive decoration—the beds of **ivory**, the lattice work—that the wealthy used to beautify their homes while they neglected the Lord's house (Amos 3:15; Ps. 45:8; Hag. 1:4). These references provide evidence of alien influences creeping into the life-style of God's chosen people, polluting their taste and encouraging them to worship human creativity rather than God's.

Apparently, some Hebrew craftsmen did eventually learn the arts of **pottery** decoration, **seal**-engraving, metal-casting, ivory-carving, and wood-carving. The Jewish leaders, however, seem never to have allowed sculpture or painting—only carving on flat surfaces. Their pottery is much plainer than that of their neighbors, the **Philistines** and the **Greeks**. And their loathing of foreign **idols** kept them from making any stone or clay images of those human figures that were so common all through the Fertile Crescent. Some believe that the Hebrews were not as sensitive as their neighbors to color, especially the Greeks and Egyptians who perfected the painting of pottery and walls (Morris Jastrow and Immanuel Benzinger 2004).

During the period of the Second Temple (450 B.C.–70 A.D.), Jewish taste began to change. Under the influence of the Greeks and **Romans**, they were both attracted to and repulsed by the art and architecture they saw in their cities. The sculptures of the human form, the wall-paintings, and the beautiful public buildings apparently tempted them to relax their prohibitions. With the great revolt that broke out in 66 A.D., the nationalistic feeling and hatred of all things Roman encouraged the orthodox Jewish leadership to ban all representation, even of **animals**.

In later years, with the rise of Christianity and the use of images among this group of believers, the Jews tended to relax their rules once again, allowing mosaics in their **synagogues** and some sculptured animal forms and human masks. Depiction of biblical scenes, probably even wall-painting, as well as illuminated manuscripts of the Scripture, were further evidences of Christian influence. Many of these came to a halt in the Middle Ages as a result of the Moslem example (strictly forbidding images) and the iconoclastic debate within Catholicism.

Modern times have seen the rise of some talented Jewish artists, such as Chagall, Pissarro, and Soutine, but there is still no such thing as distinctive "Jewish art" (Harold Osborne, 612–615). In orthodox Judaism, the synagogues remain bare of images. *See also* Art: Christian; Ivory; Metal: Gold; Pots and Pottery; Seals; Stone.

Further Reading

Jacobs, Joseph, Kaufmann Kohler, Judah David Eisenstein. "Art, Attitude of Judaism Toward," http://www.jewishencyclopedia.com (accessed December 20, 2004). Jastrow, Morris, Jr., Immanuel Benzinger. "Art Among the Ancient Hebrews. http://www.jewishencyclopedia.com (accessed December 20, 2004). Osborne, Harold. *The Oxford Companion to Art.* Oxford: The Oxford Press, 1970.

Artemis. *See Asherah, Ashtoreth, Ashtaroth; Idols, Idolatry*

Asherah, Ashtoreth, Ashtaroth

(1 Kings 11:5, 16:33, 18:19; Jer. 7:18) The name *Asherah* (pl. *Asherim*), or the variants such as *Ashtoreth* (pl. *Ashtaroth*) or *Astarte*, appear frequently in the Old Testament. This Mother Goddess figure, akin to Diana or Venus of the Romans and Ishtar of the Babylonians, was a fertility figure, a kind of Mother Earth. The "Lady of Byblos" was one of the oldest forms of "the Great Goddess in the Middle East, identified with Egypt's Hathor, Mycenae's Demeter, and Cyprus's Aprhrodite" (Barbara Walker 1983, 69). The parallel Syrian goddess appears to have been the mother/wife figure in the pantheon of gods, which included El and **Baal**. In **Palestine**, she was thought to be the wife of Baal.

Her Nature and Worship

The goddess was worshipped in "high places," and that worship was usually connected with groves of trees. The terms *Asherah* or *Asherim* were sometimes used for the goddess herself, sometimes for her image, sometimes for a wooden pole or sacred tree. Poles used as fuel for the sacrifice of animals to Baal were often referred to as "asherim." Sometimes they were set up under living trees, sometimes carved into disgusting shapes. In the Bible, the term is often connected with pillars, representing both the god and the **altar** (William Robertson Smith 1995, 204).

The goddess was often pictured as pregnant, while being also considered a virgin. She is supposed to have borne a sizable family—70 gods and goddesses (G. Ernest Wright 1996, 107). Curiously, she is also both the life-creator and life-destroyer goddess, typified by Kali, a symbol of Nature. Temples of Asherah were centers of legalized vice, where priestesses engaged in sacred prostitution. One scholar notes that the Canaanite cult was "highly erotic," with the ritual enactment of the sacred **marriage** between Baal and Ashterah at the center of the magical act of fertility. The worshipper would identify himself with Baal and the cult prostitute would represent Ashterah. "It was believed that human pairs, by imitating the action of Baal and his partner, could bring the divine pair together in fertilizing union" thereby restoring fertility to the soil (Bernhard Anderson 1966, 103).

She was also seen as the ruler of the spirits of the dead who lived in Heaven as stars, therefore known as "Queen of the Stars." She was sometimes portrayed as the Moon, surrounded by her star-children. In this mode, she is thought to have been a foreshadowing of the Virgin Mary, pictured in Revelation with parallel imagery.

Among Solomon's numerous wives were adherents to the cult of Ashterah, which the **king** allowed to flourish during his reign. Some believe that the wife of Hosea, who fell into "harlotry," may have been such a "priestess." **Priests** of this cult were among those imported by the imperious queen Jezebel, who introduced 400 prophets of Asherah into Israel (1 Kings18:19). Manasseh even had her image placed in the **Temple** (2 Kings 21:7). Her lure led numerous of the **prophets** to proclaim against her insidious influence. At various times in Hebrew history, the people were instructed to cut down, burn, or pull up the sacred trees or poles that were leading Israel astray (Deut. 7:5, 12:3, 16:21; Micah 5:14).

Sometimes called the "Hebrew Goddess" or "Queen of Heaven," this shadowy figure apparently had shrine houses at various places in Palestine, some of which have been excavated by archaeologists. In the Ras Shamara texts, she is characterized as a goddess of the sea and the consort of El, contrary to the Old Testament references to her and her ties with Baal. Differences in spelling and in history can be easily explained as the result of localized religious cults, which developed independent patterns of worship and created their own mythology.

An early stone mold has been uncovered that shows the Mother Goddess as a tall figure with a horned hat. Hundreds of clay plaques have also been discovered; one of them found at Lachish, dating from around 1000 B.C. "is typical in its emphasis on prominent breasts, sensuous smiles, accented eyes, and nudity" (Madeleine S. Miller and J. Lane Miller 1961 , 47). Sumerian cylinder seals from Lagash portray her squatting on top of her consort's body (Barbara Walker 1983, 70).

Christianity and the Mother Goddess

Some feminist scholars believe that Christians perceived a threat to their new faith in Astarte-Ashtoreh and transformed her into a devil. Her pervasive influence may still be seen in the New Testament, in Paul's experience with the silversmiths in Ephesus. They were exercised over the threat that this new religion, Christianity, posed to their worship of the fertility goddess and their sales of goddess statues. When Paul preached in the amphitheatre there, they shouted, "Great is Diana!" and forced him to flee for his life.

In John's Revelation, the pagan Mother Goddess is transformed into the beautiful image of the Queen of Heaven, the woman with the moon at her feet. In both Syria and Egypt, ancient sacred dramas in honor of the Queen of Heaven celebrated the rebirth of the solar god from the celestial Virgin each 25th of December. "A newborn child was exhibited, while the cry went up that the Virgin had brought forth" (Barbara Walker 1983, 70). The Christians were compelled to replace this old and pervasive worship of the Great Goddess with a new faith. John's brilliant use of this figure in his Revelation transforms this universal, abiding hunger for a transcendent female deity into one of the images of motherhood that fill his vision. Over the centuries, the Church herself was able to blend the ancient solar rites into the calendar of Christ's life, death, and resurrection, making Christmas a joyous celebration of the birth of the Savior.

The periodic temptation of Israel to turn away from God to this fertility goddess had been characterized as prostitution by his people—"Virgin Israel." Their covenant relationship is portrayed as a marriage, as is the relationship between Christ and his **Church**. John touches on all these female images in the elegant and intricate imagery of his great revelation: He draws the Queen of Heaven as a source for images of the Virgin Mary, as well as the whore of Babylon, who tempts the powerful of the earth. In the powerful climactic scene of Revelation, the pure virgin joins her bridegroom in the Marriage Feast of the Lamb, the union of Christ and his Church. *See also* Baal, Baalim; Idols, Idolatry.

Further Reading

Anderson, Bernhard W. *Understanding the Old Testament.* Englewood Cliffs, N.J.: Prentice-Hall, 1966. Walker, Barbara G. *The Woman's Encyclopedia of Myths and Secrets.* San Francisco: HarperSanFrancisco, 1983. Miller, Madeleine S., and J. Lane Miller. *Harper's Bible Dictionary.* New York: Harper and Row, 1961. Smith, William Robertson. *Lectures on the Religion of the Semites.* Sheffield, England: Sheffield Academic Press, 1995. Tischler, Nancy M. *Legacy of Eve: Women of the Bible.* Atlanta, Ga.: John Knox Press, 1977. Wright, G. Ernest. *Biblical Archaeology.* Philadelphia: The Westminster Press, 1966.

Assyria, Assyrians

(Isa. 7:17–25; 2 Kings 15:27–16:9, 18:7, 8, 19:20:12; 2 Chron. 33:11–13) Assyria was a land of constant **warfare** for centuries, attractive to the wild tribesmen of the desert and mountains, a place that invited battle with its envious neighbors. For the Israelites, *Assyria* was a name that conjured up great dread. The Assyrian Empire stretched from **Babylonia** to **Egypt** at one time, under such kings as Ashur-nasir-pal II (883–859 B.C.), Shalmaneser V (858–824 B.C.), Tiglash-pileser III (745–727 B.C.), Shalmaneser V (727–722 B.C.), Sargon II (722–705 B.C.), Sennacherib (705–681 B.C.), and Asshurbanapal (669–633 B.C.).

References in Scripture

Assyria and its people are mentioned 150 times in Scripture, usually in connection with attacks and captivity. Some of the main events involving both the Israelites and the Assyrians include the following:

- Shalmaneser II fought King Ahab.
- Tiglath-pileser III took North Israel even after Menahem had paid tribute. He also carried off many of the people of the Northern Kingdom into captivity (2 Kings 15:19, 20).
- Shalmaneser V laid siege to the capital of Samaria for three years and perished during the siege. Again the Israelites were carried off to Assyria, and they were replaced by new settlers from Babylonia, Elam, and Syria. These immigrants intermarried with the remaining Israelites to become the Samaritans.
- Sargon II completed the captivity of Israel, leading off thousands of its leading citizens. The Bible takes particular note of the Assyrians during the final years of Israel. Amos and Hosea, **prophets** of the north, and Isaiah all pronounced judgments based on Assyria's rise.

The people of Judah had a compact with the Assyrians, promising tribute, which Hezekiah refused to pay; he joined in a rebellion against Assyrian control. Sennacherib dealt brutally with this rebel king, besieging his cities and deporting his people until he agreed to pay tribute to Nineveh. Sennacherib captured the great city of Lachish and other walled cities, but ran into a catastrophe on the eve of his attack on Jerusalem, when his army was decimated by the **"angel** of death," thought to have been a plague. He shut King Hezekiah up in Jerusalem and demanded tribute from him, including most of the treasures of the **Temple**.

Asshurbanapal was known for his long reign (36 years) during which time he beautified the capital city of Nineveh, his capital on the Tigris River. In 612 B.C., this city was taken captive by the Chaldeans, a group of Semitic nomads who were allied with the Medes. They gained control of Babylon, forming the Chaldean-Babylonia Empire or "New Babylonian Empire" (612–539 B.C.), which succeeded the Assyrians, with Nebuchadnezzar as their most famous ruler. These peoples were in turn succeeded by the **Persians**, under Cyrus.

The Assyrian Culture

The Assyrian people called their country, their god, and their main city by one name "Ashur." In Hebrew Scripture, Assur was one of the sons of Shem, who founded several cities, including Nineveh (Gen.10:11, 22). Records dating back to 2000 B.C. indicate that they were a Semitic people who used a language closely related to Babylonian. They also used the Babylonian (or Sumerian) system of **writing**.

Although they were ruthless in battle, they tended to be practical and generous in peacetime. They opened their government posts to people from other nationalities including Israelites such as Daniel and his friends. This great empire collected enormous wealth from **taxation** and trade, allowing the **kings** to build great **palaces** and construct great public works. For example, inscriptions inform us that "Tiglath-pileser I was also a daring hunter, for in one of his campaigns, he tells us, he killed no fewer than one hundred and twenty lions on foot, and eight hundred with spears while in his **chariot**, caught elephants alive, and killed ten in his chariot. He kept at the city of Asshur a park of **animals** suitable for the chase. At Nineveh he had a botanical **garden**, in which he planted specimens of foreign trees gathered during his campaigns. He built also many temples, palaces, and canals" (Gabriel Oussani, 2004). Their walls were lined with carved panels; their furniture was decorated with carved **ivory** panels and often plated with gold.

Modern Discoveries in Assyriology

Archaeologists have discovered numerous ruins of Assyrian cities and palaces in the northern part of modern Iraq, with a host of documents and inscriptions that verify the biblical references. The study of Assyriology has become increasingly sophisticated in the last century, allowing scholars to decipher many of the cuneiform tablets of the Babylonians and the Assyrians, and thus to reveal a great deal about history. King lists, for example, tell us which kings of Israel and Judah interacted with the kings of Assyria, thus helping the Bible student to determine the approximate dates of certain events.

A great deal of the writing on clay tablets describes the commercial transactions, thus indicating the business practices and trading partners of the time. Goodspeed, one of the great scholars of the period notes: "Asshurbanipal, Esarhaddon's successor, was undoubtedly the greatest of all Assyrian monarchs. For generalship, military conquests, diplomacy, love of splendor and luxury, and passion for the arts and letters, he has neither superior nor equal in the annals of that empire. To him we owe the greatest part of our knowledge of Assyrian-Babylonian history, art, and civilization. Endowed with a rare taste for letters, he caused all the most important historical, religious, mythological, legal, astronomical, mathematical, grammatical, and lexico-graphical texts and inscriptions known to his day to be copied and placed in a magnificent library that he built in his own palace. Goodspeed notes, "Tens of thousands of clay tablets systematically arranged on shelves for easy consultation," along with official dispatches and other archives that contained "the choicest religious, historical, and scientific literature of the Babylonian-Assyrian world." Inspired by Asshurbanipal's literary zeal, "scribes copied and translated the ancient sacred classics of primitive Babylonia for this library so that from its remains, can be reconstructed, not merely the details of the government and administration of the Assyria of his time, but the life and thought of the far distant Babylonian world" (Goodspeed, *History of the Babylonians and Assyrians,* 315, 316, qtd. in Oussini, 2004).

The Winged Bull from the throne room of Sargon II was probably a symbol of imperial power, combining the human face, bird wings, and bull body. Cults of bull worship were common throughout the Near East.

The images in the wall carvings and statuary also tell much about the styles of the time, the activities, and the culture. The king is seen on his throne facing his obsequious cupbearer, or lying on a couch drinking from a golden goblet shaped like an animal's head. Impressive weapons of warfare are seen along with the boasts of the cities the king has conquered. Most of these works reveal a strong Babylonian influence and use the cuneiform writing system first developed in Babylonia.

The Religion of Assyria

The religion of Assyria was much like that of Babylon in its doctrines, cults, and rites. The main difference was that the Babylonians' chief god was Marduk and the Assyrians' was Asshur. They both had three chief deities: Anue, the god of the heavens; Bel, the earth god, who was also the creator of mankind; and Ea, the god of water and of humanity. The mother of humankind and consort of Bel was Ishtar; their son was Bel, the father of wisdom, personified in the moon. There was also a sun god, Shamash, and a god of the netherworld, Nergal. Adad or Ramman was the god of storms, thunders, and lightening. Nebo was the god of wisdom and the source of writing and science. Others were in charge of fire, demons, evil spirits, and so forth. All of these, of course, required temples, priests and priestesses, rituals, sacrifices, and myths.

A great deal of this information appears in the great libraries whose contents are currently being transcribed and translated. Much more will undoubtedly come to light once Iraq is once again a hospitable place for archaeologists and historians to work in peace. *See also* History in the Bible.

Further Reading

Alexander, Pat. "The Assyrians," *Eerdmans' Family Encyclopedia of the Bible*. Grand Rapids, Mich.: William B. Eerdmans Publishing Co., 1978. Jastrow, Morris, Jr. and J. Frederic McCurdy. "Assyria," http://www.jewishencyclopedia. com (accessed December 25, 2004). Miller, Madeleine S. and J. Lane Miller. "Assyria, Empire of," in *Harper's Bible Dictionary*. New York: Harper and Row, 1961. Oussani, Gabriel. "Assyria," http://www.newadvent.org (accessed December 25, 2004).

Atonement, Day of

(**Lev. 16, 23:26–32, 25:9; Num. 29:7–11**) The concept of *atonement* is "at one"—the reconciliation of God and humans. Observed since the time of Moses, Yom Kippur follows the traditional beginning of the Jewish New Year. This annual day of judgment, which prefigures the final great Day of Judgment, occurs on the tenth day of the seventh month of the old year and was called the "**Sabbath** of the Sabbaths." It falls before the **Feast of Tabernacles** or Ingathering. It is so important a holiday that even nonpracticing Jews continue to observe this particular sacred event (Morris Jastrow, Jr. and Max. L. Margolis 2005).

Unlike many of the **festival** days, this is a solemn day of **fasting** and repentance, when the people consider the sins they have committed during the previous year and atone for them with **blood sacrifice**. In Mosaic **Law**, it was to be called with the sound of the trumpet (or ram's horn) and to be marked by the cessation of work and denial of **food** and drink. Later more denials were added to this listing, including **bathing, cosmetics**, and sex.

The people were to spend the day recalling and repenting their iniquities of the year, chanting a liturgy especially designed for the occasion, asking God for particular blessings in the year to come, and blessing him for his mercies. After the building of the **Temple**, it was a day to be celebrated in Jerusalem at the Temple, the day of the year when the high **priest** entered the Holy of Holies, stripped of his golden vestments, clothed only in a simple white robe. There he would plead for his people.

> The post-exilic view was summed up the general view of the day in these words: God, seated on His **throne** to judge the world, at the same time Judge, Pleader, Expert, and Witness, openeth the Book of Records; it is read, every man's signature being found therein. The great trumpet is sounded; a still, small voice is heard; the **angels** shudder, saying, this is the day of judgment: for His very ministers are not pure before God. As a **shepherd** mustereth his flock, causing them to pass under his rod, so doth God cause every living soul to pass before Him to fix the limit of every creature's life and to foreordain its destiny. On New-Year's Day the decree is written; on the Day of Atonement it is sealed who shall live and who are to die, etc. But penitence, prayer, and charity may avert the evil decree. (Morris Jastrow, Jr. and Max L. Margolis 2005)

The **apocryphal** book of Ecclesiasticus, which was written about 200 B.C., has a description of the service for this day:

> They gave him the **wine** for the drink-offering, and the Prefect stood by each horn of the **altar** with a towel in his hand, and two priests stood at the table of the fat pieces with two silver trumpets in their hands. They blew a prolonged, a quavering (?) and a prolonged blast. Then they came and stood by Ben Arza one at his right hand and the other on his left. When he stooped and poured out the drink-offering the Prefect waved the towel and Ben Arza clashed the cymbals and the Levites broke forth into singing. When they reached a break in the

singing they blew upon the trumpet and at every blowing of the trumpet a prostration. (Eccles. 50:1–21)

Because of its ties to Judgment, this was also seen as the day on which the Year of the Jubilee would begin—in the fiftieth year when all debts were forgiven, **slaves** freed, and land was restored to its original owner. In modern times, this has been translated to an offering for those in need.

The sacrificial portion of the day involved the offering of a calf, a ram, seven lambs, and two goats (Num. 29:7–11). One of the more curious traditions connected with the Day of Atonement was the placing of the sins of the community by the priest on a **goat**—the scapegoat. The **animal** would be presented live before the Lord (Lev. 16:9–10). Placing the animal on the altar, the high priest would place his hands on the goat's head and confess over him the iniquities of the children of Israel and then send him away into the wilderness to be "let go." A second goat would be sacrificed on the altar, the flesh consumed in a fire outside the camp. Christians, of course, connected this sacrificial scapegoat with the sacrifice of Christ "outside the gate" of Jerusalem (Camille LaBossière 1992, 684).

Reference in the Book of Acts to the "day of the Fast" indicates it was still a part of life in the early days of the **Church**, but the old Jewish fast day became irrelevant to a people who believed in the atonement of Christ's shed blood on the cross. Hebrews describes the ritual of the sacrifice and the high priest's entrance into the Holy of Holies, noting that this ritual is no longer necessary for Christians, having a more perfect priest in Christ. Among most Christians, the concept of Christ's atonement for the sins of humankind is expressed in the broken body and blood, the **bread** and wine of the communion service.

The destruction of the Temple in 70 A.D. changed much of the Jewish ritual, leaving only the modern modified ceremony. Today, this begins with a recitation or singing of the *Kol Nidre*, a prayer for the cancellation of unpaid vows and promises, and concludes with the *Neilah,* the service that ends with "Next year in Jerusalem." Because of the belief in the judgments rendered on this day, the traditional prayer is, "Enter us in the Book of Life" and the formula of salutation on New Year's Eve: "May you be inscribed [in the Book of Life] for a happy year" (Morris Jastrow Jr., and Max L. Margolis 2005). *See also* Festivals; Time.

Further Reading

Morris, Jastrow, Jr., and Max L. Margolis, "Day of Atonement," http://www.jewishencyclopedia.com (accessed February 28, 2005). Kent, W. H. "Atonement, Day of," http://www.newadvent.org (accessed February 28, 2005). LaBossière, Camille. "Scapegoat," in *A Dictionary of the Biblical*

Tradition in English Literature. Grand Rapids, Mich.: William B. Eerdmans Publishing Company, 1992. Wacholder, Ben Zion. "Day of Atonement" in *The Oxford Companion to the Bible.* New York: Oxford University Press, 1993. Wright, Robert E. and Leon Morris. *A Dictionary of Biblical Tradition in English Literature.* Grand Rapids, Mich.: William B. Eerdmans Publishing Company, 1992.

B

Baal, Baalim

(**Judg. 2:11–14; 1 Kings 18:18; 2 Chron. 33; Hos. 2:8; Amos 5:26; Rom. 11:4**) *Baal* or *Baalim* for plural, the name of the god or gods prevalent among the **Canaanites**, literally means "possess" or "master." The word could be used for humans—as in "master of the **house**." A wife might address her **husband** as "baal" or "master." In its simplest form, this is simply a term of relationship—ownership of persons, **animals**, or things.

The Semitic god Baal, or Hadad, was the chief of the Canaanite pantheon, which included his father, El (or **Dagon**) and his consort Baalat (also **Asherah**, Astarte, or Anath). He was a storm god, pictured in statuary throwing or holding clubs and thunderbolts. Ancient texts that have been discovered reveal myths that describe his conflicts with death, infertility, floods, and other gods.

The use of the plural form in Scripture, *Baalim*, suggests that different Baals were referenced or that the Hebrews were not especially sensitive to variations among pagan deities. Baal was worshipped under different names in different towns, sometimes called Baal-gad (Lord of good fortune), Baal-hamon (Lord of riches), Baal-hazor (Baal's village), Baal-meon (Lord of the dwelling), Baal-zephon (Lord of darkness), and so forth. The title even appears in the names of men, such as Ishk-baal or Hannibal, indicating that the culture was permeated with Baal-worship.

As a rain god, Baal was thought to be responsible for the fertility of the land and the abundance of crops. Like other fertility gods, he was thought to have died every autumn and been resurrected every spring. The worship of Baal on the "high places" was frequently lamented by the **prophets**, who recognized his appeal for the people of Israel

The Hebrews probably first learned about the worship of Baal from the Canaanites, who were an agricultural people. When the Israelites settled in Canaan, they found that the festivities connected with this pagan god were appealing, as was the carefree lifestyle, an alluring contrast to their own austere and legalistic monotheism. They lived among these people, even intermarried with them, and found themselves appropriating their religion. Judah was able to resist the temptation of syncretism somewhat because of the prominence of religious activities at the **Temple** in Jerusalem, but the Northern Kingdom succumbed to Baal worship. Some believe that the Baal feasts had considerable influence on the Jewish **festivals**, which are also often tied to the cycle of harvests.

Queen Jezebel was the most notorious of the Baal cultists. The contest between the prophets of Baal and Elijah, the prophet of Jehovah, on Mt. Carmel established the clear superiority of the God of the Hebrews. The Baal cult nonetheless continued, in spite of the protests of the prophets, until Josiah tossed the Baal images into the Kidron, burned them, and sent the ashes to Bethel (2 Kings 23). The Babylonian god Bel, prominent in the **apocryphal** story of Daniel and Bel, appears to have had much in common with the Canaanite Baal and may have derived from the same source.

The name has come down in modern times as *Beelzebub*, or Baal-zebub. This "Lord of the Flies" title was used in ancient Jewish literature in legends regarding Solomon's perversion of wisdom as he grew older and more corrupt. It also appeared in stories about Satan's rule over all the lesser spirits in the Underworld. Their enemies used the term in attacks on both John the Baptist and Jesus (Matt. 12:24, 27; Mark 3:22; Luke 11:15, 18). It comes from the Greek and also can mean "master of the heavenly dwelling" (David Jeffrey 1992, 81). The term was clearly intended to signify demon possession, probably sorcery. In later literature, this is frequently a name assigned to demons, or Satan the Prince of Demons, as in John Bunyan's *Pilgrim's Progress,* John Milton's *Paradise Lost,* and in William Golding's novel *Lord of the Flies. See also* Canaan, Canaanites; Festivals; Idols, Idolatry; Witchcraft, Witches.

Further Reading

Albright, W. F. *Yahweh and the Gods of Canaan.* Garden City, N.Y.: Doubleday, 1986. Day, John. *Yahweh and the Gods of Canaan.* Sheffield: Sheffield Academic Press, 2000. Jastrow, Morris, Jr., J. Frederic McCurdy, and Duncan B. McDonald. "Ba'al and Ba'al -worship," http://www.jewishencyclopedia.com. (Accessed December 30, 2004). Jeffrey, David Lyle. "Beelzebub," in *A Dictionary of the Biblical Tradition in English Literature.* Grand Rapids, Mich.: William B. Eerdmans Publishing Company, 1992. Ringgren, Helmer. *Religions of the Ancient Near East.* Philadelphia: Westminster Press, 1973.

Babel, Tower of

(Gen. 11:1–9) *Babel* like *Babylon* means "gate of god." The story of the building of the Tower of Babel is a narrative of hubris. Seeking to be like God, humans brought judgment on themselves, causing God to turn the single language into a cacophony of tongues—or "babel." This confusion of tongues foreshadowed a contrasting scene in the New Testament, when the response to the coming of the **Holy Spirit** at **Pentecost** was accompanied by the speaking in tongues (Acts 2:4). On this occasion, the people understood different languages, bringing them together rather than separating them.

Baal, the storm god, depicted in relief on a limestone stele at Ras Shamra (Ugarit) in Syria (mid-second millennium B.C.).

The tower itself may well have been a ziggurat in ancient Sumeria, later **Babylonia**. "Etemenanki" or "the Building of the Foundation-platform of **Heaven** and Earth" whose "top reaches to the heaven" was probably the sacred edifice described by Herodotus in 460 B.C. (D. J. Wiseman 1980, 154–157.) It was a stepped pyramid with five (or perhaps seven) platforms, crowned with a **temple** where the god was thought to meet with humans. On the sides were ramps and stairways. The tradition of high places—towers or mountains—as appropriate places to worship gods is practically universal, paralleling Jacob's vision of a ladder to heaven with angels ascending and descending (Gen. 10:25).

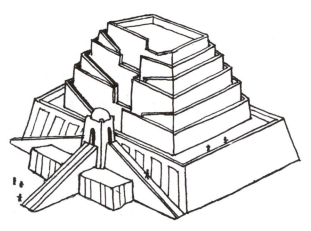

A Babylonian ziggurat may have been the original concept for the biblical story of the Tower of Babel (Gen. 11:3ff). Early Sumerian temples had brick platforms building up into a stepped pyramid. The tower was topped with a temple or heavenly house of a god, which was reached by impressive outer staircases, sometimes made of 100 steps. The terraces also might have had shrines on them, and the whole was protected by a strong gated outer wall.

Visitors note that the Tower of Babel is now "a swampy pit. Looming above the sad heaps of brick is an imperious palace built in 1987 by Saddam Hussein." At the center of the ruins of ancient Babylon are the remains of numerous **temples** where the scores of **priests** catered to the Mesopotamian gods and their followers. "The most elaborate temple, in the city center, was dedicated to Marduk, the patron god of Babylon, whose name was too holy to speak. Nearby, rising 300 feet, was the seven-stepped and brightly painted ziggurat called *Etemanki*, which the Jews dubbed the Tower of Babel." At the time of the spring festival, "Pilgrims thronged the streets, and statues of gods brought by people from all over Mesopotamia were carried by singing crowds, taken to the river and placed on boats, then ceremoniously carried in chariots to a special temple in the north part of the city" (Andrew Lawler 2003, 50). *See also* Babylon, Babylonia.

Further Reading

Lawler, Andrew. "Saving Iraq's Treasures," in *Smithsonian* 14, no. 1 (June 2003): 42–55. Wiseman, D. J. "Babel," in *The Illustrated Bible Dictionary*. Sydney, Australia: Tyndale House Publishers, 1980.

Babylon, Babylonia

(Gen. 10:10, 22:1–9; 2 Kings 17:24, 30; Ps. 137; Is 13; Jer. 51:6; Rev. 14:8, 16:9, 17:5, 18:2, 10, 21) References to the great city of Babylon, which became the term for the nation of Babylonia, appear all through the historical books (2 Kings, 2 Chronicles) and in the books of the **prophets**. The experiences of the Jews in this great, beautiful, decadent city made the city itself a metaphor for power, exile, and corruption.

In Jewish history, Babylon was the place to which the **Temple** treasures were taken after the king of Judah had been blinded; it was the place to which the exiles were transported when Jerusalem had fallen and the Temple had been destroyed. They lamented this time with the beautiful Psalm 137: "By the waters of Babylon, we sat down and wept." Daniel's exalted position in the **palace** of Nebuchadnezzar, the ruler of the Neo-Babylonian Empire (605–562 B.C.) indicates a change of status and treatment over time. The Jews had become a part of the society, even of the court, assuming positions of power. Yet Babylon itself remained a fearful symbol for the prophets. As late as the New Testament Book of Revelation, Babylon was seen as the "great whore," perhaps a metaphor for the new Babylon, Rome.

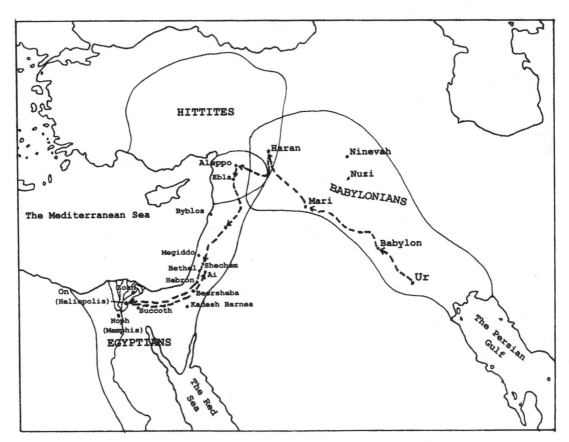

Map showing the path of Abram (Abraham) from Ur of the Chaldees, to Haran, to the Promised Land, to Egypt, and back to Hebron in Canaan.

The beautiful **gates**, the hanging **gardens**, and the splendid palaces described by Herodotus have been partially uncovered by archaeologists. It is thought that the **Tower of Babel** was part of this grand city. The ruins identified as ancient Babylon are about 50 miles from Bagdad, on the east bank of the Euphrates (Morris Jastrow, Robert W. Rogers et al., 2004). *Smithsonian* magazine noted that Babylon ("gate of the gods") "was a city where living was beautiful . . . a free city for refugees, a holy city, a kind of Jerusalem." It was a "trading city," with caravans bringing woods silver, gold, bronze, ivory, frankincense, marble, **wine** and **grains**, and all kinds of fruits and vegetables. The people of the city prized learning, including astronomy and mathematics. The city, as noted by Daniel, boasted many sages in the palace and temples (Andrew Lawler 2003, 50). For the Jews, it was the very antithesis of Jerusalem. Babylon was the city that worshipped pagan gods and flourished while their holy city Jerusalem lay in ruins. *See also* Babel, Tower of; History in the Bible.

Further Reading

Jastrow, Morris, Jr., Robert W. Rogers, Richard Gottheil, and Samuel Krauss. "Babylon," http://www.jewishencyclopedia.com (accessed December 30, 2004). Lawler, Andrew. "Saving Iraq's Treasures," in *Smithsonian* 14 (2003):1, 42–55.

Balances. *See Measures*

Baptism

(Matt. 3:13–17; Mark 1:4–11; Luke 3:21–22; John 1:25–34) All four of the Gospels describe the baptism of Christ by John the Baptizer. These are the first scriptural references to the rite of baptism. Before this, the Jews knew ablution, or the cleansing with water during and after sacrificial ceremonies (Num. 19:7). They also knew the sprinkling with **blood** and the **anointing** with oil, both rites of **blessing**. Baptism, however, as a ritual that washed a person of sins, was practiced in Greek mystery religions and by the **Essenes**, but not regularly by mainstream Jews, except perhaps in the case of proselyte baptism.

John the Baptist apparently adapted this older ceremony as a means of repentance and purification in preparation for the reign of the **Messiah** (Madeleine S. Miller and J. Lane Miller 1961, 60). As Jesus was the Messiah, John argued that a mere mortal was not fit to baptize him, but Jesus insisted on submitting himself to the ritual, perhaps to "fulfil all righteousness" and perhaps as a mark of his humanity, resulting in a magnificent display of the **Trinity** with the **Holy Spirit** descending and the voice of God thundering from the **heavens**, "This is my beloved son, in whom I am well pleased" (Mark 1:11). This is usually seen as the beginning of Jesus's earthly ministry. The **Disciples**, some of whom were probably baptized by John, continued the practice, but apparently Jesus did not (John 3:22, 26, 4:1). In an interesting exchange with the chief priests in Jerusalem, shortly before his **crucifixion**, Jesus asked them, "The baptism of John, was it from heaven, or of men?" (Mark 11:30). Their reluctance to respond indicates that even the **Sadducees** were of two minds regarding the efficacy of baptism.

Although Jesus refrained from baptizing any of his followers during his lifetime, after the **resurrection**, he did instruct his Disciples to "Go ye therefore, and teach all nations, baptizing them in the name of the Father, and of the Son, and of the Holy Ghost" (Matt. 28:19). From earliest times, the Disciples baptized new converts "in the name of Jesus" (Acts 2:38, 8:16, 10:48, 19:5). This practice appears to represent an act of commitment, a seal of entry into the new sect, and even a deed of transfer, indicating that the baptisand was giving himself over to be the property of Christ.

In some ways for these Jewish-Christians, baptism replaced the old ritual of **circumcision** as the rite of initiation for new converts to their faith. The resurrected Christ, before his ascension, told his gathered followers of the "promise of the Father, which saith he, ye have heard of me. For John truly baptized with water, but ye shall be baptized with the Holy Ghost, not many days hence" (Acts 1:5). Therefore, after the coming of the Spirit at **Pentecost**, when they were "baptized of the Spirit" (Acts 2:4), they were convinced of the importance of this ritual.

Peter, in his first sermon after Pentecost, ended by encouraging the converted peoples: "Repent, and be baptized every one of you in the name of Jesus Christ for the remission of sins, and ye shall receive the gift of the Holy Ghost" (Acts 2:38). That he followed this by reference of this promise to "you and to your children" has led some Christians to believe that baptism might also be administered to children of believers, as well as to converts to the faith. (Other Christians believe that only adults are to be baptized.)

Paul repeated the need for the baptism that went beyond John's water baptism, the "baptism of repentance," telling the people of Ephesus, "John verily baptized with the baptism of repentance, saying unto the people, that they should believe on him which should come after him, that is, on Christ Jesus. When they heard this, they were baptized in the name of the Lord Jesus. And when Paul had laid his hands upon them, the **Holy Ghost** came on them, and they spake with **tongues**, and prophesied" (Acts 19:3–6). The importance of the Spirit's role in baptism had been stressed earlier when some who had been baptized had not yet received the gift of the Spirit:

When Philip was preaching in Samaria, a new follower, Simon—even after he was baptized—tried to purchase the power of the Holy Spirit that seemed to come from the laying on of hands, but he was called to repentance for his wrongful act (Acts 8:14–24). From this time on, those who sought to buy and sell church offices were known as "Simoniacs." (Dante had a special place in **Hell** designed just for them.)

Another concern was whether baptism would have any effect if it had not been preceded by circumcision. This was settled first by evidence that uncircumcised gentiles, in great numbers, had been baptized and received the Holy Spirit. It was then also settled by Peter's response: "Can any man forbid water, that these should not be baptized, which have received the Holy Ghost as well as we?" (Acts 10:44–48, 11:15–17). At that point, he insisted that the baptism should be open to converted gentiles, a position he later defended, and which was finally settled in the Council of Jerusalem.

In the early days of the Church, total immersion, often in streams or rivers, seems to have been most commonly used (Mark 1:9; Acts 8:38). It is not clear whether all baptism was through total immersion. In the prison at Phillippi (Acts 16:33) or in the house of Cornelius (Acts 10:48), a symbolic use of the water, such as sprinkling or pouring, would appear more likely. This debate over the appropriate form of the ritual has separated religions over the years, being particularly important to the Baptists, who insist on total immersion. The Trinitarian formula is almost universal among Christians, as is the belief that the ritual need not be repeated. Most denominations believe that it is a ritual that is effective once and for all, whether offered to a young child or an old man. Paul also made it clear to the Corinthians that the baptism is in the name of Christ, not of Paul or Apollos (1 Cor. 1:13–17). The person performing the rite is not so significant as the power of the Sprit in coming into the heart of the convert.

It is one of only two universally accepted Christian sacraments, the other being the **Lord's Supper**. *See also* Lord's Supper, Mass, Eucharist, Communion; Sacrifice.

Further Reading

Dunn, J.D.G. "Baptism," in *The Illustrated Bible Dictionary*. Sydney, Australia: Tyndale House Publishers, 1980. Miller, Madeleine S. and J. Lane Miller. "Baptism," in *Harper's Bible Dictionary*. New York: Harper and Row, 1961.

Bath, Bathing

(Lev. 14:8; 2 Kings 5:10–14) Jewish **law** stipulated several occasions for bathing. For worshippers, a ceremonial cleansing of part or all of the body, as well as the clothing, was a prelude to the act of **sacrifice** and followed any defilement during the **worship**, for example, the touching of anything unclean, such as **blood**. The **priest** was expected to wash himself before the beginning of the service to enter the realm of sacred things and functions (Exod. 29:4, 30:17–21; Lev. 8:6, 16:4). On the Temple Mount, a *mikweh,* or bath, has been discovered that was apparently used for this purpose. It is carved out of the stone, with steps leading down to a deep depression that could hold water for bathing.

A traditional Jewish saying is "Cleanliness is next to godliness." The ritual washing of hands, mentioned in Psalm 26:6 was interpreted to apply to any act of worship, including prayer. The water was to be "in a state of natural purity, not discolored or defiled by the admixture of any foreign substance; it must not have been previously used for any purpose, and must be poured out by human act." This act of ablution was usually performed by one person for another (Bernard Drachman and Kaufmann Kohler 2004). This ritual washing before meals was ignored by Jesus's disciples, causing the **Pharisees** and **scribes** to note that they had "hands defiled, that is unwashed"—and eliciting the response: "You leave the commandments of God and hold fast the tradition of men" (Mark 7:1–7). Outward defilement was less a problem than inner filth.

For **women**, a cleansing was essential after the **birth** of a child or the issue of blood. The woman was considered unclean until after she had washed herself. Jesus, ignoring this prohibition in the law, allowed the woman who had an "issue of blood" to touch his garment. Rather than turning from her, he healed her of the hemorrhaging.

Bathing was also part of the law connected with diseases. No leper could eat of holy flesh until he had performed an ablution, either in a natural fountain, stream, or mikweh. He was expected to shave his hair, wash his clothing, and bathe his whole body to become clean (Lev. 22:4–6). In some parts of Scripture, bathing is a curative act, as in the case of Elisha, who ordered Naaman to dip himself "seven times in the Jordan" (2 Kings 5:14). Jesus also commanded the blind man to wash in the Pool of Siloam (John 9:11).

Certain scriptural and **apocryphal** passages indicate that bathing was also an accepted part of aristocratic life in ancient times. Bathing had apparently been more common among the **Egyptians:** the princess was bathing in the Nile when she discovered the infant Moses (Exod. 2:5); Egyptian priests were expected to bathe four times during each 24-hour day (Madeleine S. Miller and J. Lane Miller 1961, 63). When King David heard about the death of his child, he rose, washed, smeared himself with oil, and changed his **clothes** (2 Sam. 12:20). Because the ritual of **mourning** involved sackcloth and ashes, the follow-up of thorough cleansing would suggest that the mourning is complete.

The cosmetic aspect of bathing is also apparent in Scripture: Ruth's mother-in-law directed her to "wash, smear yourself with oil, and put on your best clothes" (Ruth 3:3). In the harem where Queen Esther resided, the bath was an expected prelude to any meeting with the **king**. Bathsheba had her bath on the roof of her house, allowing King David to see her and lust after her. Susanna bathed in her **garden**, with the elders secretly watching. These may have been ceremonial bathings to cleanse the women of their "unclean" status after **birth** or menstruation. Or they may have been designed for beautification. The bath, of course, was followed by **anointment** with precious oils and careful dressing in one's best clothing.

A terracotta figurine of a woman bathing in a tub has been uncovered and is now in the Israel Museum, indicating that tub bathing was a practice as early as the seventh century B.C. (Philip J. King and Lawrence Stager 2001, 70). Among the **Greeks** and **Romans**, the bathing experience grew far more elaborate, especially among the classical athletes. These cultures built great baths near natural hot springs, with graduated water temperatures moving from hot to cold. For those Jews who were influenced by the Hellenists, the bathing became a part of their religious rituals. Jesus noted that the **Pharisees** had become obsessed with hand washing while they were oblivious to their unclean hearts (Mark 7:2–6). The bath came to be seen as more than the cleansing of the body. It was also the cleansing of the soul, thus **baptism**.

A woman in a tub in this ancient ceramic statue may have been performing the cleansing required by law after menstruation or giving birth.

Different washing rituals occur at many points in Scripture, as acts of **hospitality**, healing, cleansing, refreshing, and love. In a hot and dusty land where water is so precious, the act of washing hands, feet, or body takes on a ceremonial meaning. *See also* Anointing; Baptism; Clean, Unclean; Sacrifice; Washing of Feet.

Further Reading

DeVaux, Roland. *Ancient Israel: Its Life and Institutions*. Grand Rapids, Mich.: William B. Eerdmans Publishing Company, 1961. Drachman, Bernard and Kaufmann Kohler, "Ablution," http://www. jewishencyclopedia. com (accessed December 30, 2004). King, Philip J. and Lawrence E. Stager. *Life in Biblical Israel*. Louisville, Ky.: Westminster John Knox Press, 2001. Miller, Madeleine S. and J. Lane Miller. "Bathing," in *Harper's Bible Dictionary*. New York: Harper and Row, 1961.

Beard

(Lev. 21:5; 2 Sam. 10:4; Isa. 15:2; Jer. 9:26) Hebrew men usually wore beards, which they considered a symbol of manly beauty. As one medieval writer noted, "The adornment of a man's face is his beard" (Cyrus Adler,

W. Max Muller, and Louis Ginzberg 2004). The beard was thought to have been given to man by God to distinguish him from woman.

Therefore, it was a humiliation to shave, pluck, or mutilate the beard. Lepers were shaven to separate them from others because of their dreaded disease. Mourners cut or plucked some of their beards as a sign of distress, a practice decried by the **priests**. But for the most part, the Jews appear to have worn a full, round beard, including a trimmed moustache. The barber was used for ceremonial shaving and for occasional trimming. The priests were forbidden to trim the corners of their beards. One of the means by which **warriors** could demean the enemy or emasculate him was to cut off his beard.

We can gather from the bas reliefs and other relics of the ancient world that other nations with which the Hebrews had regular relations had different beard styles. When Joseph was in **Egypt**, he apparently shaved (Gen. 41:140), in accordance with the Egyptian customs. Curiously, the Egyptian

Beards of different nationalities. Egyptian (first two), Hittite, Amorite, Assyrian, Median, Syrian, and Philistine. Both men and women among the Egyptians wore beards, some artificial and held on with a string. The Assyrians and the Medes curled their beards; others preferred to shave the mustache or trim the beards in special patterns. Left to right: Egyptian, Egyptian, Hittite, Amorite, Assyrian, Median, Syrian, and Philistine.

women wore artificial beards tied to their chins on state occasions, and the men had tiny tufts of hair under theirs. Nomadic Semites clipped the sides of their beards, producing a pointed beard. **Babylonians** and **Assyrians** had elaborate, curled ceremonial beards, and **Greeks** were close-shaven.

During the period of Greek dominance of Palestine, this custom led many Jews to abandon their beards, a sign of their abandonment of rabbinical Judaism. In modern times, the full beard with sidelocks has become the mark of the Hasidic Jew. Beards also mark the mature, married men of certain Christian denominations. *See also* Mourning; War, Warfare: General.

Further Reading

Adler, Cyrus, W. Max Muller, and Louis Ginzberg, "Beard," http://www.jewishencyclopedia.com (accessed December 30, 2004).

Beatitudes

(Matt. 5:3–12; Luke 6:20–23) *Beatitudo* comes from the Latin word that means "made happy." The name is applied to Jesus's poetic listing of qualities of character or attitudes that make a person blessed. (The listing in Matthew is fuller than the one in Luke.) These include those who are poor in spirit, those that mourn, and those that hunger and thirst after righteousness. The catalogue concludes with comfort for those who will be persecuted unjustly in the name of Jesus. In each case, the nature of the blessings forms the second part of the verse, demonstrating that the joy that is promised is spiritual rather than physical. For example, "Blessed are they that mourn, for they shall be comforted."

These Beatitudes introduce the **Sermon on the Mount**, the fullest statement of Jesus's teachings. Other statements of blessedness occur elsewhere in the Gospels (Matt. 11:6; Luke 7:23), but the term is usually applied to the listing in Matthew. *See also* Sermon on the Mount.

Bees, Honey

(Exod. 3:17; Deut. 32:13; Josh. 5:6; Judg. 14:8–14) John the Baptist lived on locusts and honey when he was preaching in the wilderness. The honey produced by bees was a great favorite of ancient peoples because it was their chief source of sweet flavoring for other foods. "Honey from the rock" (Exod. 3:17; Deut. 32:13; Josh. 5:6) became a lovely image of the natural occurrence of honey, with the bees leaving their honey in cavities in rocks. Some of these reservoirs of honey were so large that great quantities could be hauled out. In fact, honey became one of the Israelites' favorite products for trade with other peoples. This makes the recurrent image of "a land flowing with milk and honey" a realistic description of Palestine, the home of many bees.

Another nesting place for honey bees was in dead **animals**. After Samson killed the lion and left it by the side of the road, he returned to find the carcass had become a home for a bee hive. He scooped the honey out with his hands and ate it with relish, taking some to his bride and her family. Honey was commonly used as a gift among the Israelites. Samson later used his adventure as the basis for a riddle that puzzled and infuriated his wedding guests: "Out of the eater came forth meat, and out of the strong came forth sweetness" (Judges 14:8–14).

Bees also made their hives in trees. Jonathan and his army had an adventure in the woods with bees: Saul had uttered a curse on any that would break the **fast** he had proclaimed until he avenged himself on his enemies, but Jonathan and his men came into woods where they found honey all over the ground. It was dripping from the trees, but they were afraid to put their sticky hands to their mouths because of the curse. Jonathan, who had not heard the curse, took a rod and "dipped it in an honeycomb, and put his hand to his mouth; and his eyes were enlightened" (1 Sam. 14:27). When informed of his violation of his father's orders, he complained that these were poor orders, starving men who were expected to fight. There followed scenes of confession and condemnation, but the young man's popularity with the people eventually saved his life.

Honey bees were apparently domesticated at some point in Israel's history. Honey was extensively produced in highland apiaries and shipped abroad. By Ezekiel's day, candies made of dates, honey, nuts, and gum arabic were plentiful and were exported to Tyre (Ezek. 27:17; Madeleine S. Miller and J. Lane Miller 1961, 203). It was included among the "firstfruits" that the fields produced, along with **grain**, new **wine**, and oil and therefore required as a portion of the tithe dedicated to the Lord (2 Chron. 31:5) Considered a treat, it was used in candies, fancy cakes, and sticky sweetmeats sold at bazaars.

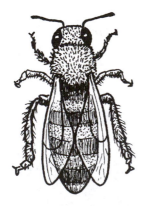

Honeybee, a favorite among ancient peoples as a source of "sweetness and light"— honey and wax.

As the favorite sweetening ingredient of most foods, honey became synonymous with sweetness. Thus "honeyed words" could mean eloquence, and the Psalmist could sing, "How sweet are your words to my taste, sweeter than honey to my mouth" (Ps. 119:103). On the other hand, the honey could be tantalizing and dangerous. Proverbs warns that the "lips of an adulteress drip honey, and her speech is smoother than oil" (Prov. 5:3). Yet, in another place, the wise writer also notes that it is a natural pleasure to enjoy: "Eat honey, my son, for it is good; honey from the comb is sweet to your taste" (Prov. 24:13). Like all good and natural things, one can indulge it to excess: "If you find honey, eat just enough—too much of it, and you will vomit" (Prov. 25:27).

King Solomon loved the imagery of honey, using it famously in his great wedding song, the Song of Solomon: "I have come into my garden, my sister, my bride; I have gathered my myrrh with my spice. I have eaten my honeycomb and my honey; I have drunk my wine and my milk." Then he invites the other guests to join him (Song of Sol. 5:1). In fact, his favorite description of his bride is that her "lips drop sweetness as the honeycomb . . . milk and honey are under your tongue" (Song of Sol. 4:11).

Given this long tradition of honey imagery, it is no surprise that the scroll the **angel** gives to John in his Revelation, which he is instructed to eat, "will be as sweet as honey," although his stomach turned sour (Rev. 10:9–10).

In later years, artists used the bee, with its industrious habits as a symbol of diligence, hard work, and good order. The beehive became an image of the ideal community—the **church**, with every member working hard toward a common goal (George Ferguson 1966, 12). In the nineteenth century, the author Matthew Arnold ((in *Culture or Anarchy*) drew on the honeybee for his image of the ideal critic, as one who like the honeybee produced honey and wax—"sweetness and light." *See also* Food; Insects.

Further Reading

Ferguson, George. *Signs and Symbols in Christian Art*. New York: Oxford University Press, 1966. Miller, Madeleine S. and Lane S. Miller. "Food," in *Harper's Bible Dictionary*. New York: Harper and Row, 1961.

Behemoth, Leviathan

(**Job 40:15**) Although the term *behemoth* occurs at other points in Scripture, apparently referring to large beasts or cattle, the meaning in Job seems to be a great beast, such as the hippopotamus. Hebrew mythology identifies the behemoth as the first land beast ever created, resembling "a prodigious hippopotamus: with a tail bigger than the trunk of a cedar, and bones like pipes of brass. He rules the land-creatures, as Leviathan does the sea. They gambol around him, where he takes his ease among lotus, reed, fern and willows, or grazes on the Thousand Mountains" (Robert Graves and Raphael Patai 1964, 49).

Some scholars believe it to be "the primeval monster of chaos, defeated at the beginning of the process of creation" (Michael D. Coogan 1993, 76). This would appear to be a reference to the **Babylonian** creation myth. Jewish **apocryphal** literature, such as the Book of Enoch, notes that the leviathan and behemoth were both created on the fifth day. Of the two monsters, one was male and one female, with the Behemoth representing the male. In 2 Esdras 6:49–53, God gave the behemoth the dry land with a thousand mountains so that he might have necessary **food**, and he gave the watery part to the leviathan. At some future time, both were to be eaten at a great feast for the elect "who will survive in the days of the Messiah" (Emil G. Hirsch, Kaufmann Kohler, Solomon Schecter, and Isaac Broydé 2004). The **Gnostics** included both of these creatures in their system of stations, which the soul had to pass through to be purged and obtain bliss.

The actual animal to which Job is referring remains in doubt. It might well be a primal memory of prehistoric animals or a speculation based on discovery of giant bones. The term as it is used today simply means an enormous animal. *See also* Animals; Babylon, Babylonia; Creation; Monsters.

Further Reading

Coogan, Michael D. "Behemoth," in *The Oxford Companion to the Bible*. New York: Oxford University Press, 1993. Graves, Robert and Raphael Patai, *Hebrew Myths: The Book of Genesis*. New York: McGraw-Hill Book Company, 1964. Hirsch, Emil G., Kaufmann Kohler, Solomon Schecter, and Isaac Broydé, "Leviathan and Behemoth," http://www.jewishencyclopedia.com (accessed September 20, 2004).

Betrothal

(2 Sam. 3:14; Deut. 22:23–24) The most famous betrothal in history was that between Mary and Joseph, the earthly parents of Jesus. In that case, the couple were betrothed, but not married when Joseph discovered that Mary was "with child." He had to decide whether to break the agreement, offering to "put her away" quietly so as to avoid scandal. The appearance of an **angel** with the message that Mary would bear the **Messiah** changed his mind, convincing him to take her as wife (Matt. 1:18–25).

This scene reveals a number of the characteristics of the betrothal: it was a formal ceremony that preceded the **wedding**, often arranged by members of the two families well ahead of time. A matchmaker might be engaged to negotiate the contract, which set the payment of the price paid for the bride, the amount of the dowry, and confirmed the consent of the parent or guardian of the girl. The **rabbis** regarded it as improper for couples to marry without an engagement or betrothal.

The suitor often brought a *bride price* to the family of the bride—a sum or duty he was willing to pay. In Jacob's case, he pledged his service and paid Laban seven years' labor for each of his daughters. The *dowry* by contrast, was the money or property that the bride's family gave to her and the groom. In that same wedding ceremony, Laban gave **slaves** or "maidservants" to Jacob along with each of his daughters. The wife's dowry was considered an indication of her worth and set the level at which she expected to be supported.

In some cases, the man would hand a coin to the woman in the presence of two competent witnesses, pronouncing the words, "Be thou consecrated to me," or he might hand to the rabbi the contract with parallel phrasing on it. He might already be cohabiting with the bride, a path that was frowned on by the clergy. Over time, the coin was replaced by a plain gold ring, which remains the custom in modern marriage ceremonies. Sometimes the betrothal was performed by proxies, but the recommended ceremony involved the principals in person (Solomon Schechter and Julius H. Greenstone 2004).

Jewish **law** added numerous details to this ceremony: After the ordinary benediction over **wine**, the person performing the ceremony continued as follows:

> Blessed art Thou, O Lord, our God, **King** of the universe, who hast sanctified us with Thy commandments and given us commandments concerning forbidden connections, and hast forbidden unto us those who are merely betrothed, and permitted unto us those lawfully married to us through 'canopy' ["huppah"] and 'betrothal' ["kiddushin"]. Blessed are Thou, O Lord, who sanctifiest Thy people Israel through huppah and kiddushin.

After this, the groom hands to the bride a ring or some object of value (not less than the smallest current coin), saying, "Be thou betrothed unto me with this ring [or object] in accordance with the laws of Moses and Israel" (Marcus Jastrow and Bernard Drachman 2004).

In two of the passages of Scripture in which it occurs, the betrothed woman is directly designated as "wife": 2 Sam. 3:14, "my wife whom I have betrothed" (*erasti*), and Deut. 22:.24, where the betrothed is designated as "the wife of his neighbor." In strict accordance with this sense, the rabbinical law declares that the betrothal is equivalent to an actual marriage, dissolved only by a formal **divorce** or by death (Marcus Jastrow, Bernard Drachman 2004). If the woman proved unfaithful during the period of the engagement, she was considered an adulteress and might be stoned, just like any unfaithful married woman (Deut. 22:23–24). This was the fate from which Joseph protected Mary by taking her as his lawfully wedded wife in spite of her pregnancy.

The period of the betrothal was used for the bride to prepare her trousseau and to plan for the wedding festivities. The wedding itself came only with the handing over of the marriage contract and the entrance into the bridal chamber.

The tradition of betrothals and dowries has lingered in numerous cultures into modern times. Orthodox Jews continue to observe much of these customs (as we see in such popular stage presentations as *The Matchmaker* and *Fiddler on the Roof*). Many Eastern cultures have formal contracts of betrothal for children far in advance of their actual marriage age. In the West, the engagement, that period between the proposal and the formal wedding, is usually fairly short, and the dowry has been replaced by wedding presents. *See also* Law; Marriage.

Further Reading

Jastrow, Marcus, and Bernard Drachman, "Betrothal," http://www.jewishencyclopedia.com (accessed September 20, 2004). Schechter, Solomon and Julius H. Greenstone, "Marriage Laws," http://www.jewishencyclopedia.com (accessed September 20, 2004).

Birds

(Deut. 14:12–18; Job 39:12–30; Ps. 91:3, 124:7; Song of Sol. 2:12; Hos 9:8; Amos 3:5; Matt. 13:4, 6:26, 23:27; Luke 13:19, 9:58, 12:6, 12:24) The **creation** of "every winged fowl" (Gen. 1:21) on the fifth day introduced a wide diversity of life to the earth and the skies. During the **Great Flood**, they, along with other living creatures, were destroyed in large numbers, and yet a remnant was preserved in God's providence.

Noah used a raven and doves to seek out the dry land when the waters had had time to dry. The return of a dove with an olive leaf in her mouth marked the end of the trial (Gen. 8:6–11). The dove with the olive branch subsequently became the international symbol of peace. It was also, like the pigeon or ring-dove, used for **sacrifice**, especially among the poor who could not afford a **sheep**, **goat**, or **ox**. Thus Joseph brought two white doves with him for the consecration at the **Temple** ((Luke 2:22–24). In a more expansive image, the dove descended from **Heaven** at the time of Jesus's **baptism** (John 1:32), marking the **blessing** of God the Father and the descent of the Holy Spirit, transforming this small white bird into the symbol of the **Holy Spirit** in **Christian art** and thought.

The raven's adventuresome spirit, leaving Noah's **ark** first, and going back and forth in search of land, made him a symbol of evil in Jewish tradition, which asserted that he had been white until he failed to return to the ark, at which time his feathers turned black (George Ferguson 1966, 34). Yet later, it was a raven (or crow) that brought Elijah bread and meat in the wilderness (1 Kings 17:6). Students of American literature will remember that Edgar Allan Poe's ominous version of the raven in his famous poem with the haunting refrain: "Quoth the Raven 'Never more.'"

Quail, the smallest of the game birds, also miraculously provided food for God's people during their sojourn in the wilderness (Exod. 16:13). A great mass of fowl came up and covered the camp of the weary wanderers. Quail are powerful fliers over short distances, but rely on the wind to help them in their migration. Some believe that these birds traveled in large flocks, often landing in such a state of exhaustion that they were then comparatively easy to catch.

Archaeology demonstrates that birds were a part of the diet of the people of the Fertile Crescent from very early times. Bones of domestic fowl have been discovered in various parts of the region, some dating back to 2000 B.C. Like the other **animals**, birds are cited for their cleanliness or uncleanliness in Mosaic **law**, which lists more than 20 birds to avoid. Birds of prey, in particular, were considered disgusting, largely because of their contact with carrion (Deut. 14). Those that were considered **clean** were the pigeon or dove; waterfowl (ducks, geese, and swans); and domestic fowl, turkey, and guinea fowl. Chickens were also a regular part of the diet of the people of Palestine.

Other Old Testament references to birds include the law of Moses, which protected nesting birds, commanding that their eggs not be touched while the hen was sitting on them. Solomon probably enjoyed roast fowl. The earliest evidence of fighting cocks in Palestine is a **seal** that was unearthed at Tell en-Nashbeh, dated circa 600 B.C. Job has a great variety of bird references; the **Psalms** are full of references to birds, as are the books of the **prophets**. Nehemiah (5:18) mentions the preparation of fowl after the return from exile (George Cansdale 1970, 163–164).

In the New Testament, there are even more bird references. Sparrows, thought to be the smallest of the birds, sold two for a farthing (a fourth of a penny) "and yet one of them shall not fall on the ground without your Father" (Matt. 10:29). Jesus is here citing the lowliest of the birds to make his point that even the fall of the sparrow is known and arranged by God. The most famous references to birds in the New Testament are the dove descending at the baptism of Jesus and the crowing of the cock as Peter betrayed Christ. In Jerusalem, there is a church named St. Peter of the Cock Crow, where tradition places Peter when he had just denied Christ the third time. As he stood near the spot where Jesus was beaten and humiliated, he heard the piercing crow of the cock, marking the sunrise (John 13:38; 18:25–27). One of Jesus's more touching and homey images is his reference to himself as a mother hen: "O Jerusalem ... how often would I have gathered thy children together, even as a hen gathereth her chickens under her wings, but ye would not" (Matt 23:37).

A host of birds fly across the pages of Scripture: sea gulls, nighthawks, owls, ospreys, water hens, hawks, herons, hoopoes, storks, cranes, cormorants, swallows, swifts, martins, peacocks, thrush, geese, partridge, pelicans, ostriches, vultures, and eagles. The eagle, with its beautiful soaring mode and its eyrie high on the mountains overlooking human activity, was a

The quail provided food for the children of Israel at the time of the Exodus. Jesus mentioned that God notices even the fall of the sparrow, suggesting the little bird is so common it is of little worth. The pigeon or turtle dove was the poor man's sacrifice at the Temple. The vulture was one of the birds forbidden to the Jews by law because of its predatory nature, rendering it "unclean."

majestic bird for biblical imagery, becoming the symbol of royalty, of high aspirations, and of daring. "They shall mount up with wings as eagles," says Isaiah (40:31). Later the eagle became the image of John, the Disciple. (The four "living creatures," including the eagle, in Ezekiel 1:5, 10 became the icons of the four **Gospel** writers.) For this reason, artists chose to shape lecterns as eagles with wings outspread, on which were placed the Bible for public readings in **churches**. *See also* Art: Christian; Creation; Food; Flood, the Great; Hunting; Law.

Further Reading

Cansdale, George. *All the Animals of the Bible Lands*. Grand Rapids, Mich.: Zondervan Publishing House, 1970. Ferguson, George. *Signs and Symbols in Christian Art*. New York: Oxford University Press, 1966.

Birth

(Gen. 3:126; Ps 22:9, 139:13–14; Eccles. 11:5; Isa. 26:17, 44:2; John 16:21; Rev. 12:1–6) Among ancient peoples, a barren womb was thought to be a **curse**. Jewish women regularly prayed for male children so that they might be honored as wives and mothers. A **husband** might **divorce** his wife if she failed to produce children to carry on his family line. The blessedness of children is a repeated refrain throughout Scripture: the long-delayed birth of Isaac, the almost comic battle among Jacob's wives and maidservants to outproduce one another to gain his favor, the plot to protect the baby Moses, and Hannah's fervent prayer for the child who proved to be the **prophet** Samuel. The Psalms repeat this tribute to the blessedness of bearing children and their significance to the life of Israel. The image of the children growing up around their parents like sprouts around an olive tree is particularly beautiful (Ps. 128:3). The Proverbs give advice regarding children, and the prophets speak frequently of children, who were considered a **blessing** from God.

In the New Testament, the events leading to the birth of John the Baptist and of Christ are carefully chronicled by Luke, indicating once again that the mother is "blessed among women," as Elizabeth said of Mary. The importance of a Savior being born of woman, fully human, as well as fully divine, is a central concept in the doctrine of the **Incarnation**.

Revelation echoes the Old Testament image of Hagar protecting her child in the wilderness, this time apparently picturing the frightened woman as an image of God's chosen people, Israel. Christ is portrayed as the endangered child: The mother figure, this time a queen-image, first appears in **Heaven**, with the sun and the moon under her feet, "and upon her head a crown of twelve stars. And she being with child cried, travailing in birth, and pained to be delivered.... And she brought forth a man child, who was to rule all nations with a rod of iron.... And the woman fled into the wilderness, where she hath a place prepared of God" (Rev. 12:1–6). This passage elevates the experience of childbirth to cosmic implications, involving whole nations and the future of humankind.

Given this emphasis on fertility and the care with which wives were selected and sheltered, it is not a surprise that abortion is not discussed in Scripture except in the laments of Job and Jeremiah (Job 10:19; Jer. 20:17). The ancient world was full of abortfacients—herbs and more violent means used to bring on miscarriages—but the Hebrews scorned them. Because the divine command was to "Be fruitful and multiply" (Gen. 1:28), and the covenant with Abraham promised that his "seed" would be as numerous as the sands, the drive to procreate was pervasive.

The importance of children is underscored by the **law** of Moses: Exodus 21:22–25 notes that, if a pregnant woman had a miscarriage as a result of a fight, the woman's husband might demand a fine. If the woman died as a result, he might demand a life for a life. This would suggest that the law was against feticide because the fetus was considered to be a human being. Using Luke 1:41–44, when John "leapt in the womb" at the presence of the unborn Jesus, some Christians argue that the unborn child is a cognizant human being (Drorah O'Donnell Stetel 1993, 4). Psalm 139, noting that God "covers" the child when in the mother's womb, also remarks that "I was fearfully and wonderfully made" (Ps. 139:13–14). This is generally interpreted to mean that the child is in God's hands from conception, under his loving care.

Although Genesis clearly indicates that after the Fall, woman will have sorrow in conception and in childbirth (Gen. 3:16), Scripture records little evidence of pain, perhaps because pangs of birth were an accepted part of life. The midwives in **Egypt** found that the Israelite children came quickly and abundantly, suggesting that easy births were common. Of course, this same record (Exod. 1:15–20), which notes that the Hebrew women were lively "and are delivered ere the midwives come in unto them," may in fact have been a lie intended to protect the newborn babes from the threat of death at the order of the Pharaoh.

There were undoubtedly deaths in childbirth, although only that of Rachel bearing Benjamin is recorded. The failure to record these deaths, at a time when medical procedures were primitive at best, might be attributed to the sense that this was not unexpected. The prophets frequently used birth pangs as measure of extreme pain (Isa. 13:8, 21:3, 26:17; Jer. 4:31, 6:24, 13:21).

The delivery process itself, at least in Egypt, involved birthing stools (Exod. 1:16). This is explained as having a woman in labor sit on two stones, placed slightly apart, like a childbirth chair which is still used, with the midwife poised under the chair to receive the child. This would explain Rachel's request that Bilhah give birth "on her knees" (Gen. 30:3), and Job's cursing the day that he found two knees to receive him (Job 3:12) (Roland deVaux, 1961, 42). (A modern novelist, Margaret Atwood, in *A Handmaid's Tale*, pictures this birth process in detail.)

At birth, the umbilical cord was cut; the baby was washed, rubbed with salt, and wrapped in swaddling clothes (Ezek. 16:4). Swaddling clothes, also mentioned in the story of Jesus's birth, were long strips of linen or cotton bandages, four to five inches wide and five or six yards long, which were wound around the baby from head to foot, including the hands so that he was a "helpless bundle like a mummy." "The band was also placed under the chin and over the forehead" (Fred H. Wight 1953, 106–107).

A newborn in swaddling clothes. This long strip of cloth was sometimes wrapped over the head as well, keeping the child completely covered.

If the child was born with a caul, this was considered a sign of good luck, and preserved. A boy child—much to be preferred—was welcomed with the words: "A boy is born to the world, a blessing has come into the world." If the child were a girl, "the walls weep" according to some ancient records (Cyrus Adler, M. Grunwald 2004).

The new baby was usually suckled by his own mother, but wet nurses were also available if the mother was unable to provide sufficient milk. The aged Sarah was especially pleased that she was able to nurse her baby herself, and apparently continued to nurse him for the regular period of three years, after which the clan celebrated with a **feast** (Gen. 21:8). Samuel's mother also nursed him until he was three years old (1 Sam. 1:20–23). Some believe this extended nursing was intended, in part, to reduce fertility. They apparently thought that a woman would not become pregnant again while she was nursing.

Immediately after birth, the child was named and **circumcised**. The mother was considered unclean for 33 days after the birth of a male child and 66 days after the birth of a female (Lev. 12:2ff.). At the end of that period, she was expected to cleanse herself and, if the child was a boy, make a **sacrifice** to express her gratitude for the birth. The sacrifice depended on the income of the family and might be as little as a pair of doves, as in the case of Mary: "And when the days of her purification according to the law of Moses were accomplished, they brought him to Jerusalem, to present him to the Lord. . . . And to offer a sacrifice according to that which is said in the law of the Lord, A pair of turtledoves, or two young pigeons" (Luke 2:22–24).

The birth of children, evidence of the "seed" of the forefathers carrying on to future generations, was the Israelites' great treasure, a blessing from God, and insurance of a life after death. *See also* Bath, Bathing; Circumcision; Husband and Wife; Law; Names: Personal.

Further Reading
Adler, Cyrus, M. Grunwald, "Childbirth," http://www.jewishencyclopedia.com (accessed June 20, 2004). DeVaux, Roland. *Ancient Israel: Its Life and Institutions.* Grand Rapids, Mich.: William B. Eerdmans Publishing Company,

1961. Stetel, Drorah O'Donnell. "Abortion," in *The Oxford Companion to the Bible,* New York: Oxford University Press, 1993. Wight, Fred H. *Manners and Customs of Bible Lands.* Chicago: Moody Press, 1953.

Birthright

(Gen. 25:29–34, 43:33; Deut. 21:15–16; 2 Chron. 21:3; Heb. 12:16–17) From early times in Bible history, the firstborn son of the family was honored and dedicated to God. By the order of his **birth**, he had special privileges: he was given authority over his brothers (Gen. 4:7; 27:29, 37, 49; 3:2). He was also given a special **blessing** from his father (Gen. 27:4). Under the **law**, he was given a double portion of the inheritance (Deut 21:17), even when he was the child of a "hated" wife. He also expected to inherit his father's position after his death, whether **king** or **priest**. In fact, he might substitute for his father even before ascending to that honored position, serving as head of **government** or leader of worship when his father was absent or ill.

The first real discussion of the birthright in Scripture occurs when Jacob tricks his twin brother, Esau, into trading his birthright for a mess of pottage (Gen. 12:1–8). Many scholars believe that Esau's careless ways with this precious heritage testified to his unworthiness to inherit the birthright. Scripture is full of examples of reversals of this rule of primogeniture (*i.e.,* preference for the firstborn). Abel was loved more than Cain, Joseph more than his elder brothers, and David more than his older brothers. David, in turn, left his throne to one of his younger sons, Solomon.

Because the firstborn has a certain sacredness associated with his birth, his family was obliged to consecrate him to God and set aside an offering to "redeem" him. One of the more significant arguments over the role of the firstborn involves the conflict between Ishmael and Isaac. The Moslems argue that Ishmael, as the firstborn, rather than Isaac, would have been the son offered to God on Mt. Moriah. Although Scripture refutes this assertion, this belief is very strong in Islamic thought.

In later days, under **Roman** law, the distinction between legitimate and illegitimate children made legitimacy a requirement for the birthright (Marris Jastrow Jr, B. Eerdmans, Marcus Jastrow, and Louis Ginzberg 2004). Identification of the firstborn, especially with twins such as Jacob and Esau, was performed by the midwife, who could testify to the order of the babies' arrival. If there were no witnesses, the father had the right to stipulate which child was born first.

That Jesus was frequently referred to as the firstborn—and only—son of God, born of a virgin, and that he "opened the womb" would also have been a powerful concept for Hebrews. It would have seemed natural to the early **Disciples** that Jesus, as the firstborn, was consecrated (Luke 2:23) and finally served as a sacrificial offering. This had been the customary recognition of the firstborn since the days of Genesis. A significant theme in discussions of Christ was his role as "the firstborn over all creation" (Col. 1:15), whose followers became "the **church** of the firstborn" (Heb. 12:23). The author of Hebrews tied the salvation of **Christians** to the salvation of the firstborn sons of Israel at the **Passover**, through the sprinkling of **blood** (Heb. 11:28). John continues this theme in his Revelation, noting that Jesus Christ was "the firstborn from the dead" (Rev. 1:5). *See also* Birth; Law.

Further Reading

Jastrow, Morris, Jr., B. Eerdmans, Marcus Jastrow, and Louis Ginzberg, "Birthright," http://www.jewishencyclopedia.com (accessed June 15, 2004).

Blasphemy

(Exod. 20:7; Deut. 5:11; Lev. 19:12; Matt. 5:34–36; James 5:12)
Blasphemy is the evil or profane speaking of God. Leviticus 24:11–16 records the story of a young man who "blasphemed the name of the Lord and cursed." "Blasphemed" here means "to pierce" with the "intent of debilitating a person" (*The King James Study Bible*, fn. 214). The Israelites brought the man to Moses, who told them to lay their hands on his head (apparently to transfer to him the guilt of the entire community that heard his blasphemy), and then "let all the congregation stone him. And thou shalt speak unto the children of Israel, saying, Whosoever curseth his God shall bear his sin. And he that blasphemeth the **name** of the Lord, he shall surely be put to death, and all the congregation shall certainly stone him: as well the stranger, as he that is born in the land, when he blasphemeth the name of the Lord shall be put to death."

Blasphemy was clearly a violation of the commandment handed down to Moses on Mount Sinai, "Thou shalt not take the name of the Lord thy God in vain, for the Lord will not hold him guiltless that taketh his name in vain" (Exod. 20:7). The Jewish tradition held that blasphemy was one of the seven crimes prohibited to Noah and his descendants—a part of natural **law** (Kaufmann Kohler and David Werner Aram 2004). Over time, the Jews came to believe that the mere pronunciation of the sacred name was a profanation, forcing them to substitute other words or letters for *Yahweh*. A witness testifying to the violation of God's name was not allowed to repeat the blasphemy in court. The **judges** cleared the court to hear the name and then rent their garments as a sign of mourning. It became a pattern for bystanders who heard such words to tear their garments and refuse to mend them. After the fall of the **Temple**, however, this custom was discontinued. According to one witness, blasphemy became so common that "garments would be nothing but tatters." Later law, however, restored the practice (Kaufmann Kohler and David Werner Aram 2004).

The crime was so serious that the Sanhedrin chose to prosecute Jesus on this basis. Earlier, the **Pharisees** and teachers noted that he claimed he could forgive sin: "Who is this fellow who speaks blasphemy? Who can forgive sins but God alone?" (Luke 5:21). At the trial of Jesus, this was repeated: "Then the **high priest** tore his clothes and said, 'He has spoken blasphemy! Why do we need more witnesses?'" (Matt. 26:65). His prosecutors noted, "We are not stoning you for any of these [sins], but for blasphemy, because you, a mere man, claim to be God" (John 10:33). They wanted to execute him and were not allowed to kill him, forcing them to hand him over to the Romans for **crucifixion**. His frequent use of the phrase "I am"—words with which God had identified himself to Moses—reinforced their argument against him. He was claiming to be God.

In the case of Stephen, the young apostle who was stoned, the charge was again blasphemy—this time against Moses as well as God (Acts 6:11). This suggests that the charge became more liberally adapted to cases where different interpretations of history or theology seemed sacrilegious. Saul of Tarsus (later, Paul) tried to compel the early **Christians** to **curse** the saving name of Jesus and renounce their baptismal vows (1 Cor. 12:3; James 2:7; Acts 24:11). To do so would have involved their commission of a blasphemous act.

Blasphemy against the Holy Spirit is mentioned in the New Testament (Matt. 12:22–32; Mark 3:22–30). This is interpreted as attributing his work to Satan rather than recognizing him as the third person of the Trinity. It also means rejection of salvific grace, or salvation, thus resulting in damnation. *See also* Court Officials; Curse; Judges; Law; Names for God; Pharisees; Punishments; Sanhedrin.

Further Reading
Kohler, Kaufmann, and David Werner Aram, "Blasphemy," http://www.jewishencyclopedia.com (accessed June 15, 2004). Falk, Ze'ev W. *Hebrew Law in Biblical Times*. Provo, Utah: Brigham Young University Press, 2001.

Blessing

(1 Kings 8:56–61; Ps. 18:20–21; Matt. 5:3–10, 11–12) "Bless you," we say casually when someone sneezes. The original meaning of the blessing was deeply serious. Like the **oath** and the **curse,** the blessing was based on the almost mystical use of words. Blessings derive from God, the source of all good things.

On the occasion of their oath of obedience of the **law** at Mount Sinai, Moses reminded his people that the Lord would bring blessings or curses on them according to the manner in which they honored their promises: "If thou shalt hearken unto the voice of the Lord thy God, to keep his commandments and his statutes which are written in this book of the law, and if thou turn unto the Lord thy God with all thine heart, and with all thy soul" (Deut. 30:10). This powerful covenant statement concluded with this choice: "I call **heaven** and earth to record this day against you, that I have set before you life and death, blessing and cursing: therefore choose life, that thou and thy seed may live" (Deut. 30:19). Other leaders and **priests** reminded the Hebrews of this oath over the years and of the blessings they were promised if they were obedient.

Individuals were also blessed: The most famous case was the blessing and promise God gave Abraham in his **covenant** with him: "I will make you into a great nation and I will bless you; I will make your **name** great, and you will be a blessing" (Gen. 12:2). The blessing was apparently passed on as a heritage from father to son by a special act. When Jacob tricked his blind old father into the granting of the **birthright** that should ordinarily have gone to the eldest son, Esau, he also won from Isaac the paternal blessing. After Jacob departed, Esau complained that he had stolen his blessing, begging his father, "Haven't you reserved any blessing for me?... Do you have only one blessing, my father?" (Gen. 27:36, 38). "The father's voice was the instrument through which God spoke, and the words, once pronounced, were regarded as the declaration of the Deity" (Kaufmann Kohler, David Philipson 2004). They could not be revoked or repeated. Apparently the blessing first given to Abraham could pass to only one of the sons; yet years later, Jacob was able to give to each of his sons the "blessing appropriate to him" (Gen. 49:28). The 12 sons, who became the 12 tribes, each received a detailed blessing from the dying Jacob as a kind of prophecy and legacy. Jewish literature demonstrates the importance of the father's blessing, indicating the high esteem in which ancient Hebrews held their parents.

Later, others recognized special favor from God as blessedness—the family of Moses and Aaron, and some of the **kings** of Israel. David was particularly aware that he had been richly blessed when God "placed a **crown** of pure gold on his head" and "granted him eternal blessings," for he "trusteth in the Lord" (Psalm 21). The paternal blessing became a more specific matter of granting permission in the case of David's "blessing" of his vengeful son Absalom (2 Sam. 13:25).

In his use of the term *blessed* in each of the **Beatitudes**, Jesus was drawing on this rich heritage of individual and corporate blessing, indicating that people who were "poor in spirit" or "persecuted" for his sake, although they appeared to be cursed, were actually eventually to be "blessed" (Matthew 5: 3–11). He is using the term as a state of happiness—a deep sense of well-being and joy a person experiences who is at one with God.

The term was also used in a far less powerful sense: showers of blessings were thought to descend on those who performed specific services or who avoided forbidden acts. A household could be blessed for generosity, and blessings could be taken away (Mic. 2:9). It appears to suggest material prosperity rather than spiritual well-being. In fact, some considered wealth an indication of God's blessing that was justified by the good works of the beneficiary.

In each case, the blessing itself came from God, not from the person invoking it. This suggests the idea of a benediction, the "actual transference of blessing from its source to a recipient" (J. G. Davies 1992, 83). As the Psalmist said, "The blessing of the Lord be upon you; we bless you in the name of the Lord" (Ps. 129:8). The benediction is actually a **prayer**, invoking God's blessing on the person, places, or object involved. Jesus signaled his deity in his blessing of the **Disciples** before he was "taken up into heaven" (Luke 24:51). The Disciples then also pronounced "the blessing of peace" on those they sent away (Acts 15:33). Paul picked up on this interpretation, noting that he came "in the full measure of the blessing of Christ" (Rom. 15:29). He traced this blessing back to the original Abrahamic covenant (Gal. 3:14).

The blessing or benediction became a standard part of New Testament **epistles**, the usual conclusion to a letter, and also to a sermon or a religious service. It is probably the source of *Goodbye*—an abbreviated form of "God be with you" or "God by wy you" as Shakespeare expressed it in *Love's Labors Lost* (III.3.1.151; *Oxford English Dictionary*).

The use of the benediction continues in Jewish tradition; the blessing of the children by their parents on **Sabbath** eve or on entering the **house** is "highly prized by the children. The value thus laid upon the benediction spoken by the father and mother represents the constancy in Jewish life of the working of forces that make for righteousness; and it is one of the constituent factors of ... the 'continuity of the Jewish spirit'" (Kaufmann Kohler and David Philipson 2005). *See also* Beatitudes.

Further Reading

Davies, J. G. "Benediction," in *A Dictionary of Biblical Tradition in English Literature*. Grand Rapids, Mich.: William B. Eerdmans Publishing Company, 1992. Kohler, Kaufmann and David Philipson, "Blessing of Children," http://www. jewishencyclopedia.com (accessed March 3, 2005). *Oxford English Dictionary* Web site: http://www.oed.com (accessed June 20, 2004).

𝔅lood

(Gen. 9:4; 1 Sam. 14:31–33; Exod. 12:7, 24:8; Lev. 4:6; Num. 19:4; Heb. 11:28, 12:24; 1 Pet. 1:2) Scripture has 405 mentions of blood, beginning with the blood of Abel, which "cries out from the ground" (Gen. 4:10).

This concept that the blood-soaked ground cries out for vengeance continues to excite the imagination of writers, including such modern Americans as William Faulkner, who made this thematic in dealing with the American South. Scholars regularly debate whether blood is a symbol of life or **death**. It seems to represent both: In his **covenant** with Noah, the Lord gave him everything, "Only you shall not eat flesh with its life, that is, its blood. For your lifeblood I will surely require a reckoning; of every beast I will require it and of man; of every man's brother I will require the life of man. Whoever shed the blood of man, by man shall his blood be shed; for God made man in his own image" (Gen. 9:4–6). In Jewish law, the "avenger of blood" is fully justified in requiring a life for a life (Num. 35:19–27).

This idea that blood represents life, and the spilling of blood is death is repeated regularly. The brothers of Joseph dipped his coat of many colors in **goat**'s blood to prove to their father that this favored son had died (Gen. 37:31). When Moses's wife circumcised him, she referred to him as the "bridegroom of blood" (Exod. 4:26). One of the **plagues** that struck Egypt was the turning of the waters of the country into blood (Exod. 7:19). When the Israelites were preparing for their final night in **Egypt**, they were told to paint the doorframes of their houses with the blood of **sheep** or goats to protect their firstborn sons (Exod. 12:7–13).

When Moses handed down the **law** to his people, he stipulated that they must refrain from eating **animals'** blood. Leviticus and Deuteronomy are full of references to this prohibition against partaking of the blood of beasts or **birds**, even of meat that is still full of blood. Eating such meat was regarded as a sin. For this reason, foods were prepared carefully, soaking and salting the meat, scouring the vessels, so as to keep the faithful from even accidental contact with blood. In the New Testament, the **apostle** Paul acknowledged this tradition, admonishing **Christian**s to avoid blood and things strangled because they had become a stumbling block to new believers (Acts 15:29).

Blood was thought to belong to God and was therefore a significant part of **sacrifices**. **Priests** sprinkled, poured, and threw blood at various times in accordance with the law. This ritual sacrifice was also central to the Christian message, imaged in both the **Last Supper** and the **Crucifixion**.

The blood of Christ became an important part of Christian thought, with the concept of redemption through his shed blood (as explained in Hebrews). Roman Catholics include in their liturgical calendar the festival of "the Sacred Heart commemorating the piercing of the heart of Christ so that the water and blood flowed from the wound" (Dom Robert Le Gall, *Symbols of Catholicism*, 122). A famous hymn by a Protestant poet, Thomas Cowper (1731–1800), also celebrates the "fountain filled with blood which flowed from Emmanuel's veins."

Practical results of this deep concern with blood and reverence for it include the legal restrictions against murder and the Jewish restrictions regarding menstruating women or those giving **birth**. It also kept generations from making any use of a corpse, whether for anatomical studies or other purposes, because the body with the blood in it was considered unclean. And the Mosaic view of blood also served as the source for medical theories regarding bleeding as a means of curing many ills, a practice that continued well into the nineteenth century. *See also* Crucifixion; Last Supper; Law, Dietary; Sacrifice.

Further Reading

Jastrow, Marcus, and Hermann L. Stack. "Blood," http://www.jewishencyclopedia.com (accessed June 12, 2004). Le Gall, Dom Robert. *Symbols of Catholicism*. New York: Assouline Publishing, 2000.

Boats and Ships

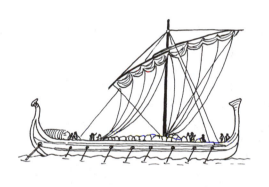

A Phoenician top-merchant ship and battleship. The Phoenicians were the great sailors of the ancient world; their ships were used by King Solomon to bring treasures from all over the world.

(Gen. 6:14; 1 Kings 9:26–28, 10:11, 22; 2 Chron. 8:18, 9:21; John 1:3; Isa. 33:23; Ezek. 27; Mark 6:47–52) Aside from Noah's construction of the **ark** and Jonah's frightening time aboard a storm-tossed ship, the Jews had little occasion to deal with ships; they were an agrarian people. In fact, Noah's ark was probably not a ship at all, but a kind of enclosed box without either sail or oars (Mary Joan Winn Leith 1993, 694). Ships, or sea-faring vessels, were less common than small boats in Jewish experience, largely because of the poor ports available. The reference in the Song of Deborah (Judg. 5:17) to Dan and Asher as seafaring tribes may mean that they were dockworkers or clients at the port of Acco.

The **Philistines**, Phoenicians, and Syrians controlled most of the coastline. Even these Sea People probably had only modest ships that hugged the coastline to avoid the angry winds and waves of the "Great Sea," the Mediterranean. Actual examples of Phoenician ships have been discovered sunk in waters west of the seaport of Ashkelon, dating from 750 to 700 B.C. They were heavy laden with amphoras of fine wine when they sank, probably as a result of the treacherous east wind. The Phoenician "hippos" ships had "gently curving hulls ending in nearly perpendicular posts capped with bird-head devices facing outboard" (Philip J. King and Lawrence E. Stager 2001, 179).

During Solomon's reign, Israel joined with Tyre to build a commercial fleet that traveled from Tarshish to Ophir in southern Arabia and perhaps to East Africa and even the Indian Ocean for spices and **gold**. The legendary seamanship of the Phoenicians made these grand voyages possible. They had even earlier been important traders with the **Egyptians**, bringing commodities, such as the cedars of Lebanon, from Syria and Cilicia. Subsequent **kings**, however, do not seem to have continued this trade. Ezekiel 27 describes the building of the ships in Tyre, with planks of fir, masts of cedar, oars of oak, and decks of pine, each from different regions. The decks were inlaid with **ivory** and there was embroidered linen from Egypt for sails. Blue and purple awnings decorated them. Skilled pilots and rowers are mentioned, indicating that the ships combined sails with oars for speed.

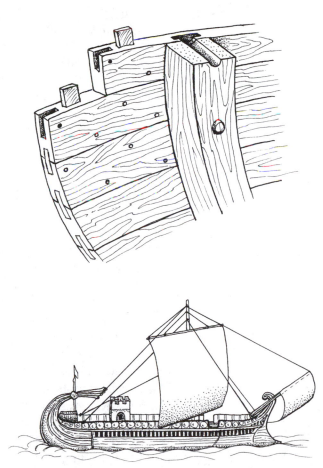

Small fishing craft were the most common Jewish boats, although they are not mentioned in the Old Testament. Apparently, barges pulled by **animals** were a common means of transporting goods. When the focus of attention moved from Jerusalem to the Galilee—in the New Testament, with descriptions of the fishermen Jesus called to follow him—the references to boats suddenly became more common. All through the **Gospels**, we find mention of the **fishermen** who became **Disciples**, their boats, and their nets. In recent years, archaeologists have discovered a fishing

A Roman warship and a detail of the hull of Roman ship. In the days of the Acts of the Apostles, Paul and others traveled on both Greek and Roman vessels.

boat from that period, indicating the approximate size and construction. It is on display in a museum adjacent to the Sea of Galilee.

In the New Testament, especially during the journeys of Paul, we see constant references to ships sailing to different ports around the Mediterranean Sea. The Book of Acts ends with a voyage to **Rome**. The ships on which he would have sailed were probably a commercial ship so common in the ancient world. Luke describes the boat in detail, noting that it was large enough to hold 276 people. It had a significant cargo as well, and was equipped with sails and more than one anchor. Even with expert sailors, the ship ran aground on a shoal in the rough seas, forcing the crew and passengers to spend three months on the island of Malta (Acts 27–28). *See also* Ark; Fish; Fishermen, Fishing.

Further Reading

Casson, Lionel. *Ships and Seamanship in the Ancient World.* Princeton, N.J.: Princeton University Press, 1971. King, Philip J. and Lawrence E. Stager. *Life in Biblical Israel.* Louisville, Ky.: Westminster John Knox Press, 2001. Leith, Mary Joan Winn, "Ships and Sailing," in *The Oxford Companion to the Bible.* New York: Oxford University Press, 1993. Wachsmann, Shelley. *The Sea of Galilee Boat.* New York: Plenum Press, 1995.

Bread

(Gen. 14:18, 1 Sam. 25:18, Jer. 7:18, Matt. 6:11, John 6:32–35, 1 Cor. 11:26) In Scripture as in modern life, bread was and is a food made of **grain**, usually wheat or barley, but sometimes other ingredients, and frequently blended with some leavening device, a moistening ingredient and oil, and even an sweetener, before being kneaded, allowed to rise, and baked, either on a rock or in an oven.

Bread is one of the most basic and pervasive of biblical foods, mentioned regularly over a period of 2,000 years. It is the "staff of life." When Abraham was greeted by Melchizedek, king of Salem, after the rescue of Lot from the **kings** who had taken him captive, the gracious "**priest** of the most high God" "brought forth bread and **wine**" for his visitor (Gen. 14:18). Abraham himself greeted his angelic visitors at a later time by offering to "fetch a morsel of bread" to comfort them, turning to Sarah and saying, "Make ready quickly three measures of fine meal, kneed it, and make cakes upon the hearth" (Gen. 18:5–6). This citation hints that the loaves were cooked on the stone hearth and presupposes the grinding of meal, the mixing and kneading of the dough, and the shaping into either small cakes or larger loaves.

The offering of bread became a standard indication of **hospitality** and generosity. It was Abigail's provision of 200 loaves of bread, along with other food and drink, that impressed David (1 Sam. 25:18), and Tamar's consideration was demonstrated in her baking of bread for her sick brother, ironically increasing Amnon's illicit lust for her (2 Sam. 13:6–8). In the New Testament, Jesus's concern for the 5,000 who had listened to his message all day without food led to his multiplication of the loaves and the fishes (Matt. 14:17). When Jesus instructed his **disciples** to go on their journey without bread, bag, or money, (Mark 6:8), he was forcing them to rely on the generosity of strangers.

Refusal to eat bread and drink water with a man became the mark of disapproval (1 Kings 13:15–22). The man of God in this story, tricked into disobeying angelic directions by eating with Jeroboam, met with a lion, which slew him for his disobedience. Refusal to provide bread for one's children was a sign of brutality, as indicated in Jesus's rhetorical question, "Which of you, if his son asks for bread, will give him a stone?" (Matt. 7:9). In fact, Jesus made the case that children must be provided their daily bread. It is clearly wrong to "take the children's bread and toss it to" the dogs (Mark 7:27). He knew the necessity of bread for survival, having faced hunger as his first temptation, when Satan suggested that he should use his powers to turn stones into bread (Matt 4:3). Even in his resurrected body, Christ shared bread and **fish** with his disciples, cooking them on a fire of "burning coals" by the shore of Galilee (John 21:9). He also knew that man does not live by bread alone, "but on every word that comes from the mouth of God" (Matt. 4:4).

Not all bread was a simple blend of wheat and oil. Ezekiel indicates that it can be made of beans and lentils, as well as millet and spelt (a kind of wheat) (Ezek. 4:9). It must have been a very special bread that Jacob gave to his brother Esau, along with his lentil stew, that made him trade his birthright for it (Gen. 25:34). When Joseph was thrown in an Egyptian prison, he found one of his fellow prisoners was the pharaoh's baker, who dreamed a fatal dream of white baskets full of "all manner of bakemeats" (Gen. 40:17). The richness and variety of baked products in **Egypt** became a fond memory for the Israelites, who recalled Egypt as a place where they "ate bread to the full" (Exod. 16:3). The Egyptians had more herbs, more sophistication, and vast storage bins for grains, making the delicious breads they ate in Egypt a much lamented memory for the Israelites.

By the time the children of Israel escaped Egypt, they had become accustomed to leavened bread, probably a process of leaving some of the previous day's dough in the mixing trough as modern cooks do with "sour dough" bread, using the old dough as a "starter." This yeast was forbidden to the Israelites as they planned their **exodus** from Egypt, when they were told to eat "bread made without yeast" along with "meat roasted over the fire" and "bitter herbs" (Exod. 12:8). This served as the basis for the Feast of Unleavened Bread, to be celebrated throughout their history (Exod. 12:17). On the first day of this seven-day **festival**, they were to remove all yeast from their homes. During the seven days, they were to eat no leavening, as a memorial to the haste of their departure from captivity.

During the Exodus, when passing through the barren desert region, the Israelites found themselves without the means to make bread, having no store of barley or wheat. In response to Moses's prayers on their behalf, the Lord said, "I will rain down bread from **heaven** for you" (Exod. 16:4). The people were to go out each morning, taking only so much as they needed, except on the **Sabbath**, the day before which they would gather a double-store. Later, when God provided Moses with instructions for the **Ark of the Covenant**, he told him to take "an omer of manna and keep it for generations to come" in memory of this gracious provision for their needs (Exod. 16:32).

In the laws handed down to Moses, a table with the "bread of the Presence" was to be a regular part of the **Tabernacle**, and later the **Temple** (Exod. 25:30). Specifications for the Bread of the Presence reveal that it was to be in wafer form, made without leavening, mixed with oil, shaped, and then spread with oil (Exod. 29: 23). The basket of these wafers were to be "before me at all times" according to God's instructions (Exod. 25:30, 29:23). This sacred bread was to be eaten by Aaron and his sons, the priests, and any that was left over until morning was to be burned: "it must not be eaten, because it is holy" (Exod. 29:34). Unless God instructed a man to eat of this holy bread, as in the case of David (2 Sam. 1:4–6), such an action was considered a desecration.

The miraculous use of bread continues through the Scriptures. When Gideon sought proof that God was choosing him to be his **warrior**, he was told to make unleavened cakes, which he was to place along with the flesh of a kid and some broth on a rock. "Then the **angel** of the Lord put forth the end of the **staff** . . . and touched the flesh and the unleavened cakes; and there rose up fire out of the rock, and consumed the flesh and the unleavened cakes" (Judg. 6:21). When Elijah the Tishbite began his ministry, ravens brought him bread morning and evening (1 Kings 17:6). Later, when he sought to test the widow, he asked that she make him "a little cake" (1 Kings 17:14), and she soon found her generosity in providing for the **prophet** from her meager store resulted in the multiplication of her store of meal and oil.

The symbolic meanings for bread became firmly implanted in Hebrew thought with the **Psalms**, Proverbs, and the Prophets, which speak of the "bread of angels" (Ps. 78:85), "bread of tears" (Ps. 80:5), the "bread of Heaven" (Ps. 105:40), the "bread of wickedness" (Prov. 4:17), the "bread of idleness" (Prov. 31:27), and the "bread of adversity" (Isa. 30:20). It became a metonym for life itself; as the standard daily fare of humankind, it represents the tone of his existence. In Wisdom literature, "daily bread" (Job 23:12; Prov. 30:8) was already used as a metaphor for manna, even before Jesus used the phrase in the **Lord's Prayer** (Matt. 6:11).

Jesus took the imagery of bread a step further by telling his disciples, "I am the bread of life. He who comes to me will never go hungry, and he who believes in me will never hunger" (John 6:35). The "true bread from heaven" comes from God, the Father, not from Moses (John 6:32). Jews, angry with this identification of Jesus with manna, sought to make him retract the statement; but he went on to elaborate that the bread was the flesh of the "Son of man," and "whoso eateth my flesh and drinketh my blood, hath eternal life; and I will raise him up at the last day" (John 6:54). On the night he was arrested, Jesus celebrated the Passover with his disciples, using the bread as a foreshadowing that Judas was to betray him. He then "took bread, gave thanks and broke it, and gave it to them, saying, 'This is my body given for you; do this in remembrance of me'" (Luke 22:19). It is this action that Paul elaborates in his instructions to the young **church** in Corinth, telling them, "For whenever you eat this bread and drink this cup, you proclaim the Lord's death until he comes" (1 Cor. 11:26).

From the time that Abram and Sarai left Mesopotamia until the days when Paul carried the Christian message to people across the **Roman** Empire, bread was the staple of diet, varied in its preparation and significance, but always essential to human life. The people of Ur, with their advanced civilization, surely had ovens and varied techniques for baking bread. Some scholars also believe that their "Queen of Heaven" was honored by baked cakes of grain, left on her **altar**. Jeremiah cited the common practice in Judah and in the streets of Jerusalem, of gathering wood and lighting a fire and kneading the dough, not just to feed the family, but to involve the entire group—children, men, and women—in making cakes for the queen of heaven (Jer. 7:18).

The **Passover**, of course, still celebrated in the springtime by Jews, continues the tradition of the unleavened bread. For Christians, the **Last Supper** became the basis of the Communion or Mass. For Roman Catholics, a wafer is the preferred bread; in Protestant circles, any bread may serve. A long-standing English Easter tradition has been to blend the symbol of the bread with the image of the **cross**, in the hot-cross bun. In each of these cases, the image involves a shared meal deeply embedded in tradition and richly resonant with meaning. Breaking bread together has become the image of harmony, eating the

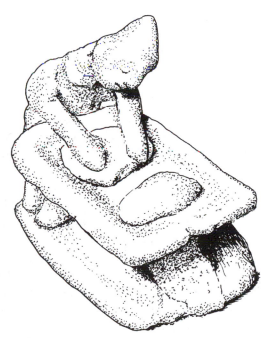

Palestinian terra-cotta statue of woman making bread.

bread an image of life, and blessing the bread a recognition that it comes from God. *See also* Ark of the Covenant; Last Supper; Passover or the Feast of Unleavened Bread.

Further Reading

King, Philip J. and Lawrence Stager. *Life in Biblical Israel*. Louisville, Ky.: Westminster John Knox Press, 2001. Le Gall, Dom Robert. *Symbols of Catholicism*. New York: Assouline Publishing, 2000.

Bricks, Bricklayers

(**Exod. 5:7, Ezek. 13:10–15**) During their long sojourn in **Egypt**, the Israelites learned the skill of brick-making. As **slaves**, they were tasked with making and laying bricks for the monumental building projects of the Pharaoh. When they returned to Palestine and settled the land, they continued to use mud brick as their primary construction material for their buildings and walls, especially in the coastal plain and the valleys where clay was readily available and timber was more scarce (Philip J. King and Lawrence E. Stager 2001, 28).

Mud was in fact used for both bricks and mortar. The raw mud was mixed with other materials, most notably water and straw (Exod. 5:7), and then kneaded to the right consistency and packed into molds. For the kneading, the workers might use either their hands or feet. The brick-maker would prepare the ground for molding the bricks by sprinkling finely chopped straw on it to keep the wet mud from sticking. He would press the damp clay into a portable wooden mold the size of a single brick and then lift the mold away, using a wooden handle. He would then place the mold next to the newly made brick and begin on the next one. The whole brickyard would eventually be covered by bricks arranged in rows, left for two days in the sun, and stamped with a trademark of some sort.

Heaton notes that sometimes stray **dogs** would scurry about the brick yard among the drying bricks, leaving paw prints that still survive. One of the more interesting discoveries at Ezion-geber, Solomon's factory town on the Red Sea, is the brickyard with "hundreds of half-finished and unused bricks still in position, as they have been for nearly three thousand years" (E.W. Heaton 1956, 132–134).

The bricks were of various sizes, usually much larger than those used today—21 inches × 10 inches × 4 inches. Unbaked bricks, when used in above-ground construction, needed a layer of plaster to weatherproof them, an annual task. Ezekiel (13:10–15) speaks of "daubing" a wall with "untempered mortar." With the hot, dry climate of the country, this process produced fairly strong bricks, but not as long-lasting as kiln-baked bricks,

Brick-making (from an Egyptian tomb painting, fifteenth century B.C.), showing the wet clay being formed into bricks, then carried to construction sites to build walls, all under the eye of the Egyptian overseer carrying his flail.

a technique that was probably not used in Israel until the early **Roman** era (Philip King and Lawrence Stager 2001, 28).

A debate regarding this process and the date when it was first used hinges on the translation of *brickmold* as *brickkiln* in 2 Sam. 12:31 and Nahum 3:14. Nahum tells his people to "go into the clay, and tread the mortar, make strong the brickmold" or "brickkiln." This scene describes the preparation of the wall against the coming siege.

The Israelites' experience of building with bricks was not limited to the brick-layer. Even the simplest peasant knew how to make his own sun-dried bricks, which he might use to construct his own home. A regular part of the seasonal work of the peasant was to cover his mud-brick "house with clay or thatch spread over roof timbers. Such buildings

Brick mold for forming the wet clay into bricks.

require constant attention" (D. J. Wiseman 1980,125). Later, when bricks were baked in the kiln, this was probably the work of the **potter**.

The larger construction, such as a city wall or a public building, would have involved more than one set of craftsmen. Building sites were surveyed with a measuring line—a rope, cord, string, or twisted thread of linen that was marked in cubits (1 Kings 7:15, 23). Later, a reed was used to mark the furlongs (Rev. 11:1, 21:15). After the surveyor completed his work, a builder took charge of the peasants, sometimes conscripts, who actually did the work of digging, carrying, laying brick with mortar, and coordinating their work with any **stonemasons** and **carpenters** who might also have a role in the construction. The builder would have used the plumbline to make sure the walls were straight and true. *See also* Measures; Slavery, Laws of.

Further Reading

Heaton, E. W. *Everyday Life in Old Testament Times.* New York: Charles Scribner's Sons, 1956. King, Philip J. and Lawrence E. Stager, *Life in Biblical Israel.* Louisville, Ky.: Westminster John Knox Press, 2001. Wiseman, D. J. "Arts and Crafts," in *The Illustrated Bible Dictionary.* Sydney, Australia: Tyndale House Publishers, 1980.

Bride/Bridegroom. *See Weddings*

Burial. *See Graves*

C

Calendar. *See Time*

Camel

(Judg. 7:12; Job 1:3; 1 Kings 10:1f.; 2 Kings 8:9; Matt. 19:24) The camel was the truck of the ancient world. The one-humped variety (dromedary or Arabian camel) was the long-distance carrier of heavy burdens for 30 centuries before Christ. Wild camels were domesticated early because of their great utility. They require little **grain**, can stock up on **water** and **food** using the unique paunches in their hump, and can travel long distances over desert sands, covering as much as three miles an hour if heavily loaded, or 9 or 10 miles an hour if lightly encumbered (Fred H. Wight 1953, 257). They can carry as much as 400 pounds and a rider for normal trips, less if expected to go on long stretches across deserts. The camels' abilities to chew dry twigs and sharp thorns, and go for three or four days without drinking make them ideal for long journeys. They may be hitched together by rope, requiring only a lead camel or donkey to guide a long line of camels through the desert. A fast dromedary, carrying only its driver, has been known to go nearly a hundred miles in 13 hours (George Cansdale 1970, 68).

Camels' milk, relished by many, is used to make cheese. It is rich but not sweet or so plentiful as cow's milk. (Scripture makes no mention of the Hebrews' drinking camels' milk.) Their hides were used for shoes and bags, and their manure was dried and burned for fuel (Madeleine S. Miller 1961, 88). Although some ancient peoples ate the meat of the camel, this was forbidden by Jewish **law**. Leviticus 11:4 includes camels with "unclean" **animals**, those that do not have cloven hooves.

Camels grow thick protective coats of hair, which is shed "in great patches before the end of April, leaving thinner summer hair underneath but looking very tatty during the moult" (George Cansdale 1970, 69). These lumps of hair were gathered and used for weaving fabric. In addition, hair was cut annually from the neck, back, and hump of the camels and woven into a durable and water-resistant fabric that could last a lifetime. A camel's hair cloak, a shelter against both heat and cold, was a treasured possession, as is indicated in

A caravan with camels, ideal animals for long treks across the desert, carrying great loads and needing little water.

references to the mantle of Elijah, passed on to Elisha (2 Kings 2:13). It was also the main **clothing** of John the Baptist (Mark 1:6). (Camels' hair coats and scarves are still treasured today.) It was frequently used, as was **goat**'s hair, for **tents** or blankets. Depending on the weaving process and the quality of the hair (whether it came from the soft undercoat of the camel), it could be a rough sackcloth or a smooth fine fabric.

Although the Israelites were proud of their camels, they preferred **donkeys** as beasts of burden. Living in hilly country, which camels could not easily traverse, they found that donkeys had greater flexibility, were more useful in domestic chores, and could be stalled in the home because of their smaller size. The early Hebrews had limited need for long trips, except for occasional trade with other peoples.

Nonetheless, they counted camels in their enumeration of wealth from the time of Abraham (Gen. 12:16). Some scholars argue that Abraham would have lived too early to use camels, but others insist that domesticated camels had appeared in history even before his time. Camels are mentioned as possessions of his **family**. His grandson Jacob "had much cattle, asses, and camels" (Gen. 12:16). And the Ishmaelites were traveling with a caravan of camels when they purchased Joseph and carried him to **Egypt** (Gen. 37:25, 28).

In Egypt, the Israelites found that the Egyptians used camels for work and transport. In the period of the **Judges**, enemies of the Israelites used camels in **warfare:** the Midianites came riding against Gideon on camels (Judg. 6–8), and later Saul and David faced camel-riding Amalekites (1 Sam. 15:3, 27:9, 30:17). Job was said to have had 3,000 camels (Job 1:3), suggesting that he was a camel-breeder. This remains a lucrative business east of the Jordan even today (Madeleine S. Miller and J. Lane Miller 1961, 87). It is a slow process: camels bear one offspring at a time and the pregnancy lasts 12 months.

Kindness to camels was used as a test for Isaac's potential bride, Rebekah, who offered to water the camels of Isaac's servant (Gen. 24:20). The vast thirst of the camel at the end of a trip, when it was likely to drink as much as nine gallons of **water**, makes the gesture of drawing water for a stranger's camels an act of genuine generosity.

Foreign peoples were more likely than Israelites to appear on camels; their height and decorations signified wealth and power. The animal was often elaborately decorated with bangles. Crescent-shaped ornaments and shells sewn on red cloth covered the collars, and sometimes the cloth was lavishly embroidered. These might be topped with a palanquin, a seat that fits over the hump and looks like a wooden box. Some had saddles, which were fastened crosswise, and could carry more than one person. These saddles were often used in tents as makeshift chairs. It may have been under such a saddle that Rachel hid Laban's household gods. (Genesis 24:61 indicates Rebekah rode on a camel to become Isaac's bride.)

When the Queen of Sheba visited King Solomon, she brought camels laden with gifts (1 Kings 10:2; 2 Chron. 5:21). Because the decorative camel was an indicator of wealth and royalty, Jesus himself twice used camels for subjects of **parables**, in both cases referring to their size. The first parable mentioned their difficulty in going through the "eye of the needle" (Matt. 19:24). (This may refer to the small emergency **gate** that was next to the main gate of the city, used for travelers who needed to enter after the regular gates were closed for the night. Or it may simply refer to a needle and be hyperbole.) Christ's other reference was to the difficulty in "swallowing of the camel" (Matt 23:24).

Artists have found the camel a useful means to establish the exotic atmosphere of Bible illustrations, associating the animal with royalty and dignity. Renaissance artists enjoyed the elaborate trappings with which camels were harnessed (George Ferguson 1966, 13). *See also* Animals; Art: Christian; Cloth; Clothing; Parable; Tents.

Further Reading

Cansdale, George. *All the Animals of the Bible Lands.* Grand Rapids, Mich.: Zondervan Publishing House, 1970. Ferguson, George. *Signs and Symbols in Christian Art.* New York: Oxford University Press, 1966. Miller, Madeleine S. and J. Lane Miller. "Camels," in *Harper's Bible Dictionary.* New York: Harper and Row, Publishers, 1961. Wight, Fred H. *Manners and Customs of Bible Lands.* Chicago: Moody Press, 1953.

Canaan, Canaanites

(Gen. 6:15–18; Deut. 7:1; Num. 34:1–12) Canaan was the "Promised Land" to which Abraham and Sarah (a.k.a., Abram and Sarai) traveled, a land of "milk and honey" that eventually became Israel. This is also the land to which Moses returned, leading his clan as far as the Jordan River, and leaving the task of conquering the land and settling it to Joshua and subsequent Israelites. It was the land divided among the **Tribes of Israel**. Its peoples continued through Bible history to serve as neighbors, enemies, friends, and spouses of the Israelites.

The borders of Canaan appear in Numbers 34:1–12. It lay between the Mediterranean Coast and the Jordan rift, extending as far as the Dead Sea on the one side and the Wadi of **Egypt** near Gaza on the other. On the north, it went as far as the Pass of Hamath on the upper Orontes, north of modern Lebanon. In the Bible, the term "Canaanite" is often a general designation "for all the indigenous inhabitants of ancient Palestine without ethnic or political distinction"—sometimes also called "**Amorites**" (P. Kyle McCarter, Jr. 1993, 98).

Canaan was an Egyptian province when the Hebrews first sojourned there. Like numerous other peoples of the region, such as the Phoenicians, the **Hittites**, and the Jebusites, the Canaanites were thought to have descended from Ham (Gen. 6:15–18). Deuteronomy 7:1 indicates that the Canaanites were one of seven nations the Israelites drove out of the land, forcing them to settle along the coast. In much of later Scripture, "Canaanite" is interchangeable with "Phoenician."

In Mesopotamia, Canaan was also a term for red or purple dye, which came from the murex shell. The Canaanites were famous for this product, and it is not clear whether they derived their name from the dye, or the dye from the people who discovered and produced it. Their name also came to mean "merchant,"(Zech 14:21), probably because of their seaports and active seafaring (Kyle McCarter 1993, 98).

The Canaanites never were a united people, largely because of the geography of the region. The country is so cut up with mountains, rivers, and valleys that city states prevailed, with local **kings** or warlords building **fortresses** to protect themselves and their territories. Joshua noted that five such kings of city-states banded against him: the kings of Jerusalem, Hebron, Jarmuth, Lachish, and Eglon (Josh.10–12). Other important city-states in Canaan were Debir, Libnah, Gezer, Bethel, Jericho, Shechem, Dor, Megiddo, Beth-shan, Pell, Hazor, Kedesh, Yano'am, Tyre, Sidon, and Damascus. Most were in the Judean lowlands, along the coast, or in the valleys of Jezreel and along the Jordan, avoiding the hill country that was probably thickly wooded with good grazing for the herds of the Joseph tribes. It was here, in the hill country, that the Israelites first settled, gradually attacking one city after another until they had taken much of the land (George Ernest Wright 1956, 34). Some modern scholars suspect that many of the aboriginal peoples remained among the Hebrews even after defeat and that the "settlement" of the region actually took generations.

This victory (or this series of battles) seems miraculous in retrospect. After all, the Canaanites were thought to be superior fighters: They were better protected and better armed than the invaders; they had iron **chariots** and heavily fortified cities. Even so, they were not a unified people fighting with a coherent strategy. After 1600 B.C., the population of the country became increasingly mixed with Hittites, Amorites, Pezzirites, Hivites, and Jebusites, each group considering itself distinct from the others. The Jebusites, for instance, were possibly Canaanites who lived in the city of Jebus. The Amorites were survivors of a great invasion from earlier times. The Hivites (possibly the same as Horites) seem to have come from northern Mesopotamia to **Edom** or Seir. At the time of Joshua, the Hivites controlled the four federated cities northwest of Jerusalem and cleverly negotiated a treaty with Joshua. The Perizzites and Girgashites are both names of people lost to history except as references in Joshua (Josh. 3:30, 24:1; G. Ernest Wright 1956, 35–36).

The religion of Canaan, which often seemed both shocking and appealing to the Israelites, was primitive and barbarous. Like the **Greeks**, the Canaanites believed in a family of gods. The father was El, "the father of years," "creator of creatures," also known as the "bull." His wife was **Asherah**, and their large family included a grandson named Hadad, called "**Baal**" or "Lord" by the people. He personified fertility—all of the heavenly forces that produced rain and vegetation. His wives were Anath and another known as *Ashtoreh* in Palestine, who seemed to be parallel to Astarte. She personified love and fertility. Other gods were Mot (Death), Resheph, (pestilence and Lord of the Underworld, Baal's enemy), Shulman or Shalim (bringer of health), and Koshar or Kothar (god of arts, including **music** and crafts) (G. Earnest Wright 1956, 36).

The numerous stories about this divine family show them to have been of lower morality than most humans, without constraints or sympathy; they were bloodthirsty and brutal. They required worship of especially cruel nature, including child sacrifice, sacred prostitution, and snake-worship. The temptations of these pagan gods and their worship challenged the Israelites, who had been firmly admonished to "have no other gods" before Jehovah. God had ordered that everything connected with the Canaanite religion be destroyed (Deut. 7, 12:1–3). Yet the worship on "high places" and the celebration of the Baalim continued through much of Jewish history.

The languages of both the Canaanites and Israelites were Semitic, making it easy for Israelites to communicate with their neighbors and to trade with them. The Canaanites living along the coast engaged in commerce with many lands. From them the Hebrews and others bought cedar wood (as for Solomon's **Temple** and palace), jars of oil and **wine**, **writing** paper, **pottery**, and of course the famous dye. Trading with Egypt, Crete, and Greece and sailing from their numerous ports at Tyre, Sidon, Beirut, and Byblos, the Canaanites served as a bridge between Asia and Egypt, carrying the various cultures as well as the material goods. Their own cities blended many styles of architecture and decoration; they used **Babylonian** cylinder **seals** and enjoyed Hittite gold-work from Turkey; they imported Egyptian scarabs and **jewelry**.

Their great legacy was the alphabet, which was invented between 2000 and 1600 B.C. Using Egyptian paper (papyrus), they shared this simplified mode of writing with other cultures around the Mediterranean and throughout the Fertile Crescent (Pat Alexander, 1978, 16). It is no wonder that Solomon would have reached out to Hiram to bring architects and craftsmen, goods, and services from Sidon and Tyre to his kingdom when he set out to become a renowned ruler surrounded by a rich culture.

Although intermarriage was forbidden by the priests, it became common. After the return from Exile, the **prophets** and other religious leaders felt compelled to prohibit this practice and cleanse their community of such

Canaan and her neighbors Egypt, Ammon, Edom, and Midian.

outsiders. *See also* Asherah, Ashtoreth, Ashtaroth; Baal, Baalim; Boats and Ships; Hittites; Warfare; Writing and Reading; Writing Materials.

Further Reading

Alexander, Pat. *Eerdmans' Family Encyclopedia of the Bible*. Grand Rapids, Mich.: William B. Eerdmans Publishing Co., 1978. McCarter, P. Kyle, Jr. "Canaan," in *The Oxford Companion the Bible*. New York: Oxford University Press, 1993. Wright, George Ernest. *The Westminster Historical Atlas to the Bible*. Philadelphia: The Westminster Press, 1956.

Candle, Candlestick

(Exod. 25:31–40; 2 Kings 4:10; 2 Chron. 4:7; Matt. 5:15; Mark 4:21; Luke 8:16) In Scripture, candles were not usually wax tapers, but clay or metal lamps with nozzles through which flax wicks carried the oil (Madeleine S. Miller and J. Lane Miller 1961, 90). The most ancient **lamps** were simple dishes of clay that held a wick and oil. Fire at the end of the wick kept burning until the oil in the dish was used up. It was later and only among the wealthier peoples that wax was used for tapers. Because most poor people lived in homes without many windows, some light was required day and night. Lamps were kept burning all of the time.

The Psalmist used the metaphor of the light for the brightness of God's glory. As in John 1, the light shining in the darkness is evidence that God has seen fit to "light my candle: the Lord my God will enlighten my darkness" (Ps. 18:28). For God's dwelling, candles were preferred to **olive oil** lamps. In the original design for the **Tabernacle**, the lamp stand with seven branches was to be made of gold (Exod. 25:31–40). This menorah design was repeated in the plan for the **Temple**, this time with five treelike candlesticks in the Holy Place (1 Kings 7:49; 2 Chron. 4:7). In the famous marble Arch of Titus in **Rome**, we can see the candelabrum taken when the Romans looted and destroyed the Temple in 70 A.D.

Even today, Jews continue the use of the menorah, both in communal and private worship. The celebration of Yom Kippur involves the lighting of a special candle on the eve of the **Sabbath**. And in the **festival** of Hanukkah, which celebrates the rededication of the Temple by Judas Maccabeus, four lamps are used on each side of the stand and the central kindling light (Madeleine S. Miller and J. Lane Miller 1961, 90).

The tradition continues in **Christian** worship as well, largely because of the consistent use of light and candle imagery by Jesus. He spoke of himself as the Light of the World and of his followers as Children of the Light. In the catacombs, where the Christians worshipped during the Roman period, light was essential. Such Scripture as the story of the 10 virgins (Mat. 25:1–13) increasingly gave the candles a symbolic meaning.

Roman Catholics light the especially designed Paschal Candle as a symbol of the risen Christ. They have also traditionally used Eucharistic candles to symbolize the coming of Christ in Communion and the six lights on the **altar** to represent the Church's constant round of **prayer**. When arranged in groups of three, they represent the Trinity, seven signify the Seven Sacraments (George Ferguson 1966, 162).

Following the Jewish custom of lighting lamps on Friday evening at the beginning of the Sabbath, many **churches** begin their services by the ceremonial lighting of candles. A great favorite in many modern churches is the Christmas Eve service, ending with the lighting

The Menorah, or the seven-branched candelabrum, is pictured on the Arch of Titus in Rome. In 70 A.D., this was one of the relics from the Temple that the victorious Romans carried away to Rome.

of candles of the entire congregation as they sing "Silent Night, Holy Night."

The final scriptural reference to candles is in Revelation 22:5. John realizes that, in the New Jerusalem, "There shall be no night there; and they need no candle, neither light of the sun; for the Lord God giveth them light; and they shall reign for ever and ever." *See also* Hanukkah or Festival of Lights; Lamp; Sabbath; Tabernacle; Temple.

Further Reading

Ferguson, George. *Signs and Symbols in Christian Art.* New York: Oxford University Press, 1966. Le Gall, Dom Robert. *Symbols of Catholicism.* New York: Assouline Publishing, 2000. Miller, Madeleine S. and J. Lane Miller. "Candle," "Candlestick," in *Harper's Bible Dictionary.* New York: Harper and Row, Publishers, 1961.

Carpenters, Carpentry

(2 Sam. 5:11; Eccles. 1:18; Mark 6:1–18; Heb. 3:3) "Isn't this the carpenter?" (Mark 6:3). This was the question that the amazed observers asked regarding Jesus of Nazareth. Every little town and village had its carpenters who made many of the implements needed by the local **farmers:** the ladders, **yokes**, **plows**, **threshing** sledges, handles for mattocks, and pitchforks. The carpenter also constructed carts and in time of **war** made **chariots** for the **king.**

In ancient Israel, carpenters probably made the wooden portions of **temples,** such as the pillars and the roofs. They would also have been called on to repair the city **gates** and panel some of the homes that Haggai mentions (1:3). They made some modest **furnishings** for homes: looms, tables, stools, benches, and chests, including wooden coffins. In **house** construction, the roof beams and joists, window frames, lintels, doors, beams in the ceiling or roof constructions, and posts and columns that shored up the roof beams were the work of the carpenter (Philip J. King and Lawrence E. Stager 2001, 23–24). Smaller items, such as keys and locks, were also frequently made of wood, as was the latticework for windows. In the tombs at Jericho (ca.1800 B.C.) were found finely carved bowls, spoons, and boxes, perhaps the work of clever carpenters.

The Jewish carpenters, unlike those more skilled craftsmen in **Egypt** and elsewhere, seem not to have made the fine cabinets or other intricate carpentry for the wealthy homes. In fact, Jesus and Joseph—and most of the Jewish carpenters—probably did not perform many of the tasks for which the skilled craftsmen of Egypt or **Babylonia** or Tyre became famous—construction of fine buildings and ships. When Solomon prepared for the building of his Temple and **palace** in Jerusalem, he arranged for foreign artisans to do much of the work (2 Sam. 5:11), suggesting that they were superior to the Israelites, who had been transformed from **tent**-dwellers to inhabitants of settled dwellings and carpentry shops late in their history. Although they had seen the workmanship of the Egyptians, they remained mostly peasants with minimal exposure to royal tastes. Some believe that foreigners considered their tools and methods quite primitive, adopting only the "modern innovation" of the workbench as opposed to sitting on the floor (Fred. H. Wight 1953, 207).

Solomon, in ordering the very best possible materials for the Temple, specified cedar from Lebanon. In the Temple, the design involved alternating hewn stone and cedar beams (1 Kings 7:12). This king, who bragged about the many dwellings he had built, also complained about bad workmanship and lazy workers: "By much slothfulness the building decayeth; and through idleness of the hands, the house droppeth through" (Eccles. 10:18). (Given his use of forced labor for much of this work and his preference for foreigners over his own fellow citizens, idleness might well have been expected.) The work in his palaces, stables, and other buildings at places such as Meggido testify to his ambitious schemes, as well as his extensive use of foreign craftsmen.

The tools the carpenter would have used were the compass, plane, pencil, saw, hammer, and nails or pegs. He made his saw by mounting flint teeth with serrated edges on a curved frame. Ancient handsaws were pulled against the wood in the opposite direction from that used by modern craftsmen (Madeleine S. Miller and J. Lane Miller 1961, 93). He would also have had a plumb line for keeping lines straight, an image used by the **prophet** Amos (7:7–8). He used his ax to chop down trees and shape timber, often in a rough manner. Archaeologists have also discovered at Gezer ribbon-flint knives that were made into saws by making their edges irregular, and they have also found an abundance of bronze and iron nails (Fred Wight 1953, 209). The drill and awl (Exod. 231:6; Deut. 15:17) would have been used to bore holes.

Isaiah describes the Babylonian carpenter using his tools to craft an **idol:** he "measures with a line and makes an outline with a marker; he roughs it out with chisels and marks it with compasses" (Isa. 44:13). It is difficult to establish whether Jewish craftsmen also used the same tools and skills, but the prophet's use of the imagery suggests that the scene is well known to his people. Wood, of course, deteriorates, making the carpenter's work and

Carpenter with bow drill sitting on the floor, using a section of a tree for his workbench, typical in ancient Israel, where tables and benches were rarely used until late in history.

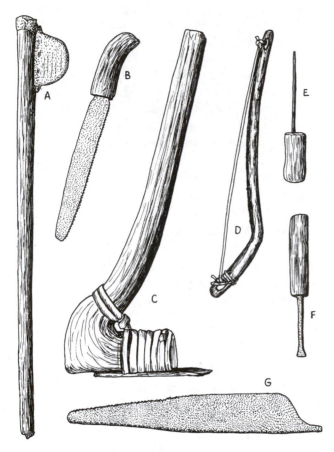

Carpenter's tools: (A) Bronze-headed axe. (B) Small handsaw with bronze blade. (C) Adze with bronze blade. (D) Wooden bow-drill. (E) Bit used with bow-drill. (F) Chisel. (G) Bronze saw blade. Note the minimal use of metal in these essential tools.

materials scarce in archaeological digs. Most have rotted or burned, leaving few traces of this craft.

Jesus, who rarely used imagery from either carpenter's tools or chores in his sermons and **parables**, did mention the importance of planning before building (Luke 14:28–30) and of building on a sure foundation (Matt 7:24–27), but these are concerns of any builder— the **bricklayer** or the **stonemason** as much as the carpenter whose role in home construction seems to have been limited to doorways, windows, and roof. Many of the homes in Palestine appear to have been made of **brick** or stone, although wood was then far more abundant in ancient Israel than it is today. The skilled carpenter, who knew how to use his chisel, could also have acted as the carver of **ivory** furnishings mentioned by the prophet Amos (6:4), but such luxuries probably were imported from other more opulent countries.

Nonetheless, the "builder" became a recurrent image for the early Christians. Paul spoke of himself as an "expert builder" who began the work among the Corinthians for someone else to finish (1 Cor. 3:10). The author of Hebrews compares Jesus to the "builder of the house" who has more honor than the "house itself" (Heb. 3:3). In this remarkable letter, the writer notes that ultimately, God is the builder of everything (Heb. 3:4), including the "city with foundations" of which he is "the architect and builder" (Heb. 11:10). *See also* Agriculture; Temple; War, Warfare: General.

Further Reading

King, Philip J. and Lawrence E. Stager, *Life in Biblical Israel.* Louisville, Ky.: Westminster John Knox Press, 2001. Madeleine S. Miller and J. Lane Miller. "Carpenters," in *Harper's Bible Dictionary.* New York: Harper and Row, 1961. Wight, Fred H. *Manners and Customs of Bible Lands.* Chicago: Moody Press, 1953.

Cattle. *See Ox, Oxen*

Caves

(Gen. 19:30, 23:17–19, 25:9; Josh. 10:16; 1 Sam. 13:6, 24:7; Ps. 142)
A ready dwelling place for early peoples was the cave. The countryside around **Canaan** is honeycombed with caves as is much of the region around the Dead Sea. It was in one of these caves that Lot and his daughters hid after their escape from the doomed city of Sodom. As late as David's day, the young **king**-apparent spent occasional nights in caves. So did King Saul and his men. They made excellent hiding places for **warriors** away from home, for **shepherds**, and for robbers and other men on the run from their enemies.

The caves in the Galilee were considered ideal hiding places for the **Zealots** and for bandits, who could attack and retreat with little fear of being discovered. The rocky mountainside, hidden entranceways, and deep, interconnected passages made them nearly impossible to track, parallel to some modern terrorists in Afghanistan.

Apparently caves were also used for more benign purposes by the **Essenes**, who gathered in at least one community near the Dead Sea. John the Baptist may well have been one of their number or at least lived much as they did in the same region. It was in one of these enormous caves at Qumran that the Dead Sea Scrolls were discovered.

Caves were also ideal burial vaults, as Abraham understood. It was his sad task, when he arrived in the Promised Land, to purchase the cave of Machpelah as a burial place for himself and his family (Gen. 23:17–19). His wife Sarah was the first to be buried there. And it was there that his sons buried him some years later (Gen. 50:30). *See also* Essenes; Graves; Zealots.

Chaff

(Isa. 5:24, Job 21:18) This dry grass or hay, which is left over in the **threshing**, formed an ideal image for poets and prophets for the transience of human life. The **farmer** would lift the dry, harvested **grain** on his winnowing fork and allow the wind to blow away the unwanted portion—the chaff. *See also* Agriculture; Grain; Threshing, Threshing Floor.

Chariots

(Exod. 14:7; Josh.11:4; 2 Kings 2:11; Ezek. 1:5–13; Jer. 4:13, 17:25; Rev. 9:9) The Hebrews did not have **war** chariots until the time of **King** Solomon, largely because they did not have the **iron** for wheels. They did know other peoples who had chariots and used them, often to their disadvantage. The clatter of the **horses'** hooves, the roar of the wheels, and the speed

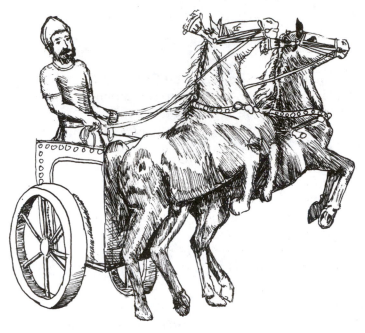

Solomon was the first king of Israel to make use of horses and chariots, which had proven powerful in warfare waged by Egyptians and the sea peoples.

of the chariot's movement proved powerful against these more primitive riders of **donkeys** and **camels**.

Hebrews probably had primitive chariots (or wagons) with wooden wheels, but found them cumbersome conveyances compared with the simple backpacks that they could load on their donkeys. **Egyptians** used chariots even before Joseph came to the land. In fact, Joseph rode in a chariot to meet his father in what must have been an impressive reunion (Gen. 46:29). The Egyptian war chariots, 600 of which were selected for a special royal force, are described as being open at the rear, with a semicircular standing board made of wood. Each chariot had two wheels and was drawn by two small horses. The Hyksos period (ca.1732–1570 B.C.) is thought to have been the first time that **warriors** used chariots (Exod. 14:7; *The King James Study Bible*, fn.125). These grand vehicles, however, were lost in the sea as they chased after the fleeing Israelite **slaves**.

When the Hebrews settled in **Canaan**, their neighbors and enemies often overpowered them with their chariot **warfare**. The **Philistines**, who had a flourishing iron industry, had chariots but found them useless against Barak's forces once the rainy season bogged them down in mire. Warriors on iron chariots attacked and killed King Saul, but David later turned the tables on them, defeating them in large numbers and ham stringing their horses. It is probable that the hill country of Israel was not good terrain for warriors encumbered with wheeled vehicles. The crafty David could hide, run, climb, and leap out to surprise the larger forces he faced.

Chariot imagery is common in Scripture. The chariot of fire appeared, along with horses of fire, when the whirlwind took Elijah up to **Heaven** (2 Kings 2:11). The most interesting use of chariot imagery is in Ezekiel and is repeated with variations in Daniel and Revelation 4. In his vision, Ezekiel saw God on an amazing chariot, which was like a **throne**, with **cherubim** and flaming wheels. The wheels—and the wheels within the wheels—have been interpreted various ways over the years. Matthew Henry

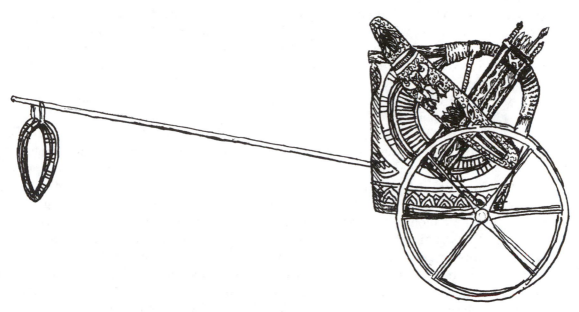

An Egyptian chariot, such as that used to race after the Israelites. Notice there was place for only one rider in these early chariots. Later warriors found it handier to have a driver and a fighter, and sometimes even a third person in the chariot, requiring somewhat larger conveyances.

thinks they represent God's work on earth—with eyes to see everything, **angels** to guide the work, and forward movement that allows secondary causes to continue all events in a grand movement according to God's providence (Matthew Henry 1961,1034–1035).

Chaucer, Milton, Blake, and others have used the fiery chariot imagery with great power over the years (David Sten Herrstrom 1992, 823–824). *See also* Metal: Iron; War, Warfare: General.

Further Readings

Henry, Matthew. *Matthew Henry's Commentary in One Volume*. Grand Rapids, Mich.: Zondervan Publishing House, 1961. Herrstrom, David Sten. "Wheels within Wheels," in *A Dictionary of Biblical Tradition in English Literature*. Grand Rapids, Mich.: William B. Eerdmans Publishing Company, 1992.

Chemosh

(Num. 21:19; Judg. 11:24; 1 Kings 11:7, 11:33; 2 Kings 23:13; Jer. 48:7, 48:46) The name *Chemosh* or *Kemosh* means "fire," or "hearth." Some believe it also means "destroyer," and "subduer," pointing to his role as a war god. He was the national idol of the **Moabites** and the **Ammonites**, like **Moloch**, but apparently not identical with him. He also seems to have kinship with **Baal**-peor and Baal-zebub. Scripture speaks of his "abominations," and the **prophets** proclaim the eventual downfall of those who follow him. Like Baal, he descended from the primitive mother goddess, sometimes called Athtar, sometimes Shtar, and sometimes Astarte. He required human **sacrifice** to secure his favor (2 Kings 3:27) and expected his worshippers to build him **sanctuaries** when he answered their **prayers**.

The Moabites were called the "children of Chemosh," but from the days of Solomon he was also a god worshipped by the Israelites. Solomon built a temple to him on the Mount of Olives (1 Kings 11:7, 33), which remained until Josiah's reforms took effect (2 Kings 23:13), a period of nearly 400 years (Morris Jastrow, Jr. and George A. Barton 2004). Albright notes that the 10 mentions of Chemosh as god of Moab in the inscription on the Moabite Stone and elsewhere mean "we may safely assume he was identified with the morning star, the lord of **heaven**" (William Foxwell Albright 1969, 239).

The Moabite Stone, a famous discovery by archaeologists, describes some of his "commands" and his "**punishments**" of the Moabite peoples. King Mesha, a ninth century B.C. ruler of the Moabites, attributes his victories and defeats to Chemosh: "I built this sanctuary to Chemosh in Qerihoh, a sanctuary of refuge, for he saved me from all my oppressors and gave me dominion over all my enemies. Omri was king of Israel and oppressed Moab many days, for Chemosh was angry with his land" (Werner Keller 1982, 250–251). These few words on a broken stone and the random references in Scripture constitute the entirety of our understanding of this once significant deity. Ironically, the message on the stone proclaims triumphantly, "And Israel perished for ever." *See also* Ammon, Ammonites; Asherah, Ashtoreth, Ashtaroth; Baal, Baalim; Moab, Moabites.

Further Reading

Albright, William Foxwell. *Yahweh and the Gods of Canaan*. Garden City, N.Y.: Doubleday & Company, Inc., 1969. Jastrow, Morris, Jr. and George A. Barton. "Chemosh," http://www.jewishencyclopedia.com (accessed November 15, 2004). Keller, Werner. *The Bible as History*. New York: Bantam Books, 1982.

Cherub, Cherubim (pl.)

(Gen. 3:24; Exod. 25:18–22, 26:1, 37:9; 1 Kings 6:23–35, 8:6–7; Ps. 80:1, 99:1; Ezek. 10:1–20, 41:18–20) The word *cherub* in Akkadian is *karibu*, meaning "one who prays" or "one who intercedes" (Gustav Davidson 1967, 86). As noted in the section on **angels**, the cherubim are among the most elevated of the angelic orders. The early theologian Philo called them symbols of God's highest and chiefest potency, sovereignty, and goodness. They are thought to be the guardians of the gates of the Garden of Eden and they also stand guard over the **Ark of the Covenant**. In Revelation 4:8, they are living creatures who praise their Maker unceasingly.

In Genesis, they seem to be enormous presences, guarding the Tree of Life and holding flaming swords. They are pictured as a combination of human and **animal**, with wings and faces: Ezekiel saw four wings, while John notes that they have six. Ezekiel described them as having eagle wings, and appearing to have a blend of human and animal features. "And every one had four faces: the first face was the face of a cherub, and the second face was the face of a man, and the third the face of a lion, and the fourth the face of an eagle" (Ezek. 10:14). The sound of their great wings frightened the astonished **prophet**, as they mounted up from the earth, taking the glory of the Lord with them.

This vision and the cherubim's role in standing guard suggest the great human-faced winged bulls on palaces in **Assyria** and **Canaan**. They also bear resemblance to the **Egyptian** sphinx and the Hittite griffin. The visions, however, should not be taken so literally, as the faces and wings described in ecstatic states are often metaphors for inexpressible elements such as power and glory.

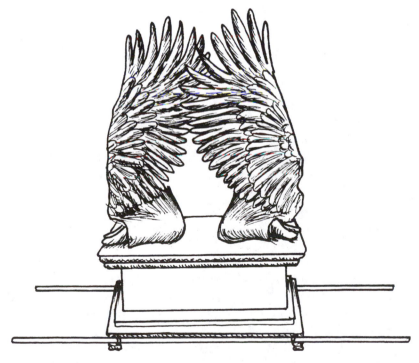

Cherubim, as they may have appeared on the Ark of the Covenant.
Notice the human shape of the body, as opposed to the form they have in other descriptions.

Images of the cherubim became a decorative element in both the **Tabernacle** and the Temple. Like their role as guardians of the Tree of Life in the Garden, so they became guardians of the Ark and later of the **Temple**. These colossal figures, carved of olive wood and covered with **gold** had great outstretched wings, forming a **throne** for God. Cherubim also seem to serve as **chariots** for Jehovah, who is said to ride on a cherub, apparently a figurative way of saying that God rides on the wings of the wind (David G. Burke 1993, 109). *See also* Angels; Ark of the Covenant; Art: Jewish; Tabernacle; Temple.

Further Reading

Burke, David G. *The Oxford Companion to the Bible*. New York: Oxford University Press, 1993. Davidson, Gustav. *A Dictionary of Angels including the Fallen Angels*. New York: The Free Press, 1967. McCurdy, J. Frederic and Louis Ginzberg, "Cherub." http://www.jewishencyclopedia.com (accessed November 12, 2004).

Children. *See Family*

Christian

(Acts 11:26, 26:28; 1 Pet. 4:16) The word *Christian* derives from *Christ,* or Greek *Christos,* meaning "the anointed." Jesus spoke of his followers as **disciples** or **apostles**, also referring to clusters of believers as the **Church**. The early followers of Jesus spoke of themselves as followers of "the Way," and being "of Christ," "brothers," or "saints," but not as "Christians."

It was in Antioch, possibly as a term of derision, that Paul and Barnabas were first labeled "Christians" (Madeleine S. Miller and J. Lane Miller 1961, 98). Some suspect that the term would have been a natural one for **Romans** or Latin-speakers. Pagans would have understood their worship in the name "of Christ" to suggest that they were followers of a leader by that name, hence "Christian" as others might be called "Herodians" for following Herod (Kaufmann Kohler 2004).

Both of the contemporary Roman historians, Tacitus and Suetonius, refer to the earlier believers as *Christians*. Tacitus says they were a people hated for their evil deeds, and Suetonious called them "a new and evil superstition" (Edwin D. Freed 1993,111). The name appears in the first epistle of Peter as if it was a widely understood term. Agrippa used it when speaking to Paul as if it were a common term of the time. After the Christians became separated from Judaism and were seen as a separate religion, this term was generally used for them, as it continues to be today. *See also* Apostle; Church; Disciples; Messiah.

Christian symbol of the fish, used by early believers because the Greek word for fish is *ichthus*. The five component letters contain the initials of the five Greek words that mean "Jesus Christ, Son of God, Savior."

Further Reading

Freed, Edwin D. "Christian," in *The Oxford Companion to the Bible*. New York: Oxford University Press, 1993. Kohler, Kaufmann. "Christian," http://www.jewishencyclopedia.com (accessed November 18, 2004). Miller, Madeleine S. and Lane S. Miller. *Harper's Bible Dictionary*. New York: Harper and Row, Publishers, 1961.

Church

(Matt. 16:18, 18:17; Eph. 1:22; Col. 1:18) Some believe that the English word *church* derives from the Latin word *circus* ("circle"), indicating a place near a crossroads that was set apart for preaching. The actual English word *church* comes from a usage later than the New Testament. It may derive from the adjective in a Greek phrase meaning the "Lord's house" (*kyriake oikia*). But it is the New Testament term *eklesia* that the English word *church* is trying to represent in our Bible translations. This Greek word referred to citizens who were "called out" (Daniel N. Schowalter 1993, 121).

When Jesus called the 12 **Disciples** and gave them instructions, he empowered them to continue his work when he was no longer with them. He even referred to this power in speaking to Peter, who had proclaimed of Jesus: "Thou art the Christ, the Son of the Living God." Christ then answered, "Blessed art thou, Simon Bar-jona; for flesh and blood hath not revealed it unto thee, but my Father which is in **heaven**. And I say also unto thee, That thou art Peter, and upon this rock I will build my church; and the gates of **hell** shall not prevail against it" (Matt.16:16–18).

The concept of the church is parallel to the assembly of Israel that received the **law** through Moses, which was referred to as the "congregation of Israel." Churches are usually considered a logical development from the Jewish pattern of **synagogues** as places of teaching and **prayer**. In fact, most of the earliest **Christian** churches grew from groups within the Jewish community. Paul, for example, regularly preached in synagogues.

Some of the earliest meetings were held in homes of the wealthier members. When the persecutions began, the meetings were moved to underground passageways, or catacombs. In Ephesus, St. Peter's Church is in a natural **cave** on the western slope of Mt. Silpius. It has an interior of limestone broken by erosion. Here is the cave church where Peter, Luke, and Paul are all thought to have preached.

Places and buildings, however, are not the real Church. Rather, it is the congregation of believers, even where two or three were gathered together in the name of Christ form the real Christian Church. In the New Testament, "church" refers most often to the local group of Christians, an assembly of baptized believers under the discipline of the Word of God. The various churches are not referred to as a collective "Church," meaning the "Church universal" or the "Catholic Church," until somewhat later.

The best known of these early churches, or congregations of believers, were located in such cities as Jerusalem, Antioch, Thessalonica, Philippi, Corinth, Ephesus, Rome, and elsewhere. Revelation 2 and 3 speaks of the

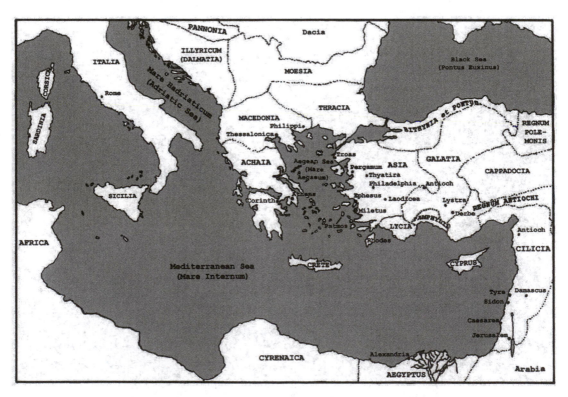

The Christian Church, with leadership from Paul and other apostles, spread out into much of the Roman Empire, from Egypt to Rome and beyond.

seven churches to which the **epistle** is addressed. Most of the New Testament is either an account of the founding of such churches (the Book of Acts) or the problems and concerns of the various churches (the various epistles).

The early organization of the Christian Church was quite loose, with the **apostles** as the natural leaders. This group of 13 men was not replaced. Over time, their duties became too onerous, leading them to appoint deacons to handle the mundane work of caring for widows and orphans, managing the day-to-day programs of the group. Stephen was one of these early deacons who relieved the senior church officials of some of their tasks. Then as the new churches were established, elders were appointed to lead them. Later, Paul gave Timothy good advice on the kind of elders (leaders, or bishops) and deacons that the new churches should have (1 Tim. 5:17). The epistles include numerous discussions of the proper qualities of church leaders. They also focused on certain issues that each of the congregations was facing at the time of the writing.

Some consider the **Pentecost** the birth of the Church, that is the universal Christian fellowship of believers in the world, under the guidance of the **Holy Spirit** and in fulfillment of the Great Commission: "Go ye therefore and teach all nations, baptizing them in the name of the Father, and of the Son, and of the Holy Ghost" (Matt 28:19). Over time, the Church Militant (those still on earth) and the Church Triumphant (those in **Heaven**) have come to be seen as the saints who compose the universal Church. *See also* Apostle; Baptism; Disciples; Epistles; Holy Spirit, Holy Ghost; Pentecost or the Day of the First Fruits.

Further Reading

Robinson, D. W. B. "Church," in *The Illustrated Bible Dictionary*. Sydney, Australia: Tyndale House Publishers, 1980. Schowalter, Daniel N. "Church," in *The Oxford Companion to the Bible*. New York: Oxford University Press, 1993.

Circumcision

(Gen. 17:10–11; Exod. 4:25–26; Luke 2:21) When God made his **covenant** with Abraham, promising him and his seed after him that they would inherit the Promised Land and that he would be their God, he asked that Abraham seal the covenant with circumcision, a rite in which the prepuce, or foreskin, of the penis is cut off. This was to be a sign of the covenant on his flesh. This dramatic action signified that his offspring would be uniquely dedicated to God. Abraham performed the ritual on himself when he was 90 years old. He also circumcised all of the male members of his household, including Ishmael, who was 13 at the time. This established the tradition that all of Abraham's males descendants were to be circumcised, and the time set was on the eighth day after birth, apparently an ideal time for the health of the child. Arabs, following the precedent of Ishmael, continue the tradition of circumcising adolescents at age 13 years.

Scripture is explicit about the ritual, which was performed in the home, not in the **Temple**: "And ye shall circumcise the flesh of your foreskin, and it shall be a token of the covenant . . . . and my covenant shall be in your flesh for an everlasting covenant. And the uncircumcised man child whose flesh of his foreskin is not circumcised, that soul shall be cut off from his people; he hath broken my covenant" (Gen. 17:11–14). The ritual has continued from ancient times through the time of Christ, into modern day practice. After the Exile, the ceremony was transferred from the house of the parents to the **synagogue**, where it took place after the service in the presence of the whole congregation (Emil G. Hirsch, Kaufmann et al. 2004). Jesus, a Jewish child of the covenant, was duly circumcised at the time he was named, on the eighth day after his birth (Luke 2:21).

The ritual was apparently respected by most of Abraham's descendants but was neglected by Moses, perhaps because of his **Egyptian** acculturation (although there is also evidence of circumcision among Egyptians). Moses's **Midianite** wife, Zipporah, realized that he was violating the terms of the covenant and performed the circumcision on their son—with a sharp **stone**—and cast the foreskin on her husband's feet (Exod. 4:25–26). (Before **metal** was available in most households, flint was used for precise cutting.) During the sojourn in the wilderness, the Israelites discontinued the custom, returning to it when they entered the Promised Land. The Lord told Joshua to make "sharp knives" and circumcise the "children of Israel at the hill of foreskins" (Josh. 5:2–3).

The refusal to allow circumcision during the days of Antiochus Epiphanes, who had women and their circumcised sons killed (1 Macc. 1:60), was considered a grotesque violation of the Jewish faith and practice. Nonetheless, after their return from the Exile, many of the Jews became so completely Hellenized that the orthodox Jews relented and agreed that Jewish men no longer needed to be circumcised. When Jews mingled with gentiles at the baths of the times, where the men were unclothed, the Greeks called the circumcised Jews "harlots" (George Wesley Buchanan 1993, 123). During that period, some Jews even sought to reverse their circumcision through surgery.

Even in ancient days, not all Hebrew practices of circumcision were strictly orthodox. For example, when Judah planned revenge for the seduction of his sister Dinah's rape, he required that the men of Sechem be circumcised in anticipation of the **wedding**. He and his brothers then attacked and slaughtered them three days later, while they were still recovering from the painful surgery (Gen. 34). In **warfare**, the forcible circumcision of enemies, such as David's cutting the foreskins off his adversaries, appears a cruel distortion of this sacred sign. That Saul required a hundred foreskins of the Philistines as a marriage present for Michal (1 Sam. 18:25) suggests that these were trophies of victory rather than symbols of God's covenant with his people.

The **prophets** pointed to the need to circumcise the heart, not just the body. Just as sacrifices and phylacteries were only outward symbols of an inner experience, so the circumcision was not a saving **sacrament** but only a sign of God's mark on his people. For Jews, noncircumcision was considered a blemish, keeping the man from being perfect in God's eyes (Emil G. Hirsch, Kaufmann Kohler, Joseph Jacobs et al. 2004).

Changes in custom and the evangelism of the gentiles led to a reconsideration of the rite by the **Christian** era. On numerous occasions, Paul discussed this particular sign of the covenant, seeking to show that the real circumcision must be a spiritual experience, not just a physical one, just as Jeremiah had spoken of both the "uncircumcised heart" and the "uncircumcised ear" (Jer. 9:25–26; 6:10). The **crucifixion** rendered this sign on the flesh unnecessary, and Paul argued that it should not be imposed on gentiles seeking to be baptized (Rom. 3, 4, 15; Gal. 5; Phil. 3:3; John 7:22; Acts 15; Col. 2:11).

This belief in the sacredness of the flesh is reflected in many of the Hebrew **laws** and customs regarding sexuality. Because the seed of Abraham and his descendants is precious, it must not be "spilled" nor used on another man nor withdrawn before fulfillment. The purpose of sexuality was thought to be the planting of the seed and the production of young souls who would carry on the faith and the **blessing**. Such sexual crimes as rape or adultery were considered particularly heinous, not only because they attacked another man's property—his wife or daughter or sister—but also because they led to a misuse of the blessed seed. *See also* Baptism; Covenant; Law; War, Warfare: General.

Further Reading

Buchanan, George Wesley. "Circumcision," in *The Oxford Companion to the Bible*. New York: Oxford University Press, 1993. Emil G. Hirsch, Kaufmann Kohler, Joseph Jacobs, Aaron Friedenwald, and Isaac Broydé. "Circumcision," http://www.jewishencyclopedia.com(accessed December 10, 2004).

Cistern

(Gen. 37:22–24; Lev. 11:36; Prov. 5:15; Isa. 36:16; Jer. 38:6–13, 41: 7–9) A cistern is a reservoir that may be used for the storage of water. Cisterns in ancient Israel were usually circular shafts that are larger at the bottom than at the top, lined with plaster or cut into stone. As Leviticus notes, "A spring . . . or a cistern for collecting water remains **clean**" (Lev. 11:36). In a dry **climate**,

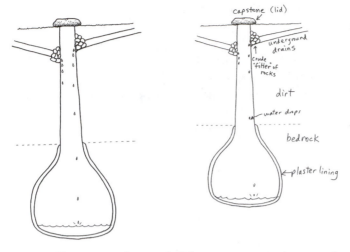

Cistern (from top to bottom): lid or capstone, underground drains, crude filter of rocks, dirt, water drops, bedrock, plaster lining, and water collected in bottom.

such containers are essential because the rain **waters** run off quickly, not soaking the hard earth.

Cisterns may be fed by springs, as well as rain, and are sometimes dry enough that they may be used as informal prisons, as seen in several Bible stories. Joseph was thrown into a cistern by his brothers while they considered how to dispose of him (Gen. 37:24). Jeremiah was also thrown into a cistern that was deep enough that his enemies had to lower him by ropes. It was still wet at the bottom so that Jeremiah sank down into the mud (Jer. 38:6).

In old Jerusalem, the Pool of Hezekiah was a large reservoir that drew water from considerable distance. In preparation for the anticipated siege of the city by **Assyrian** forces, this **king** "made a pool, and a conduit, and brought water into the city" (2 Kings 20). When Sennacherib sought to lure the people of Judah to his side, he promised a cistern for every man: "Do not listen to Hezekiah. This is what the king of Assyria says: Make peace with me and come out to me. Then every one of you will eat from his own vine and fig tree and drink water from his own cistern" (2 Kings 18:31). Such a promise of clean water available at hand must have been a strong incentive to the besieged Jews.

The writer of Proverbs notes that a man should "drink water from your own cistern, running water from your own **well**" (Prov. 5:15) probably meaning much more than limiting oneself to clean water. He uses the cistern—and the well—as metaphors for the pure and upright life.

The most disgusting use for the cistern that Scripture records is at the conclusion of Jeremiah's incarceration. When he was raised from the cistern, Ishmael and his men went throughout the city slaughtering their enemies. He then threw all the bodies of those he had killed into the cistern and "filled it with the dead" (Jer. 41:7–9). *See also* Climate; Waters; Wells.

Further Reading

Keller, Werner. *The Bible as History.* New York: Bantam Books, 1982. Miller, Madeleine S. and J. Lane Miller. "Cisterns," in *Harper's Bible Dictionary.* New York: Harper and Row, Publishers, 1961.

Cities of Refuge

(Num. 35:9–34; Deut 4:41–43, 19:1–13; Josh. 20:1–9) In his extended explication of the **law**, God ordered the Israelites to have cities where an involuntary killer could take refuge from **blood** vengeance (Num. 35:11–32). There were to be three cities of refuge in Transjordan and three west of the Jordan, not indicated by name. Asylum was granted only to the involuntary killer: the willful murderer might not be received in the city of refuge, but must die at the hands of the avenger of blood. The community was to decide the question of guilt, reject the murder, and watch over the involuntary killer, who was expected to stay in the city until the death of the high **priest** (Roland deVaux 1961, 160–161).

Out of these practices dating from Moses developed the institution of the "holy towns," which were linked with the right of asylum, recognized as sanctuaries—an early idea that continued as the medieval concept of **churches** as sanctuaries, protected from the law—and even used occasionally today. Illegal immigrants, for example, sometimes seek refuge in church buildings, finding that the officials are reluctant to invade sacred space. *See also* Law: Civil and Criminal.

Further Reading

DeVaux, Roland. *Ancient Israel: Its Life and Institutions*. Grand Rapids, Mich.: William B. Eerdmans Publishing Company, 1961. Falk, Ze'ev W. *Hebrew Law in Biblical Times*. Provo, Utah: Brigham Young University Press, 2001.

Clean, Unclean

(Gen 9:3; Lev. 11; Deut. 14; Acts 10:9–15) Cleanliness was an obsession with the Jews from earliest times. "The clean body as an index ... of a clean soul, and thus of an approximation to holiness, is so natural a conception in the human mind that the records of early Jewish legislation accept the theory" without any need to explain or justify it (Cyrus Adler, Frederick de Sola Mendes 2004). Clean **sacrifices**, clean **food**, clean body, clean **clothing**, and clean heart all go together in Hebrew thought.

The division of **animals** into "clean and unclean" categories dates at least from the time of Noah, when God instructed him to save pairs of each type from the **Flood**. Afterwards, Noah sacrificed clean animals (Gen. 9:3), apparently fully aware of the definition. When Rachel sat on the household gods, insisting that the "custom of women is upon me," Laban was reluctant to search her clothing for them (Gen. 31:35), suggesting that she realized and Laban understood that woman was considered unclean during and after menstruation. Further evidence of the concept's acceptance even in

The vulture's habits, picking over carcasses and garbage for food, were probably why the law of Moses judged the bird "unclean."

patriarchal times before the Mosaic **law**, is that Jacob, in preparing his family to visit the shrine at Beth-el, instructed them to "purify" themselves. Certainly the sojourn in **Egypt** must have reinforced the Israelites' concern with cleanliness in ritual practices. Scholars note that Egyptian priests washed twice during the day and twice at night (C. L. Feinberg 1980, 299). The fullest admonitions for the need for purity, of course, are in the Mosaic law.

As a rule, being "unclean" was primarily a concept of ceremonial defilement, not physical or moral filth. Unclean animals were those that did not chew the cud or have a cloven hoof. Only noncarnivorous **birds** were allowed, and only certain **insects**. Shellfish were forbidden, although **fish** with scales and fins were acceptable. There is an extended list of unclean birds and fish in Leviticus 11 and Deuteronomy 14. Eating one of these forbidden creatures rendered the human himself or herself unclean. Only unblemished clean animals, and not all of them, were considered suitable for sacrifice. The manner of their slaughter was also carefully prescribed. For instance, an animal that had been slain violently or was torn apart by other animals was considered unclean—unfit for eating. The **blood** was to be carefully drained from the body when the animal was slain in order for it to be kosher.

In addition, certain physical activities or experiences rendered a person unclean: coming in contact with a dead body (Num. 19:11–22), contracting leprosy (Lev. 13–14), having sexual relations (Lev. 12; 15), having a menstrual period or any discharge of blood, childbirth, touching a woman with such discharges, having murdered someone without being punished (Deut. 21:1–9), and worshipping idols (Hos. 6:10).

For the most part, a man or woman might be purified by a combination of the passage of time and the completion of other rituals, that is waiting 30 days after the **birth** of a child, and then performing a **bathing** ceremony in running **water**. Other cleansing rituals involved fire and the ashes of a red heifer. Before sacrifice, the **priest** and the person bringing the sacrifice were expected to bathe and put on clean clothes. During the ceremony, there were additional ceremonies of washing, and even of changing clothes. There were public bath houses, as well as streams and ponds for cleansing, and later the *mikweh,* a stone bath near the **Temple**, where worshippers might cleanse and clothe themselves before offering their sacrifices.

Everything connected with worship was to be washed before and after sacrifice, including the **metal** vessel in which the meat was boiled. If an earthenware vessel was used, it was broken so that it might not be reused.

On the **Day of Atonement**, the high **priest** changed his clothes and washed his entire body after coming out of the Holy of Holies, apparently as a signal that he was leaving the realm of the holy and reentering the profane world of normal life (deVaux 1961, 460–461).

Every regulation regarding cleanliness was expanded and explained by the **scribes** in post-exilic times so that it eventually became an elaborate and burdensome system. The **Psalms** and the **prophets** spoke of ethical purity, as well as physical and ritual purity (Ps. 19:9, 51:7, 10), but the leaders of the **synagogues** and the Temple often ignored the deeper meaning of the law. As a consequence, Jesus argued with the **scribes** and **Pharisees**, insisting that they were rejecting the clear commands of God in favor of their own traditions (Mark 7:9). Later, Peter was to have a **vision** in which God admonished him not to call that "unclean" which God called "clean" (Acts 10: 9–15), again noting that the regulations had become more important than the word of God. This vision and Peter's interpretation of it were discussed by the **Church** leaders at the Council of Jerusalem. They decided to allow gentiles to omit the legalistic practices of Judaism when they became **Christians**.

The Book of Hebrews picks up this theme, that the only pollution that matters to the person of faith is that of the conscience, from which the sacrifice of Christ alone can cleanse the worshipper. "For if the blood of bulls and of **goats**, and the ashes of a heifer sprinkling the unclean, sanctifieth to the purifying of the flesh, How much more shall the blood of Christ, who through the eternal Spirit offered himself without spot to God, purge your conscience from dead works to serve the living God?" (Heb. 9:13). In John's great Revelation, the Bride of the Lamb makes herself ready, "And to her was granted that she should be arrayed in fine linen, clean and white: for the fine linen is the righteousness of saints" (Rev. 19:8). *See also* Baptism; Bath, Bathing.

Further Reading

Adler, Cyrus, and Frederick de Sola Mendes, "Baths, Bathing," http://www.jewishencyclopedia.com (accessed November 20, 2004). DeVaux, Roland. *Ancient Israel: Its Life and Institutions.* Grand Rapids, Mich.: William B. Eerdmans Publishing Company, 1961. Feinberg, C. L. "Clean and Unclean," in *Illustrated Bible Dictionary.* Sydney, Australia: Tyndale House Publishers, 1980.

Climate

Various lands are described in Scripture, from **Egypt**, with its floods and long growing season, to Mesopotamia, with its fierce dry summers. The climate of Palestine is essentially Mediterranean in pattern, midway between temperate and tropical. The summers are so hot and dry that plant growth may cease for weeks or even months, but the winter is comparatively mild and wet. Frost or snow is rare, except in the higher hills. Sometimes snow lies on the coastal mountains while tropical fruits ripen on the plain (Pat Alexander 1978, 2).

The temperature in the Dead Sea region on a summer's day may often reach 40 degrees Celsius; a wet winter's day in the Galilee may have a freezing rain. In spite of the heat, cool breezes often blow from the Mediterranean in summer. The mid-day sun is often so fierce that people stay indoors or in the shade, preferring early morning and early evening for their major outdoor activities.

Rainfall varies according to the height above sea level: the mountains have more rain than the lowlands. Most of the rain falls between October and April, with the hills determining where it falls. The general rules are that the rainfall decreases as the traveler goes south and inland. Because the rain varies so much from year to year, averages are meaningless, especially in the drier zones. "The wettest parts of the hills enjoy up to 32 in., and on the border with the Lebanon upwards of 40 in. South of Beersheba 12 in. is the most farmers can ever hope for, and they *cannot be sure of even half of that*" (George Cansdale 1970, 21). The absence of April rains (the "latter rain") can create a devastating drought.

Dew is particularly important to those regions that have little rain. This moisture, which comes in from the Mediterranean during the summer nights, sometimes provides as much as a quarter of the moisture for the region. This would explain the importance of the miracle involving Gideon and the fleece, as well as Elijah's prophesy that there would be no dew or rain (1 Kings 17:1). As God promised: It is "a good land.... A land of wheat, and barley, and **vineyards**, wherein fig trees, and pomegranates, and **olive** yards grow: a land of oil and honey. Where without any want thou shalt eat thy **bread**, and enjoy abundance of all things" (Deut. 8:7–9). *See also* Geography.

Further Reading

Alexander, Pat, ed. *Eerdmans' Family Encyclopedia of the Bible*. Grand Rapids, Mich.: Wm. B. Eerdmans Publishing Co., 1978. Carsdale, George, *All the Animals of the Bible Lands*. Grand Rapids, Mich.: Zondervan Publishing House, 1970. Souvay, Charles L. "Biblical Geography," http://www.newadvent.org (accessed September 15, 2004).

Cloth

(Job 7:6; Song of Sol. 4:2; Isa. 36:2; John 19:23) For most of the Old Testament period, cloth was manufactured in the home, and was largely the work of women. Men would tend the **sheep**, wash them, and shear them; but the women had the task of carding the fleece, dyeing it, spinning it into thread, and weaving it on a loom into fabric that might be fashioned into a garment or a **tent**. The textile industry gradually developed into a major part of Israel's economic life, second only to agriculture (Philip J. King and Lawrence E. Stager 2001,146). As the people grew more urban, the textile industry grew increasingly segmented with professionals performing the specialized tasks of dyeing, fulling, and so on. Solomon, in love with elegant materials, imported fabrics from far-flung countries; but many of the materials, such as linen, were also imported. Most of the references in Scripture are to clothing or to specific materials, such as linen, wool, **goat's** hair, or **leather**, not to the generic term *cloth*.

Although Scripture provides no clear descriptions of the processes used in the making of textiles, archaeologists have uncovered many of the techniques used. For example, when producing wool, the

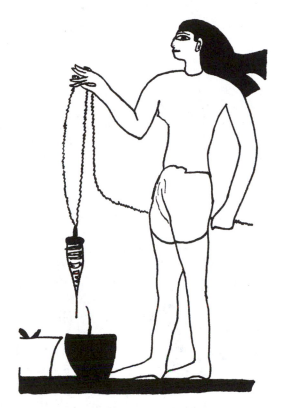

An Egyptian spinning wool, cotton, or flax (taken from painting in the tomb in Amenenhet II, twelfth dynasty, ca. 1900 B.C.).

primary animal fiber used in antiquity, the **sheep** were dipped in water to clean their fleece. Then they were sheared and the fleece was collected and washed a second time to remove grease and produce the beautiful white appearance celebrated in the Song of Solomon (4:2). White wool (Ezek 27:18) was considered the best type, a prized merchandise (Philip J. King and Lawrence Stager 2001, 148).

The white fleece was combed or "carded" in preparation for spinning (or twisting) it into thread. The distaff, a large stick, would hold the unspun flax or wool from which the thread was to be drawn (or the wool might be in a bowl), while the spinning was done on a hand spindle (a rotating stick), using "whorls" (or weights) that were made of stone, clay, or bone. The spindle was a thin wooden stick about a foot long with a notch at the top and was stuck through a whorl so that the weight came in the lower half. The spinster would hold the strands of combed wool in her left hand or under her left arm. With her right hand, she would draw out enough wool to twist into a yarn between her thumb and forefinger. She attached this yarn to the notch in her spindle, gave it a sharp twist, and let it fall in front of her, giving it another twist as it fell. When it got near the ground, she

Simple loom and weight. Weights such as these have been found in large numbers in archaeological digs.

stopped it and wound the thread on the spindle shaft, repeating this mechanical operation over and over.

Exodus pays special tribute to the skill of the Israelite women as spinners: "All the women who were expert spinners brought hand-spun blue-purple, red-purple, and scarlet yarn, and fine linen. All the women who possessed the skill spun goat hair" (Exod. 35:25–26). This ancient process was put to a holy use in the outfitting of the **Tabernacle**, with its coverings and tapestries.

While spinning was an exclusively female occupation, men would also work with the weaving, laboring long hours in uncomfortable positions. There was often a village weaver to whom the family would carry their thread. The weaving was done on a loom, either horizontal or vertical. The most primitive of the ancient looms had a top beam with warp threads suspended from it, kept taut by loom weights. The weaver would stand to work the weft thread back and forth, alternating among the threads. Eventually, the Israelites discovered a means of threading the weft so that the shuttle could be sent back and forth quickly. A simple stick could help in half of the process, but the second half—the reversal—took the invention of the leash-rod before it also became less labor intensive. We know that looms were a regular part of the Israelites' homes—even in Samson's day. Delilah used a domestic loom to weave her sleeping lover's luxurious hair into the weft of her work, probably using a horizontal type of loom (E. W. Heaton 1956, 120). Job made reference to the speed of a weaver's shuttle (Job 7:6), indicating that the more advanced kind of loom was in use by his very early period.

Cloth was woven in long pieces that were useful for clothing, curtains, rugs, or hangings. These long pieces might also be used as winding sheets or shrouds for the dead. An especially long piece might serve for a **tent** cover. A single garment could also be woven on the loom, like the seamless robe Jesus wore to his **crucifixion** (John 19:23).

An expert weaver could develop patterns, using various colored threads in his work. Some of the most ancient illustrations of Hebrews show them wearing clothing with vertical stripes, suggesting that these were woven with dyed threads interspersed among the natural colored ones.

As a finishing touch, these garments could also be decorated with fancy needlework, usually around the neckline of the women's clothing. The wall hangings of the Tabernacle were decorated with specific patterns and interweavings. Ezekiel mentions that **Egypt** and **Edom** were famous for their embroidery (Ezek. 27:7, 16). The process is one of interweaving threads of various colors on the cloth to form patterns. The vivid colors against the white fabric were much prized, usually a sign of royalty. When Sisera's mother waited for her son, she speculated that he was gathering the booty of war, including "dyed stuffs embroidered, two pieces of dyed work embroidered for my neck as spoil" (Judg. 5:30, Philip J. King and Lawrence Stager 2001, 158).

Archaeologists have discovered that in the later times, cloth manufacture was concentrated into industrial centers in places such as Debir, where basketfuls of loom weights and dyeing installations have been excavated (E. W. Heaton 1956, 116–117). *See also* Cloth: Dyeing and Fulling; Cloth: Goat's Hair and Wool; Cloth: Linen; Clothing; Work: Women's.

Further Reading

Heaton, E. W. *Everyday Life in Old Testament Times*. New York: Charles Scribner's Sons, 1956. King, Philip J. and Lawrence E. Stager. *Life in Biblical Israel*. Louisville, Ky.: Westminster John Knox Press, 2001.

Cloth: Dyeing and Fulling

(Mal. 3:2; Mark 9:3; Acts 16:14) By New Testament times, cloth production had changed from a cottage industry to commercial, specialized businesses. Making cloth involved numerous people, from the **shepherd** or the **farmer** to the dyer and fuller. Although the activities were a well-understood part of everyday life in ancient Palestine, many of the terms, materials, and activities seem quite alien to the modern reader.

All through Scripture, colored garments were highly prized. Dyeing had been practiced since 2500 B.C. in Egypt, as the linen mummy wrappings indicate (Philip J. King and Lawrence E. Stager 2001, 159). The most famous dye dealer in Scripture was Lydia, the "seller of purple" whom Paul met in Philippi, his first European convert. Lydia, who invited the missionaries into her home and saw her whole household converted (Acts 16:14), lived in Thyatira, a region famous for its purple dye. The entire Phoenician Coast was known for its dye industry; the very names *Canaan* and *Phoenician* probably meant "purple."

The Jews were not particularly sensitive to color, naming only a few colors in their scripture, crimson or scarlet, purple, and white being the most prominent. They did dye heifer skins red for **festival** offering, and noted with apparent admiration Joseph's coat of many colors (if that is the proper translation). But generally, only royal or rich people wore colors. In fact, the Hebrew language has no single word for *color,* "and their words for describing the various colours and shades of colours are so few that they cannot have been used much in general conversation. Even such obvious colours as blue and yellow do not occur as distinct terms" (E. W. Heaton 1956, 122).

They found their pigments in nature. Scarlet dye was produced by an **insect** such as the cochineal, which lived on a particular kind of tree. When crushed and put into hot water, it produced a vivid red liquid. The purple came from the murex shell**fish** found off the coast of Phoenicia around Tyre. The top of the shellfish was cut off and the yellowish secretion collected. Two colors resulted from the two ingredients in it, one a dark blue (called "blue" in Scripture) and the other a purple red (called "purple").

In Israel, purple goods were probably imported, thus limiting their use to the wealthier, aristocratic citizens. Purple was used for the adornment of the high **priest** (Exod. 28:6) and the inner drapery of the **Tabernacle**. Jeremiah complained that it was also used for the clothing that decked the images of pagan gods (Jer. 10:9).

Other dyes were produced from vegetables such as almond for yellow and madder (an herb) for red. The actual shades depended on the use of other chemicals in the processing (for example, lye, alkaline salt) Jeremiah mentions washing cloth in lye, probably a primitive form of soap.

Although the thread was usually dyed before it was woven into cloth, an easier method was immersing the finished fabric in the dye bath (Philip J. King and Lawrence Stager 2001, 159). Archaeologists have discovered dye plant sites in Palestine. The vats were made of solid blocks of stone about a yard in height and in diameter. They were hollowed out at the top into a basin with a narrow mouth (6 inches across), and a deep channel cut all round and pierced at one point around the rim to allow the surplus to drain back into the basin. Heaton believed this testifies to the value of the dye

Egyptian fullers at work cleaning cloth.

itself: "It was too valuable for a drop to be wasted" (Heaton 1956, 121). Near the vats were found jars containing slaked lime and decomposed potash, various stone basins and water cisterns.

The person who "fulled" or thickened, cleansed, bleached, or dyed the cloth was called a "fuller." He was often a trader in textiles and was able to help with the upkeep of woven garments. Because **clothing** was very precious, the fuller's role was respected to the point that Jerusalem had a "fuller's field" at the conduit of the upper pool of the Gihon Spring. There the fullers spread out "garments to dry after washing them in copper tubs. After the grime had been loosened by lye or soap, they trod it out with their feet" (Mal. 3:2).

The fuller's guild was an important organization in first century **Roman** towns such as Pompeii, "where today the ruins of their headquarters are still seen facing the principal forum" (Miller and Miller 1961, 208).

Mark pays tribute to the effectiveness of the fuller in his description of the Transfiguration: "And his raiment became shining, exceeding white as snow; so as no fuller on earth can white them" (Mark 9:3). *See also* Cloth; Clothing.

Further Reading

Heaton, E.W. *Everyday Life in Old Testament Times*. New York: Charles Scribner's Sons, 1956. King, Philip J. and Lawrence E. Stager. *Life in Biblical Israel*. Louisville, Ky.: Westminster John Knox Press, 2001. Miller, Madeleine S. and J. Lane, *Harper's Bible Dictionary*. New York: Harper and Row, 1961.

Cloth: Goat's Hair and Wool

(**Deut. 22:11; Ezek. 44:17; Mark 1:6**) Wool or hair from **animals** proved a durable and abundant material for the migratory Hebrews. The fabric from **goat's** hair could be made into waterproof **tents** that sheltered the inhabitants from heat in summer and cold in winter. (Paul was a "tentmaker," as were his friends Priscilla and Aquila, perhaps making the tents of goat's hair, although perhaps of leather.) The same goat's hair fabric could be used for tunics or cloaks.

Sackcloth, a loosely woven fabric of rough goat's or **camel's** hair, was frequently mentioned as a sign of poverty and **mourning**. This material was woven of the roughest and least desirable part of the thread. As the name suggests, it was akin to the material used for making sacks to carry supplies. When David lamented his child's illness, he was clad in sackcloth and covered with ashes. He was following traditional mourning practices in doing this. This simple homespun "sackcloth" furnished material for clothing that even the poorest man could own. John the Baptist, preaching in the desert, was dressed in camel's hair, "with a girdle of skin about his loins" (Mark

1:6). Such simple bits of **clothing** might serve for a lifetime and be handed down to the next generation. It may have been such a cloak that the prophet Elijah gave to Elisha, transferring his ministry in the gesture.

Wool fabric, especially after washing, was very heavy, but was durable and warm. It became the most popular of the heavy fabrics. There was a law against blending wool with linen (Deut. 22:11), which would have lightened its heft. In addition, it was rarely washed and became matted and dirty over time. Wool proved ideal for heavy cloaks and outer clothing, but not for more intimate garments. Moderns continue to find that wool is irritating to the skin and is most useful for winter coats. Levitical priests were forbidden to wear any wool, probably because of possible pollution with **blood**, they limited their clothing to linen (Ezek. 44:17).

In Mesopotamia, wool became the principal fiber used, with archaeological evidence from earliest times. The prevalence of sheep and shepherding references in Scripture testifies to the importance of wool among the Israelites as well. *See also* Cloth: Linen.

Further Reading

King, Philip J. and Lawrence E. Stager. *Life in Biblical Israel*. Louisville, Ky.: Westminster John Knox Press, 2001.

Cloth: Linen

(**Exod. 9:31; Josh. 2:6; Ezek. 44:17**) Linen was manufactured from flax, which was grown in both **Egypt** and Palestine. The plant requires wetlands or intense irrigation for cultivation.

The flax stalks were pulled up by the roots and beaten with sticks to free them from their seed and pods, then dried in the sun. Rooftops were convenient places for such a process (Josh. 2:6). The stripped flax stalks were then steeped for a week or so in water to separate the inner fibers from the woody part of the stalk, a process known as "retting." Then they were dried and beaten a second time. After they were dried, they were sorted and combed before spinning.

The plant itself is mentioned in the Bible only one time: "Now the flax and barley were ruined, for the barley was in the ear and the flax was in bud" (Exod. 9:31). The linen fabric, however, is mentioned numerous times. For example, to show the high esteem in which the Pharaoh held Joseph, he arrayed him in fine Egyptian linen (Gen. 41:42). When David brought the **Ark of the Covenant** to Jerusalem, he "was clothed with a robe of fine linen" as were the Levites who carried the Ark (1 Chron. 15:27).

The finest linen was very fine indeed—light and smooth to the touch, demanding an experienced hand to produce—and was generally imported from Egypt where centuries of the craft had refined the production into an art with remarkable results. This fabric was used in **Temple** vestments, even the priests' linen underpants, a kind of double-apron that covered the hips.

The Israelites produced a much coarser type of linen than the Egyptians, some of which was used to wrap the documents discovered with the Dead Sea Scrolls (E.W. Heaton 1956, 121). The fabric was used for all kinds of clothing among the wealthy people. One evidence that the ideal woman of Proverbs (31:13, 24) is virtuous and smart is that she "seeks wool and flax, and works with willing hands." She also "makes linen garments and sells them." Ezekiel speaks of a stately sailing ship with a fine embroidered linen sail for its ensign (Ezek. 27:7). The long fibers were the most precious for producing good thread. Broken fibers were used for lamp wicks.

The use of flax for textiles dates back at least to the eighth century B.C. Evidence in neolithic Jericho suggests that it was also considered valuable for the oil that came from flax seeds. Philip King believes that Jericho may have been the source of flax found in the Nahal Hemar Cave, situated in cliffs near the Dead Sea. Remnants of yellow, red, green, and black fabric, as well as a horizontal loom and loom weights found there, are thought to have come from flax grown at 'Ein-Gedi (Philip J. King and Lawrence E. Stager 2001, 149). The Gezer Calendar (ca. 900 B.C.) names Adar-Nisan as the month for the uprooting of flax. Another impressive discovery in the Sinai revealed several linen fabrics, loom weights, wooden beams, and flax fibers, as well as spun yarn, and twisted thread, indicating that this was the site of textile manufacturing from a very early time.

Clean linen became symbolic of spiritual purity. To the end of Scripture, white linen robes were the standard clothing for the saints, just as they had been for the **priests**. They were also the dress of the **angels**. The "**clean**" garments John mentions in Revelation 16:15 would seem to refer to the brilliant white linen clothing kept ready for the Last Days. *See also* Agriculture; Cloth; Clothing; Priest, High Priest.

Further Reading
Heaton, E.W. *Everyday Life in Old Testament Times*. New York: Charles Scribner's Sons, 1956. Hirsch, Emil G. and I.M. Casanowicz. "Linen," http://www.jewishencyclopedia.com (accessed March 16, 2001). King, Philip J. and Lawrence E. Stager. *Life in Biblical Israel*. Louisville, Ky.: Westminster John Knox Press, 2001.

Clothing

(2 Kings 2:24, Isa. 3:16–25, Eph. 6:14–17) When Adam and Eve realized they were naked, they "sewed fig leaves together, and made themselves aprons" (Gen. 3:7), thus forming the first human clothing. In later generations, the hides and hair of **sheep**, **camels**, and **goats** were widely used for modesty and warmth. Some believe that, before **metal** instruments were available for cutting the **animals**' hair, tufts were plucked out of the animal. Camels moult, making it unnecessary to cut their hair, although the finer camel's hair is procured by clipping it. Later, sheep shearing became a festive time for the **Israelites**. In **Egypt**, the Israelites undoubtedly came to enjoy linen, the more versatile and cooler fabric made from flax. By the time they were developing the clothing for their **priests**, the Israelites considered fine linen the appropriate fabric to use. Evidence from archaeology also indicates the early presence of cotton in **Canaan**.

Later, much more splendid fabrics, dyed with rich colors became part of the royal tastes of Solomon and his offspring. Imported from cities in Asia, Europe, and Africa, the fabrics were increasingly varied and beautiful. The silk must have come from China, although there is evidence of efforts to cultivate mulberries to feed the silk worms and produce silk locally for Jewish consumption.

Little material evidence has survived of any of these fabrics, as all are easily destroyed by moth, rot, fire, or mildew. The Hebrews' prohibition against graven images limits the pictorial evidence of ancient Israelite garments to those pictures that have survived among other cultures: the Egyptians or **Assyrians** or **Romans**. The Scripture record alone tells us the major details of their cloth and of clothing. We know far more about what the conquerors wore: the loin cloths of the Egyptians and their simple headdresses, the short togas and robes of the Romans, and the fringed garments and round head coverings of the Assyrians and **Persians**. The Bible, however, is full of references to Hebrew clothing—cloaks and girdles, veils, and sandals—the normal garb of Palestinian peasants.

The elaborate garments of later times were embroidered and ornamented far more

Simple Egyptian loincloth (1300 B.C.) and sheath dress (200 B.C.), as pictured in wall paintings.

lavishly, the layers of clothing and **jewelry** suggesting an opulent lifestyle. Isaiah sneers at the haughty daughters of Zion with their:

> tinkling ornaments about their feet, and their cauls, and their round tires [headbands and crescent-shaped ornaments] like the moon. The chains, and the bracelets, and the mufflers, The bonnets, and the ornaments of the legs, and the headbands, and the tablets, and the earrings, The rings, and nose jewels, The changeable suits of apparel, and the mantles, and the wimples, and the crisping pins, The glasses, and the linen, and the hoods, and the veils. (Isa. 3:16–25)

These will finally be replaced by a "girding of sackcloth" when the lavish lifestyle is ripped away and Jerusalem is left desolate, sitting on the ground.

Much later, Paul spoke symbolically of the "whole armor of God"—telling us a great deal about the garments of the Roman soldier:

> having your loins girt about with truth, and having on the breastplate of righteousness; And your feet shod with the preparation of the gospel of peace; Above all, taking the shield of faith, wherewith ye shall be able to quench all the fiery darts of the wicked. and take the helmet of salvation, and the sword of the Spirit, which is the word of God. (Eph. 6:14–17)

This symbolism of clothing permeates Scripture: the head coverings may indicate the regal authority or the modesty of the wearer, the phylacteries on the forehead or breast reveal the love of God's word, the fringes of the corners of the mantle show faithfulness to that word, and the lowly sandals reveal the humility of the servant. When there was a tragedy, the Hebrews often tore their clothing to express their anguish, putting on new clothes to signal a new beginning. When **King** Jehoiachin was released from prison, he changed his clothing (2 Kings 2:24), putting aside his prison garb. Although most poor people did not own a change of clothing, they understood the symbolism of changing clothing. When a person changed his life, cleaned up after a battle, or prepared to meet his king, he would change his clothes to mark the very special occasion.

In a traditional society, each detail of clothing is significant in a way that it is hard for Westerners with closets full of ready-made outfits to understand. For the ancient Hebrew, each bit of fabric, each layer, and each color were significant. Just as heirloom quilts are often made from fragments of cloth, each of which has special meaning to the family, so the items of apparel

Clothing of a rich man of the Middle East.

Roman soldier's clothing (from a Roman statue in the Christian era).

were significant to these people. From the skin outward, from the head to the foot, each item had potential meaning. Nakedness was a sign of humiliation. Multiple changes of clothing signified great wealth. A coat of many colors could render the owner an object of envy and violence. *See also* Cloth; Jewelry.

Clothing: Basic—Shift and Tunic

The shift was the usual garment worn by both men and women against the body, and among the poor it was often the only garment. A **linen** or **leather** loincloth, held in place by a belt, looking somewhat like a kilt, was the basic garment of Israelite soldiers and laborers. Priests wore linen underpants, covering them with their flowing robes.

The tunic, which was worn over the shift, might be made of **leather**, camel's or goat's hair, **wool**, **linen**, or even cotton. Usually it was without sleeves and fell straight from the shoulders to the knees. A mark of the more expensive garment was that it might have sleeves and extend to the ankles, perhaps an explanation for Joseph's "coat of many colors," which is now translated to read "a long robe with sleeves" or a richly ornamented robe (Gen. 37:3; NIV). This garment was draped over one shoulder and secured with a belt.

There must have been differences in design between the women's and men's garments because Scripture specifically forbids men wearing women's clothing (Deut. 22:5). One difference was that the **law** required men to have distinctive fringes on this mantle. These involved a blue cord, and long strings on the four corners of their outside garments as a perpetual reminder to fulfill divine commandments rather than one's own desires (Num. 15:38–41, Deut. 22:12). "Fringes may also have indicated covenantal affiliation, serving both to differentiate male from female and to distinguish between Israelite and gentile" (Judith R. Baskin 1993, 236). Many orthodox Jews still follow this admonition.

The woman's outer garment was draped around the body and over the left shoulder, leaving the right shoulder uncovered. Some of the ancient pictures and carvings show women wearing mantles pulled over their heads like hoods, and one shows a long shawl covering the head and shoulders, reaching to the ankles. It was held in place by a toggle pin, which was finally replaced by a fibula, which looks like a modern safety pin. Some women seem to have worn garments rounded at the neck. Although usually no garment was worn over the tunic, which reached just above the ankles, women occasionally had longer shawls (Philip J. King and Lawrence Stager 2001, 272).

The outer robe was a looser and longer type of tunic, not generally used by ordinary people. **Kings** were more likely to wear heavier robes of more exotic materials (1 Sam. 24:4). It is not clear whether there was also a third garment that some wore as well (Fred H. Wight 1953, 91–93). When a man was clad only in his shift, he was called "naked" (Isa. 20:2–4, Micah 1:8, John 21:7). To remove the clothing or to tear it was a sign of **mourning**. *See also* Cloth; Jewelry; Leather; Mourning.

Further Reading

Baskin, Judith R. "Fringes," in *The Oxford Companion to the Bible*. New York: Oxford University Press, 1993. King, Philip J. and Lawrence E. Stager. *Life in Biblical Israel*. Louisville, Ky.: Westminster John Knox Press, 2001. Wight, Fred H. *Manners and Customs of Bible Lands*. Chicago: Moody Press, 1953.

Clothing: Girdle or Belt

(Luke 12:35; Eph. 6:14) Moderns think of the *girdle* as a woman's undergarment, enhancing her figure, but the older meaning of the word was a large belt. John the Baptist and Elijah both wore wide (6-inch) leather belts around their waists. These were fastened with clasps and were used to hold up the tunic and robe for easier walking or for working. This girdle might also be made of a long, folded linen cloth, or even of silk or embroidered material. It was first folded and then wound around the waist, over the tunic, like a sash. It formed a useful pouch for keeping money and other possessions or for fastening a man's sword to his body.

Everyday dress for women in ancient Israel.

The image of the girdle was frequently used in Scripture: "Let your loins be girded [or "wrapped"] about," (Luke 12:35) Christ admonished his disciples—meaning, "Be ready to run." Paul called truth the Christian's belt in his warfare with Satan (Eph. 6:14).

Clothing: Headdress

(Gen. 24:64–65; Deut. 24:1; Exod. 13:9, 16; Song of Sol. 4:1, 6:5) The manner in which both Jews and Christians were to wear their hair and to cover their heads has been a matter of controversy from early times. It is unlikely that the head was covered except for warmth or protection in ancient times, but the style of the hair and the symbolism of the headdress soon became a subject of **law** and of custom. The symbolism and traditions associated with hair styles and head coverings continue to be a source of contention within religious communities and in the secular world today. Many see certain hair styles as symbols of conformity or of rebellion. For example, the tight and high cut of the military versus the long hair and pony tails of free spirits. Some countries (France, for instance) forbid the wearing of distinctive headdresses in public schools, fearing that they may cause strife.

Men's Hair and Head Coverings

In ancient Scripture, bareheadedness was the usual practice, especially among the young. Both men and women were proud of their hair and considered it one of their prize attributes. Absalom's flowing mane was so long that it trapped him in the trees (2 Sam. 15:26), and Samson's hair was so long that Delilah could weave it into fabric and later cut it off (Judg. 13–16). Because uncut hair was a sign of Samson's Nazirite vow; cutting it demonstrated either the violation of that vow or the proper completion of it (Num. 6:5). (It was thought to be the source of his power.)

Baldness was seen as a flaw, as suggested by the youth who confronted Elisha, saying, "Go up, thou bald head" (2 Kings 2:23). Baldness was also considered a sign of leprosy, so a bald man might be suspected of having that disease. Generally, young men loved to wear their hair long and curled and were proud of abundant hair (Fred Wight 1953, 96). Hair was considered so sacred by Jews that they often swore by it or by their heads. Jesus admonished his followers, "And do not swear by your head, for you cannot make even one hair white or black" (Matt. 5:36).

Because Moses hid his face before the Shekinah at the burning bush (Exod. 3:6), men were expected to cover themselves during prayer. "Accordingly, a man with uncovered head is, like one in rags and half-covered, forbidden to recite the Shema" and considered an offense to God and fellow worshippers. Although boys were allowed to be bareheaded in worship, men were expected to wear at least a skullcap. Gradually, the orthodox Jews came to believe that their heads should be covered most of the time, even when walking. On the other hand, modern Reform Jews often insist that it is a sign of respect to stand bareheaded before a person in authority, thus praying with head uncovered is proper (Kaufmann Kohler and Gotthard Deutsch 2005).

A thick turban became the usual headdress for married men. It was wrapped carefully around the head. Their long hair was bound up in this headdress. The fabric from which the head covering was made and the manner in which it was folded signified the clan and the region from which the man came. Among many Arabs, this continues to the practice even today in the wearing of the "Kaffieh." For example, Yassir Arafat's head covering, which had a fixed design of his people, was folded and draped so that the part that covered his shoulder was thought to be the shape of Israel, which he claimed for the Palestinians.

Covering the head also signaled dignity, like the "head-tires" or turbans of the **priests**, which were prescribed "for glory and beauty" (Exod. 28:40). The high priest was to wear a golden diadem on a miter that bore the sign "Holy to the Lord." Some interpreted the words in Leviticus 10:6, "uncover not your heads" as meaning, "Let not the hair of your heads go loose" (Kaufmann Kohler and Gotthard Deutsch 2005). The priests wore more elaborate head coverings than most men, more like great **crowns**, and had phylacteries—boxes of metal or bands of parchment—fastened to their foreheads by straps (Exod. 13:9, 16). (They might wear the phylacteries on their hands as well.) The conspicuous use of such marks of their piety was an element of the **Pharisees'** garb that Jesus specifically criticized (Matt. 23:5).

A woman's veil; men with two kinds of turbans.

In addition, **kings** had crowns to show their elevated status, giving them additional height and splendor. Each of the regions of the Fertile Crescent had its own distinct head coverings and traditions. In addition, the Greeks and Romans influenced the hairstyles and head coverings of the early Christians. Christ is portrayed in early images with long hair parted in the middle and flowing to his shoulders. Later, the monks and priests of the Church adopted various styles, including long hair, **beards**, and tonsures (a circle of hair like a crown around the skull).

Thus, by close study of the hair and head covering, one might determine the age, nationality, rank, tribe, and religious convictions of a man.

Women's Hair and Head Coverings

Jewish custom has changed over time regarding women's hair. In the Song of Songs, the Shulammite's flowing locks thrilled Solomon (Song of Sol. 4:1, 6:5). The art of braiding was noted in several places in Scripture (Isa. 3:24; 2 Sam. 14:26; Judg. 13).Women's hair was considered so beautiful that it was a snare even for the **angels**, causing Paul to insist that women keep their heads covered. In early Christian (or Roman) fashions, the women wore their hair waved, curled, frizzed with irons, arranged in tiers, and twined about the head like a high diadem with locks reserved to fall over the forehead and on the temples (H. LeClercq 2005). This elaboration of hair styles may have been part of Paul's concern about the distractions women's uncovered hair brought to the worship service, or he may have been continuing to echo the Jewish tradition in which he was raised.

Bareheadedness, among the Hebrews, came to be seen as "nakedness" (Deut. 24:1), tempting men to improper glances. In Mishnaic times, Jewish customs developed that women should not be seen on the street with their hair uncovered. A married woman who violated this rule was deemed to have given her husband sufficient grounds for divorce (Kohler and Deutsch 2005). Both Jewish and Christian thought indicates that the covering of the head was a sign of mourning for Eve's sin and of her consequent subordination to the lordship of her husband (1 Cor. 11:3–12).

A woman might be shamed by having her hair disheveled by the priest or by having it shaved, an insult inflicted on captive women (Jer. 7:29; 1 Cor. 11:15) in both the ancient and modern world. Those women who fraternized with the enemy in World War II, for example, were shaved to signify their perfidy. In some religious orders, shaving the head signals repentance and rejection of the secular world, an act of mortification of the flesh.

Among Jews, married women were expected to be particularly scrupulous in covering their hair. In some cultures, the hair was clipped off before the marriage and a cap was placed on the woman's head. Even today, some orthodox Jewish women cover their hair in conformity with this tradition.

In most of the period covered by Scripture, women usually wore a mantle or a veil over their hair, both for protection against the elements and for modesty. This piece of cloth might be as long as six feet and was often decorated with embroidery work. Most women were veiled at all times except in private moments in the home. Any visitor in the home would have been greeted by a veiled hostess, accompanied by a maid. The exceptions would have been prostitutes and servants, women of low status.

Young girls were especially protected from the lustful glances of men by veils. The veil might be worn over a high cap which had gold and silver coins sewn in the front. These precious coins, which were often included in the woman's dowry, might decorate the edges of the veil. When Rebekah first met Isaac, she covered her face with such a veil (Gen. 24:64–65). And it was the veil over the head and face of Leah that allowed her to marry Jacob in place of her sister Rachel.

The continued use of the veil in Moslem society has been a frequent source of debate in modern Saudi Arabia, where American women with uncovered heads are thought to be immodest. The custom survives in Western countries as the bridal veil, a symbol of chastity. After the wedding vows, it is lifted by the groom for the connubial kiss.

Some modern churches require that women (but not men) have their heads covered during worship. Female tourists in Israel find that they are not allowed in many of the holy places bareheaded (or in shorts or sleeveless blouses). This is also the case in many cathedrals in Europe. The custom of wearing hats has declined in Protestant America, where only the most conservative congregations require head coverings. For example, Amish or Mennonite women wear prayer caps almost all the time.

Further Reading

Adler, Cyrus and Judah David Eisenstein. "Veil," http:www.jewishencyclopedia. com (accessed April 1, 2004). Kohler, Kaufmann and Gotthard Deutsch. "Bareheadedness," http://www.jewishencyclopedia.com (accessed April 23, 2005). LeClercq, H. "Hair (in Christian Antiquity). http://www. newadvent.org (accessed April 23, 2005). Wight, Fred Hartley. *Manners and Customs of Bible Lands*. Chicago: Moody Press, 1953.

Clothing: Mantle or Cloak

(Exod. 22:26–27; Luke 6:29) The heavy outer garment worn by most Israelites was a large cloak, more useful than an overcoat, for it could serve as a bag for carrying loads or as a cover for sleeping. It was a shelter from sun, wind, and rain; a blanket at night; and even a makeshift **tent**. Daniel and his companions wore their cloaks when they went into the fiery furnace.

It was an important garment, protected by the **law** of Moses (Exod. 22:26–27) and mentioned by Christ as an emblem of generosity when shared willingly: "Do not keep back your undergarment from the one who robs you of the outer one" (Luke 6:29). If such a garment were taken, it was to be returned by sunset (Fred Wight 1953, 94–96).

When the Israelites prepared to escape from **Egypt**, they wrapped their unleavened dough and their kneading bowls in their cloaks and carried them on their shoulders (Exod. 12:34). When Gideon was collecting the booty from battle, the Israelites spread out their cloaks and threw the earrings they had taken into them (Judg. 8:25). When David and Jonathan made their **covenant**, Jonathan stripped off his robe, armor, sword, bow and belt, giving all of these to David (1 Sam. 18:4), signifying in the act a transference of royal succession (Philip J. King and Lawrence E. Stager 2001, 271). A parallel scene is found in 2 Kings, when Elijah left his mantle with Elisha as he crossed over Jordan (2 Kings 2:8–13). The transfer of this garment symbolized the transfer of power or prophetic prerogative. In an even more dramatic move, the **king** of Nineveh removed his robe and covered himself with sackcloth in response to Jonah's teaching (Jonah 3:6).

Further Reading

King, Philip J. and Lawrence E. Stager. *Life in Biblical Israel*. Louisville, Ky.: Westminster John Knox Press, 2001. Wight, Fred Hartley. *Manners and Customs of Bible Lands*. Chicago: Moody Press, 1953.

Clothing: Sandals

(Mark 6:9, Acts 12:8) Simple sandals, made of **leather** or **wood** and held by leather thongs to the foot, were common footwear among ancient Near Eastern peoples. More commonly, shoes were not even a part of the clothing unless the person planned an extended walk or if the ground was particularly hot, cold, or wet. In the household, most people went without shoes—thus the custom of **foot-washing** for those entering the home. This was the task of the **slave** or the humble host, as Jesus demonstrated by washing his **disciples**' feet. When John spoke of being unfit to loosen the latchet of Jesus's sandal, he was referring to the leather thongs that held the sole in place. It was a custom to go barefoot when **mourning**, even if the person was a noble (Joseph Jacobs, Immanuel Benzinger, Wilhelm Bacher, M. Seligsohn 2004).

Peasants would have a single pair of sandals held on with straps (or thongs) that crossed from the back over the instep and a third, narrower strap, fastened in front, that passed between the toes and was tied to the instep strap. The more affluent would have had various kinds of sandals.

Archaeological evidence shows that shoes had turned-up toes or fitted heel-caps, leggings or boots on occasion, probably as a result of foreign influences (Philip J. King and Lawrence E. Stager 2001, 273).

Curiously, the sandal was sometimes used as a **seal** of a contract. In the story of Ruth, Boaz gave his sandal to his kinsman as surety for their agreement about the planned levirate **marriage**. In rabbinical literature, the **judge** and the teacher were allowed to use a sandal to strike the miscreant or pupil who disobeyed their instructions or rebelled against their decisions (Jacobs et al. 2004) In modern Arab countries, hitting with the sole of the shoe is a sign of insult, demonstrated by the angry crowd striking the statue of Saddam Hussein with their shoes as it was dragged down the street in Baghdad.

Further Reading

Jacobs, Joseph, Immanuel Benzinger, Wilhelm Bacher, and M. Seligsohn. "Sandals," http://www.jewishencyclopedia.com (accessed March 20, 2004).
King, Philip J. and Lawrence E. Stager. *Life in Biblical Israel.* Louisville, Ky.: Westminster John Knox Press, 2001.

Clouds. *See Weather*

Coins. *See Measures; Money*

Cooking, Cooking Utensils

(Lev. 6:2; Ezek. 34) Kitchens were a luxury that came late in Hebrew history. Tent-dwellers used a portion of the **tent** or the out-of doors for their simple cooking activities. The pots for the **grain** and oil, the skins of **wine**, and the fire all had to be portable. As **slaves** in **Egypt**, although they may have had simple houses in which to live, they probably added only a few of the utensils they saw among the more sophisticated Egyptians. After they settled in **Canaan**, they replaced their tents with houses. Many of the peasants continued to cook their meals in the courtyard or in the middle of the family room, with an open clay-baked box or a thick jar with holes in the sides serving as a stove. The smoke might escape through an opening in the ceiling or window (Hos. 13:3, Fred H. Wight 1953, 30–31). They gathered into cities and developed a more lavish lifestyle, finding the need for more elaborate **food** preparation facilities and more varied cooking utensils, and borrowing ideas from their new neighbors. Over time, the homes became larger and the kings built palaces, which were far more richly furnished.

The typical fuel for cooking was wood—often in the form of small sticks, pieces of charcoal or dried dung—all of which were readily available to the migratory peoples (1 Kings 17:10, John 18:18). Like modern Arabs, they also used thorny shrubs or bundles of dried grass. Even the most primitive household probably had a flint to ignite the blaze (Isa. 50:11). Without this, the family had to bring fire from another home or from the local baker's embers. They also needed fans to encourage the flame, shovels to add more fuel, and tongs to move coals about. The most primitive hearths were built on a mud floor, with a few stones around the fire, and pots placed on top. The tent-dwellers also had small portable cooking stoves that could accommodate two pots at a time (Emil G. Hirsch and Immanuel Benziner 2004). The scarcity of **metal** made such constructions rare in ancient times.

Bread was baked by kindling a fire on the sand or on small stones. When they were hot, the baker brushed away the fire and ashes from the surface and placing the thin cakes of dough on the hot **stones** or sand, covering them with glowing ashes. When iron plates were available, these might be substituted for stones, with the flat surface serving as a griddle for the flat bread (1 Chron. 9:31). Other forms of stoves were used, including a clay oven, shaped like a beehive that is narrower at the top than the bottom, with space at the bottom for fire. When the inside was heated, the cakes of bread were stuck on the inside walls to bake. Egyptians used the outside walls of such ovens for their baking. Later, the **Temple** ovens were made of metal (Morris Jastrow Jr, Immanuel Benzinger, Margus Jastrow, and Louis Ginzberg 2004).

Other basic utensils included a pestle for crushing the grain, a hand mill to grind it, sieves for straining the flour, a kneading trough for preparing dough, and clay pans (or later metal ones in the Temple) for final baking of the bread loaves. In addition, many homes had a tin plate or a deep pan for baking cake or bread. Such a plate might also be used for carrying fire.

Metal forks for lifting meat out of pots.

For the liquids, the families had large earthen jugs in which they brought water from the local well (Gen. 24:15, 1 Kings 28:34) and stored it. (Earthen jugs have the virtue of keeping water cool, even in hot weather.) Smaller vessels, formed like a ladle or cup, must have been used to offer a drink to visitors. The large pots were also used for storing meal or corn, as well as for cooking (Gen. 24:15, 1 Kings 17:12, 18:34).

The most commonly mentioned vessel was the cooking pot in which the meat was boiled and the daily fare prepared (Ezekiel 34). Small serving bowls were often used for individual helpings. The homes also were furnished with basins, probably made of clay or metal, for washing and ewers for pouring the water over the hands and feet (2 Kings 3:11).

Goat skins were used for the milk and wine; small earthen (or later metal) jugs were used for oil and honey (1 Kings 17:12) and baskets held fruits and pastry (Hirsch et al. 2004) These would have been arranged around the tent or home, sometimes on shelves, sometimes hanging from the rafters, and sometimes on the floor—depending on the danger of infiltration by rats, household **animals**, or **insects**.

The common folk, throughout much of the Old Testament, probably used crude earthen vessels (Lev. 6:21) made by the village **potter**. Even these must have been enriched by commerce with the **Philistines**, who had a heritage of elegant pottery design. From them they probably enlarged their household collection to include a much wider variety of pot designs than the Israelites had previously known. From the Canaanites and Philistines, whom they plundered, the Israelites also acquired metal bowls, which usually were found in the homes of the wealthy. These were far more durable and could be cleaned and reused, making them ideal for usage in the Temple.

The usual household would also have had at minimum a few standard utensils: a three-pronged fork was used to lift meat out of the pot (1 Sam. 2:13) and knives for slaughtering animals and dressing the meat (Gen. 22:6, 10). Spoons must also have been available, although for special uses such as dishing out cream. For the most part, forks, knives, and spoons were unnecessary for eating the meal. Bread was often used to lift food to the mouth from the common serving dish. Under the **law**, which outlined the regulations for **clean** and unclean procedures, certain dishes were reserved for certain kinds of food, with a clear separation between the meat and the milk products.

Food was such an intrinsic consideration in Hebrew life and thought that even the sacred spaces—the **Tabernacle** and **Temple**—had requirements for cooking facilities and utensils. After all, the sacrifices involved the killing of animals, the preparation of the meat, as well as cooking and eating it. The sanctuaries had **altars** for burning the meat, pots for boiling it, utensils for tending the fires, and various bowls for related activities. The preparation, serving, and eating of meals became a ritual of considerable importance among the Hebrews, rich with sacred meanings in the observance of the law of Moses and the various mandated **feast** days. By the time that the **Pharisees** appeared on the scene, the cooking process had acquired hundreds of ordinances. Some commentators note that they brought back both meaning and joy to the shared family meals with all their rituals. *See also* Bread; Clean, Unclean; Meals; Pharisees; Pots and Pottery; Sacrifice.

Further Reading

Hirsch, Emil G., Immanuel Benziner, "Cooking Utensils," http://www. jewish-encyclopedia.com (accessed March 21, 2004). Jastrow, Morris, Jr., Immanuel Benzinger, Margus Jastrow, and Louis Ginzberg. "Baking," http://www. jewishencyclopedia.com (accessed March 22, 2004). King, Philip J. and Lawrence E. Stager. *Life in Biblical Israel*. Louisville, Ky.: Westminster John Knox Press, 2001. Wight, Fred H. *Manners and Customs of Bible Lands*. Chicago: Moody Press, 1953.

Cornerstone. *See Stonemasons*

Cosmetics, Ornamentation

As soon as people had mirrors, they began using cosmetics to enhance their appearance. The earliest mirrors that have been discovered in **Egypt** and Palestine were made of highly polished metal (Job 37:18). Glass may also have been used by the Egyptians and was probably used by the first century A.D., when Paul spoke of their imperfect reflection: "Now we see through a glass darkly" (1 Cor. 13:12, A.R. Millard 1980,1011–12). Even with such cloudy reflections, ancient folk must have noticed their gray hair and pale cheeks.

For both men and women, hair had a special attraction, to the point that Paul recommended that women cover their heads rather than distract others from worship. Apparently women learned to braid their hair in elaborate designs. Curling rods have been discovered, as well as **ivory**, bone, and **metal** hair pins and ivory combs, suggesting some more complex patterns of hair arrangement (Madeleine S. Miller and J. Lane Miller 1961, 115).

Men also wore their hair long. Absalom was so proud of his beautiful hair that it caused his death, trapping him in the trees as he rode through the forest (2 Sam. 18:9). Samson, who had taken the Nazirite vow never to cut his hair, wore his long, luxuriant hair in seven locks; when his beloved Delilah weaved his hair into her web and cut it, he was deprived of his strength (Judg. 16:13–14).

The discovery that the ancient Israelites knew and used henna indicates that some dyed their hair and **beard**s a deep red hue. Archaeologists have discovered razor blades among ancient artifacts in Israel, suggesting that beards were sometimes shaved, although generally the Hebrews were proud of their beards. Other cultures, such as the Egyptians and the **Greeks**, were likely influences in this radical adoption of shaving. Cutting of the beard was a sign of impending doom or of mourning (Jer. 41:5), like the tearing of clothes and gashing of the body. To cut off part of a beard was symbolic of castration (2 Sam. 10:14, Philip J. King and Lawrence E. Stager 2001, 283). But a full beard, untrimmed, by law, marked mature men. The

Torah instructed, "You shall not round off the hair on your temples or mar the edges of your beard" (Lev. 19:27). (This admonition is the source of the modern Hassidic tradition of keeping their long ear locks uncut.) The men's hair and beards were regularly oiled, either with perfumed oil or **olive oil**, a very different concept of beauty from moderns.

The most frequently noted form of face painting or beautification was eye paint. Jezebel painted her eyes and "attired her head" (2 Kings 9:30), probably using heavy black lines under her eyes to make them look larger. This was a common practice among the Egyptians and Babylonians, perhaps originally designed "to protect them from the bright sun, to relieve eye ailments, and to protect the eyes from insects" (Philip J. King and Lawrence E. Stager 2001, 281). Curiously, Job had named one of his daughters Karen-happuch or "horn of eye paint" (Job 42:14). The eye liners and shadows were of various colors depending on the materials used. The most common was black kohl,

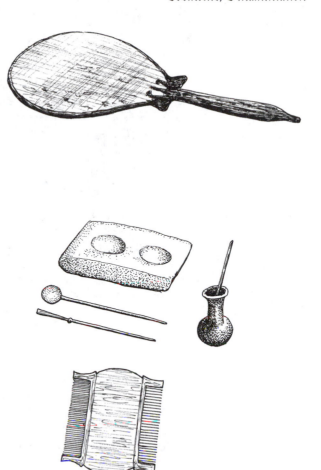

Cosmetic tools used in New Testament times: polished metal mirror; container and tiny basins for holding colors, kohl, and so on, to be used for lining eyes, coloring lips or skin; and comb.

made from either soot or galena. Green was made from malachite. The mineral was ground to a fine powder and then mixed with water or gum to form a paste. The mixture was stored in a receptacle, a small horn or vase (as Job's daughter's name would suggest), and applied with a tiny stick or spatula, which might be made of wood, bone, ivory, glass, or bronze. Such objects, as well as ivory spoons for kohl and cosmetic palettes of limestone, have been discovered in Palestine. "Egyptian women would paint the upper eyelids and eyebrows black and the lower eyelids green" (Philip J. King and Lawrence E. Stager 2001, 281). The Israelites were more conservative, considering such ornamentation of the body as a sign of the prostitute. As Ezekiel notes, in speaking of the unfaithful harlot Jerusalem: "For them you bathed yourself, painted your eyes, and decked yourself with ornaments" (Ezek. 23:40).

A mortar and pestle for grinding ingredients into fine powder or smooth paste. The bowl-shaped vessel of hard material such as stone or basalt was used for cosmetics, perfumes, unguents, grain, spices, and other materials that required the user to pulverize them (Num. 11:8; Prov. 27:22).

In addition, in Babylonia and Egypt, henna juice was used on feet, hands, and nails to give them a bright red color. Yellow ochre, also called "golden clay" or "face bloom," was used by the Sumerians. Rouge and paint were applied to faces of both men and women (Madeleine S. Miller and J. Lane Miller 1961, 115). Red ochre has been found in Egyptian tombs, probably used as rouge for coloring the cheeks. Egyptian ladies also had powder-puffs and lipstick (K. A. Kitchen 1980, 322).

The absence of pictorial evidence from ancient Israel gives us only a few hints of the actual practices of face painting,. The source for much of our knowledge of these ancient practices lies in the discovering of innumerable cosmetic containers: juglets for oil, carrot-shaped and spherical perfume bottles, ivory and wood cosmetic containers, and decorated bowls for grinding and mixing cosmetics. These have been found in various burial sites from Persia, Jerusalem, Megiddo, Dan, Lachish, Gezer, and Egypt. Egyptian wall paintings show hair stylists at work and portray the colored eyes and faces of the royalty. It is clear that Jezebel was not the only woman who painted her face in an effort to enhance her beauty. *See also* Clothing; Pots and Pottery.

Further Reading

King, Philip J. and Lawrence E. Stager, *Life in Biblical Israel*. Louisville, Ky.: Westminster John Knox Press, 2001. Millard, A. R. "Mirror," in *The Illustrated Bible Dictionary*. Sydney, Australia: Tyndale House Publishers, 1980. Miller, Madeleine S. and J. Lane Miller. "Cosmetics," in *Harper's Bible Dictionary*. New York: Harper and Row, Publishers, 1961.

Cosmology

(Gen. 1; Psalm 104; Job 38) We can perceive the universe as it was understood by the ancient Hebrews from the poetic narrative of the **creation** story, as well as other references in Scripture and from their incidental references to the physical world. The ancient Hebrews were not a scientific people, and we should not take scriptural imagery literally. When God commanded them through Moses: "Thou shalt not make unto thee a graven image, nor the likeness of any form that is in **heaven** above, or that is in the earth beneath, or that is in the water under the earth" (Exod. 20:4), this summary picture gives us a three-storied universe, with heaven stretching above the earth, and the **water** beneath. Or, when God proclaimed to Job that he was not one of those present when the Lord "laid the foundations of the earth" (Job 38:4), this was a well-known way of conceiving such hidden matters: pillars that held up the earth, keeping it from the waters below.

Scripture provides a large number of references that expand this image of the universe in Psalm 104, Job 38, and numerous examples in the prophetic writings. Most of the references are glancing, allowing the faithful to consider the joyous moment of creation, as well as its nature, its order, and its ultimate meaning for their lives. The poetic context allows most readers to interpret the words as poetic imagery, not as scientific explanations of the nature of the universe.

Most of the world beneath the heavens was thought to consist of water, with oceans circumscribing the earth and filling the void beneath it, except perhaps for a space allotted to Sheol, the place of the dead. The firmament covered the entire earth like a giant dome. The heavenly region above the firmament was the section where God was thought to live.

The Firmament

The firmament, the framework that held things in place, mentioned in the Old Testament but not the New, was thought to be the vault of the sky, or the heavens. It was thought to be a rigid dome rising above the earth and the oceans. It had several chambers, in the highest of which God was thought to dwell (Deut. 26:15). Above the firmament was the heavenly ocean, the "waters above the firmament," and below it the clouds and all the celestial creations. It rested on "foundations" or "pillars" (2 Sam. 22:8; Job 26:11, 37:18).

Firmament was a favorite word of Hebrew writers wishing to demonstrate the majestic presence of God the Creator. It was a feature of Ezekiel's vision (1:22), and Daniel used it to describe the wise man (12:3). The nature of the "firmament" itself has been debated vigorously, some believing it to be transparent dome—like ice—a thin sphere covering the earth, a strong substance two or three fingers in thickness, or perhaps a metallic substance that never tarnishes. The Psalmist thought of it as a gigantic tent or curtain (Ps. 19:1; Madeleine S. Miller and J. Lane Miller 1961, 194). There were scholars who even decided it was a "journey of 500 years" above the surface of the earth (Kaufmann Kohler and Emil G. Hirsch 2004).

The Heavenly Bodies

The sun, moon, and stars were thought to hang from the firmament in such a manner that they could move in their orbits. Other peoples might have studied the stars and even worshipped them, but the Hebrews saw them only as the work of God—not deities like Venus or Saturn.

When Job spoke of the creation as an occasion, "when the morning stars sang together and all the sons of God shouted for joy" (Job 33:7), he appears to suggest that the stars were supposed to be living creatures. In fact they not only shout and sing but also "walk on the way," "come out in the morning," and "go in" at night (Judg. 5:20). In fact Lucifer, considered by some to be another name for Satan, was spoken of as a fallen star (Luke 10:18). (This is one of several hints in Scripture of an ancient story of a Battle of Angels, ending with the casting out of Satan and his hosts.)

John Milton drew heavily on these passages, as well as on medieval legend to develop his work *Paradise Lost,* which includes vivid pictures of the whole scene of Creation. William Blake, an English poet writing at the end of the eighteenth and beginning of the nineteenth centuries, developed a mystical epic picturing the stars as living creatures—the heavenly hosts—of whom some were cast out for their disobedience to God. God himself was spoken of frequently as "Lord of hosts," as if he were the actual leader of a heavenly array (Morris Jastrow, Jr, Peter Jensen, Marcus Jastrow et al. 2004).

"Lucifer" (or Phosphorus, the "light-bearer") has been thought to refer to the planet Venus, the morning star. Apparently, the Hebrews had also recognized Saturn, the farthest removed from the earth and the highest in the heavens, which was frequently referred to by the Assyrians. This may be what Daniel means in referring to the "captain of the army" (Dan. 8:11). Other references to individual stars indicate that the Jews knew about Orion, Sirius or the Pleiades, the Great Bear, and the Twins or Gemini. The ancient forms of the names make it difficult to determine exactly which stars are referred to by Isaiah, Amos, Job, and others.

They would have made no great distinction between the stars and the planets, although they speak of seven of the planets, which appear to be Saturn, Jupiter, Mars, the sun, Venus, Mercury, and the moon. (These names, of course, were assigned by Romans, and were not the names used by the Hebrews or their neighbors.) In later times, Jewish writers, after their stay in Babylon, speak of the 12 constellations of the zodiac: Aries (Taleh), Gemini (Teomim), Cancer (Sarton), Leo (Ari), Virgo (Betulah), Libra (Moznayim), Scorpio (Akrab), Sagittarius, the Archer (Kasshat),

Capricornus (Gedi), Aquarius (Deli), Tarus (Eglah), and Pisces (Dagim). Each of the constellations was thought by pagans to rule one month—Aries ruled Nisan (March), Taurus Iyyar (April). Such ideas, although tempting, were not part of orthodox Hebrew thought.

On clear nights, with little light around them to interfere with their observations, these ancient people could see the starry heavens clearly, even though they lacked the details provided by our telescopes and observatories. *See also* Afterlife; Angels; Creation; Heaven(s), New Jerusalem, Paradise; Time; Waters.

Further Reading

Kohler, Kaufmann and Emil G. Hirsch. "Cosmogony," http://www.jewishencyclopedia.com (accessed June 12, 2004). Jastrow, Morris, Jr., Peter Jensen, Marcus Jastrow, Ludwig Blau, Richard Gottheil, Joseph Jacobs. "Astronomy," http://www:jewishencyclopedia.com (accessed June 13, 2004). Miller, Madeleine S. and J. Lane Miller. "Firmament," *Harper's Bible Dictionary*. New York: Harper and Row, 1961.

Court Officials

(2 Sam. 8:16–18, 20:23–26;1 Kings 4:1–6; 1 Chron. 18: 14–17) The entourage of the **king**, those who "saw the king's face" (2 Kings 25:19), included his bodyguard (2 Sam. 15:18; 2 Kings 11:4) and the leading military officials (1 Sam. 14:50, 18:13; 1 Kings 16:9, 16). The "captain of the host" was considered his chief officer. The Bible lists both David's and Solomon's attendants (2 Sam. 8:16–18, 20:23–26; 1 Kings 4:1–6; 1 Chron. 18: 14–17).

In these listings we see the primacy of the military command, with a division of power between the commander of the army and the commander of the guard. When the king went to **war**, he was accompanied by an armor-bearer, who served as a kind of squire and charioteer. He also might have a royal guard, a corps of foreign mercenaries, with charioteers, runners, and watchmen, who protected the **palace** (Roland deVaux 1961, 123–124).

The king also had **priests** in his entourage, probably to perform sacred functions, although it is not clear exactly what their connection to the king might have been. Saul had discovered that the king was not a priest and was forbidden to perform the rites designated for the descendants of Levi and Aaron. Nonetheless, David did participate actively in religious functions, such as the development of the **Psalms** and the transporting of the **Ark of the Covenant** to Jerusalem. It is obvious that the high priests were involved in political activities, especially in the decision in favor of Solomon over his elder brother who would have had the normal right of succession. One of the two high priests was cast out of Jerusalem as a result of this power struggle. The king's priest, however, may have functioned as a kind of chaplain to the court. This became a common role in medieval times, when royal families had their own chapels. David also had a **prophet** on whom he also relied for advice, which Nathan delivered without hesitation or fear in the case of Bathsheba.

Among the civilian posts was an officer "over the household" (1 Kings 4:6, 18:3; 2 Kings 18:18, 37). This "master of the palace," whose position was hereditary, was apparently sufficiently important that he might also serve as a governor in the absence of the king (Roland deVaux 1961, 129–130). Some believe he served much as the Egyptian or **Assyrian** vizier did, or a modern chief of staff does, reporting every morning to the monarch, and receiving his instructions, opening the gates of the royal **house**, and opening the official day, screening visitors and documents, giving the king's orders to the other officials, serving his monarch as Joseph had served the Pharaoh in **Egypt**. Either he or another functionary may have acted as the "king's servant," whose role may have been keeper of the **seal**.

His civil attendants included the recorder or private secretary, who was probably his chronicler and **scribe** (2 Sam. 8:16–17, 20:24–25; 1 Kings 4:3). The royal secretary, who was also in charge of **taxes**, served as both a private secretary and secretary of state. He was responsible for all collections and correspondence, and was ranked just below the master of the palace (2 Kings 18: 18; Isa. 36: 3). The royal scribe may well have been the chronicler and tax collector, or he may have simply performed tasks as assigned by the king and his officers. This role again seems to have been a copy of the Egyptian job description.

Within the household was also a historiographer to keep a record of the great accomplishments of the king, on the same order of presidential historians in modern times.

The royal herald was charged with palace ceremonies, introduction of people to audiences, and reporting to the people the commands of their king (Roland deVaux 1961, 132). From medieval and Renaissance history, we picture the herald blowing a trumpet to announce the king, although this may not be an accurate picture of the Israelite herald.

There was also a "keeper of the wardrobe" (2 Kings 22:14); the cupbearer (Neh. 1:11), chamberlains, bakers, someone designated his "friend" (1 Kings 4:5; 2 Sam. 15:37, 16:16); and another who served as his counselor (2 Sam. 15:12).In addition, there was the overseer of conscript labor (2 Sam. 20:24; 1 Kings 4:6, 5:14, 12:18) and many other minor attachés (Madeleine S. Miller and J. Lane Miller 1961, 366).

In the household of Solomon, there must also have been poets, musicians, and others who helped with his multitude of cultural projects. After all David, his father, also had male and female singers in his cortege, probably singing the Psalms he wrote. David himself had served as a musician for Saul. As we see from ancient Greek literature, the singer or bard was a revered part of the court, providing entertainment and wisdom. For the

Cupbearer to the king in Nehemiah's time, an important official at court and one who often tasted the king's meal to ensure he was not poisoned. Notice also the throne of the king and his scepter.

Hebrews who relied on the Scripture rather than epics, the musicians probably had a more limited role. We do know that Herod had music and dance with his banquets. It was on such an occasion that his stepdaughter performed the dance that led to the beheading of John the Baptist.

Although the Hebrew royal entourage did not match that of the other monarchies of the time, it was a modest copy of the Egyptian, **Assyrian**, and **Babylonian** courts. For a man to display his authority, he surrounded himself with officers and helpers who became his eyes and ears throughout the kingdom. The pomp and circumstance that signaled his appearance on the scene reinforced his power. *See also* Kings; Palaces; Warriors.

Further Reading

DeVaux, Roland. *Ancient Israel: Its Life and Institutions.* Grand Rapids, Mich.: William B. Eerdmans Publishing Company, 1961. Miller, Madeleine S. and J. Lane Miller, *Harper's Bible Dictionary.* New York: Harper and Row, Publishers, 1961.

Covenant

(Gen. 9:13, 15:18–21, 17:4–14; Exod. 34; Ezek. 16:59–63) Covenants mark many of the great moments in Scripture. These sacred agreements have been central to the continuing relationship between God and his people. The Hebrew term for *covenant* may derive from a word meaning "bond" or "fetter," which suggests the binding relationship and mutual obligations agreed to by the participants. The concept is a compact between individuals or groups that involves promises on both sides.

The covenant is formal and usually sealed by some symbolic act—a seal, a rite, an **oath**, a sacred **meal**, a **blood sacrifice**, or an invocation of **blessings** and **curses** that make it solemn and binding (Bernard W. Anderson 1993, 138). Humankind discovered early in history that few could be trusted to be true to their promises. Even in earliest literature, the Gilgamesh epic (2750–2500 B.C.), for example, we find the need for blood brotherhood—fidelity to acting for one another's good. Such a totally committed friendship appears in the oath that Jonathan and David swear (1 Sam. 18:1–3).

The Ritual

"In primitive times covenants were sealed by swallowing a drop of each other's **blood**" (Madeleine S. Miller and J. Lane Miller 1961, 116). It is clear that the original idea was a "blood covenant," sometimes marked by cutting the flesh and co-mingling the blood of the two principals. When Abraham entered into a covenant with El Shaddai (Gen. 15:17–21), the word used for the covenant was "cutting." God told Abraham to prepare for the covenant by slaughtering several animals, cutting them in half and placing the two parts of each on the ground so that the parts would lie opposite one another. "The two parties would then walk around those two halves in a figure of eight path through the blood. In that ritual they would pledge themselves to each other to the extent of all they had, even to their very lives" (Markus Reins 2005). The covenant was then sealed with a naming of all the blessings to come as a benefit of keeping the covenant, all the curses that would follow the breaking of it.

In the agreement between Abraham and God, **circumcision** became the designated **seal** for all of the males in his family. Paul and other Christians interpreted the shedding of the blood of Christ as the seal of the New Covenant, replacing the circumcision.

For human covenants, this bloody ritual of the slain animals was simplified to a handclasp or, in the case of Boaz and his relative, handing over a sandal.

Examples of Covenants

Examples of covenants began as early as Genesis, when Adam was placed in the Garden of Eden and offered eternal life, if he obeyed the restriction to avoid eating of the Tree of the Knowledge of Good and Evil. His violation of this prohibition broke the covenant relationship. Later, Noah had another covenant with God, this time sealed with the sign of the rainbow, signifying that God would never again destroy mankind (Gen. 9:13). The most detailed covenants were with Abraham, who was promised a land for his descendants, a son by Sarah, and progeny as numerous as the stars in the sky or the sands in the sea. These covenant promises were repeated, expanded on several occasions during the long life of Abraham (Gen. 15:18–21, 17:4–14).

One of the most extended statements of covenant promise in the Bible was in the **law** of Moses, or the Covenant Code (Exod. 14:7), an extended instruction in the law, which the people of the **Exodus** were to follow as evidence of their faith in and love of God. This is explained in considerable detail in Exodus, Leviticus, Numbers, and Deuteronomy—most of the Torah. In return for obedience to the law of God and a promise to worship only Yahweh (Exod. 34:14), God promised to bring them safely into the Promised land (Exod. 34:11). They were to be his special people, protected by him.

Later covenants include the promise of God to David that he and his heirs would inherit the **throne**. It is this covenant that led the Hebrews to assume that the **King** of Kings would come from the line of David, from the root of Jesse. This explains the detailed genealogies in both Luke and Matthew, tracing Jesus's lineage back to David.

Types of Covenant

In the ancient world, various types of treaties and covenants governed relations between peoples, in particular parity treaties between two equal states, and overlord treaties between a powerful monarch and a vassal state. The scriptural covenants usually took the form that was ordinarily used between a sovereign and a subject people, a common pattern in the Near East. It also had parallels to the traditional marriage contract, a formal agreement to the terms that we see in negotiations between Jacob and Laban for the hand of Rachael. Scripture clearly indicates that God's promises are based on his forgiving grace, and when the covenant peoples act rebelliously, the covenant may be annulled (Ezek. 16:59–63; Hos. 1:9).

Secular and lesser covenants also appear in Scripture, marking agreements and treaties between brothers, leaders, or tribes as signals of peaceful resolution of conflicts. They could be treaties between nations (1 Sam. 11:1), leaders of two peoples (Gen. 21:25:32), or the king and his people (1 Chron. 11:3) and agreements among individuals (Gen. 21:27), between a conquering king and a vassal (Ezek. 17:13–19), or between friends (1 Sam. 18:3–4).

The **prophets** considered the covenant relationship to be more spiritual than physical. They interpreted the sufferings of Israel to be a result of a broken covenant, requiring a need for a spiritual awakening. Jeremiah noted that God was willing to forgive his people's transgressions and write in their hearts a new covenant (Jer. 31:30), which would be universally available. And Ezekiel associated the new covenant with the coming of the **Messiah** (Ezek. 37:21). It was this prophesy that Luke echoed (1:20) in the narrative of the Incarnation.

In the New Testament, Jesus announced at the **Last Supper**, that the cup of **wine** he offered his disciples was " the New Covenant" in his blood, a sign and seal of his death and **resurrection** and a promise of his coming again. Believers were encouraged to perform the ritual of drinking the cup and eating the **bread** in remembrance of him, until he should return. In the book of Hebrews, the author expands on the gracious covenant relationship between God and his people, which he interprets as applying to those who accept the sacrificial death of Christ and follow him—"the mediator of a new covenant" (Heb. 7:22, 8–10, 9:15). *See also* Blessing; Curse; Oaths; Seals.

Further Reading

Anderson, Bernard W. "Covenant," in *Oxford Companion to the Bible*. New York: Oxford University Press, 1993. Miller, Madeleine S. and J. Lane Miller. "Covenant," in *Harper's Bible Dictionary*. New York: Harper and Row, 1961.

Creation

(Gen. 1–3) "In the beginning, God created the **heaven** and the earth." Thus begins Genesis, the book of beginnings. The Hebrews believed that God spoke and the universe came into being, revealing him to be a powerful, creative, preexistent deity. Unlike the other creation stories of the Fertile Crescent, this great poetic narrative in Scripture reveals an orderly God, who created the heaven and "the earth, which was without form, and void; and darkness was upon the face of the deep," moved "upon the face of the **waters**," and then proclaimed: "Let there be light; and there was light." He separated the light from the darkness, and named the Day and the Night, establishing time by calling this "the first day."

He then created the firmament, separating the waters from the earth, dividing the waters below from the waters above. He gathered the waters together, making the seas and the dry land. He filled the earth with grass, fruit trees, and all manner of herbs. He set lights in the firmament, the sun and the moon, and the stars, providing for light and for the marking of seasons, days, and years.

He then filled this physical setting with living things: the waters with whales and **fish**, the air with **birds**, the earth with cattle and every kind of beast and creeping thing. And finally, on the last day of creation, "So God created man in his own image, in the image of God created he him, male and female created he them." Looking at his creation, he called each day's work "good," finally blessing it all, and admonishing the humans to "Be fruitful, and multiply, and replenish the earth, and subdue it: and have dominion over the fish of the sea, and over the fowl of the air, and over every living thing that moveth upon the earth." On the seventh day, God rested, blessing and sanctifying the day—the only day for which the Hebrews had a name—the **Sabbath**.

In the following chapters of Genesis, a more detailed story emerges, telling of the **Garden of Eden,** locating it "eastward" with rivers and plants and gold and onyx. In this garden were the "tree of life, and the tree of knowledge of good and evil." Here God formed Adam, and later—from his rib—Eve, admonishing them to eat the fruit of any of the trees except from the tree of knowledge. This ideal human existence in perfect harmony with both God and nature was broken by the violation of the single rule, the subsequent lies and judgment, and finally the expulsion from the garden.

These remarkable opening chapters of Genesis tell us a great deal about the God of the Hebrews, Christians, and Moslems. He is a benevolent and thoughtful god, who created and sustains the entire world in all its variety. He created humans in his image, as guardians of his creation, as social creatures, free to disobey their maker. He provided a rich and plentiful world for human existence. He talked with Adam in the morning mists, suggesting that he enjoyed communion with his creatures. He even provided, by his own example, the day of rest. But he is also a law-giving and judging deity. On each day of creation, he pronounced his work "good." And when the man and woman in the garden fell for the blandishments of the **serpent,** ignoring the clear command of God, he cast them out of Eden, but did not abandon them.

This systematic, intelligent, moral, self-sustaining, and harmonious creation, placed under the stewardship of humans, who themselves remain under the dominion of God, contrasts dramatically with stories from other primitive peoples, whose myths tell of primal eggs, monstrous dragons, and primordial battles. The **Egyptian**, **Greek**, and **Babylonian** myths revealed gods that were cruel, chaotic, limited, brutal, and sexual. These variant creation myths gave shape to and reflect very different religions and cultures. The Hebrew narratives of the seven days of creation and the brief sojourn in the Garden of Eden provided this remarkable people with an image of a stern, creative, and loving God. He acted justly while showing mercy and revealed that he lived both in and out of time, knowing their hidden sins and predestined the lives of them and their descendants until the end of the world. He revealed himself here as the **Alpha and Omega**.

From these first chapters in Genesis, which were undoubtedly passed in oral form from generation to generation over the centuries, the Hebrews came to understand their own special calling, their relationship to their physical surrounding, their relationships with other peoples, and the nature of their god.

Later portions of Scripture reinforce the Creation narrative and expand on it—Job presents the Creator's perspective (Job 38:4–11); the Psalmist proclaims God's glory and power, revealed in his remarkable works (Ps. 8:3–4, 19, 36:5–6, 90:5–9, 104, 139, 148, etc.); Solomon speaks of God's wisdom (Prov. 3:19–20, 8:24–31); and the **prophets** wonder at the power of God and his purpose in the Creation and envision a new creation of a new heaven and a new earth (Isa. 40:12, 45:18, 65:17; Jer. 31:22, 32:17–21, 51:15–16, etc.).

In the New Testament, John places Christ at the Creation, calling him "the Word" or the *Logos* (John 1:1–4). The **Epistles** also speak of the creation (Rom. 8:18–23; 1 Cor. 15:39; Heb. 1:3, 10–11, 11:3). And Revelation notes the creation of man, the "breath of life" (Rev. 13:15).

The powerful narrative of Creation undergirds most of Scripture, providing the foundation for the worship of God and evidence of his power and majesty. It also establishes relationships on earth—between man and woman, humans and animals. And it sets in place the concepts of justice, mercy, sin, foreknowledge, free will, and love. *See also* Cosmology.

Further Reading

Sproul, Barbara C. *Primal Myths: Creating the World*. New York: Harper and Row, Publishers, 1979. Tischler, Nancy M. *Legacy of Eve: Women of the Bible*. Atlanta: John Knox Press, 1977.

Crown

A crown is a headdress that signifies the role of the wearer, often a royal role. Crowns may range from twisted bands of gold or vine to elaborate turbans. The purpose is to signify honor accorded to a person or significant object. The word, especially when used as a verb, frequently becomes a metaphor, using the physical action or accomplishment as an image: to be "crowned with glory" (Ps. 8:5) or to have children or wisdom providing ones "crown."

Scripture makes various uses of the word "crown," using five different terms. *Crown* serves as either a verb or a noun. The term *zer*, which was used in Exodus, referred to the twisted bands of gold molding that were placed around the **Ark of the Covenant**, the **incense**, and the table of showbread (Exod. 25:11, 25:24, 25, 30:3; Emil G. Hirsch, Frank Knight Sanders, and Kaufmann Kohler 2004).

A second word for crown, *nezer*, was used for the crown worn by the high **priest**, carrying the words "Holy to Jehovah" (Exod. 28:36). This term was also used for the headdress of the **king**, but crowns were not invariably used by the Hebrews as the mark of the king.

Pagan crowns and pagan usages had other words: The *kether,* or diadem, was used by any monarch, including the queen Vashti (Esther 1:11). The term *atarah,* meaning the crown of any king, was used in the case of David's coronation (2 Sam. 12:30). He was crowned with a heavy gold crown set with precious **stones**, which had been previously worn by an Ammonite monarch (1 Chron. 20:2).

Atarah is also used to signify the rewards given at pagan games. This is similar to the New Testament meaning of the word, as a crown of victory or triumph. Paul, in particular, with his background in Greek culture, was interested in sports and used terminology of sports in numerous of his epistles (Phil. 4:1).

In the New Testament, the most common term for the crown is the Greek word *stephanos,* which indicates the "garland or wreath awarded the victor in a contest (1 Cor. 9:25). In derision, a *stephanos* of thorns platted by soldiers was placed on Christ's brow" (John 19:5; Matt. 27:29; Madeleine S. Miller and J. Lane Miller 1961, 120). This crown of thorns, which was pressed down on Jesus's head as he was pronounced "King of the Jews," was an ironic combination of the garland and the traditional regal crown. The final term, *diadema,* also used in the New Testament, denotes royalty, as in Revelation 19:12.

Because the crown was so important to the ceremony and person of the king, it was often used, like **throne**, as a simple way to refer to the king himself. Unfortunately, images or artifacts that reveal the designs of the Hebrew crowns have not been discovered. We can picture the possibilities only by looking at the grand crowns worn by monarchs in the region and speculating that there were probably similarities. Most of them seem more like elegant turbans than the sharp, pointed, gem-encrusted crowns used in modern times.

One of the more memorable examples is God's promise of the "incorruptible crown" (1 Peter 4). With the New Testament writers, the crown was often associated with the triumph of the life to come. In Revelation, the four and twenty elders in heaven have "crowns of gold," which they cast before the throne of the Lord (Rev. 4:4, 11).

At various times in history, crowns served as a popular adornment for all the guests at a feast. They were standard for revelers at Bacchic **feasts**. Before the destruction of the **Temple**, even the Jews would sit adorned with crowns on their heads at feasts (Emil G. Hirsch, Frank Knight Sanders et al. 2004.) They were also used to adorn the bride and bridegroom at weddings. At certain points in Jewish history, even the steer that was to be sacrificed might be crowned with a garland of **olives** to mark his role in the thanksgiving ceremonies. Eventually, however, because the gentiles placed crowns, or garlands, on their idols, garlands were forbidden to the Jews.

For the **Christians** of biblical times, the crown was usually the enemy's symbol, as the emperors persecuted the early **Church**. Later, it was accepted by the Church for ceremonial purposes, designating the king the Lord's anointed. In some modern churches, the pontiff wears a head covering that resembles the ancient crowns of Israel. In Roman Catholicism, for example, part of the pontifical insignia is the miter, a headdress that adapts the high priest's turban with a triangular crown that points heavenward (Dom Robert LeGall 2000, 80). *See also* Clothing; Sports.

Further Reading

Hirsch, Emil G., Frank Knight Sanders, and Kaufmann Kohler, "Crown," http://www.jewishencyclopedia.com (accessed November 11, 2004). LeGall, Dom Robert. *Symbols of Catholicism.* New York: Assouline Publishing, 2000. Miller, Madeleine S. and J. Lane Miller, *Harper's Bible Dictionary.* New York: Harper and Row, Publishers, 1961.

Crucifixion, Cross

(Matt 27:37; Mark 15:26; Luke 23:38; John 19:19–22) The term *crucifixion* refers to the execution on a cross, a construct with intersecting pieces of wood on which the victim was nailed or tied. All four **Gospel** writers describe the crucifixion of Jesus Christ.

Romans used crosses for the execution of criminals, a particularly painful and humiliating form of punishment. **Assyrians**, Persians, Phoenicians of Carthage, **Egyptians**, and **Greeks** were also known to have used the cross

Different forms of crosses were used by the Romans and Greeks, with the cross bar at various positions, sometimes using a simple tree for the upright and sometimes nothing more than a post, with the hands nailed above the head.

as an instrument of execution (Madeleine S. Miller and J. Lane Miller 1961, 118). In the Old Testament, criminals who had been judged guilty of blasphemy—the crime with which Jesus was charged—were usually stoned to death. The dead bodies, however, might be hung on a tree as a warning to the community (Deut. 21:22–23). This may explain the New Testament use of the term *tree* when referring to the cross of Christ (Acts 5:30, 1 Pet. 2:24). The dead bodies, which were considered accursed, were removed and buried in the night (J. B. Torrance 1980, 340).

Where crucifixion was used, it was limited to **slaves** and the worst kind of criminals. There were at least three types of cross: the single upright post on which a victim was tied or impaled, the T-shaped cross with two beams, and the X-shaped cross, often thought to be the actual one used in Jesus's crucifixion. The cross of Jesus, however, had space above his head for the sign that read "King of the Jews." The very use of the cross as the instrument of death indicates that the final orders were issued by Romans, not Jews, and the charge was sedition rather than the theologically specific one of blasphemy.

The victim was usually scourged before the crucifixion using a whip of leather thongs. He then carried his own cross through the streets to the place of execution, in this case Golgotha. For Jesus, this public humiliation was intensified by the mockery connected with dressing him in a robe, a **crown** of thorns, and fixing a to the cross.

Because death was considered a defilement, executions in Jewish culture took place outside the city walls. The person to be crucified was secured to the cross by nails driven through his hands and feet. Archaeologists have discovered remnants of a crucified man's heel, indicating that the nails went through both heels together. This means that his legs would have been twisted to allow this awkward and painful act. Some believe that a small shelf under the feet braced the body to avoid asphyxiation (a death deemed too quick to provide sufficient suffering). A final act to hasten death was the breaking of the legs, done to the two thieves, but not to Christ, as he had already died. The spear thrust in his side was to ensure that the crucified man was dead. The process ensured maximum pain, hurried at the end only because of Sabbath requirements.

While this was happening, the soldiers were allowed to divide his **clothing**—in this case casting lots for his robe, which would have been spoiled by tearing it into parts. The crucifixion was public, with friends and family as well as strangers able to witness the suffering. After the death, the body was lowered to the ground and taken away for burial. On some occasions, it remained exposed on the cross as a lesson to others.

The arrest, trial, flagellation, and condemnation that preceded the final crucifixion are all detailed in the various passion stories, most vividly in Mark. This series of events marks the Christian Easter week commemorations, beginning with the **Last Supper** on Thursday, through the time on the cross on Friday, to the **Resurrection** on Easter Sunday.

Christians saw the suffering and death on the cross as the fulfillment of **prophecy**. The unblemished Lamb of God, sacrificed for the sins of the world, became a central tenet of Christian thought. The sign of the cross thus symbolized this remarkable scene. The Apostles' Creed, accepted by many Christian **churches**, asserts that Christ "suffered under Pontius Pilate, was crucified dead and buried, descended into **Hell** and rose the third day from the dead and ascended into **Heaven**, where he sitteth on the right hand of God the Father Almighty."

Much of Christian theology, ritual, art, and drama derive from the Crucifixion. Paul spoke often of Christ's triumph over Death, and the recitation of the Apostles' Creed reminds Christians of the event regularly. Artists through the ages have painted and sculpted the different scenes attendant to the Crucifixion; great musicians have written oratorios in tribute to the Passion; the Passion plays that date from the Middle Ages continue in some venues even today. Catholics venerate the Stations of the Cross, specific scenes in the great drama of the Passion.

The empty cross and the crucifix with the figure of the dying Christ have become standard symbols for many Christians. One writer expressed the powerful symbolism in the image of the Cross: a "combination of the horizontal and vertical axes," This "intersection of those two lines is a point of meeting, of convergence and of synthesis. Conversely, the cross also evokes images of torture, suffering and confrontation" (Dom Robert Le Gall 2000, 22). *See also* Law; Punishments; Trials, Courts.

Further Reading

Le Gall, Dom Robert. *Symbols of Catholicism*. New York: Assouline Publishing, 2000. Miller, Madeleine and J. Lane Miller, "Cross," in *Harper's Bible Dictionary*. New York: Harper and Row, 1961. Torrance, J. B. "Cross, Crucifixion," in *The Illustrated Bible Dictionary*. Sydney, Australia: Tyndale House Publishers, 1980.

Cures, Medicine

(**Deut. 32:39, Exod. 15:26, Lev. 13–14**) Inasmuch as ancient Jews believed the words of Deuteronomy 32:39: "I kill, and I make alive; I have wounded, and I heal," there was little impetus for the study of human medicine. Sickness was thought by many to be a punishment for sin. Some may also have thought that it resulted from the **curses** hurled at them by enemies. If a man fell ill, he usually went to the sanctuary or to a holy man— a **prophet** or a **priest**—on the assumption that his basic problem was sin.

Yet the practice of medicine was sanctioned by the **law** of Moses, which noted possible cures for those wounded when "men strive together, and one smites another" (Exod. 15:26). There were "wound dressers" and surgeons from early times: Joseph employed a house physician (Gen. 50:2) and Isaiah mentioned physicians as well (Isa. 3:7). Wounds in different parts of the body, caused by swords, arrows, hammers, and so forth, are noted frequently in the history books. Some led to inflammation and abscesses, gangrene, and putrid discharges (Deut. 28:27, 35; Ps. 38:6; Prov. 7:4, 14:30). These were usually treated with wine or oil, bandages, and sutures.

Priests did not monopolize the practice of medicine, as in some other ancient cultures, but they were assigned the task of supervising contagious diseases. Mosaic law is full of details about the treatment of **disease**, which was linked to ritual impurity. "Priests diagnosed diseases according to a system of purity, which determined whether or not a person should be quarantined from the community and administered purification rites for the malady" (Philip J. King and Lawrence E. Stager 2001, 77).

A ritual for diagnosing and treating the dreaded disease leprosy takes up two extended chapters in Leviticus (13–14). At the end of his separation from the rest of the people, the recovering leper had a ceremony of purification that involved killing a **bird** so that its blood dripped in **water**, and throwing another bird alive into the water, along with cedar wood, red cochineal, and hyssop; then releasing a live bird in the open country, and finally sprinkling the leper with water and pronouncing him **clean**. Seven days later, he shaved all the hair off his body, washed his **clothes**, took a **bath**, and was finally considered cured (Lev. 14:2–9). This whole ceremony was followed on the eighth day with a **sacrifice** of reparation—a sacrifice for sin and a holocaust, with a detailed ritual involving the right ear, the right thumb, and the right big toe of the man who had been cured; and ending with an anointment of oil (Roland deVaux 1961, 462–463). This elaborate description may well point to the quasi-magical manner in which many diseases were treated.

Herbal remedies were probably used with some frequency in ancient times. We know that Rachel and her sister thought that the mandrake root could cure barrenness in women. It was thought to increase sexual desire (Gen. 30:14–16). Among many ancient people, various plants were thought to encourage the abortion of fetuses and to cure various ills, but these are not mentioned in Scripture. We do know of the "balm in Gilead" (Jer. 8:22), medicinal leaves (Ezek. 47:12), painkillers (Mark 15:23), and even Jesus's use of earth and saliva (John 9:6–7). Red things were thought to be especially effective—red cochineal, red water, the ashes of a red heifer. Wormwood, gall water (a concoction of bitter herbs), and various oils were probably used by families for medical emergencies. Other, more nauseating, possibilities included dog's dung, human excreta and urine, all of which were thought to help drive away demonic forces. They discovered that belladonna helped check bladder spasms and poppy relieved pain and produced sleep (Robert T. Boyd 1969, 37). Like other practitioners of folk medicine, the Jews considered the possibilities of magical causes for their aches and pains—evil spirits, the supernatural powers of the enemy, and the ill will of the dead (Joseph Jacobs 2005). They were particularly concerned with the power of **demons** over the human body and mind.

A fig poultice was placed on Hezekiah's boil to cure it (Isa. 38:21). Mineral baths, especially at natural springs or in the Dead Sea, were popular among the Romans, who built spas for their use. A standard treatment of wounds was the use of **wine** and **oil**, probably effective as the wine would wash and sterilize and the oil would soothe and protect the wound. Isaiah shows of something of contemporary medicine in his description of his people as sick unto death: "From the sole of the foot even unto the head there is no soundness in it; but wounds, and bruises, and fresh stripes; they have not been squeezed, neither bound up, neither mollified with oil" (Isa. 1:6). The Good Samaritan used this treatment for the wounded stranger. Paul also recommended a little wine "for the stomach's sake" (1 Tim. 5:23), indicating that it was seen as an aid to good digestion. And King Lemuel suggested wine as a restorative for a dying man (Prov. 31:6).

For broken bones, there was a primitive form of bone setting in use (Ezek. 30:21). The Psalmist spoke of broken bones, leading us to believe that they were fairly common. Isaiah mentioned crutches, which like walking sticks must have been used for handicapped people. There is evidence that the Jews of the Talmudic period had a fairly thorough knowledge of the bones and muscles of the body, based on careful study of dead animals and humans. (One problem lay in the Hebrews' prohibition against touching the dead, requiring the purification of a body that they chose to examine.)

The only surgeries mentioned in the Bible are **circumcision** and castration (the latter being forbidden), but archaeologists have found skulls indicating that even brain surgery was practiced. The **Egyptians**, who appear to have been skilled in medicine quite early, left a surgical papyrus that is thought to date from the seventeenth B.C., which includes a surgeon's notebook (Madeleine S. Miller and J. Lane Miller 1961,138). The Ebers Papyrus deals with internal diseases, and the Edwin-Smith Papyrus, which is the oldest surgical document known, analyzes many disorders common to humans, such as wounds, dislocation, fractures, tumors, ulcers, and abscesses. The Egyptians knew about lint for absorbing moisture, adhesive plaster and stitching to close incisions, and salves to soothe and protect wounds (Robert T. Boyd 1969, 37). Archaeologists have discovered evidence in Palestine of some fairly invasive medical practices. Human skulls have been found with cuts that indicate "trepanning," an operation in which the skull bone is sawed away to relieve pressure on the brain. Signs of healing indicate that the surgery was successful and the patient recovered, at least for a time.

Apparently mental illness was thought to be soothed by music, as David performed for Saul. And demonic possession was treated by exorcism. In the most spectacular case recorded, Jesus drove the demons from the Gadarene demoniac into swine, which then fled over the cliff into the Sea of Galilee (Mark 5:1–13). As in his other healing miracles, Christ was able to cleanse the mind or body of pollutants by a simple act or word, testifying to his authority over demons and diseases.

The **Greeks** attributed medical science to Aesculapius, who was thought to restore men to health by means of healing oracles. A priestly caste grew up in Thessaly and other places where he was worshipped. In these places, temple physicians kept records of sickness that serve as interesting chronicles of ancient diseases and physical problems. The subsequent tradition of Hippocrates (the source of the Hippocratic oath, still used by doctors) is also chronicled in documents three centuries before Christ. He was followed by Galen and others, but medicine did not flourish until the wave of scientific experimentation that came with the Renaissance made it less of an art and more of a science.

When kings and others consulted foreign physicians from Egypt or Mesopotamia, they undoubtedly received more sophisticated treatment than the common peasant or soldier. Herod the Great, with his final diseases, surely had a host of physicians in attendance, but this is not documented in Scripture, which sees human health in God's hands. *See also* Clean, Unclean; Disease; Physicians; Wine.

Further Reading

Boyd, Robert T. *Tells, Tombs and Treasure: A Pictorial Guide to Biblical Archaeology*. New York: Bonanza Books, 1969. DeVaux, Roland. *Ancient Israel: Its Life and Institutions*. Grand Rapids, Mich.: William B. Eerdmans Publishing Company, 1961. King, Philip J. and Lawrence E. Stager. *Life in Biblical Israel*. Louisville, Ky.: Westminster John Knox Press, 2001. Jacobs, Joseph. "Folk Medicine," http://www.jewishencyclopedia.com (accessed April 22, 2005). Miller, Madeleine S. and J. Lane Miller. "Diseases and Healing," in *Harper's Bible Dictionary*. New York: Harper and Row, 1961. Schechter, Solomon, C. D. Spivak, Joseph Jacobs, and Frederick T. Haneman. "Medicine," http://www.jewishencyclopedia.com (accessed April 22, 2005). Senfelde, Leopold. "History of Medicine," http://www.newadvent.org (accessed April 22, 2005).

Curse

(Num 22:6, 17, Deut. 27, Luke 6:28) A curse is the opposite of a **blessing**. It is a prayer that God will bring harm to the person involved. It rests on the premise that one can bring calamity on people or things merely by the power of the spoken word, regardless of the moral justification. Like blessing, cursing was based on the belief that words had power, that the word once pronounced would accomplish its mission. The concept of cursing and blessing was modified somewhat over time, with a growing awareness that the "causeless curse" would not be fulfilled (Prov. 26:2).

For Hebrews, one of the worst curses a person could utter was against God (Exod. 22:28), parents (Exod. 21:17), authorities (Exod. 22:28), and the helpless deaf (Lev. 19:14). The child who cursed his parents might be put to death; the man who cursed God was guilty of **blasphemy** and might be stoned.

Cursing was permissible when prompted by religious motives. The **priests**, the Psalmist, or the **prophets** might curse those who misled their people or denied that the Messiah would come. The enemies of Israel were also cursed, largely because they were standing in the way of God's plan for history. God himself cursed the serpent in the Garden of Eden (Gen. 3:14). Noah cursed Canaan (Gen. 9:25). And Christ cursed the barren fig tree (Mark 11:14), in addition to the cities that failed to believe (Matt. 11:21), the **scribes**, the **Pharisees**, and the damned (Matt. 25:41).

Conditional curses were often used as the threats in **oaths**. If the person swearing the oath should break it, he would bring on himself the evil he names. Thus, pronouncing a curse on a potential thief will protect property (Judg. 17:2, Prov. 29:24). A curse pronounced on an accused person, if it should come to pass, established the person's guilt (Num. 5:21–28, 1 Kings 8:31, 2 Chron. 6:22). Pronouncing a curse on anyone who should disobey enforced a command by persons in authority (1 Sam. 14:24; Gen. 24:41). Pronouncing a curse on anyone who might break a treaty guaranteed loyalty to the treaty (Gen. 26:28). It is in this last sense that curse was used in connection with Israel's **covenant** with the Lord, which bore similarities to a treaty (Deut. 29:18). In all these senses, the curse was understood as conditional, that is, efficacious only if some legal right or agreement had been violated.

Sometimes an individual may be referred to as a "curse" (Num. 5:21; Jer. 290:18), meaning that such a person is in so calamitous a situation that he or she embodies the consequence of a curse that one might wish on another. (In literature, especially sea stories such as "The Rime of the Ancient Mariner" and *Moby Dick*, this proves a powerful concept, probably deriving from both the story of Jonah and the traditions of the sea. Calling a person a "Jonah" indicated that he was cursed and the source of bad luck for all who were around him.)

Curses tend to follow formulaic patterns: "Cursed be" (Deut. 27:15–25, 28:16–19). spoken by person in authority and directed against a subordinate (Gen. 4:11; 1 Sam. 14:24, 28). The same general usage continues into the New Testament. Paul speaks of "being under a curse"(Gal. 3:10) because anyone who has heard the **Law** and failed to obey it is cursed

(Deut. 27:26). Jesus changed the view of curses by insisting that his followers should "bless them that curse you" (Luke 6:28).

Modern usage of the term *curse* is quite different and often much more flippant. People speak of foul language as "cursing." Actually, this usage is correct only when damnation is called down on one's adversary. In cultures where voodoo is practiced or superstition has considerable influence, people think of curses as bad luck caused by spells cast by **witches** or evil spirits. The conditional curse remains common in some societies, when people assert, "May lightening strike me if I am not speaking the truth." The ancient deep theological concept is rarely intended by moderns, who tend to use the terminology frivolously. *See also* Blessing; Covenant.

Further Reading

Conrad, Edgar W. "Curse," in *The Oxford Companion to the Bible.* New York: Oxford University Press, 1993. Fisher, J. H. "Cursing," http://www.newadvent.org (accessed April 24, 2005). Ginzberg, Louis and Caspar Levias. "Cursing," http://www.jewishencyclopedia.com (accessed April 24, 2005). Jastrow, Morris, Jr. and Wilhelm Nowack. "Blessing and Cursing," http://www.jewishencyclopedia.com (accessed April 24, 2005).

Dagon

(Josh.15:41, 19:27; Judg. 16:23–30; 1 Sam. 5:1–5) Dagon, a fertility god, was called the father of **Baal**, although in other places, Baal's father was named El. He was a nature god, with a name that derived from the Phoenician word for "grain." According to Ugaritic texts, he was worshipped from earliest times in the Euphrates Valley. Sargon of Accad was supposed to have paid homage to him in the twenty-third century B.C.

Some have speculated that he was a merman, the upper half of his body a man, the lower half a fish. It is not clear how the Israelites pictured him or what statues of him they might have seen. The first reference in Scripture leaves his image ambiguous, and the second seems to belie the portrayal of a fish-man.

In the Hebrew Bible, Dagon is mentioned only in connection with the **Philistines**. In the first case, these traditional enemies of the Hebrews chained Samson, captive and blinded, to the pillars of Dagon's temple. In his final heroic act, Samson pulled down the pillars on the worshippers of Dagon at Gaza (Judg. 16:23–30).

In a later scene, the Philistines captured the **Ark of the Covenant** and carried it to the house of Dagon "and set it by Dagon. And when they of Ashdod arose early on the morrow, behold Dagon was fallen upon his face to the earth before the ark of the Lord" (1 Sam. 5:3–4). When they tried again, the head of the statue came off and the palms of his hands were cut off, leaving only the stump of the fallen idol. The episode ends, "Therefore neither the priests of Dagon, nor any that come unto Dagon's house, tread on the threshold of Dagon in Ashdod unto this day" (1 Sam. 5:5). *See also* Ark of the Covenant; Baal, Baalim.

Further Reading

Albright, William F. *Yahweh and the Gods of Canaan*. Garden City, N.Y.: Doubleday & Company, Inc., 1969. Jeffries, David Lyle. "Dagon," in *A Dictionary of Biblical Tradition in English Literature*. Grand Rapids, Mich.: Williams B. Eerdmans Publishing Company, 1992.

Dance

(Exod. 15:20, 32:19, 2; Judg. 21:21, Sam. 6:5) Miriam and the other Israelite women danced and sang after the escape from the Egyptians. One of the most famous examples of dance occurred when David and his procession danced and sang their way to Jerusalem carrying the **Ark of the Covenant** (2 Sam. 6:5). In a more pagan episode, the children of Israel

Woman playing a tambourine and dancing in celebration, as Miriam and the other women would have done at the Exodus.

danced around the Golden Calf when Moses left them to spend time on the mountain with Jehovah.

The reference to David's dancing is a rare example of male dancers. In Scripture, it was usually the women who danced, whether the victory dances, the round dances, or the dances for simple entertainment. Job mentioned the children dancing (Job 21:11), and Ecclesiastes spoke of an appropriate time to dance (Eccles 3:4). The **Psalms** spoke of dancers accompanied by the sound of timbrels, probably a common practice (Ps. 150:4). Another Psalm told of turning **mourning** into dancing, suggesting that the people saw dance as a sign of joy (Ps. 30:11).

Scholars believe that most joyful occasions were celebrated with **music** and dance, whether the yearly festival at Shiloh (Judg. 21:21) or David's special delight at the bringing of the Ark of the Covenant to its final home. Most of the dancing noted in Scripture had a religious function and was accompanied with instrumental music and singing. The happy folk dancing of the grape gatherers (Judg. 21:21) and other dancing at community gatherings seem, for the most part, more wholesome than the **Canaanite** fertility dances or the **Greek** bacchanalia. There was music to praise God (Ps. 149:3, 150:4) and to express joy. One of the happier of Christ's **parables** ends with dancing children at the Prodigal Son's homecoming activities (Luke 15:25). Surely ancient **wedding feasts** must have involved dancing just as modern weddings often do.

The saddest occasion for a dance in the New Testament was the apparently lascivious dance of Salome—the famous dance of the seven veils—for which she was rewarded by King Herod with the head of John the Baptist (Mark 6:21–22). This event seems to follow the Greek custom of employing professional women dancers rather than having a dance shared by the whole community. Unfortunately, it was Salome's sinister abuse of this joyous expression that became the basis for later judgments against pagan forms of dance, and eventually a prohibition against dance in **Christian** circles. The ecstatic dancers of certain cults probably also alienated Christians, who have often condemned the practice as unworthy of the faithful believers. In early Christendom, the lascivious dances of their pagan neighbors led the Church Fathers to proscribe dancing, as well as instrumental music, relating it to the practices of prostitutes.

At various times in Christian history, the "dire warnings and deep suspicions" of the Church Fathers regarding this ecstatic dimension of music and dance have been ignored. The heavily rhythmic music and dance, which is described in the Old Testament, can produce a physical response that bypasses the intellect. This has repeatedly drawn interest toward dance and has alarmed concerned critics.

The Ethiopian Church, from earliest times, used dance as a part of sacred ceremony. When Africans came to America as slaves, they brought their sacred dance traditions with them, carrying some of them into modern times. The old camp meetings, for instance, had leaping and shuffling that approximated David's ecstatic dance. Mahalia Jackson (1911–1972) recounted the services of African American worshippers she knew in her childhood:

> These people had no choir and no organ. They used the drum, the cymbal, the tambourine and the steel triangle. Everybody in there sang, and they clapped and stomped their feet, and sang with their whole bodies. They had a beat, a rhythm we held onto from slavery days, and their music was so strong and expressive. It used to bring tears to my eyes. (Andrew Wilson-Dickenson 1992, 192–193, 202)

Some of this tradition has even continued in Protestant worship in spite of Calvin's firm banishment of dance from worship, in accord with its denial of the flesh. Even Bach's Christian music, hardly a place one would expect physical abandon, has been described as "an apotheosis of the dance." The chorus of his B Minor Mass leads some musicologists to recall Bernard of Clairvaux's words:

> Jesus the dancers' master is,
> A great skill at the dance he is,
> He turns to the right, he turns to the left,
> All must follow his teaching deft
> (Andrew Wilson-Dickenson 1992, 98–99).

Contemporaries noted that Bach, when directing rehearsals, was almost like Orpheus, swaying and letting the rhythm take possession of his limbs.

In modern times, a number of churches have revived religious dance as part of the worship service. Even fairly staid denominations, such as Episcopal and Presbyterian, have encouraged the limited use of artistic modern dance as part of worship, although not usually the ecstatic dance reminiscent of the whirling dervishes. The song "Lord of the Dance," referring back to Bernard of Clairvaux's image of Christ-the-Dancer, has become quite popular in recent times, played even on Christian radio stations, which generally promote evangelical Protestant music. Modern Gospel music and much charismatic worship follow rhythmic uses of ecstatic music, with practitioners often breaking into dance with hands in the air and bodies swaying to the beat of the music.

A more restrained, historical use of dance has also continued. Classical ballet has often used dance to tell Bible stories. This is particularly true of Jewish choreographers. Giora Manor traces a number of dance troupes among the Israelis who have delighted audiences with their use of the material from Scripture—"heroes and heroines, kings and sinners" (Giora Manor

1993, 148–149). One of the more famous of the modern Broadway musicals, *Fiddler on the Roof,* makes entertaining use of traditional Jewish folk dances. *See also* Festivals; Music; Song.

Further Reading

Manor, Giora. "Dance and the Bible," in *The Oxford Companion to the Bible*. New York: Oxford University Press, 1993. Wilson-Dickson, Andrew. *The Story of Christian Music: From Gregorian Chant to Black Gospel*. Minneapolis: Fortress Press, 1992.

Day of Atonement. *See Atonement, Day of*

Day of Judgment, Day of the Lord

(Ezek. 38–39; Isa. 2:11–17; Rev. 6:17) From earliest Scripture, the **Hebrews** anticipated an end to time. The **blessings** promised to the children of the **Covenant** were seen as events of some far distant time, a time when the Lord would reveal himself in thunder and lightening to smash the opposing powers of this world (Emil G. Hirsch 2004). The early **prophets** expanded on this anticipated day of judgment (Amos 3:2, 5:18, 8:9; Hosea 10:8). This process of purification by the devouring fire of God's judgment would leave the pure gold of God's chosen people. They anticipated at first that the judgment would fall on the gentiles, not on Israel, but this changed over time to a belief that the righteous remnant of the Jews would remain after the great Judgment Day. The day of the Lord was seen as a day of distress and desolation for most of humankind.

During the Exile, this vision was amplified so that judgment was aimed at individuals, not just the collective nations, and the individuals who were refined and redeemed would form the nucleus of the Messianic kingdom (Jer. 1:11–16; 23:7, 8; 24:33, 34). Isaiah expanded this to include the blessings on all nations, not just Israel (Isa 3:17; 12:14, 15; 16:19). This "New Covenant" was the one carried into New Testament times, when the idea of the **Messiah** became a living force.

After the Exile, Malachi focused on the judgment to come, emphasizing the role of the **Temple**, to which he expected God to come for his great judgment on that "great and dreadful day" (Mal. 4:23–24). These ideas were much debated during the time between the testaments, with some of the **Pharisees** and the **Essenes** expanding on the concepts.

Jesus referred to the Day of Judgment when discussing his **resurrection** and the Kingdom of God. The description of his Second Coming, described in Matthew 24, is vivid:

> immediately shall the sun be darkened, and the moon shall not give her light, and the stars shall fall from **heaven**, and the powers of the

heavens shall be shaken. And then shall appear the sign of the Son of man in heaven: and then shall all the **tribes** of the earth mourn, and they shall see the Son of man coming in the clouds of heaven with power and great glory. And he shall send his **angels** with a great sound of trumpet, and they shall gather together his elect from the four winds, from one end of heaven to the other. (Matt 24:29–31)

Jesus also quoted many of the prophets in his references to the Day of the Lord, emphasizing that he was continuing the well-known tradition.

Both Hebrew and Christian apocalyptic literature have references to the Day of the Lord or Judgment Day. As noted, the prophets looked forward to that time when God will come in judgment, the final battle against the forces of evil—"Israel's final combat with the combined forces of the heathen nations under the leadership of Gog and Magog, barbarian tribes of the North" (Ezek. 38–39). "Assembled for a fierce attack upon Israel in the mountains near Jerusalem, they will suffer a terrible and crushing defeat, and Israel's land will thenceforth forever remain the seat of God's kingdom" (Kaufmann Kohler 2004). This final cataclysmic scene of **Armageddon** will end with the defeat of the heathen nations forever, and God's kingdom will be established on earth. According to the New Testament writers, the New Jerusalem will be a city that needed no temple, for God himself will dwell in it.

In these final days, God will judge the nations as well as the secrets of hearts (Ezek. 30; Isa. 2:12, 3:18). Images of thunder and lightening, earthquakes, and tidal waves emphasize how terrible this great day will be when humankind falls into the hands of the living God (Isa. 13:22, Jer. 46:10; Lam. 2; Heb. 10:31; Rev. 16:12–21). In those days, there will also be the coming of a Messiah and a travail of the Messianic time. There will also be false prophets and false messiahs. After the final victory, at the sound of a trumpet, the dead will be resurrected. The saints will join the Son of Man in a great banquet and celebration among those enjoying the blessing of God.

Although Jewish scripture teems with references to the Last Judgment, the prophets, especially at the time of the Exile, found great comfort in this idea that Israel would finally be redeemed by God, and the pagan nations would be defeated in that great day when justice would roar down like a mighty stream. Rather than a day of doom, the prophets predicted the downfall of the heathen nations and the triumph of God's people over the idolaters of the earth.

The Christian tradition continued this belief, with emphasis on the defeat of **Babylon** the Great (now seen as **Rome**) and the Second Coming of Christ, who will invite all believers to the wedding feast of the Lamb. Much of Revelation deals with this vision. The Messiah will first undergo a time of plagues and travails, but will finally preside over a world of perfect peace and harmony, where the resurrected will live forever in a condition of eternal bliss. This will be the "new heaven and the new earth" to which Isaiah referred (Isa. 11:1–10, 65:17–25).

Scholars over the centuries have studied and interpreted these various and scattered bits of Scripture in an effort to divine what the last days will bring and when they will come. Much of **apocryphal** literature deals with predictions regarding the end times. Jewish and Christian scholars have both written about the subject. Sermons picturing sinners in the hands of an angry God and novels dealing with the millennium have excited and frightened many over the years. Perennially, new prophets proclaim that the end of the world is at hand, identifying signs of the great day of judgment. *See also* Afterlife; Apocalypse, Apocalyptic Literature; Kingdom of God; Messiah.

Further Reading

Jeffrey, David Lyle. "Second Coming," in *A Dictionary of Biblical Tradition in English Literature*. Grand Rapids, Mich.: William B. Eerdmans Publishing Company, 1992. Hirsch, Emil G. "Day of the Lord," http://www.jewishencyclopedia.com (accessed December 23, 2004). Kohler, Kaufmann. "Eschatology," http://www.jewishencyclopedia.com. (accessed December 23, 2004). Minear, Paul S. "Day of the Lord," in *The Oxford Companion to the Bible*. New York: Oxford University Press, 1993.

Dead Sea. See Geography

Demons

(Gen. 6:1–4; Num. 5:14; Judg. 9:23; 1 Sam. 16:124; 1 Kings 22:22; Hos. 4:12; Matt. 4:1–11, 24; Luke 10:17, 17:20, 9:34; Acts 19:11–16; Rev. 12:9) Many ancient people—and many moderns—have believed in a vast supernatural world, populated by good and bad spirits, which influence many of the day-to-day events in human life.

Having come from Mesopotamia, a land full of demonology, the Israelites retained strong superstitions about the powers of evil spirits, believing that they were controlled by God. In Mesopotamian culture, demons were thought to dwell in deserts and solitary places, including ruins. Magical incantations speak of them as haunting the wilderness, sometimes appearing as black ravens (Theodor H. Gaster 1969, 577–578). They were seen as mischievous, but not diabolical, nor under the orders of a satanic power. Some believed them to be independent of both God and Satan, living in a kind of nether world (Isa. 38:11; Job 14:13; Ps. 16:10, 49:16, 139:8). Others believed they were semi-celestial and semi-infernal and had no supernatural power beyond that allowed by God. Some believed they were the idols of the **Canaanites**, which were thought to seduce humans into worshipping pagan gods (Emil G. Hirsch, Richard Gottheil, Kaufmann Kohler, and Isaac Broydé 2004).

The demons mentioned in the Bible divide into two classes: the *se'irim* ("hairy beings") and the *shedim* ("devils"). The satyr-like demons were thought to dance in the wilderness (Isa. 8:21) and may even have been nothing more than **goats** (thus serving as an explanation of the ritual of the scapegoat which was driven out to Azael, the goatlike demon of the wilderness) (Lev. 16:10). Because leprosy was thought to come from such creatures, a sacrifice was essential to free one of the **disease**. The ritual of the **bird** sent off into the wilderness may have been a means of carrying the disease back from whence it came.

Demons were sometimes seen as evil spirits; sometimes as night, midday, or morning spirits; sometimes as the cause of famine and earthquake. They were thought to surround humans on all sides, a thousand on the left, and ten thousand on the right (Ps. 91:7), hovering around the house and field, dwelling in groups in nut trees, shady spots, roofs of **houses**, under gutters, near ruins, cemeteries, and privies, in water, oil and breadcrumbs cast on the ground (Emil G. Hirsch, Richard Gottheil et al. 2004). They were thought to be particularly dangerous at night, Lilith (the night-hag) being the chief danger in the dark.

Their main task was to cause harm to humankind. Of the numerous diseases thought to have been caused by demons, brain disorders, blindness, epilepsy, melancholy, and illnesses attendant to childbirth were the most frequent. They would enter the body and seize the person, taking possession and even speaking through the victim in a different voice. To cure the diseased person, the demons had to be drawn out or ordered out through exorcism.

They were thought to be under the dominion of a chief, sometimes called "Ashmodai" or "Samael" (the angel of death) or Satan. The queen of the demons was Lilith, pictured with wings and long flowing hair. In the New Testament, Beelzebub or Lucifer is named as their chief. Some believed that Lilith was their mother, bearing them to Adam. More generally, **Christians** have tended to believe that they are the offspring of the **angels** who fell with Lucifer, those who mingled with the daughters of Adam. They were disembodied spirits who were allowed to do the work of destruction until the **Day of Judgment**. This concept seems to explain the image in Revelation 12:9: "And the great dragon was cast out, that old serpent, called the Devil, and Satan, which deceiveth the whole world: he was cast out into the earth, and his angels were cast out with him."

Dealing with evil spirits was a complex matter. The best prophylactic against demons was obedience to the **law**. In numerous cases, washing of hands was thought to be the cure for diseases and the best preventive. Obedience to the other commandments was also thought to be a protection. There were also rituals, much like **witchcraft**, and there were **prayers**, which were thought to be especially effective before going to bed at night. There were also incantations, to be recited before drinking **wine** or performing other activities. The superstitions were numerous and local, communicated largely by word of mouth.

In the Old Testament, the term "evil spirit" usually is followed with the words "from the Lord." Thus the evil spirit that tormented Saul was recognized to be God-sent (1 Sam. 16:14–23). When David played the harp to soothe Saul's madness, the spirit returned with even greater force, motivating him to violence (1 Sam. 19:9). Only in the apocryphal book Tobit do evil angels or spirits play a significant role.

By New Testament times, however, the greater part of the Jewish and gentile world believed in the evil powers of demons and magic formulas by which these spirits could be subdued. The **Essenes** in particular and many of the Gnostics were interested in studies of the occult and **magic**. Those who first saw John the Baptist preaching in the wilderness, neither eating nor drinking, insisted, "He has a demon" (Matt. 11:18). It was a common view among the early Christians, like their Jewish relatives, that the devil brought diseases and that demons must be driven out of those afflicted with madness.

Jesus himself describes the restless evil spirit that possesses a man or woman and is driven out of him or her (Matt. 12:43; Luke 11:24). Numerous of the afflictions that he healed were attributed to evil spirits or demons (Luke 4:33, 9:42; Mark 3:30, 7:25). When he drove the demons out of the men or women, they would depart with a shriek (Mark 1:26). Most notable among the examples of the demon-possessed were Mary Magdalene, who was possessed of seven demons (Luke 8:2) and the demoniac who called himself "Legion" because "many demons had gone into him. In this case, Jesus drove the demons into a large herd of pigs, which fled over the cliff into the sea (Luke 8:30–35). His command of these spirits indicated that he was master of demonic forces, able to exorcise them. This, of course, led the **Pharisees** to suspect he was the prince of demons, or Beelzebub (Matt. 9:34; 12:27). Jesus responded that he drove out demons "by the Spirit of God" ((Matt. 12:28) or "the finger of God" (Luke 11:20), for he had the authority to do this work.

Some believe that the spirit world was particularly active during Jesus's ministry on earth, with the forces of good and evil in violent combat. The early scene of the **Temptation**, when Jesus confronted the enticements of Satan in the wilderness, appears to confirm this vigorous activity of Satanic forces during his time on earth.

The gift of healing by exorcising demons was handed on to the **Disciples**, who also "drove out demons and anointed many sick people with oil and healed them" (Mark 6:13). The gift of healing was to mark many of the early Christians. As Jesus said: "In my name they will drive out demons" (Mark 16:17). Luke also mentions that Jesus called the Twelve together and "gave them power and authority to drive out all demons and to cure diseases" (9:1). As obedient servants of Satan, the ultimate adversary of God, demons have the power to deceive and torment only to the end of "this evil age" (Paul S. Minear 1993, 162).

The early **Church** had its own battles with demons, whom many people continued to worship. Paul spoke of his concern that Christians were using foods that had been sacrificed by pagans to demons, asserting, "You cannot drink the cup of the Lord and the cup of demons too; you cannot have a part in both the Lord's table and the table of demons" (1 Cor. 10:20–21). In a letter to Timothy, he noted that, "The Spirit clearly says that in later times some will abandon the faith and follow deceiving spirits and things taught by demons" (1 Tim. 4:1). John picked up on this same concern in Revelation, noting that demons—or idols—continued to be objects of worship and were actively tempting mankind in the final days. Babylon the Great eventually would become "a home for demons and a haunt for every evil spirit, a haunt for every unclean and detestable bird" (Rev. 16:4, 18:2). *See also* Cures, Medicine; Curse; Disease; Witchcraft, Witches.

Further Reading

Gaster, Theodor H. *Myth, Legend, and Custom in the Old Testament.* New York: Harper & Row, Publishers, 1969. Hirsch, Emil G., Richard Gottheil, Kaufmann Kohler, and Isaac Broydé, "Demonology," http://www.jewishencyclopedia. com (accessed December 26, 2004). Minear, Paul S. "Demons," in *The Oxford Companion to the Bible.* New York: Oxford University Press, 1993.

Desert. *See* Geography

Diana of the Ephesians. *See* Asherah, Ashtoreh, Ashtaroth

Disciples

(**Matt. 14:26, 20:17; Mark 2:18; Luke 11:1; John 9:28**) The term *disciple* derives from the Greek word for "follower" or "learner." It might refer to the follower of any leader or teacher, such as Moses, the Pharisees, or Jesus. It was a common practice in the ancient world for men to cluster around a great teacher, as the disciples of Socrates did, learning from him on an informal basis. Some of the men who eventually followed Jesus were thought to have previously been disciples of John the Baptist.

The **Gospels** use the term to speak of the 12 men who followed Jesus longest and most closely and who were given power to preach and heal. Remarkably, these men were not highly educated or sophisticated; they were relatives and neighbors of Jesus, from Galilee, who were mostly fishermen. One was a tax collector and others probably tradespeople. In most cases, we know only their names and relationships to one another, not their work or status in society. Certainly none were **priests** or **rabbis**. Some were married and had businesses, but all left their homes and work to follow the Master. With the exception of Judas Iscariot, who betrayed Jesus, the Disciples gradually came to understand Jesus's teaching and believe that he was the **Messiah**, the chosen one of Israel. After the death of Judas, the remaining Disciples cast lots to replace him with Matthias.

Various of the Disciples were among those who provided the information for the Gospel writers: Matthew, John, and Peter (who is thought to have influenced Mark). A number of the Gnostic Gospels were also attributed to the Disciples, who became the leaders of the early **Church**. It is astonishing that these simple peasants became the first evangelists, taking the Gospel message to all of the known world. They were also involved in making the major decisions of the new faith, such as how the Church should be organized, how the money was to be shared, and how Gentiles were to be brought into the fold. Some of them—Peter, James, and John—became writers of **epistles** full of wisdom and power. Some also became martyrs for their faith and were exiled or executed. The Scripture does not trace their eventual careers, although popular mythology has filled in numerous stories of martyrdom.

The Disciples differ from the **apostles** ("someone who has been sent") in that they were specifically called by Jesus and followed him in the flesh. Paul, on the other hand, was called by the resurrected Christ, and is known as an *apostle* instead (1 Cor. 12:29). Luke used the designation "apostle" for those Disciples who were companions of Jesus and witnesses to the resurrection (Acts 1:21–22). A more recent debate has arisen among feminist critics as to whether the women who followed Jesus, including his mother and Mary Magdalene, might also be designated "Disciples." The attention paid to the Gnostic Gospel of Mary Magdalene has intensified this debate. Although women followers did refer to him as *rabboni,* or teacher, and clearly engaged in discussions with him, Scripture does not designate them among the Disciples.

Other interpretations suggest that all the followers, pupils, or adherents of Jesus should be called *disciples.* The term is used for the 72 sent out by Jesus (Luke 10:1). It is also used in regard to the new believers in Acts (6:1, 2, 7; 9:1, 10, 19, etc.) It is, in fact, the name assumed by one denomination of the Church, "Disciples of Christ."

For the most part, the term refers to the 12: Simon Peter and his brother Andrew; James and John, the sons of Zebedee; Philip; Bartholomew; Matthew (also called "Levi"); Thomas; James, the son of Alphaeus; Thaddeus; Simon the Canaanite; and Judas Iscariot (Mark 3:16–19). Some believe that Jesus chose 12 as a symbol of the 12 **Tribes** of Israel, indicating that his Church under the New **Covenant** would become the New Israel. *See also* Apostle; Christian; Church; Gospel, Gospels; Rabbi.

Further Reading

Miller, Madeleine S. and J. Lane Miller. "Rabbi, Rabboni," in *Harper's Bible Dictionary*. New York: Harper and Row, 1961. Singer, Isidore, Isaac Broydé, Joseph Jacobs, Judah David Eisenstein, Kaufmann Kohler, and Max Landsberg, "Rabbi," www.jewishencyclopedia.com (accessed November 20, 2004). Souvay, Charles "Disciple," www.newadvent.org (accessed March 19, 2005). Stern, Philip. "Rabbi," in *The Oxford Companion to the Bible*. New York: Oxford University Press, 1993.

Disease

Scripture is quite vague about illness, noting primarily that one has a "sickness" or is "weak." The opposite condition is to have "wholeness, well-being" (Philip J. King and Lawrence E. Stager 2001, 69). Some problems are named, but with such vague reference that we can only speculate as to what their actual meaning might be in modern medicine: alcoholism (Prov. 23:30–35); blindness and eye diseases (Gen. 27:1, 29:17; Prov. 23:20); cancer (2 Kings 20:1; 2 Chron. 21:18); consumption or tuberculosis (Lev. 26:16; Deut. 28:22); boils, tumors, itches, and sores (Exod. 9:9; Lev. 13:18; Deut. 28:27, 35; 2 Kings 20:7; Isa. 1:6); dropsy (Luke 14:2); dumbness (Matt. 9:32, 12:22); dysentery (2 Chron. 21:15; Acts 28:8); epilepsy (Matt. 17:15); fever (Luke 4:38; John 4:46–54); venereal disease (Gen. 20:17); gout or foot disease (2 Chron. 16:12); leprosy (Exod. 4:6; Lev. 13:1–17; etc.); mental disorders (1 Sam. 21:13; Matt. 4:24, 17:15; Mark 3:11; Acts 26:24); paralysis (2 Sam. 4:4); palsy (Matt. 12:10); plague and pestilence (Jer. 21:6; Ezek. 6:11; Mark 3:16); and worms (Acts 12:32; Madeleine S. Miller and J. Lane Miller 1961, 135–6).

Archaeologists have studied bones and other relics of biblical times, including the residue from outhouses, only to determine that some of the diseases of ancient times included arthritis, tuberculosis, septic infection, and malignancies. In ancient pits, fossilized excrement has revealed beef or pork tapeworm and whipworm. Some form of worms were thought to have brought on the death of Herod Agrippa: he was "eaten of worms" (Acts 12:1–6).

Ancient combs had lice and lice eggs still clinging to them, suggesting that the treatment for lice was much as it is today, combing the hair with a fine-toothed comb. Putting oil on the hair also killed the lice, providing an added inducement to the tradition of anointment.

There are numerous mentions of blindness, which specialists attribute to trachoma. The very old—such as Isaac—may have had the traditional eye diseases of the elderly—cataracts and glaucoma.

Infertility was also considered a disease, which Rachel and her sisters thought could be cured with herbs—mandrakes in her case. For Hannah and others with "barren wombs," **prayer** was the ultimate answer. In Rachel's case, although she was able to bear two sons to Jacob, she finally died in childbirth, undoubtedly a frequent but unmentioned cause of death among females.

Plagues are mentioned several times, with the **Egyptians** (Exod. 15:26) and the army of Sennacherib (2 Kings 19:35) being the most dramatic. Plagues probably occurred with some frequency, as they are mentioned even in the Psalms. Given the primitive sanitary conditions, the closeness of people to animals, the poor sewage, the use of untreated waste on crops, and the general ignorance of causes of diseases or their treatments, those plagues carried by rats and fleas or by parasites must have moved quickly though a community. The "pestilence" mentioned in the Bible was probably the bubonic plague, which was especially prevalent in Egypt (Emil G. Shirsch and Schulim Ochser 2004).

One of the most frequently mentioned diseases was leprosy, which apparently was different from the modern disease. Leviticus 13–14 describes the purification rites for cleansing the victim, referring to the person "stricken with scale disease," which sounds more like psoriasis than the hideous wasting disease we now call "leprosy." Miriam was stricken with this after her act of rebellion, but the disease was short-lived and she was soon able to return to the camp.

Mental illness, such as that that struck down King Saul, was thought to be caused by demonic possession and cured by **music**, in this case provided by David. Nebuchadnezzar was also thought to have been afflicted by mental illness late in his life, which ended with the pitiful image of the old king crawling about on all fours like an **animal**. In the New Testament, this is explained explicitly as **demon**-possession, with the cure being exorcism. The Gospel of Mark is particularly consistent in its portrayal of demons causing psychological disorders.

In most cases, **cures** were thought to lie in God's hands. Thus the **priest** was a more likely attendant than the **physician**. Prayers and miracles, such as those performed by Elisha (2 Kings 4:18–37) or Jesus and his **disciples**, were considered the ultimate medicine. God had promised the Israelites that, if they would "diligently hearken to the voice of the Lord" and "do what is right in his sight," they would have "none of these diseases upon thee which I have brought upon the Egyptians" (Exod. 15:26). The **law** of Moses proved a mighty blessing to the Hebrews, encouraging them to bathe and anoint themselves regularly, making them among the cleanest community in the ancient world. Health, they believed, was a reward for obedience, sickness the punishment for disobedience.

This was the mindset that Jesus confronted when curing the sick. As in the earlier story, Job's comforters had assumed sin was the root cause of his calamities, so the crowd believed that those coming to Jesus with paralysis, bloody flux, blindness, or other problems were either guilty of sin or were being cursed for the sins of their fathers (John 9:2). Miracles and miracle workers were their last hope: Apparently, the blind and crippled thought that they could find cures by virtue of an **angel** that would come and trouble the waters of the pool of Bethesda (John 5:1–4). They had little faith in the cures of a physician (Mark 5:26). By New Testament times, the crippled and diseased people of the land were numerous: the laws of **purity** were ignored, unscrupulous **rabbis** proposed magical rituals as cures, and modern medicine was in the far distant future: "One travelling through the land would scarcely ever be out of sight of blind beggars, or crippled people, or lepers" (Fred Wight 1953, 140–141). *See also* Anointing; Bath, Bathing; Cures, Medicine.

Further Reading

Hirsch, Emil G. and Schulim Ochser. "Pestilence," http://www.jewishencyclopedia.com (accessed December 26, 2004). King, Philip J. and Lawrence E. Stager. *Life in Biblical Israel*. Louisville, Ky.: Westminster John Knox Press, 2001. Miller, Madeleine S. and J. Lane Miller. "Diseases and Healing," in *Harper's Bible Dictionary*. New York: Harper and Row, 1961. Schechter, Solomon, C. D. Spivak, Joseph Jacobs, Frederick T. Haneman. "Medicine," http://www.jewishencyclopedia.com (accessed April 23, 2005). Senfelde, Leopold. "History of Medicine," http://www.newadvent.org (accessed April 23, 2005). Wight, Fred Hartley. *Manners and Customs of Bible Lands*. Chicago: Moody Press, 1953.

Divorce

(Gen. 1:27; Lev. 21:7; Num. 30:10; Deut. 22:19; Mark 10:6–8) "What God hath joined together, let no man put asunder!" These words of the traditional **wedding** service, taken from the **Gospel** of Mark, represent the strongest possible view of **marriage**—as holy and permanent. When Jesus used these words, he first quoted Genesis, "from the beginning of **Creation**, 'God made them male and female.... For this reason a man shall leave his father and be joined to his wife, and the two shall become one flesh'" (Gen. 1:27). He then added, "So they are no longer two but one flesh. What therefore God has joined together, let not man put asunder" (Mark 10:6–8).

The **Pharisees** asked Jesus whether it was lawful for a man to divorce his wife; they noted that "Moses allowed a man to write a certificate of divorce, and put her away" (Mark 10:2, 4). Quoting the Mosaic **law**, found in Leviticus, Numbers, and Deuteronomy, they assumed that divorce, like marriage, was the prerogative of the **husband** (Lev. 21:7; Num. 30:10; Deut. 22:19, 29). As the marriage was a unilateral **covenant**, with the woman "given" and "taken," it was only natural that the man would also be the one to elect to end the marriage by a divorce. There were some provisions for a wife who wished to terminate the marriage: A wife whose husband refused her conjugal rights was permitted to leave him (Exod. 21:10–11) and return to her father's house. But only in post-exilic times might a wife be the one who sought to dissolve the marriage.

The grounds for divorce were that the husband had discovered that his bride was not a virgin at the time of their marriage or had found some indecency in her (Deut. 24:1), that he had found someone fairer (therefore she no longer "found favor in his sight"), that she was barren, or that she was a scold or a fornicator (Magen Broshi 2004, 36). For a proven charge of adultery, rather than being divorced and sent quietly to her father's home, the woman could be stoned to death.

On occasion, the man could be blocked from seeking a divorce: If the husband was found to have accused his wife falsely of not being a virgin, he lost his right to divorce her (Deut. 22:13–19). (This was one reason the shrewd wife preserved the blood-stained bridal sheet, as evidence of her virginity.) Also, if he had been forced to marry a woman he had previously violated, he had no right to divorce her (Deut. 22:28–29).

During the Rabbinic Age, the discussion of marriage and divorce grew heated, probably precipitating the questions asked by the Pharisees of Jesus. The "rigorist" school of Shammai admitted only adultery and misconduct, but the more liberal school of Hillel would accept even trivial reasons such as the wife's spoiling a dish of food or the husband's preferring another woman. One scholar recommended, "If thy wife does not obey thee at a signal and a glance, separate from her" (Roland deVaux 1961, 34–35).

The law was more specific about remarriage, noting that taking a second wife while the first was still alive was fornication. As a matter of practice, polygany was common in Judaism, especially among the upper classes. To get a divorce from his wife, the husband was required to get a "writing of divorce" (Deut. 24:1). She might remarry, although she might not marry this husband again, even after becoming divorced or widowed. The woman at the well, whom Jesus confronted, appears to have had several husbands who apparently had either divorced her or had died. Jesus's teaching was that remarriage of either party was appropriate only on the grounds of adultery (Matt. 31–32, Mark 10:10–12, Luke 16:18). The writing of divorce, which specifically stated: "You are free to marry any man," allowed her to remarry without fear of charges of adultery (Bruce M. Metzger and Michael D. Coogan 1993, 170).

As summarized in Falk's study of Hebrew law, "divorce was an arbitrary, unilateral, private act on the part of the husband and consisted of the wife's expulsion from the husband's house" (Ze'ev W. Falk 2001, 150). One formula for the separation, recited in front of witnesses, was: "She is not my wife and I am not her husband" (Hosea 2:4). If she had brought a substantial dowry with her to the marriage, she might expect to have this returned. In post-exilic times, there are also notations regarding "divorce money," apparently an early form of alimony.

The **prophet**s saw the marriage ceremony as a permanent covenant, akin to the covenant between God and Israel. The formula used at the wedding ceremony was, "I am your husband forever." This oath gave the relationship a sacred aspect, making any violation of it a serious breach of the covenant. In fact, scholars suspect that divorce was a rare occurrence in ancient Israel but became more common later.

The symbolism of marriage and divorce, especially after the Exile, took on an increasingly spiritual aspect, making divorce an image of man's hardness of heart. Malachi 2:13–16 summarizes God's displeasure with easy divorces:

> You cover the Lord's **altar** with tears, with weeping and groaning because he no longer regards the offering or accepts it with favor at your hand. You ask: Why does He not? Because the Lord was witness to the covenant between you and the wife of your youth, to whom you have been faithless, though she is your companion and your wife by covenant.... So take heed to yourselves and let none be so faithless to the wife of his youth. For He hates divorce, says the Lord the God of Israel.

Paul saw the single life as the ideal for Christians, especially those who had separated (1 Cor. 7:10–11; Rom. 7:1–3). If a Christian should marry an unbeliever, Paul indicated that the Christian might grant his or her partner a divorce (1 Cor. 7:15), but did not recommend remarriage. The celibate life (making oneself a **"eunuch"** for Christ) allowed the evangelist to focus all of his energies on spreading the Gospel message. *See also* Covenant; Husband and Wife; Law; Marriage; Punishments; Weddings.

Further Reading

Broshi, Magen. "What Jesus Learned from the Essenes," in *Biblical Archaeology*, January/February 2004, 36. DeVaux, Roland. *Ancient Israel: Its Life and Institutions*. Grand Rapids, Mich.: William B. Eerdmans Publishing Company, 1961. Falk, Ze'ev W. *Hebrew Law in Biblical Times*. Provo, Utah: Brigham Young University Press, 2001. Metzger, Bruce M. and Michael D. Coogan. "Divorce," *The Oxford Companion to the Bible*. New York: Oxford University Press, 1993.

Dogs

(**Exod. 11:7; Matt. 15:26**) Unlike moderns, families in biblical times did not usually keep dogs as pets. These descendants of wolves had been domesticated since the late Stone Age (George S. Cansdale 1970, 57). They proved to be exceedingly useful for herding **animals**, especially **sheep**. They may also have served as protectors against thieves and predatory animals. Exodus has a mention of a dog's failing to bark "at man or animal" (Exod. 11:7). Some people may have kept them in the house as companions, a possible explanation for the dog mentioned by the Syro-Phoenician woman who spoke with Jesus (Matt. 15:26). (The term used in this Gospel is a diminutive, suggesting this was a small house pet.)

Ordinarily, when they are mentioned in Scripture, dogs were lowly scavengers, snapping up the **food** tossed from the table. They also sorted through refuse piles, finding edibles wherever they could. In disposing of garbage, they undoubtedly provided a valuable service, but they were nonetheless viewed with disgust by people who were particular about their dietary rules. The habit also made dogs potential carriers of disease. One colorful reference (2 Kings 9:35–36), prophesied earlier, notes that the wicked Queen Jezebel was eaten by dogs, which consumed her carcass, but wisely declined "to eat her feet which have run on errands of mischief, the palms of her hands which have wrought cruelty, and her head which has designed evil deeds" (Mary Ellen Chase 1945, 71).

The packs of semi-wild dogs that roamed on the outskirts of cities and villages, waiting for "rubbish or dead bodies to be thrown over" the walls would clearly be untouchable bearers of defilement. Their disgusting eating habits appalled the Israelites. Consider also the two references to a dog returning to its vomit (Prov. 26:11; 2 Pet. 2:22). Proverbs also mentions seizing a dog by its ears, possibly a means to controlling a stray animal or an unruly pet.

By and large, biblical references to dogs are negative: Gideon chose his men from among those who did not drink like dogs (Judg. 7:5), and the Philistine Goliath compared David's lack of armor reducing their heroic combat to disciplining of a canine: "Am I a dog that you come at me with sticks?"(1 Sam. 17:43). Apparently, one of the worst things one man could call another was a "dog" or a "dead dog." That Hazael used this insulting term of himself—"a mere dog" (2 Kings 8:13)—suggests that this was considered the lowest form of life. When the Judaizing intruders ("dogs") were excluded from the **Church** (Phil. 3:2), the pattern was set for Revelation, where they are also excluded from the New Jerusalem. In fact, the term *dog* here and elsewhere may have been the more "technical term for a male temple prostitute" (George Cansdale 1970, 57).

Not all peoples of the ancient world shared this disdain for animals. Egyptians used them in **hunting** expeditions and held them in reverence, as they did a host of animal deities. Tobias had a faithful dog who accompanied him on his travels. Not surprisingly, as humankind has become more enamored of this animal, dog imagery has improved. Over time, the dog's intelligence, usefulness, and faithfulness have made him a symbol of fidelity—hence the name "Fido." Thus, in medieval paintings of married women, dogs are often shown in their laps or at their feet, as icons of loyalty. St. Dominic was later symbolized as a dog with a flaming torch in its mouth, and Dominicans were known as "*Domini canes,* dogs of the Lord" who wore black-and-white habits (George Ferguson 1966, 15). *See also* Animals; Shepherds.

Further Reading

Cansdale, George S. *All the Animals of the Bible Lands.* Grand Rapids, Mich.: Zondervan Publishing House, 1970. Chase, Mary Ellen. *The Bible and the Common Reader.* New York: The Macmillan Company, 1945. Ferguson, George. *Signs and Symbols in Christian Art.* New York: Oxford University Press, 1966.

Donkey, Ass

(Gen. 12:16; Num. 22:22–33; Matt. 21:5) The English word *ass* is rarely used in modern translations of Scripture or in sermons because it has taken on obscene alternate meanings, but the older word came down from "ancient languages like Sumerian and Armenian, through Latin" (George Cansdale 1970, 70) and has been popular through the ages to describe one of the Bible's favorite beasts. The word *donkey* was unknown before the end of the eighteenth century and derives from the color dun—a dingy brown. Donkeys were brownish-gray, with a pale undercoating in earlier times, and most have a clearly marked line across the shoulders and along the back, which tradition fancifully attributes to the sign of the cross. Asses live longer than **horses**, often from 25 to 40 years. They sleep standing and are noted for the unearthly sound of their braying, which comes "at odd intervals for little obvious reason, the result of muscular contractions of the body" (George Carsdale 1970, 71).

The wild donkey was already well known in Abraham's day (Gen. 12:16), when the pharaoh included "male and female donkeys" among his gifts. Ishmael was prophesied to be a "wild donkey of a man" (Gen. 16:12), a man hard to civilize, with his own willful ways and hostile heart. Sumerians and others had found this hardy little beast could be easily domesticated and was an exceedingly useful member of the household. As a beast of burden, this tough and sure-footed **animal** carried enormous loads through rugged countryside, and often served as the transportation for the descendants of Abraham.

It was probably donkeys rather than **camels**—the alternative for those who planned long trips across the desert—that formed much of Abraham's caravan from Ur of the Chaldees and later Haran. It was a donkey that carried the load of wood for the burnt offering that was to be used for the **sacrifice** of Isaac (Gen. 22:3). Moses placed his wife and sons on a donkey to begin his long trip back to **Egypt** from **Midian** (Exod. 4:20).

Donkey carrying a heavy load; This was the favorite beast
of burden among the Israelites.

As late as the New Testament, the donkey is usually pictured as the beast
carrying Mary, pregnant with child, from Nazareth to Bethlehem, and
standing nearby in the stable when the child was born. In his ministry, Jesus
requisitioned a donkey to make the triumphal entry into Jerusalem on what
was to become Palm Sunday: "See, your **king** comes to you, gentle and riding on a donkey, on a colt, the foal of a donkey" (Matt. 21:5). As noted in
the Scripture, this fulfilled the **prophecy** of the **psalm** that proclaims: "Be
not afraid, O Daughter of Zion, see your king is coming, seated on a donkey's colt" (John 12:12). This echoes the earlier prophesy in Zechariah 9:9
that the king would come "gentle and riding on a donkey, on a colt, the foal
of a donkey" (Matt. 21:2; 2 Sam. 18:9; 1 Kings 1:33). Until the reign of
Solomon, the kings of Israel rode on donkeys. Warlike kings rode on horses;
the Prince of Peace was mounted on a donkey.

Apparently, donkeys were greatly valued and properly tended. They were
usually housed with the family livestock, often in the house. They had saddles to protect them from rough loads, tethers to tie them to trees and keep
them from wandering off, and feedbags to carry their **grain** when they were
on tiresome journeys.

A number of the **laws** of Moses deal with donkeys: the use of the firstborn as a sacrifice (Exod. 13:13), the prohibition against coveting the
neighbor's donkey (Exod. 20:17), and the treatment of a trapped animal.
They are among the "unclean" animals, unfit for food. Mention is also
made of stolen donkeys, overburdened ones that fall to the ground, injured
ones, and so on. It is obvious that the donkey was a cherished possession,

not to be abused or neglected. The law even orders a man who finds a donkey wandering off to bring it back to the owner (Exod. 23:4). The animal, however, was seen as one of the lesser possessions. Moses insisted, for example, that he had taken nothing from his enemies—not even "so much as a donkey" (Num. 16:15). Over time, some of the burdens assigned to the donkey were taken over by mules, the half-donkeys, half-horses, which were larger and stronger, although the Hebrews were forbidden to breed them under the law of Moses.

In one famous story, a donkey astonished his master, Baalam, who found that the animal recognized the **angel** of the Lord before he did. Baalam's ass halted, refusing to keep on his path, even when beaten by his master and threatened with slaughter. At that point, the donkey found his tongue, asserting, "Am I not your own donkey, which you have always ridden, to this day?" The intervention of the angel then saved the donkey's life (Num. 22:22–33). Later, Peter cited this as an example of a "beast without speech—who spoke with a man's voice and restrained the **prophet**'s madness" (2 Pet. 2:16).

This simple, hard-working creature, a plodding friend of humans, contrasted with the camel and the horse, both of which appear much more rarely in Scripture. The horse especially was seen as an indulgence of prideful foreigners (Isaiah 1), and the donkey became a symbol of humility, peace, and Davidic royalty (Matt. 21:2). *See also* Animals; Camel; Horse.

Further Reading

Carsdale, George. *All the Animals of the Bible Lands*. Grand Rapids, Mich.: Zondervan Publishing House, 1970.

Dowry. *See* Betrothal

Dreams

(**Gen. 28:12ff., 41:16, 25; Dan. 2: 19; Joel 2:28; Acts 2:17**) "And it shall come to pass afterward, that I will pour out my spirit upon all flesh; and your sons and daughters shall prophesy, your old men shall dream dreams, your young men shall see visions" (Joel 2:28). This was repeated at the time of the **Pentecost**, when Peter preached to the people, believing that Joel's famous prophecy of visions and dreams had finally come to pass (Acts 2:17). Dreams, like visions, were perceived as a gift from God, his way of speaking to humankind through images that sometimes demanded interpreters.

For Jacob, the dream was immediate and clear. He saw the ladder to **Heaven**, with the **angels** coming and going, and he immediately understood he was in direct communion with God. In that glorious night at Bethel, with a **stone** for a pillow, the discouraged and outcast Jacob "dreamed, and beheld a ladder set up on the earth, and the top of it reached to heaven and behold the angels of God ascending and descending on it" (Gen. 28:12). God spoke directly to Jacob, making promises that would keep his hope alive through long years of toil and estrangement from his family. He identified the place of his dream as a "dreadful" place—"this is none other but the house of God, and this is the gate of heaven" (Gen. 28:17).

Many peoples of the ancient world believed that the gods spoke through dreams to humankind. As the story of Joseph reveals, the **Egyptians** thought that dreams had validity but that they required the interpretation of wise men. In the case of Joseph, both simple folk in prison with him and great ones, such as the Pharaoh, found him a reliable interpreter of dreams. Later, Daniel displayed the same kind of skill in interpreting the dreams of Nebuchadnezzar. Both Daniel and Joseph gave God credit for their interpretations, not posing as "wise men" of their own accord (Gen. 41:16, 25; Dan. 2: 19).

This power of accurate interpretation was believed to come from God primarily because most Israelites thought that it was always the Hebrew God, not pagan deities, who spoke through dreams, either to make known his will or to announce future events (Emil G. Hirsch, Solomon Schechter, Ludwig Blau, Cyrus Adler, and Joseph Jacobs 2004). Biblical dreams were usually intended for the benefit of the seed of Abraham, not simply for individuals (Gen. 20:3; 28:12; 31:10, 24; 37:5, 9, 40, 41; Judg. 7:13; 1 Kings 3:5, 15; Dan. 2, 4). Daniel considered his dreams and interpretations as a "vision of the night."

Dreams were also taken as divine revelations even if they referred only to the dreamer himself. For example, Elihu told Job that God speaks in dreams, in "a vision of the night, when deep sleep falleth upon men, in slumberings upon the bed, Then he openeth the ears of men, and sealeth their instruction, That he may withdraw man from his purpose, and hide pride from man" (Job 33:14–17).

Only Adam, Noah, and Moses were allowed to talk to God face-to-face. Abraham, as a **prophet**, knew God's words and heard his instructions clearly. In **prayers**, he talked with God and even argued with him, as in the case of his haggling over the terms for the destruction of Sodom. Moses, however, was the last of the prophets who had the dazzling experience of seeing God and living. The aura that surrounded Moses's countenance after the experience testified to the splendor of this amazing experience. As God told Miriam and Aaron, who were angry that only Moses conversed with God "mouth-to-mouth," the time would come when God would speak to prophets, although not with the directness he spoke with Moses: "I the Lord will make myself known unto him in a vision, and will speak unto him in a dream." These "dark speeches," which used the language of symbols, would require interpretation (Num. 12:6–8). In the days of Samuel and Saul, the people believed that the Lord spoke through dreams as well as through **Urim** and the prophets (J.G.S.S. Thompson and J.S. Wright 1980, 394).

In fact, dreams could be either warnings or instructions. They could also be vehicles of evil. Sexual dreams were thought by many to be the work of evil spirits, especially Lilith and her nefarious offspring (Richard Schell 1992, 454). In Deuteronomic **law**, a dreamer whose message encourages apostasy was to be put to death (Deut. 13:2–6). Jeremiah attacked false prophets for proclaiming their dreams as revelations from God (Jer. 23:16, 25–27, 32) but differentiated true prophetic dreams as divinely inspired (31:26).

Scripture makes little distinction between dreams and visions (Job 4:12; Acts 16:9. 18:9). Visions were considered "waking dreams" that were usually reserved for prophets. Hagar's theophany in the wilderness, after she had been cast out by Sarah, provided her comfort and a clear message of the need to return for the birth of Ishmael. When she was cast out a second time, her later vision opened for her the future of the Arab people, providing prophetic words by which she and her son were given God's promise of God's protection and their survival.

Jesus's life and ministry, as recorded by Matthew, were full of visions and dreams. From the moment of the Annunciation, when Mary was told she was to blessed above all women, until Pilate's wife dreamed ominous things about his death, Jesus was marked as a special child of God. Matthew recorded several dreams in connection with the birth and infancy of Jesus (Matt. 1:20, 2:12–13, 19, 22).

One of the most famous visions of the New Testament was Paul's conversion experience on the road to Damascus. His later vision (or dream) of the Macedonian man beckoning him provided the inspiration for the missionary trip that crossed into Europe and opened a major new chapter in religious history.

It was also a dream that convinced Peter that his ministry should extend to the Gentiles. He dreamed—or had a vision—of a blanket lowered down from heaven, with all manner of **food**s on it. He refused twice to follow the Lord's clear command to eat of it, only to realize on the third occurrence that nothing that the Lord had blessed would be unclean. The early days of the **Church** was a special time for **miracles** and visions, with the **Holy Spirit** at work among the people and their minds open to leadings and messages. All of the Book of Revelation could be considered a dream-vision, which blended a host of rich images in a prophetic message.

Throughout the history of religion, dreams and visions have provided windows to God's messages. The saints throughout the ages, like the prophets and the patriarchs, have been inspired by these revelations. Poets who followed in the Christian tradition often framed their allegories as dream-visions, as we see in the works of Dante, Milton, and Bunyan. The form allows a freedom for creative expression that can be very powerful. *See also* Prophet.

Further Reading

Hirsch, Emil G., Solomon Schechter, Ludwig Blau, Cyrus Adler, and Joseph Jacobs, "Dreams," http://www.jewishencyclopedia.com (accessed December 10, 2004). Schell, Richard. "Lilith," in *A Dictionary of Biblical Tradition in England*. Grand Rapids, Mich.: William B. Eerdmans Publishing Company, 1992. Thompson, J.G.S.S. and J. S. Wright. "Dream," *The Illustrated Bible Dictionary*. Sydney, Australia: Tyndale House Publishers, 1980.

Eagle. *See Birds*

Earrings. *See Jewelry*

Eden, Garden of

(**Gen. 2–3**) "And the Lord God planted a garden eastward in Eden." This brief introduction to the earthly paradise opens the second narrative of the **Creation**. It tells of Adam and Eve and the **serpent** , the participants in the story of man's original perfection, his temptation, his **fall** into disobedience, and his final expulsion from the **garden**, to endure the torments of the life "east of Eden" from this time forward.

As all manner of **animal**s were created to live harmoniously with him in the garden, Adam named each in turn. He was tasked with tending the **trees** of the garden and was allowed to eat the fruit of all of them except for the Tree of the Knowledge of Good and Evil. God warned him that "in the day that thou eatest thereof, thou shalt surely die." One other tree of significance in the garden was the Tree of Life, which had fruit that made humans immortal. After the expulsion of the first couple from the garden, God placed **cherubim** and a flaming sword of the garden, keeping humans from reentering this paradise and tasting immortality.

The name *Eden* is thought to mean "delight, enjoyment." Some scholars think it may derive from the Arabic word for "field, depression" and associate it with a location in southern Babylonia (Emil G. Hirsch, Mary W. Montgomery, Solomon Schechter, Judah David Eisenstein, and M. Seligsohn 2004). Because of the reference to the four rivers, the Tigris, the Euphrates, the Gihon, and the Pison, this seems like a good supposition. The last two of these named rivers are thought to have been canals that may have originally been river beds that branch out from the Euphrates just below **Babylon**. As Hirsch notes, the country south of Babylon "was so beautiful in its luxuriant vegetation and abundant streams that it was known as 'Kar-Duniash,' or 'garden of the god Duniash.'" The possible location in a lush, green area near the Gulf was drained and turned into a wasteland by Saddam Hussein. Others have thought that the original garden may have been in Cush or Ethiopia, a theory possibly fueled by discoveries of ancient human skeletons in Africa. Josephus thought the last two rivers of the garden were the Ganges and the Nile (*Antiquities,* 29).

The symbolic use of the garden setting is far more important than its physical location. Ezekiel used it is as a judgment against the sinful nations, Tyre, and **Egypt** (Ezek. 28:11–19, 31:8). Joel related it to the coming **Day of the Lord** (Joel 2:3). And Isaiah used it as a metaphor for the renewal of the land of Israel (Isa. 51:3; Dennis T. Olson 1992, 178).

In later literature, especially the medieval and Renaissance periods, the image of the earthly paradise became very appealing. Dante placed it at the top of Mt. Purgatory, the end of the effort to restore original purity, but not yet Heaven. Milton pictured it as the setting for his famous epic of the **Fall** of man, *Paradise Lost*. In religious thought and history, the dream of returning to this condition of original purity in harmony with God and nature has powerfully moved humankind. Many of the immigrants from England and Europe who made their journey to America saw this as a "new Eden" where humankind could begin all over again in an earthly paradise. Nathaniel Hawthorne and William Faulkner are among those who use this imagery in their novels (Joseph Duncan and David W. Baker 1992, 223–225). *See also* Cherub, Cherubim; Creation; Gardens.

Further Reading

Duncan, Joseph, and David W. Baker. "Eden," in *A Dictionary of Biblical Tradition in English Literature*. Grand Rapids, Mich.: William B. Eerdmans Publishing Company, 1992. Hirsch, Emil G., Mary W. Montgomery, Solomon Schechter, Judah David Eisenstein, and M. Seligsohn. "Eden, Garden of," http://www.jewishencyclopedia.com (accessed December 11, 2004). Josephus, Flavius. *The Works of Josephus*. Peabody, Mass.: Hendrickson Publishers, Inc., 2001. Olson, Dennis T. "Eden, The Garden of," in *The Oxford Companion to the Bible*. New York: Oxford University Press, 1993.

Edom, Edomites

(Gen. 14:6; Deut 2:12; Judg. 11:17) The antagonism between Esau and his twin brother Jacob continued among their descendants throughout the ages. With the sale of his **birthright** for a mess of pottage, Esau was destined to live outside the boundaries of the Promised Land, in Edom. Some believe that the name *Edom,* meaning "red," came from the color of the pottage he ate; some believe it came from the red rock in such areas as Petra. Mount "Seir" or "hairy," another name for the country, was also thought to derive from Esau, a hairy man, although this name could have derived from the progenitor of the Horites who lived in the region previous to Esau and his clan (Richard Gottheil and M. Seligsohn 2004). The **Greeks** called the region "Idumea."

Edom was a rocky, mountainous country where men like Esau, a strong and skillful hunter, could survive in the rugged mountains. The Bible notes that, immediately after Isaac's death, Esau settled in Mount Seir, driving out the Horites (Deut. 2:12). This was a towering 5,000 foot ridge, which was to become the cradle of the national life of Edom (Madeleine S. Miller and J. Lane Miller 1961, 149). The land stretched along the route that the

Israelites followed—the Kings' Highway. It extended from the Gulf of Aquaba, with its seaport city Elath, to Moab and Judah on the north. Its ancient capital was Bozrah (Gen. 36:33), and at one time Selah (later the "rose-red wonder city of Petra") was its principal stronghold.

Edom was already a prosperous monarchy at the time of the Exodus (Num. 20:14-21). The Edomites appear to have had eight kings with subordinate chiefs (Exod. 15:15). Archaeologists have discovered mines, mining camps, and slag heaps, indicating that large amounts of copper and iron were mined in this region and marking them later on as a prime target for the kings of Israel. The Edomites thought themselves secure in their fortified mountain settlements, which used fire to communicate any signs of trouble to other parts of the region (Miller, 149). They created bad blood with the Israelites when they refused to allow the them to use the King's Highway, the standard route through their country.

Although God forbad the Israelites to wage war against the Edomites at this time and guided them around this country instead (Num. 20:14–21), the antipathy lingered. Some 400 years later, Saul attacked the Edomites (1 Sam. 14:47); and 40 years after that, David overthrew them in the "valley of salt." Joab, his general, killed all their males (2 Sam. 8:13, 14) but failed to slaughter the entire royal family, some of whom fled to Egypt, only to return after David's death to lead a brief unsuccessful rebellion. After this, Edom remained subject to Israel with Israelite governors. After Solomon, it became a dependency of Judah. At one point, the Edomites joined with **Ammonites** and **Moabites** to revolt against Jehoram, and then elected a king of their own to signal their independence. Amaziah attacked and killed 10,000 of the Edomites in battle and dashed 10,000 more to pieces from the cliffs. The Israelites took Selah, their stronghold, and brought them under their control, although they were never able to subdue the Edomites completely (2 Chron. 20:10–23, 21:8, 25:11–12; 2 Kings 8:20–22; Richard Gottheil and M. Seligsohn 2004). In the reign of Ahaz, Edom threw off Judean control and remained independent of Judah until the time of **Assyrian** domination.

The Assyrian presence seems to have benefited Edom economically and politically, as excavations at Buseira, probably Bozrah, suggest. The late eighth through the mid-sixth centuries B.C. saw a peak in the prosperity and power of Edom. When Nebuchadnezzar plundered Jerusalem, the Edomites joined in the slaughter of the Jews. Because of this and other activities, Edom was violently denounced by the **prophets** Isaiah, Jeremiah, and Obadiah (Isa. 34:5–8; Jer. 49:7–22; Obad. 11, 13, 14). Amos complained that they held Israelites as slaves, Joel that they mistreated innocent merchants and travelers, Obadiah that they were prideful in their rocky fortresses, and Ezekiel that they were vindictive. Even so, the Israelites showed them some respect, honoring them for their wise men and perhaps even accepting from them a remarkable contribution to Scripture, the Book of Job (Madeleine S. Miller and J. Lane Miller 1961, 149).

After the conquest of Judah by the **Babylonians**, the people of Edom were permitted to settle in southern Palestine. They were driven out of Edom by the Nabataeans, who conquered the land and built their own cities, such as Petra. They prospered in southern Palestine for the next four centuries until they were conquered by Judas Maccabeus (163 B.C.) and John Hyrcannus (ca 125 B.C.). Hyrcannus forced them to observe Jewish rites and **laws**. Under the Greeks, who called them "Idumeans" and their country "Idumea," they were incorporated into the Jewish nation. With Antipater, the Idumean dynasty, including the infamous Herods, ruled over Judea into the period of the **Romans**. According to Josephus (4:4, 5), just before the siege of Jerusalem (70 A.D.), 20,000 Idumeans fought on behalf of the **Zealots** who were besieging the **Temple**. "Idumaeans were admitted as defenders of the Holy City. Once within, they proceeded to rape, rob, and kill, sparing neither **priests** nor populace in their orgy of blood" (Madeleine S. Miller and J. Lane Miller 1961, 149–50). This was their last act as a separate people. The prophesy of Genesis 27:40 was fulfilled in the history of this people: "And by thy sword shalt thou live, and thou shalt serve thy brother, and it shall come to pass when thou shalt have the dominion, that thou shalt break his yoke from off thy neck." Unfortunately for them, the assertion of Jesus was also fulfilled: "all they that take the sword shall perish with the sword" (Matt. 26:52).

Like the other near neighbors of Israel, they were not welcome into the congregation until the fourth generation. They probably worshipped Hadad/Baal and El, as well as a god named Qaus/Qos, of whom little is known. Pitard notes that it is not even clear whether he is a war god or a storm god. They may, in fact, have included Yahweh in their pantheon (Wayne T. Pitard 1993, 179). *See also* History in the Bible.

Further Reading

Gottheil, Richard, and M. Seligsohn, "Edom, Idumea," http://www.jewishencyclopedia.com (accessed November 10, 2004). Miller, Madeleine S. and J. Lane Miller. "Edomites," in *Harper's Bible Dictionary*. New York: Harper and Row, Publishers, 1961. Pitard, Wayne T. "Edom," in *The Oxford Companion to the Bible*. New York: Oxford University Press, 1993. Wright, George Ernest. *Biblical Archaeology*. Philadelphia: The Westminster Press, 1957.

Education

(**Prov. 1:7**) For most of antiquity, Jewish children learned the rudiments of life, language, work, morality, and faith from their mothers. Until they were weaned (often at 3 years old), both boys and girls were largely in the care of their mothers. Then, until they were adolescents, the home—with both father and mother present—was their school. Here girls studied practical skills such as **cooking**, spinning, and weaving; boys watched their fathers, learning from them the secrets of plowing, herding, **hunting**, and **carpentry**. Adolescent girls remained with their mothers to learn the chores of women, and the boys moved into the masculine world, where their fathers taught them their crafts and the **rabbis** drilled them in their faith. It was usually from their fathers that all the children learned about the history of their people, the ceremonies that commemorated Jewish history, the **law** of Moses, and the elements of their faith. "The fear of the Lord is the beginning of wisdom," says the preacher (Prov. 1:7). This was the basis of Hebrew education.

The children learned primarily by word of mouth. "The teacher told his story, gave explanations and asked questions; the pupil repeated the story, and asked or answered questions." "The word comes by hearing," Jesus noted, echoing the way he learned and taught. The father handed on to his sons the national traditions (which were also religious traditions), and the divine commands given to their forefathers. They memorized literary passages, such as David's lament over Saul and Jonathan. "The father also gave his son a professional education; in practice, trades were usually hereditary, and crafts were handed down in the family workshop" (Roland deVaux 1961, 49). Mnemonic devices, such as acrostics, were common in Hebrew pedagogy and remain in modern American institutions of learning.

It is now believed that Abraham came from a highly developed culture, where he probably learned to read, write, and calculate. Archaeologists have discovered that there were schools in Ur of the Chaldees, and that pupils "had writing lessons on tablets, and dictation lessons in vocabulary. In arithmetic, they had the multiplication and division tables, and more advanced scholars had square and cube roots, with lessons in practical geometry. Grammar lessons included paradigms of the conjugation of verbs" (Fred H. Wight 1953, 112).

Moses added to the Hebrew system the knowledge he received in the **Egyptian** court. Stephen said in his final sermon that Moses was "learned in all the wisdom of the Egyptians" (Acts 7:22). If he went to school at the **Temple** of the Sun in Heliopolis, he not only learned reading and writing, but also "he had lessons in arithmetic, using duodecimal and decimal scales of notation. He must have studied geometry" as well, and perhaps some architecture, anatomy, chemistry, metallurgy, theology, and so on. "**Music** was also an important subject in Egyptian schools. Moses must have been well educated according to the standards of ancient Egypt, which were of a high calibre" (Wight, 113). After all, he was part of the Pharaoh's household.

The Hebrews who sojourned in the desert and settled **Canaan** developed their ceremonies largely for the inculcation of religious and moral lessons in the children (Exod 12:26, 13:8; Deut. 4:9, etc.) They were admonished to teach the commandments "diligently" to their children and talk "of them when thou sittest in thine house, and when thou walkest by the way, and when thou liest down, and when thou risest up" (Deut. 6:8). Various proverbs testify to concern for the education of children, including the need to train up the child in his faith from the beginning, teaching the appropriate things at the right age (Prov. 22:6), teaching throughout life (Prov. 1:2, 7, 8), and applying the "rod of correction" (Prov. 12:24). (Note: the rod was to keep students on the proper path, not to beat them.)

The various **festivals** were planned partly for the education of the children: The questions the father asks of his son in the celebration of the **Passover**, for example, require that the child explain the meaning of the different foods they are eating, for example, the unleavened **bread** and the bitter herbs. The **tribes** were also required to assemble every seventh year at the close of the Sukkot festival to hear and learn the law. "Out of this Biblical ordinance was evolved the custom of completing one consecutive reading of the Pentateuch at the **Sabbath** services within every three years" (Emil G. Hirsch, Kaufmann Kohler, Richard Gottheil, M. Gildemann, Cyrus Adler et al. 2004). Thus the study of the Torah became the central religious teaching of children, especially the boys. The **priests** and the Levites, as the keepers of the law, were the main instructors, but every father was required to teach his children the daily liturgy of his faith. One of the requirements of the faith, with special meaning to Christians, was the annual pilgrimage to Jerusalem for the feast of the Passover. Luke (2:41–42) tells of Jesus's whole family taking this traditional trip, and of Jesus's lingering behind to ask and answer questions of the **scribes** in the Temple.

In the age of the monarchy, there were more specialized schools for **prophets**, as seen in the story of Eli and Samuel, with the young Samuel forming a school for young men "mostly Levites ... to teach the Law of God to the people" (Fred Wight 1953t, 114). These apparently continued into the days of Elijah and Elisha (1 Kings 20:35), with prophets living together in communities, sometimes as large as one hundred, in places such as Gilgal, Bethel, and Jericho. Like the monks of the Middle Ages, these men spent their lives in the study of the law and history, transcribing sacred history. They also cultivated sacred music and poetry. There were schools for scribes, "at an early date in the two capitals, where civil servants were trained; similar training-schools existed in Mesopotamia, in Egypt and among the **Hittites**.... According to a Jewish tradition, it was only in 63 A.D. that the high priest Joshua ben Gimla decreed that every town and village should have a school that all children would have to attend from the age of six or seven" (Roland deVaux 1961, 50).

It was Ezra "who established Scripture" (such as it was at the time) as the basis for schooling; and his successors went on to make the **synagogue** a place of instruction, as well as a place of worship. Simon ben-Shetab enacted, about 75 B.C., that elementary schooling should be compulsory"(D. F. Payne 1980, 413). Synagogues became places of instruction in the hopes that eventually "the earth shall be full of the knowledge of the Lord as the waters cover the sea" (Isa. 11:9). The period of "book-learning or of the scribes" came after the Exile, when it was clear that real effort was needed to preserve the traditions which had been largely oral in early times. These scribes and teachers, for the first time in Jewish history, became an "organized body of teachers" who replaced the priests and prophets as the primary interpreters of Scripture (Emil Hirsch et al. 2004).

After the codification of the law during the time of Ezra (Neh. 8), professional "teachers and synagogue schools functioned all over Palestine, stressing the memorizing of portions of the sacred writings" (Madeleine S. Miller and J. Lane Miller 1961, 150). It was considered the duty of the teachers to provide free instruction for men, but not for women. R. Eleazar is said to have commented that "he who instructs his daughter in the Law is like one who teachers her indecorous things" (Emil Hirsch et al. 2004). In taking time to sit with Mary and Martha and the other women and teach them about the **resurrection**, Jesus was clearly violating very ancient Jewish customs.

By the first century B.C., even country towns had schools for those young men 16 or older. (The children were still instructed by their parents in the home.) Every synagogue had an attendant like the one described in Luke 4:20, who sat on a low platform in the midst of boys teaching them the "Law and the Prophets, and the elements of reading. The teacher gave out a verse, and the pupils repeated it after him in unison" (Madeleine S. Miller and J. Lane Miller 1961, 150). The more advanced students would read the verse or copy it on wax-covered wooden tablets. These teachers were paid by the local congregation.

By the time of Jesus, the synagogue teaching followed a clear pattern: "The study of the Bible commenced with that of the book of Leviticus. Thence it passed to the other parts of the Penateuch; then to the Prophets; and, finally, to the hagiographa.... Care was taken not to send a child too early to school, nor to overwork him when there. For this purpose, the school hours were fixed, and attendance was shortened during the summer–months" (Alfred Edersheim 2004, 161). Scholars assume that Jesus would have frequented the synagogue school after learning the rudiments of his faith from his mother and father. He would have sat at the foot of the local teacher along with the other children of Nazareth, repeating the sacrificial ordinances in the book of Leviticus. He would have attended services at the same synagogue, listening to the reading of Moses and the other prophets. His own words suggest that he read Scripture in the original Hebrew, writing this language in the "square, or Assyrian characters." Without any opportunities at a higher level of education that he might have known in Jerusalem or another large city with its academy, he was nonetheless able to argue with the **Pharisees** and **Sadducees.**

In the larger synagogues, there were classes for the more advanced students who hoped to become rabbis, scribes, or masters. For those especially talented students, like Paul, who had come to Jerusalem from Tarsus to study the Law under Gamaliel (Acts 22:3), the discussions of Judaism were sophisticated and intense. The teacher might have taught in his own house or in the Temple porticoes, where Jesus did much of his teaching. It was customary for students to sit on the ground at their teacher's feet. Benches were introduced later in history.

For the Jews, tutors were rare except among the royalty. Among the **Romans**, however, educated slaves were sometimes used as tutors. Jewish education, by contrast, continued to be considered the primary obligation of the child's family. Its content was designed for making the child a member of the faith community. *See also* Carpenters, Carpentry; Cloth; Rabbi; Scribes; Shepherds; Synagogue; Writing and Reading.

Further Reading

DeVaux, Roland. *Ancient Israel: Its Life and Institutions*. Grand Rapids, Mich.: William B. Eerdmans Publishing Company, 1961. Edersheim, Alfred. *The Life and Times of Jesus the Messiah*. Peabody, Mass.: Hendrickson Publishers, Inc., 2004. Hirsch, Emil G., Kaufmann Kohler, Richard Gottheil, M. Gildemann, Cyrus Adler, Gotthard Deutsch, and Joseph Jacobs, "Education," http://www.jewishencyclopedia.com (accessed June 12, 2004). Miller, Madeleine S. and J. Lane Miller. "Education," in *Harper's Bible Dictionary*. New York: Harper and Row, 1961. Payne, D. F. "Education," in *The Illustrated Bible Dictionary*. Sydney, Australia: Tyndale House Publishers, 1980. Wight, Fred H. *Manners and Customs of Bible Lands*. Chicago: Moody Press, 1953.

Egypt, Egyptians

(Gen. 12:10–20, 41:41–45; Exod. 1–12) Egypt, the near neighbor of Palestine, was a rich and powerful country with a long history before it had any mention in Scripture. **Canaan**, where the Hebrews settled, was of interest to the Egyptians largely because of its position between Egypt and Asia, where the main trade routes ran. Along the coastline, the Egyptians established colonies, engaged in trade, built monuments, and occasionally waged battles against Bedouin attackers, whom they called the "desert peoples" (Werner Keller 1982, 58–59). When the Semites began to settle the region, the Egyptians kept a wary eye on these "sanddwellers" and finally took possession of the whole of Canaan about 1850 B.C. Some cities proved intractable, as can be seen from ancient documents regarding the "cities of execration" (ca. nineteenth century B.C.). In these cases, the magicians cursed the hostile elements, some of whom may well have been the Semites.

This "golden age" of Egyptian literature and culture coincided with the travels of Abraham, who left Haran, going first into Canaan and then to

Egypt. Werner Keller tells the "Tale of Sinuhe," a remarkable contemporary narrative of an Egyptian nobleman who spent some time in Canaan and finally returned to Egypt at about the same time that Abram (later to be known as *Abraham*) would have migrated to Canaan and visited Egypt. Some of the phrasing of the folktale parallels that of Abram in his meeting with the Pharaoh.

When one of their periodic droughts hit Canaan, Abram took his family and his flocks to Egypt, where the food and grain were abundant. According to Scripture, Abram was welcomed there but caused problems for the pharaoh by pretending that his beautiful wife was his sister. When he was asked to leave, he was given many presents, including the pharaoh's daughter, Hagar. This Egyptian princess became a handmaiden for his wife and the mother of his child Ishmael, the progenitrix of many of the Arab peoples. Later, Abraham's great-grandson Joseph was taken to Egypt as a captive, only to become a major figure in the court by means of his native wits and God's blessings. This series of events and yet another famine in Canaan led to the migration of Jacob and the entire family, beginning a sojourn that lasted for more than four centuries (Exod. 12:40). Scholars estimate this happened around 1700 B.C. (Madeleine S. Miller and J. Lane Miller 1961, 151).

Although there is little archaeological evidence of the Hebrews' sojourn in the land of the Nile, there are documents and artifacts that mention a foreign group called *Apiru,* who were forced to build the cities of Pithom and Ramses. Some believe that the Israelites lived in Egypt at the time of the Hyksos invasion (ca. 1700 B.C.). According to this Egyptian version of history, this Asiatic group of invaders was despised by the Egyptians, who, after four centuries, finally drove them out of Egypt and chased them into Palestine, where they fought for some years more. There were thought to be Semitic slaves at the time of the Hyksos, some of whom were appointed to high office. Joseph's story (Gen. 37–50) would fit perfectly into this period when Joseph assumed the role of the Vizier.

The region in which the Israelites settled, Goshen, is now thought to be a narrow valley connecting the Nile with Lake Timsah. Wright notes that herdsmen, such as the Bedouins from Palestine and Sinai, were allowed to enter Egypt during hard times, but were restricted to the Goshen region (G. Ernest Wright 1957, 56). A number of the details of the Genesis story—the use of **coins**, the cart in which Jacob was carried, Joseph's **chariot**, the baker and the butler, the celebration of the pharaoh's birthday, and the embalming of the bodies of both Jacob and Joseph—indicate an observed knowledge of Egyptian life. Even the cycle of seven years of plenty and seven of famine is typical of this land.

By the end of their centuries in Egypt, the Hyksos had been driven from the land and the Israelites were enslaved and forced to build the great public monuments for the pharaoh (thought to be Ramses II, who undertook a massive building program throughout all Egypt and Nubia). In the meantime, Egyptian control over Syria-Palestine had slackened, petty princes there were free to fight one another, and there was constant movement back and forth between Egypt and Canaan. It was a remarkably cosmopolitan period in Egyptian history.

Because of their rapidly increasing numbers, the Hebrews were seen as something of a problem, leading the Egyptians to try to limit their population by slaughtering their newborn males. Moses, their eventual leader, having escaped this fate through the shrewd devices of his mother and sister, was adopted by the Egyptian princess and was undoubtedly educated in the court, probably during the time of Ramses II (ca. 1290 B.C.). Scholars note that the Egyptian royal family often adopted **slave** children and educated them, bringing them up in royal harems, anticipating that they would eventually hold offices of some prominence (K. A Kitchen 1980, 423).

With its high level of culture, its long history, and great wealth, Egypt appears not to have noted either the migration of the Hebrews to this land or their escape from it. It did, however, make a major difference in the lives of the Hebrews, who now knew the "fleshpots" of Egypt—the opulent lifestyle of these people. They were probably influenced by their agricultural practices; their use of certain of these native products, such as linen and papyrus; their lavish **jewelry;** their craftsmanship in **ivory**, **pottery**, and **metal;** and perhaps even their calendars and some of their religious ideas. The behavior of the Hebrews during their time in the wilderness reflected the tastes they acquired during their Egyptian sojourn: their constant laments about the superior **food** and spices they left behind in Egypt, their abundance of purloined gold jewelry that they used to make the Golden Calf, and their plans for outfitting their priests with the finest Egyptian linen. Gradually during these 40 years in the wilderness, they returned to their nomadic lifestyle. Later with their eventual conquest of Canaan, they tended to forget much of this Egyptian influence, reviving their own strong culture and finding more influences in Asia Minor than in Egypt.

God used the **plagues** to convince the pharaoh of his superiority over some of the multiplicity of Egyptian gods. Most of these plagues are thought to be echoes of powers attributed to the various deities worshiped by the Egyptians, as well as to recurrent natural events in this land. Egypt was a land of many gods: Re, the sun god; Thoth and Khons, moon gods; Nut, the sky goddess; Hopi, the god of the Nile flood; Amun, the god of hidden life-powers in nature; Maat, the goddess of truth, justice, and right order; Thoth, the god of learning and wisdom; Ptah, the god of craftsmen; Oriris, the king of the underworld; not to mention gods that looked like bulls, **birds**, and other creatures. The popular use of graven images for their gods, with constant attention to their needs, became a warning to the Hebrews of pagan practices that violated their own concept of an invisible God. The

Egyptian interest in **magic**, which Moses confronted in the Pharaoh's court, was strictly forbidden under the **law** of Moses.

Egypt continued through much of Israel's history to be of marginal interest, sometimes overrunning the country in conflicts with the other great empires, sometimes serving as a friendly neighbor offering a wife for King Solomon (1 Kings 7:8) or acting as a trading partner with his kingdom. It was from Egypt that the king got his **horses** and his linens (1 Kings 10:28–29). There were battles, such as the one in which Asa of Judah (897 B.C.) apparently ended Egypt's aggressive policy in Asia. Ahab had links with Egypt, and Hosea turned for help to the "King of Egypt" against **Assyria** (2 Kings 17:4), but found this ally too weak to be of any real help.

Like Israel, Egypt faced one great invasion after another, falling like a "bruised reed" before the Assyrians (2 Kings. 18:21). Ashurbanipal (664 B.C.) sacked the ancient Egyptian city of Thebes, taking away 14 centuries of temple treasures, leading Nahum to proclaim the ruin of Nineveh in its turn (K. A. Kitchens 1980, 425). Later Nebuchadnezzar marched against Egypt, and even later the country fell under Persian domination under Cambyses.

Alexander the Great "liberated" Egypt in 332 B.C. The country became a Hellenistic monarchy under the Ptolemies, which took large numbers of Jews to Egypt as colonists and prospective citizens. Others followed and prospered in Egypt, making Alexandria a center of Jewish learning. It was here that the first Greek translation of the Old Testament, the Septuagint, was made by Hellenistic Jews (Emil G. Hirsch and J. Frederic McCurdy 2004). In 203 B.C., Antiochus III took Judea from Egypt, and it was under his second successor, Antiochus Epiphanes, that the great profanation of the Temple took place. Ptolemaic Egypt subsequently fell to **Rome** and then Byzantium. Finally, in 641 A.D., Egypt was overrun during the Islamic conquest.

At the time of Christ's birth, in the days of Caesar Augustus, a journey into Egypt to keep the child safe from Herod the Great's slaughter of the innocents would have been a natural avenue to escape (Matt. 2:13–19). There was a large community of Jews living in Egypt at that time. In the days of the early **Church**, Egyptians are mentioned as being among those present at the time of the **Pentecost** (Acts 2:10). The ancient Coptic (**Christian**) Church, which survived for many years, was thought to be evidence of missionary activity among the earliest Christian **apostles**. Most of the Coptic literature is translations from **Greek**. Manuscripts of Gnostic Gospels have been discovered in Egypt at Oxrhynchus, containing the reputed "sayings" of Jesus. These are thought to date from the third and fourth centuries A.D. (G. Ernest Wright 1957, 242). *See also* Bricks, Brick-layers; Cloth; Exodus; History in the Bible; Plagues; Writing and Reading; Writing Materials.

Egypt's gods (left to right, upper row): Isis, Osiris, Nephtys, Set; (lower row) Hathor, Anubis, Horus, and Nut. The Egyptians also worshipped many lesser gods.

Further Reading

Hirsch, Emil G. and J. Frederic McCurdy. "Israel, People of," http://www. jewishencyclopedia.com (accessed June 14, 2004). Keller, Werner. *The Bible as History.* New York: Bantam Books, 1982. Kitchen, K. A. "Egypt," in *The Illustrated Bible Dictionary.* Sydney, Australia: Tyndale House Publishers, 1980. Miller, Madeleine S. and J. Lane Miller. "Egypt," in *Harper's Bible Dictionary.* New York: Harper and Row, Publishers, 1961. Wright, G. Ernest. *Biblical Archaeology.* Philadelphia: The Westminster Press, 1957.

Epistles

In the Old Testament, letters were an uncommon means of communication. Few people were literate, and tokens or **seals** usually functioned to communicate important information in commercial dealings. By the time of the Babylonian captivity, the Jews became accustomed to formal letters from monarchs, proclaiming a royal mandate or providing authority regarding some event. We see this in both the books of Esther and Daniel. These formal documents are often transcribed in full in the Bible, especially when they prove central to the narrative.

In New Testament times, Jesus was not known to have written any letters, although he was probably literate. He did write some words on the ground with his finger when confronting those who accused a woman taken in adultery (John 8:6–7). Rather than sitting in a study and **writing** his thoughts, he spoke directly to his friends and followers, living out the theology he was seeking to explain. Written accounts came years later, when human memory was growing faint and **Christians** feared that the original experience might be lost or misreported.

The **apostles** needed to talk with one another and with their converts in a widely dispersed range of churches over three continents. It was a propitious time for letter writing: papyrus, velum, inks, and reeds for writing were readily available; literacy was more widespread. The roads and seaways were open, and mail could be sent by messengers going on journeys. The need to communicate across the miles and the opportunity to send letters brought forth the form of the epistle, peculiar to later New Testament writings. In all, 21 of the 27 books of the New Testament are apostolic letters (all except three of the **Gospels**), mostly written between 49 and 175 A.D. By contrast, none of the Old Testament books are letters, although they contain some letters, and they were written over hundreds of years.

In the Apostolic Age, the letter became a popular means of sending news, admonishing congregations, seeking help, or expressing affection. Paul, Peter, James, and others wrote long and meditative letters to congregations they knew. The letters were probably read aloud and studied by the group. When the writer returned, these discourses were undoubtedly the subject of discussion (Madeleine S. Miller and J. Lane Miller 1961, 169).

The epistle itself usually has the same components as letters written in our own day:

1. An opening greeting that designates the sender and the addressee
2. A discussion, elaborated for the specific audience addressed
3. A closing salutation, wishing the readers a divine blessing, extending a benediction, or dispatching personal remembrances from the writer and his Christian associates

Paul was the outstanding letter writer of early Christianity He set the form for many others to follow, which was based on the Hellenistic letter type found in both Jewish and non-Jewish communities. He is credited with 18 or 20 letters or fragments of letters, including Romans, 1 and 2 Corinthians, Galatians, Philippians, 1 Thessalonians, and the letter to Philemon. Some are quite brief and specific such as Philemon. Some are composed like logical arguments (for example, Galatians or Romans). They invariably address the concerns of a specific congregation or person, mentioning the individuals he knew in the group, and providing advice that has both a direct and more general application. They sometimes include fragments of ceremonies and hymns, lists of good and bad behaviors, and warnings against false teachings (William G. Doty 1993, 447–448).

Many of the other epistles in the New Testament are considered "Pauline," that is, drawing their form and much of their substance from Paul's letters. Paul's letters are rarely private documents, aimed instead at a larger audience and intended for study and discussion, but the "Pastoral" epistles do include personal references. (These include 1 and 2 Timothy and Titus and are addressed to church officers.) The more "General" or "Catholic" epistles are more rhetorical in style and intended for wider reading. Examples of this form would be James, 1 and 2 Peter, Jude, 1 John, and Hebrews. These include few personal references. Although addressed to the seven churches and ending with a benediction, Revelation is a piece of **apocalyptic** writing, not really a letter at all. Although epistolary in form, both Luke and Acts are also more general in style, clearly addressed to an audience beyond the "Theophilus" ("Lover of God"), ostensibly the addressee named in the opening verses.

The most venerated of the early Christian letters were undoubtedly saved, passed around, copied, and finally included in the canon as inspired works. *See also* Apostle; Scribes; Writing and Reading; Writing Materials.

Further Reading

Doty, William G. "The Epistles," in *A Complete Literary Guide to the Bible*. Grand Rapids, Mich.: Zondervan Publishing House, 1993. Miller, Madeleine S. and J. Lane Miller. "Epistles," in *Harper's Bible Dictionary*. New York: Harper and Row, 1961. White, John L. "Letter-Writing in Antiquity," in *The Oxford Companion to the Bible*. New York: Oxford University Press, 1993.

Essenes

At the time of Jesus's birth, there were three major religious orders of Jews: the **Sadducees**, the **Pharisees**, and the Essenes. The Essenes, the smallest of these groups, lived in separate communities and sought to adhere strictly to the spirit of the **law**. Some commentators consider them an offshoot of the Pharisees, following the law with almost Levitical purity. Like the Pharisees, they probably arose from the Hasidim of the pre-Maccabean time. They rejected **Temple** worship in Jerusalem because they believed it had been defiled. They were especially outraged by the usurpation of the high priesthood by the Maccabean **king** Jonathan (152 B.C.), precipitating their building communities in towns or villages throughout Palestine. The First Jewish Revolt in 68 A.D. probably marked the end of their movement.

One of these Essene communities, probably the largest, was excavated in the 1950s at Qumran, revealing ruins of several buildings, a library, and the remarkable cache of documents known as the Dead Sea Scrolls. The Qumran community was probably the "city in the wilderness" that the historian Pliny mentioned in discussing this group. Some of these scrolls describe the rules of the community, which required that its members remain celibate, rejecting the "order of the earth" (George E. Wright 1961, 173). Philo, another historian who mentioned them, estimated that they numbered about 4,000 and noted that they lived in villages, worked hard at agriculture or mechanical chores, and devoted much of their time to the communal study of moral and religious questions, especially the interpretation of the sacred books (F. F. Bruce 1980, 478).

The Essenes were **apocalyptic**, expecting the final days in the immediate future, obsessed with living in a manner appropriate for this "new age" that they anticipated, and with preparing for the coming of a **Messiah**. Living an ascetic life under the leadership of the "Teacher of Righteousness," they had strict regulations about entry into the community and life within it. According to Josephus, another historian who described their rules, men could become members only after a long period of schooling in the ways of the community, followed by the purification by water and the swearing of a succession of solemn oaths, at which time they were allowed to share in the common meal. They assumed that only the men within the community, who had come to a true understanding of the law under the tutelage of their Teacher of Righteousness, were the true men of the **covenant**, the "sons of light" (John Riches 1993, 198). They held all property in common, renouncing money and women, yet their numbers were sustained over a period of almost two centuries by new entrants into the order.

The Essenes' day, Josephus tells us, began before sunrise with morning prayers, which were addressed to the sun. They then began their work, which continued until noon, when they bathed, dressed in clean linen, and had a common meal. After lunch, they changed back to their simple work clothes, usually only loin cloths, and worked until the evening meal. They were thought to have avoided speaking, but sang hymns of praise to God. Pliny speaks of 4,000 Essenes, who lived as farmers and artisans apart from the cities and in a perfect state of communism. They condemned **slavery**, avoided **sacrifice**, abstained from swearing, strove for holiness, and were particularly scrupulous regarding the **Sabbath** (Kaufmann Kohler 2004).

There are some debates about the actual life of the community and its influence: whether the Essenes forbad marriage, whether John the Baptist was one of their members, whether other of the **disciples** of Jesus—or even Jesus himself—might have been influenced by their ideas. As evidence, Kohler notes the same communism, "the same belief in **baptism** or **bathing**, and in the power of **prophecy**; the same aversion to **marriage**, enhanced by firmer belief in the Messianic advent; the same system of organization, and the same rules for the travelling brethren delegated to charity-work." Finally, "and, above all, the same love-feasts or brotherly meals" (Kaufmann Kohler 2004). Certainly, the fact that these ideas were current at the time Jesus lived and preached and that some of his disciples seem to have understood them must have helped prepare the way for his message. *See also* Pharisees; Sadducees.

Further Reading

Bruce, F. F. "Essenes," in *The Illustrated Dictionary of the Bible*. Sydney, Australia: Tyndale House Publishers, 1980. Josephus, Flavius. *The Works of Josephus*. Peabody, Mass.: Hendrickson Publishers, Inc., 2001. Kohler, Kaufmann. "Essenes," http://www.jewishencyclopedia.com (accessed October 1, 2004). Riches, John. "Essenes," in *The Oxford Companion to the Bible*. New York: Oxford University Press, 1993. Wright , George E. "Essenes," in *Harper's Bible Dictionary*. New York: Harper and Row, 1961.

Eunuchs

(Deut. 23; Acts 8:27) Although the term *eunuch* is not often used in Scripture, eunuchs were probably well known to the Jews. They usually managed the harems. Obviously a number of female servants would also be part of the harem staff—those who bathed, perfumed, and dressed the women and attended to their needs. (Although it is clear in the book of Esther that such women were in the **king**'s household, they mostly remained invisible in Scripture.)

It was contrary to Jewish **law** to castrate a male (Deut. 23). Castrati were, in fact, forbidden to worship in the **Temple**, apparently because they were regarded as unfit for worship or because self-mutilation was a part of some pagan worship rituals (Madeleine S. Miller and J. Lane Miller 1961, 176). Men who had been rendered impotent by sickness or accident, however, might serve as officers of the **court**. More likely, such officials came from other countries—Ethiopia or **Egypt**—and were non-Jews, such as the Ethiopian eunuch that Philip meets on the road (Acts 8:27).

It is thought that the **Babylonians** were accustomed to castrating those they intended for high office, leading some scholars to believe that Daniel may have been a eunuch (Jer. 41:16; Esther 1:10; Dan. 1:3). Apparently, the custom of castration was so common among Babylonians and Persians that the word for *eunuch* in Hebrew is derived from "royal attendant" or "official" (Gene McAfee 1993, 205).

Josephus notes that eunuchs were important members of a regal household, "especially under Herod the Great, the care of whose drink was entrusted to one, the bringing of his supper to another, and the putting of him to bed to a third, 'who also managed the principal affairs of the government.'"

Herod's favorite wife, Marianne, was also attended by a eunuch (Emil G. Hirsch, Wilhelm Nowack, Solomon Schecter, M. Seligsohn 2004).

In the New Testament, those who "have made themselves eunuchs for the sake of the kingdom of heaven" (Matt. 19:12) are noted as followers of Christ who have "attained a holy indifference to the delights of the married state.... Continence is a special gift of God to some, but not to others." Matthew Henry explains, "The single state must be chosen for the kingdom of heaven's sake" (Matthew Henry 1961, 1300). This is a metaphorical use of the term, as is Isaiah's (Isa. 56:4–5) and Paul's plea for those who can abstain to refrain from marriage. *See also* Court Officials.

Further Reading

Henry, Matthew. *Matthew Henry's Complete Commentary in One Volume*. Grand Rapids, Mich.: Zondervan Press, 1961. Hirsch, Emil G., Wilhelm Nowack, Solomon Schecter, M. Seligsohn, "Eunuch," http://www.jewishencyclopedia. com (accessed June 2, 2004). Josephus, Flavius. *The Works of Josephus*. Peabody, Mass.: Hendrickson Publishers, Inc., 2001. McAfee, Gene. "Eunuch," in *The Oxford Companion to the Bible*. New York: Oxford University Press, 1993. Miller, Madeleine S. and J. Lane Miller. "Eunuch," in *Harper's Bible Dictionary*. New York: Harper and Row, 1961.

Exile. *See* History in the Bible

Exodus

Exodus, "a way out," was adopted from Greek. It is the name given to both the experience of escaping from captivity in **Egypt** and the book of the Bible that follows Genesis. The title in the Hebrew Bible is *Shemoth*.

The experience, which is chronicled in Exodus, begins with a narrative of the **slave** condition of the Hebrews after Joseph was long forgotten. Moses, the leader who was to take the children of God from enslavement to freedom, is fully characterized from birth to death. The confrontations with the Pharaoh and his magicians, the series of **plagues** brought on the land because of the Pharaoh's hard heart, and the culminating experience of the **Passover** of the **angel** of God prepared the Israelites for their perilous journey. Finally allowed to escape, they collected their belongings, in addition to **jewelry** and gold taken from the Egyptians, and fled. When the Pharaoh changed his mind, he followed with his **horses** and **chariots**, only to be halted by the miracle of the parting of the Red Sea (or Reed Sea), which closed in on his army. The jubilant Israelites celebrated this escape in **dance** and **song**.

The following years are also chronicled in Exodus, the constant whining of the Israelites about the conditions of life in the wilderness, the **manna** that was miraculously provided for their "daily **bread**," the water that flowed from the cleft in the rock, the gift of the **law** of Moses, the apostasy of the Golden Calf, as well as the numerous travels, battles, arguments, challenges and changes the people saw as they wandered for 40 years before being led into the Promised Land of **Canaan** by Joshua.

Historians and archaeologists have debated the route and time of the Exodus. Some believe it was approximately 1250 B.C. The most baffling portion of the journey to map is the path out of Egypt. Recent explorations have suggested that it may have been far south of the original route suggested, leading into the area that is modern-day Saudi Arabia. This debate continues, although traditional scholars believed it to be through the Sinai, with Mt. Sinai considered the location for the theophany in which Moses received the **Ten Commandments**.

For later peoples, the Exodus became the symbol of freedom and delivery from oppression. Among slave peoples everywhere, the redemption of the Hebrews signaled God's hand in history, preserving his chosen people. *See also* Canaan, Canaanites, Egypt, Egyptians; History in the Bible; Idols, Idolatry.

Fall of Man

(Genesis 2–3) Genesis tells a profound story in few words. God made man from the dust of the earth; he then made woman from a rib he took from Adam's side. He placed them in the garden to tend it and to care for the **animals**. He asked only that they obey his simple command, that they refrain from eating of the Tree of the Knowledge of Good and Evil. From the story of the first man and first woman, their sojourn in the **Garden of Eden**, their temptation by the **serpent**, their decision to eat the forbidden fruit, and their subsequent blaming of one another and of the snake, we derive numerous theological concepts underlying both Judaism and Christianity. Among these is the Fall of humans through this first sin. The act of disobedience, echoing the Satanic decision to refuse to serve God, results in the first example of the spread of Original Sin—from Eve to Adam. It also results in knowledge of evil—the awareness that they are naked. Further, it brings deceit—lying to God regarding their choice. And finally it brings the judgment of God and the expulsion from Eden.

Other "forgotten books of Eden" that were apparently known to the Hebrews and to the early Christians tell in much more detail the sorrows that Adam and Eve knew after their loss of Eden, as they took up their new life in the Cave of Treasures. Here they felt hunger and thirst for the first time, saw their first sunrise, and discovered all of life's adversity in a land of rocks and sand. Weeping for the lost Eden, according to these **apocryphal** writers, they even contemplated suicide, only to be comforted by God with the sure knowledge that their seed would in time be saved by Christ. The editor of these noncanonical narratives indicates that many of the ancient scholars, including writers of the Talmud, must have known these manuscripts that were thought to be the work of ancient Egyptians (Rutherford H. Platt Jr 1974, 3).

Theologians see the events of the first transgression as the rationale for death, the pain of childbearing, the difficulties of work, and the general breach of the human and divine relationship. Original Sin is thought to be innate in each subsequent "child of Adam," throughout the generations, requiring the **law** for constraint and direction, and a redeemer for salvation and reconciliation. Because of this, among Christians, Christ is seen as the "Second Adam," redeeming the sin of the first through the **sacrifice** of his innocent **blood** on the **cross** (for example, Romans 5:12–21; 1 Corinthians 15:21–22, 15:45).

Each of these steps in the narrative becomes important in Scripture, as a part of the human story, the clash with Divine will, the subsequent judgment, and the loss of innocence and of **blessings**. Theologians and **prophets** have pointed out the various elements in the basic story of the Fall, which is replicated in each individual life. In more recent times, psychologists have also pored over the elements of the story, finding them embedded deep in human experience, a kind of coming-of-age journey. Augustine was particularly instrumental in emphasizing both the original innocence of Adam and the hideous decline resulting from sin (Dennis Danielson 1992, 272).

Over the years, authors have returned again and again to the narrative of the Fall, using it explicitly (e.g., Milton's *Paradise Lost*) or symbolically (e.g., *Hawthorne's The House of Seven Gables*). Romantic writers tend to reject the doctrine of the Fall, assuming instead that humans are born good and come to earth from **Heaven** "streaming clouds of glory" (Wordsworth). Rousseau was instrumental in presenting this point of view. Some writers, such as Shelley, tended to glorify Satan rather than seeing him as villain of the piece, making his rebellion and his involvement of humankind in that rebellion an act of Promethean grandeur. In modern times, William Golding (*Lord of the Flies*), C. S. Lewis (*Perelandra*), and J.R.R. Tolkien (*Lord of the Rings*) have revived the story of the Fall, relating it to all humankind.

Christian art has numerous portrayals of the moments of the **Creation** of both Adam and Eve (Michangelo), of the temptation of Eve (Botticelli), and of expulsion of Adam and Eve (di Paolo). Cynics suggest that artists were delighted to have a theologically sound rationale for drawing and painting nude studies, which were otherwise forbidden in the medieval period. The drama of the scene invites the artist to capture the torments of the first couple succumbing to temptation and losing their primal innocence. *See also* Creation; Eden, Garden of.

Further Reading

Danielson, Dennis. "The Fall," in *A Dictionary of the Biblical Tradition in English Literature*. Grand Rapids, Mich.: William B. Eerdmans Publishing Company, 1992. Ferguson, George. *Signs and Symbols in Christian Art*. New York: Oxford University Press, 1966. Platt, Rutherford H., Jr., ed. *The Forgotten Books of Eden*. New York: The New American Library, 1974.

Family

(**Exod. 20:12, 21:15, 17; Lev. 20:9; Proverbs 31**) The family has provided Jews, **Christians**, and Moslems their image of God and his people. He is the father; we are his children, brothers and sisters in the faith. For Christians, Christ is the elder brother, who taught us to pray, "Our Father." On the posts of Hebrew doorways are **prayers** indicating that the household is dedicated to God. Inside, the family worship is central to several of the holy days, notably the **Sabbath** and the **Passover**. Family members are expected to participate in the ceremonies of these days. The rituals of clearing the house of yeast, the careful handling of kosher foods, the precise delineation of tasks all testify to the impressive saturation of the Hebrew household in biblical faith. Much of this carried over into the New Testament.

Throughout the history of Judaism and continuing into modern times, no set of relationships has proven so basic to Jewish life as the family. The joint family or clan that formed the father's household consisted of **blood** relatives and women connected through **marriage** (Philip J. King and Lawrence E. Stager 2001, 39). It also included all the servants and **slaves** of the joint families that formed this basic unit. A good example of this extensive household is found in Judges 17–18: Micah lived in the hill country of Ephraim with his wife or wives, his widowed mother, his sons, a hired priest, and servants.

The head of it all was the father or *paterfamilias,* who ruled like a **king**. In this tiny kingdom, the father had command over his wife, his children, his children's children, his servants, and all of his household. Usually, when the father died, his eldest son assumed the position of leadership, becoming the ruler over the whole family, including his own mother.

The family itself determined right and wrong, made **laws**, administered justice, and maintained divine worship (Kaufmann Kohler and Adolf Guttmacher 2004). Thus, the larger state and the political arena were far less important to ancient Jews than they were to **Greeks** and **Romans**.

"Honor thy father and thy mother that thy days may be long upon the land which the Lord thy God giveth thee" (Exod. 20:12). The Jews, responding to Mosaic law, took this admonition to "honor" their parents seriously. The authority of the parents over their children was almost supreme, allowing them even to offer their children as **sacrifice** to their gods. **Moloch**, the hated god of their neighbors, regularly demanded the firstborn sons of his worshippers. Even father Abraham was ready to sacrifice his son Isaac to his god should he require it (Gen. 22). And Judah ordered Tamar, his daughter-in-law, to be burned when he thought she had broken her marriage vow (Gen. 38:24). The father could sell his young children into slavery to satisfy debts, and he could arrange **marriage**s for them with or without their agreement. There were some limits on his power: he could not sell his wife into slavery or his daughters into prostitution (Lev. 19:29).

The father was expected to support his children, to circumcise his sons, and to teach them trades. In addition, he was obliged to find wives for his sons and husbands for his daughters (Solomon Schechter and Caspar Levias 2004). They, in turn, were expected to honor him in accordance with the commandment. A son who was stubborn, rebellious, gluttonous, or a drunkard might be brought before the other elders of the **tribe** for judgment. If they so decided, he might be stoned to death. A son who hit or cursed his father could also be put to death (Exod. 21:15, 17; Lev. 20:9). Disrespect for a father or mother was considered a significant crime.

The wife and mother, although deserving and expecting the same respect as the father, was nonetheless inferior in position, both legally and ritually. She was considered the possession of her husband, who could **divorce** her if she displeased him, and who could take other wives or concubines without consulting her. If she committed adultery, her husband could bring her before the elders of the town and have her stoned to death. If she came to the marriage not a virgin, she could also be stoned. She had little standing before giving **birth** to a son and heir; and at her husband's death, as noted earlier, she became subject to her own son. In the early years of her children's lives, she was the main force, providing nourishment and training. It was her task to maintain all the rituals connected with the kosher household. In addition, her moral influence was especially strong because of her early contact with her children. The Bible is full of examples of close and loving relationships between mothers and sons.

The most impressive tribute to the "virtuous woman" is in Proverbs 31, King Lemuel's tribute to his mother:

> her price is far above rubies. The heart of her husband doth safely trust in her, so that he shall have no need of spoil. She will do him good and not evil all the days of her life. She seeketh wool, and flax, and worketh willingly with her hands. She is like the merchants ships; she bringeth her **food** from afar. She riseth also while it is night, and giveth meat to her household, and a portion to her maidens. She considereth a field, and buyeth it: with the fruit of her hands she planteth a **vineyard**. She girdeth her loins with strength, and strengtheneth her arms. She perceiveth that her merchandise is good: her candle goeth not out by night. She layeth her hands to the spindle, and her hands hold the distaff. She stretcheth out her hand to the poor; yea, she reacheth forth her hands to the needy. She is not afraid of the snow for her household: for all her household are clothed with scarlet. She maketh herself coverings of tapestry; her **clothing** is silk and purple....She maketh fine linen, and selleth it; and delivereth girdles unto the merchant. Strength and honor are her clothing; and she shall rejoice in time to come. She openeth her mouth with wisdom; and in her tongue is the law of kindness. She looketh well to the ways of her household, and eateth not the bread of idleness. Her children arise up, and call her blessed; her husband also, and he praiseth her. (Prov. 31)

Although Scripture here portrayed a woman of property and prestige, not to mention brains and enterprise, she was a realistic role model for other women to emulate. The good wife was considered a treasure beyond price. Her chastity ensured the purity of the family's lineage, and her teachings brought solidity to the family's life and faith. With so much of Hebrew ritual centered in the home and assigned to the wife, the blessedness of the household was in her hands.

In the New Testament, Jesus and his mother appear to have had a long and close relationship, perhaps suggesting that Joseph died early and left her a widow, with Jesus serving as head of the household. Jesus's refusal to "honor" her demands that he abandon his ministry (Mark 3:31–35) apparently did not offend her or his **disciples**. Along with "the other women," she henceforth seems to have followed him. His response to her enlarged the meaning of the traditional family, defining his real "mother" and "brothers" as those who followed him rather than only those who shared his bloodline. It is obvious that the bonds of familial love continued to the end, testified to by his concern for her even as he hung on the cross, telling her that John was now her son and she his mother.

The New Testament has numerous segments related to domestic relations (Eph. 5:21–26, 9; Col. 3:18–4:1; 1 Tim. 5:4, 8–16, Phil. 15:16). In these segments we see the **Church** as the Bride of Christ, the father asserting his authority and demonstrating his love over the household, and the wife gladly submitting to the leadership of her husband. Husbands are encouraged to love their wives as Christ loves the Church (Eph. 5:25). Wives are encouraged to submit to their own husbands, as they do to the Lord. And children are told to obey their parents, "for this is well-pleasing unto the Lord" (Col. 3:20). At the same time, parents are warned not to provoke their children to anger. Masters are told to treat their slaves as brothers (Phil. 16) rather than as servants. The whole Church is pictured as the family of God, an interesting image, as so many of the early churches were household churches, meeting in individual homes. Paul instructed Timothy to choose leaders of the Church who were godly men who had only one wife each and orderly homes.

Most impressive of all in the New Testament is the consistent emphasis on the Father/Son relationship between God and Jesus, the only begotten Son, who sits on the right hand of God. The love and obedience displayed in the harmony of Trinity serves as a model for human relationships for all time. The three distinct persons are nonetheless one God. The ideal is a return to the idyllic harmony of **Eden**. *See also* Festivals; Law; Marriage; Slavery, Slaves.

Further Reading

King, Philip J. and Lawrence E. Stager, *Life in Biblical Israel*. Louisville, Ky.: Westminster John Knox Press, 2001. Kohler, Kaufmann and Adolf Guttmacher, "Family and Family Life," http://www.jewishencyclopedia.com (accessed July 6, 2004). Schechter, Solomon and Caspar Levias, "Father," http://www.jewishencyclopedia.com (accessed July 7, 2004)

Farmers. See Agriculture

Fast, Fasting

(Lev. 16:29–34; Matt. 4:2; Acts 9:9) Limitations on food and drink, even total abstinence, was a common part of Hebrew and early Christian practice. The modern custom of Lenten fasts is a vestige of this mode of mortification of the flesh. Even our word "breakfast" is based on the notion that we are "breaking" the night's fast.

Certain of the Jewish **festivals** involve fasting: the **Day of Atonement**, for example, the only fast commanded by the **law** (Lev. 16:29, 23:27–32), was called "the fast" in New Testament times (Acts 27:9); the Fast of Esther is the thirteenth day of Adar, the day before **Purim**. Minor fast days, instituted after the Babylonian Exile, includes one that memorializes the destruction of the Jerusalem **Temple**, observed on the ninth of Ab (2 Kings 25:1) and one that memorializes the destruction of the Jewish state (Jer. 41).

Notice that these are times of **lamentation**, the fast often being seen as a sign of **mourning**. In fact, in Esther we have the decree for the days of Purim, "established for themselves and their descendants in regard to their times of fasting and lamentation" (Esther 9:31). This echoes the Jews' response to the brutal edict of the king: they fasted, wept, and wailed. "Many lay in sackcloth and ashes" (Esther 4:3).

Directions for universal fasting as signs of sorrow for sin or for loss were repeated several times in Scripture: Jeremiah recommended that the people observe a day of fasting when they went to the house of the Lord and heard the powerful words written on the scroll. The people in Jerusalem and those who came from different towns in Judah obeyed their **prophet**, fasted, and listened (Jer. 36:9). Joel told the people that the Lord was asking them to "return to me with all your heart, with fasting and weeping and mourning" (Joel 2:12).

Saints and prophets of the faith also found in fasting a pathway to God's revelation. In Isaiah, we see the prophet fasting to "lose the chains of injustice and untie the cords of the yoke, to set the oppressed free and break every **yoke**" (Isaiah 58:6). Daniel and Joel also found fasting a means to approach God: Daniel "pleaded … in **prayer** and petition, in fasting, and in sackcloth and ashes" (Dan. 9:3).

Not all fasting served its intended purpose. The Psalmist lamented that his knees "give way from fasting; my body is thin and gaunt" (Ps. 109:24), and yet God failed to answer him. This echoes an earlier Psalm (35:13) in which he complained that he put on sackcloth and humbled himself with fasting, but his prayers returned to him unanswered. This illustrates one typical reason for fasting: to demonstrate humility and submission at a time of petition.

Unfortunately, this public display of humility sometimes backfired. Isaiah noted that the people often ended their fasting with quarrelling and strife, even fistfights. It is no wonder that the Lord failed to respond (Isa. 58:4). He also indicates that fasting does not necessarily lead to moral improvement. After fasting, "you do as you please and exploit all your workers" (Isa. 58:3).

Later, Jesus picked up on Isaiah's critique, noting that it is not so much what goes into the mouth but what comes out of it that causes trouble. He scorned the **Pharisees** and the **"hypocrites"** who relished their public displays of fasting, even "disfiguring their faces" (Matt. 6:16). (One sign of mourning , continuing today in some cultures, was to scrape the face with fingernails, leaving bloody marks.) Jesus indicated that this kind of exhibitionism is its own reward.

Fasting continued in New Testament times among both Jews and Christians. John the Baptist certainly had a modest diet—locusts and wild honey—and his **disciples** often fasted (Mark 2:18). Jesus himself was probably fasting in the wilderness in preparation for his ministry when the Tempter used his hunger to recommend Jesus turn stones into **bread** (Matt 4:2).

Jesus's objection to fasting was that it should not be a prideful display of piety, but an honest practice of faith. The **Christians** apparently combined fasting with prayer and seeking God's will, as in the worship services before committing Paul and Barnabas to the Lord's work (Acts 13:2, 14:23). Some considered it inconsistent with the hope of the coming **Messiah**, and unnecessary (Matt. 9:14). Modern Christians, Jews, and Moslems all observe fasting on certain occasions, according to a variety of regulations. Arabs, for instance, usually fast only from sunrise until sundown. Others fast in sympathy for the hungry of the world. Some fast in preparation for service or for decision making.

Among those who choose the contemplative life—monks and saints of various sorts—fasting has became a common practice. As a result, the traditional image of the saint is in the style of El Greco, an ethereal, emaciated figure who has clearly denied the lusts of the flesh. *See also* Bread; Festivals; Food; Passover or the Feast of Unleavened Bread; Prophet; Purim; Temple; Time.

Further Reading

DeVaux, Roland. *Ancient Israel: Its Life and Institutions.* Grand Rapids, Mich.: William B. Eerdmans Publishing Company, 1961. Miller, Madeleine S. and J. Lane Miller. "Fasting," in *Harper's Bible Dictionary.* New York: Harper and Row, 1961. Suggit, John N. "Fasting," in *The Oxford Companion to the Bible.* New York: Oxford University Press, 1993.

Feasting

Feasting means the gathering for ceremonial meals to celebrate events in the year or in history. It often involves strictly specified foods, prepared in fully documented ways, and eaten in a specific manner. For the Jews, **food** has strong historical, legal, and religious meanings, often serving as a symbol for different facets of life and worship. Reading the word of God, for example, is compared in the Psalms with devouring it, relishing the taste of it: "How sweet are thy words unto my taste! yea, sweeter than honey to my mouth" (Ps. 119:103). Feasting is an outward symbol of the community's sharing of God's bounty, a recognition that all nourishment ultimately comes by the grace of God.

The religious elements of festivals grew over time to become increasingly complex. The time, place, rationale, and ceremonies of each of the major festival times expanded along with the increasing complexity of the culture. While retaining the Festival of the New Moon, the Festival of First Fruits, and the Festival of Ingathering, all of which were relics of the agricultural calendar, the people added the celebrations of religious and historical events: **Passover**, the first day of the Festival of Unleavened Bread; Rosh Hashanah; Yom Kippur; Hanukkah; and **Purim**.

From the descriptions in Scripture, these celebrations usually involved feasting rather than **fasting**, often accompanied by **music**, **dance**, and **song**. Some of the **prophets** noted that the feasts could lead to excess and sought to return the people to the basic purpose of such festivities—the celebration of God's **blessings**. In addition, the celebrators became more contentious about the proper locale for the celebrations and the proper procedures as their leaders grew more legalistic.

By the time of Christ, the festivals had become regularized, with strict requirements, including obligated travel to Jerusalem. Jesus's conversation with the woman at the well, in which she asked about the proper place of worship, signaled his kinship with the prophets, who considered the spirit of worship rather than its appearance: "But the hour cometh, and now is, when the true worshippers shall worship the Father in spirit and in truth: for the Father seeketh such to worship him" (John 4:23).

In the early Christian Church, some of the sense of the festivals was retained in the "love feasts." These became so raucous in Corinth that Paul discouraged them, instructing the believers to go back to the spirit of the common **meal**, a remembrance of Christ's sacrifice. The Church transformed many of the Jewish customs into Christian ones, thus making the spring festival of Passover into the Christian Easter. Pentecost became a celebration of the Holy Spirit's descent on the early Church, and Christmas replaced the pagan celebration of the winter solstice, which came after Hanukkah. Americans have added Thanksgiving, a time to celebrate the "ingathering." And many non-Jews use the new year in January for the same purpose that orthodox Jews use the Day of Atonement.

In recent years, some Jewish families have enlarged or added to their traditional festivals or holy days for significant reasons. Hanukkah, for example, now contends with Christmas as a time for candle lighting and gift giving. Because it also comes in December and is a time for remembering the faithfulness of God in a time of great distress, this holiday deserves its new prominence. So also Yom HaShoah, Holocaust Memorial Day, is now considered a Jewish holy day unlike any other It was established as a day of commemoration by Israel's Parliament in 1951 as a day to hold in memory the millions who were slaughtered by the Nazis.

The date was chosen to fall a few days after the end of Passover, within the Hebrew month of the famous anti-Nazi Jewish uprising in the Warsaw Ghetto. Although there is considerable debate over the proper way to observe this day, many use the lighting of candles at the evening synagogue services, prayers for the dead, somber readings, and liturgical poetry. Ultra-Orthodox Jews refuse to acknowledge this day, believing that communal mourning "is subsumed in another day of commoration, Tish B'Av" (Seth Siegel 2005).

By keeping history alive and traditions in tact, such celebrations, commemorations, and festivals make the religious communities strong. They are invaluable lessons for the children and excellent reminders for the parents. They also give the worshippers a sense of shared identify and reinforce their faith. *See also* Fast, Fasting; Passover or the Feast of Unleavened Bread; Pentecost or the Day of the First Fruits; Sabbath.

Further Reading

Siegel, Seth. "Stories of Survival," *The Wall Street Journal.* May 6, 2005, W11.

Festivals

Festivals were a joyous time for the Hebrews. They came together to celebrate their own history and God's great mercies in song, dance, sacrifice, and worship. Each festival had its own origin in history and practice; each accrued certain rituals and meanings. The table shows a partial listing of the major festivals named in Scripture:

Jewish Feasts	Time of Celebration	Scripture References
Passover	Nisan, 14th day (March/April)	Exod. 12:1–14; Matt. 26:17–20
Unleavened Bread	Nisan, 15–21st day (March/April)	Exod. 12:15–20
First Fruits	Nisan 16th day (March/April) or Sivan 6th day (May/June)	Lev. 23 9–14 Num. 28:26
Pentecost	Sivan 6th day (May/June) or Harvest or Weeks 50 days after barley harvest	Deut. 16:9–12; Acts 2:1
Rosh Hashanah	Tischr 1, 2 (September/October) or Festival of Trumpets	Num. 29:1–6
Yom Kippur	Tishri 10 (September/October) or Day of Atonement	Lev. 23:26–32; Heb. 9:7

Tabernacles	Tishri 15/22 (September/October) or Festival of Booths or Ingathering	Neh. 8:13–18; John 7:2
Hanukkah	Chislev 25 (for 8 days) (Nov/Dec) or Lights or Dedication	John 10:22
Purim or Lots	Adar 14, 15 (February/March)	Esther 9:18–32

Additional celebrations included the new moon (each month) and the Sabbath, which was celebrated each week. *See also* Atonement, Day of; Passover or the Feast of Unleavened Bread; Purim.

Firmament. *See* Cosmology

Fish

(Deut. 14:9) Fish provided an abundant and ready **food** in antiquity, yet are curiously absent from most of the Old Testament commentary on foods. In fact, the Bible does not mention any fish by name, using only the words *dag* and *nun* as generic terms (Emil G. Hirsch 2004). The streams and lakes of Palestine had been fished from earliest times, but this readily available food had no mention before the captivity in **Egypt**.

Mosaic **law** (Deut. 14:9, 10) allows "All that have fins and scales" and disallows "whatsoever hath not fins and scales." Thus, the Hebrews might eat most of the scaly fish swimming in the fresh waters of Canaan, but were forbidden the eels, water snakes, lizards, mussels, oysters, shrimp, crab, lobster, octopus, and squid. Usually, the scriptural references are simply to large and small fish: small fish were thought to be particularly wholesome food. There was no regulation against eating fish roe or using fish oil for fuel or mixing it with olive oil, all of which were apparently common practices.

The Israelites found abundant fish in the waters of Egypt, where one of the plagues turned the Nile into **blood,** so that the fish died and the water stank (Exod. 7:18–21). During their long sojourn in this foreign land, they apparently learned to fish these waters and enjoyed the fish they caught, along with cucumbers, melons, leeks, onions, and garlic that the Egyptians included in their diet (Deut 14:9–10; J. A. Thompson 1980, 509). Scripture suggests that the Israelites learned much about the varieties of fish and their preparation from the Egyptians. Numbers 11:5 notes that during their sparse meals in the desert, the Israelites looked back to a time when they "did eat in Egypt freely." In spite of this acquired taste, it is remarkable that "the eating of fish is never mentioned favorably" in the Old Testament,, although 25 of the 26 New Testament references mention fish as food (George Cansdale 1970, 212–213).

Hirsch mentions that the Talmudists made specific note of fish as delicacies—cooked or raw, salted or fresh. The Hebrews also made and sold chopped fish-meat, believing fish best when near decomposition. It was considered a wholesome food, especially good for pregnant women (Emil Hirsch 2004).

Fish was sometimes considered a curative, excellent for those being bled, nourishing a child, or suffering from eye infections. On the other hand, a fish diet during the month of Nisan might lead to leprosy (Emil Hirsch 2004). In the **apocryphal** story of Tobit, smearing the gall of a fish on the eyes cured blindness (Tobit 11:7).

Fish must have become a staple of the diet, as evidenced by their frequent mention in the writings of the **prophets** and the wisdom literature. Abundant fish are the sign of God's blessing: "Swarms of living creatures will live everywhere the river flows. There will be large numbers of fish, because this water flows there and makes the salt water fresh; so where the river flows everything will live" (Ezek. 47:9). This cleansing of the Salt Sea (the Dead Sea) would bring a purification so impressive that fishermen would stand along the shore—the whole length of the land—discovering fish of many kinds.

But it was in the "Great Sea" that the fishermen found boundless varieties of fish. Apparently the trade in fish by the men from Tyre (Neh. 13:16) became so impressive that one of the city gates was named the Fish Gate. They also violated the Sabbath with their constant fishmongering in Jerusalem.

One small sea creature of importance to the clothing industry was the murex, from which the famous tyrian purple was obtained. This was the color, sometimes described as purple, sometimes as scarlet, which was used to dye wool. Only a single drop could be extracted from each of these tiny shell creatures, making the resulting fabric very expensive and rare—therefore "royal purple" for which Tyre was famous.

For a land-bound people like the Hebrews, the great fish were creatures of mystery and peril. Genesis mentions specifically the **creation** of the great whales, while relegating the rest of the water creatures to "every living creature that moveth, which the waters brought forth abundantly" (Gen.1:21). Later, Job would wonder at the majesty of Leviathan, and Jonah would find himself in the belly of a "great fish" for three days and three nights (Jonah 1:17). In the fantastic tale of Tobit (Tobit 6:3–6), a somewhat smaller fish provided help to the hero. In this case, an **angel** told the man to cut the fish open and remove the gall, heart, and liver, "For its gall, heart , and liver are useful as medicine."

Jesus transformed the palpable fear of Jonah's monstrous fish into the image of death, saying that "as Jonah was three days and three nights in the belly of a huge fish, so the Son of Man will be three days and three nights in the heart of the earth" (Matt. 12:40).

Smaller, edible fish were found in the fresh waters of the Holy Land. In the Sea of Galilee, famous for its fishing, are found 25 native species of fish, many of which probably date back to New Testament times. The tilapia, which is known as St. Peter's fish, from the legend that he found a coin in the mouth of such a fish, makes a delicious dish. The lake sardine, a somewhat less popular fish, is caught only at night. It may be the fish involved in the story of the **Disciples** weary from their night of fishing. No one knows what kind of small fish, which became the center of the at the feeding of the 5,000, the boy had packed for his lunch (Mark 6:38). These fish that Peter and his friends caught on the Lake of Galilee apparently were a staple in Jesus's day. The lad who brought his lunch to spend the day listening to this **prophet** had five loaves and two fish (Mark 6:38). The Disciples caught nets full of the fish. This constant activity led Jesus to use fishing imagery in his beckoning them to "Come, follow me, and I will make you fishers of men" (Matt. 4:19; Mark 1:17). Even after his death and **Resurrection**, Jesus cooked fish on burning coals and offered them to his disciples (John 21:9). This would explain the imagery of the early Christians, who used the memories of Jesus and the Greek letters forming the word "fish," which were also the letters of the five words: "Jesus Christ God's Son Savior." *See also* Animals; Fishermen, Fishing; Monsters.

Further Reading

Cansdale, George. *All the Animals of the Bible Lands*. Grand Rapids, Mich.: Zondervan Publishing House, 1970. Hirsch, Emil G. "Fish and Fishing," http://www.jewishencyclopedia.com (accessed September 10, 2004). Thompson, J. A. "Fish, Fishing" in *Illustrated Bible Dictionary*. Sydney, Australia. Tyndale House Publishers, 1980.

Fishermen, Fishing

By the time of Jesus's birth and his early ministry, fishing had become a major occupation in the Galilee region. Fishing villages had grown up around the lake, little boats were harvesting the plentiful fish, and local entrepreneurs had discovered recipes for preserving and pickling fish so that they could be shipped elsewhere. There were even fish ponds or manmade hatcheries on the level land in the region (George Cansdale 1970 , 212).

Although they occasionally occupied Joppa on the coast of the Mediterranean, the Hebrews were not a seafaring folk and probably found fishing the deep waters of the sea to be too difficult and insufficiently rewarding. Most of the fishing of these waters was done by foreigners. The citizens of Sidon and Tyre, who were expert sailors, continued the earliest industry of the Phoenicians. Ezekiel mentioned Tyre's use of fishing nets in his prophesies (Ezek. 26:5, 14), and Nehemiah complained about the men of Tyre who brought fish to Jerusalem to sell them, even on the **Sabbath**. Cansdale surmises that the fishermen of Tyre had learned preservation techniques—salting, smoking, sun drying—to keep the fish edible for this 40-mile journey. One of the Jerusalem gates is known as the Fish Gate and is probably where the sales took place.

The Hebrews apparently learned to fish in these waters of **Egypt** and enjoyed the fish they ate there "at no cost," along with cucumbers, melons, leeks, onions, and garlic (Num. 11:5). Later, when Moses brought the dietary **laws** to his people, these included forbidding "water creatures having fins and scales (e.g., shellfish) as unclean" (Deut. 14:9–10; J. A. Thompson 1980, 509). All other fish were allowed.

Fishing must have become a common activity, as evidenced by the frequent mention of fishing techniques in the writings of the prophets and the wisdom literature: Ezekiel says that God will "put hooks in your jaws and make the fish of your streams stick to your scales. I will pull you out from among streams, with all the fish sticking to your scales" (Ezek. 29:4). This indicates the use of fish hooks, although not necessarily poles. Isaiah (19:8) also refers to casting "hooks in the Nile," suggesting a modern form of fishing using a barbed hook and a bait. Amos (4:2) says, "He will take ... your posterity with fish hooks." Pictures of the period indicate that captives were led away with fishhooks in their noses, making this less an imaginary image than a portrait of reality.

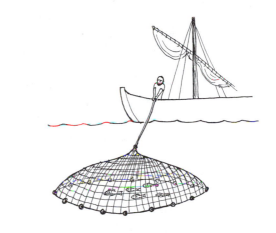

In Ecclesiastes (9:12), the writer compared men, who cannot know when their hour has come and are trapped in evil times, to fish that are "caught in a cruel net." Nets of various types were used regularly by the fishermen. Some gathered the fish, some dredged for them. The large, heavy nets required constant attention after their use. They had to be repaired and cleaned and dried before

Traditional types of fishing nets cast into the Sea of Galilee.

217

they were used again. Cansdale describes in detail the various fishing techniques, including spearing the creatures (George Cansdale 1970, 218–220). In the stories of Jesus and his disciples, they cast their nets to drag the Sea of Galilee for fish.

Ezekiel promised a wonderful time for fishermen, when "Swarms of living creatures will live everywhere the river flows. There will be large numbers of fish, because this water flows there and makes the salt water fresh; so where the river flows everything will live" (Ezek. 47:9). This cleansing of the great salt sea—the Dead Sea—would bring a purification so impressive that fishermen would stand along the shore—the whole length of the land—discovering fish of many kinds.

Jesus drew his first disciples from among the fishermen in Capernaum. Peter appears to have owned a lucrative fishing business there that included his brother Andrew. Some think that they had a fleet of small ships, and that Peter was quite prosperous. This activity led Jesus to use fishing imagery in his beckoning them to "Come, follow me, and I will make you fishers of men" (Matt. 4:19; Mark 1:17). Much of the early part of Mark's Gospel deals with travels back and forth on the Sea of Galilee in fishing craft. The men around him were mending their nets, casting their nets, and pulling in their catch. One of Jesus's miracles was to produce an enormous load of fish for the weary Disciples to haul ashore after laboring all night with no success. Even after his death and resurrection, Christ used fish as a gesture of loving concern for his followers, cooking the fish on burning coals, and offering them to his disciples (John 21:9). *See also* Boats and Ships; Fish.

Further Reading

Cansdale, George. *All the Animals of the Bible Lands.* Grand Rapids, Mich.: Zondervan Publishing House, 1970. Thompson, J. A. "Fish, Fishing," in *Illustrated Bible Dictionary.* Sydney, Australia: Tyndale House Publishers, 1980.

ℱlood, the Great

(Gen. 6:1–10, 19; Isa. 54:9; Matt. 24:37–39; Luke 17:26–27; Heb. 11:7; 1 Pet. 3:20–21; 2 Pet. 2:5) Also known as the "deluge," the great flood of Noah is one of the best known stories of the Bible. It follows the basic Old Testament paradigm: sin of humankind, anger of God, judgment on all except a remnant of humankind, and a **covenant** to mark the conclusion of the action. Seeing the evil ways of the men and women he had created, God told faithful Noah that a great deluge was coming. Only he and his family would survive. His task, acting on faith, was to build an **ark** big enough to hold two of every kind of animal—a kind of floating box. Following the Lord's orders precisely, Noah entered the ark on the day that the rains began. They lasted 40 days and 40 nights. After that time, Noah waited until the waters receded, sending out birds—first a raven and then a dove—to determine when it would be safe to open the doors and come out of the craft onto dry land. When the dove appeared with an **olive** branch in its mouth, he stepped out onto Mt. Ararat, where the ark had settled, and immediately built an **altar**, offered sacrifice, and sealed his covenant with God. God promised that he would never again obliterate humankind, marking the covenant with the sign of the rainbow. The olive branch in the dove's beak became the international symbol for peace.

The story of the Flood appears in almost every culture. "The historicity is confirmed by the tradition existing in all places and at all times as to the occurrence of a similar catastrophe. F. von Schwarz ... enumerates sixty-three such Flood stories which are in his opinion independent of the Biblical account" (A. J. Mass 2004). Mass does assert that the universality may be anthropological rather than geographical—that a memory of such an occurrence does reside in the oldest literature of many different peoples. Records from Australia, India, Polynesia, Tibet, Kashmir, and Lithuania all record it a great flood. Leonard Woolley, the famous archaeologist, described his efforts to dig deeply into the graves of the kings of Ur, only to find a layer of flood-clay separating two distinct cultures. He dated this at about 4000 B.C. (Werner Keller 1982, 22–27). This remarkable natural event made its way into the literature of the ancient world. In **Babylonia**, it appears in the epic of Gilgamesh. This Sumerian Noah is called Uta-Napishtim (C. Leonard Woolley 1965, 122–123). Greek myth has Zeus angry at the impious Pelasgians. He flooded the earth, saving only Deucalion and his wife Pyrrha, who, warned by Prometheus, built an ark and floated to Mount Parnassus. When they disembarked, they offered a sacrifice to Zeus and prayed at Themis's shrine. Zeus sent Hermes to comfort them and encourage them to renew humankind by throwing the bones of "your mother behind you." They finally interpreted this to mean "Mother Earth," and therefore threw stones over their shoulders. These became the new generation of men and women (Robert Graves and Raphael Patai 1964, 117–118).

The differences among the accounts are as instructive as their similarities: the stories outside of the Bible are polytheistic, with capricious, jealous, and quarrelsome gods. The hero is chosen simply because he is the favorite of one of the gods. Only the Bible is monotheistic, with a God who commands instant reverence and a hero saved by his faith and righteousness, as noted in Hebrews 11:7 (Emil G. Hirsch, W. Muss-Arnold, and Hartwig Hirschfeld 2004).

In recent years, a number of expeditions have been undertaken to Mt. Ararat in an effort to discover remnants of the ark, but so far to no avail. The snow-capped summit of the mountain, which lies in Eastern Turkey near the borders of Russia and Iran, is more than 16,000 feet high, making any exploration exceedingly difficult. The tiny Armenian village of Bayzit at the foot of Ararat has a story that has been recounted for generations: a mountain shepherd was said to have seen a great wooden ship on the mountain. A report in 1833 seemed to confirm this story, mentioning a wooden prow that stuck out of the south glacier in summer. Others have reported sightings, many of them mentioned in the work of Dr. Aaron Smith, an American historian and missionary, who wrote a complete history of Noah's Ark, citing 80,000 works in 72 languages, with 70,000 mentions of the "legendary wreckage of the Ark" (Keller, 38). The search continues with the dream that moderns will discover the ark with the help of new technology and verify its authenticity. *See also* Altar; Ark; Birds; Covenant.

Further Reading

Graves, Robert and Raphael Patai. *Hebrew Myths: The Book of Genesis*. New York: McGraw-Hill Book Company, 1964. Hirsch, Emil G., W. Muss-Arnold, and Hartwig Hirschfeld, "The Flood," http://www.jewishencyclopedia.com (accessed August 3, 2004). Keller, Werner. *The Bible as History*. New York: Bantam Books, 1982. Mass, A. J. "Deluge," http://www.newadvent.org (accessed August 4, 2004). Woolley, C. Leonard. *The Sumerians*. New York: W. W. Norton & Company, 1965.

ƒood

The major **work** of women was preparation of food for the family. Much of the tending and slaughter of the **animals** fell to men, who were the **shepherds**, hunters, and **priests**. Often the men also assumed the large public or commercial cooking chores, such as the baking of **bread** in large ovens for the community or for the king's household. Cooking was complicated in different times for different reasons: in early days, the limits of foods and cooking utensils restricted the diet. Later, after the introduction of the **law** of Moses, the kinds of food—**clean** and unclean—as well as the rules regarding the handling of them made the cook's chores complex and important for the spiritual and physical life of the family. Especially for the preparation of meat dishes, the prohibition against eating **blood** and the regulations for slaughter and handling made this a tightly regulated process. Vegetables and fruits were limited by the productivity of **gardens** and fields accessible to the people, and spices were determined by trade. The preparation of foods changed as the utensils became more sophisticated and the women learned techniques and recipes from other peoples. The **meals** themselves, as **festivals** proliferated and laws multiplied, became both more elaborate and more tightly regulated. There is a world of difference between a meal that Abraham offered strangers in Genesis and the **feasts** that Daniel refused in the court of Nebuchadnezzar.

In ancient times, the Hebrew people ate bread, **olives**, oil, as well as "buttermilk and cheese from their flocks; fruits and vegetables from their orchards and gardens; and meat on rare occasions" (Fred H. Wight 1953, 43). As nomads and herdsmen, they had plenty of meat to provide feasts for visitors. When they settled into a more stable lifestyle, Abraham's children must have had orchards and vineyards and gardens to enlarge their diets, providing them fruits, vegetables, and herbs. They also had access to wild game: Esau loved the meat he killed on his **hunting** expeditions and the savory stews made from lentils that he found so delicious he was willing to trade a mess of pottage (Gen. 25:33, 34) for his birthright.

During the sojourn in **Egypt**, the Hebrews discovered their favorite seasonings, leeks, onions, and garlic (Num. 11:5), which must have made the "fleshpots" very savory. By the days of the **kings** and **prophets**, gardens included cucumbers (Isa. 1:8) and a variety of vegetables. Leeks and onions were apparently eaten raw with bread for the most part. Cucumbers were also eaten raw and sometimes combined with other vegetables into a salad. Melons were probably part of their diet as well. During the Exile, Daniel and his friends preferred this healthy fare to the richer food available in the royal household (Dan. 1:12).

There is no evidence in Scripture that the Jews ate breakfast as a family, although they probably nibbled on dried fruits or grain while waiting for the noontime meal. Raw grain, plucked from the field and rubbed in their hands (Luke 6:1, Matt. 12:1, Mark 2:23) or parched corn (1 Sam. 17:17) was a common food, easy to find and easy to eat—like our snack foods. In the story of Ruth, Boaz told the maiden to come to him at mealtime—perhaps noontime—when she was invited to "eat of the bread, and dip thy morsel in the vinegar. And she sat beside the reapers: and he reached her parched corn and she did eat, and was sufficed and left" (Ruth 2:14).

The large meal of the day, however, was served in the evening. Jesus and his **disciples** were frequently invited to meals with friends—at the house of Levi or Mary and Martha or Peter—where they enjoyed meals with the family and invited friends. Among the early Christians, "love feasts" were popular, apparently after **worship** services. These appear to have been communal meals, where Christians shared their food, like a potluck supper.

Except for feasts or special occasions, the ancient Hebrews rarely ate meat. Bread made of wheat or barley was the most common food, present at every meal. Guests, even as early as Abraham's time, were given "freshly baked bread as a sign of **hospitality** and as a way to honor the guest. The bread was not cut but was always broken into pieces" (Philip J. King and Lawrence E. Stager 2001, 62). In the story of Elijah and the widow of Zarephath, the prophet asks for a "morsel of bread" (1 Kings 17:10–11). She makes a "little cake" for him—made by stirring oil into flour and shaped into a cake before being baked in an oven. The flat bread that resulted was a "pita." Bread making was a daily chore, varied with uses of ferment at times, kneading, or sweetening with honey or figs. Cakes were more like our griddle cakes, quite different from the modern pastry. For extra flavor, the cook might add salt or honey. There were also syrups made from the juice of grapes, dates, and figs (King, 66).

Honey was a favorite sweetener for dishes, and fruit was also a favorite sweet dish. Figs, for example, might be dried and pressed into square or round cakes for use well past the season when they ripened (1 Sam. 25:18, 30:12). Grapes, either fresh or sun-dried as raisins, were regular fare. Dried grapes might also be pressed into cakes: "It is doubtful whether the Israelites knew grape-syrup, although the fact that the Arabic 'dibs,' corresponding to the Hebrew 'debash,' is used to designate both the natural and this artificial honey or syrup, shows that they probably knew the latter" (Gen. 43:11; Ezek. 27:17; Emil G. Hirsch, Wilhelm Nowack, Solomon Schechter, and Samuel Krauss 2004).

Pomegranates were cherished for both the fruit and the juice, from which **wine** might be made (Deut. 8:8; Song of Sol. 4:3). The favorite drink, which was present at virtually every meal, was wine. This might be diluted with water, flavored with spices, or poured into bowls or cups in its pure form, with the server to pour it slowly, being careful to avoid stirring the lees and clouding the liquid. The fruit of the nearly ripe carob was used for flavoring water.

The Israelites may have also known apples, although the word *tappuah* is of doubtful signification. The fruit of the mulberry fig tree may have been eaten by the poor; they also ate the date-palm fruit, which they treated like figs and grapes. In addition, pistachio nuts, almonds, and walnuts were available.

Beans or lentils were typical vegetables, useful even in stews. These were often cooked with herbs and spices, and served with bread, which was used to dip the beans out of the serving dish, as spoons and forks were not available. Ezekiel is directed to mix wheat and barley, fava beans and lentils, millet and emmer to make bread for himself (Ezek. 4:9). King notes that this is an unusual mixture of foodstuffs, legally unclean, probably indicating a scarcity of food.

Spices available included cumin, dill, mint, mustard, and salt. Over time, with imports from other countries, this array was considerably enlarged. Salt was used both for seasoning and for preservation, serving as an essential element in the household store. When Jesus referred to his followers as the "salt of the world," he may have had both uses in mind.

Milk was readily available from cows, **sheep**, and **goats**, not to mention **camels**. With the hot weather, the milk soon turned into buttermilk. *Leben* or sour curdled milk was a common food. It was made by pouring milk in a dish with yeast, covering it with a warm cloth, and waiting for about a day until it set. This is the food Abraham offered his guests (Gen. 18:8) and Jael offered Sisera (Judg. 4:19, 5:15) (Fred H. Wight 1953, 49–50). The ancient Jews also knew how to churn butter (Prov. 30:33) and to make cheese (1 Sam. 17:18, 2 Sam. 17:29). Cream was frequently offered as a present, carried in cylindrical wooden vessels, and sprinkled with sugar. It was eaten out of little dishes with wooden spoons (Hirsch et al. 2004).

Ancient people ate meat much less frequently than moderns. Only the king served it daily. When a guest or a stranger—or a long-lost prodigal son—appeared, the Hebrew turned the evening meal into a feast. For this, he often kept a "fatted calf," an animal that was kept in a stall and fed better than those in the field, and exercised less. Only clean animals might be used for food, and young, tender animals were considered preferable to older ones. Abraham served veal to his guests (Gen. 18:7), and Gideon was provided with a kid (Judg. 6:19).

Because Israelites were forbidden to eat any of the animal's blood, the slaughter had to be performed correctly, the blood drained and offered to the priest, and the flesh salted and washed. Those portions of the meat that could not be cleared of blood, like the liver and brains, were roasted over a fire to cleanse them. Although roasting, perhaps over a spit, was the more typical ancient manner of cooking meat, boiling became popular. Ezekiel used the boiling pot of meat, with the scum rising to the top, as an image of God's people: "Set a pot . . . and also pour water into it. Gather the pieces thereof into it, even every good piece, the thigh, and the shoulder; fill it with the choice bones. Take the choice of the flock and burn also the bones under it, and make it boil well. . . . Woe to the bloody city, to the pot whose scum is therein, and whose scum is not gone out of it! . . . Heap on the wood, kindle the fire, consume the flesh, and spice it well" (Ezek. 24:4–11). The liquid left in the pot after the meat was cooked and cut up into serving-size pieces was used as the base for stewing vegetables, which might be poured over the meat.

Fowl are mentioned primarily in connection with sacrifices, not in descriptions of meals. Their eggs, which are mentioned only once (Luke 11:12), may have been eaten, but were not considered a tasty treat (Job 6:6). The references suggest that eggs were an available food, but not highly prized or suitable for festive meals.

Fish, except for shellfish, is clearly described in the law, and must have been used for food, especially among poor people. The story of Tobias and his miraculous fish and the Disciples and their regular fishing suggest that this was a fairly common food late in Israel's history. Some of the fish might be eaten fresh, usually fried, but much of the catch was dried in the sun or salted or pickled and preserved for future use (Neh. 3:3, 12:39; 2 Chron. 33:14). Jesus fed the five thousand by multiplying the five loaves and two fishes that a young man, planning to spend the day listening to Jesus preaching, had brought to serve for his lunch. Such fish must have been preserved to be useful for noonday nourishment in a hot climate. One of the last scenes of the resurrected Jesus shows him on the shore of the Sea of Galilee, with his disciples, cooking fish over a fire. *See also* Bees, Honey; Bread; Cooking, Cooking Utensils; Feasting; Festivals; Fish; Gardens; Grain; Meals; Olives, Olive Oil, Olive Trees; Vineyards; Wine.

Further Reading

Hirsch, Emil G., Wilhelm Nowack, Solomon Schechter, and Samuel Krauss, "Food," http://www.jewishencyclopedia.com (accessed June 4, 2004). King, Philip J. and Lawrence E. Stager. *Life in Biblical Israel*. Louisville, Ky.: Westminster John Knox Press. Wight, Fred H. *Manners and Customs of Bible Lands*. Chicago: Moody Press, 1953.

Fortifications, Fortified Cities, Fortresses

When the Israelites were semi-nomadic, they learned to be constantly vigilant. It was almost impossible to protect a caravan, a camp, or a village from marauders. **Dogs** can give warnings, and watchmen can keep a keen eye on approaching strangers, but the camps in the wilderness were always in danger of attackers. It was sensible to travel as tribes, to camp in clusters, and to have armed servants near at hand. The fact that Abraham had enough warriors in his band to fight the five **kings** who attacked Lot and his friends suggests that the old man was well aware of the perils of the road.

As the Israelites became more agrarian and had more to steal, especially after their return from **Egypt**, they found their security through settling into communities. When the ever-growing tribe of Israel had returned to the land of **Canaan**, they found a number of fortified Canaanite cities. Even as they attacked and devastated such places as Jericho, the Israelites marveled at their superior fortifications. Fortresses came to play an important role in the Hebrews' **warfare** as a means of protecting their treasures—their homes, families, and wealth.

Their few defenses included such primitive strategies as hiding in caves or mountains (Judg. 6:2, 1 Sam. 8:6). They built their small towns and villages near water sources and close to their fields and **vineyards** so that they could protect them. In the vineyards, they often built **watchtowers**. In harvest season, men would live in these towers to defend the vineyards and fields against predators, but raids were frequent and rapid. Farmers would often sequester their grain or olive oil in **caves** or cisterns to protect against bandits. They kept their livestock close, in the sheepfold or house, under constant watch. The defensive practices of the time of the Judges, when "every man did what was right in his own eyes," were designed to survive uncoordinated attacks, not great armies.

Under their monarchs, they became better fighters and developed techniques for overcoming the fortresses of the enemies, beginning with David's capture of Jerusalem (2 Sam. 7). They also began to build their own fortified cities. A listing of their fortified cities would include the following:

Jerusalem—a Canaanite city conquered by Israelites, which became "David's city"

Hazor and Megiddo—Israelite cities built by Solomon in the northeast

Gezer, Beth-horon, and Baalath—Solomon's cities protecting against invaders from the coast and from the west

Tadmor (Tamar)—a city of unknown origins, probably for protection against Idumea

Geba and Mizpah—ancient cities protected by Asa

Fifteen cities fortified by Rehoboam south and west of Jerusalem

Shechem and Penuel—cities that Jereboam fortified

Samaria—built by Omri, captured by Assyrians after a three-year siege

Masada, Machaerus, and Jotapata—Maccabean fortresses

Most of these are of interest to archaeologists, who are seeking to determine their origins and their history. Of these, the most famous are Jerusalem, which became the Holy City, and Masada, where the heroic stand was taken by the Jews in the great Jewish war (66–73 A.D.). Megiddo, which has been carefully excavated over many years, is thought by many to be the location of the final battle of Armageddon (Avraham Negev 1986).

Cities, unlike villages and fields, could be protected. The major difference between a town and an open village was the encircling rampart. In the case of fortified cities, though, this was a much more complex pattern of construction. The best strategy was situating the city on an acropolis, a steep rocky site where the height itself became a natural barrier against enemies. Jerusalem was begun on the steep western slope of the eastern hill where the old city of Salem had been since Abraham's day. Samaria was built by Omri on the top of a mountain. Pilgrims still wonder at the majesty of Masada, a natural rock fortress on the western shore of the Dead Sea, started by the high **priest** Jonathan and later improved and used by Herod. Zealots held Masada until May 2, 73 A.D., when it was finally conquered by Romans (Avraham Negev 1986, 231).

All of the fortresses were further protected by thick walls, even double walls. These were composed of large blocks of stone, often built without cement. They were so wide that large numbers of people could stand on them and fight from this elevated position. They often had battlements for the archers to secure cover. And there were towers built of large square stones, with the strongest at the corners and above the gates. From here the guards could overlook the surrounding countryside (Emil G. Hirsch and Wilhelm Nowack 2004).

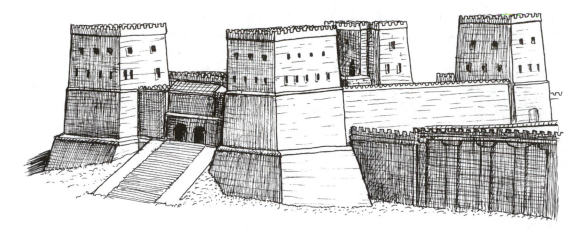

The Antonia Fortress, northwest of the Temple, built by Herod before 31 B.C. to honor Mark Antony.

The gates were usually heavy wooden doors covered with metal for reinforcement with bolts of brass or iron. These were designed for protection, often with passages of approach, which allowed the men on the walls to observe approaching forces and defend against invaders. Rules of warfare, even when besieging a gentile city, required that troops come from three sides, leaving one side free for those who wished to escape (M. Seligsohn 2004).

The fortified city was to become a symbol of the human community. Within the gates of Sodom and Gomorrah was a culture replete with corruption, brutality, and ultimately death. The city of David, the Jews' beloved Jerusalem, housed the **Temple** of Solomon. It became a foretaste of the ideal—the City of God on earth. When it was destroyed, the Jews felt their national life was also obliterated. And when they returned to rebuild it after the **Babylonian** Captivity, the shining city on a hill became an image of their national struggle for rebirth. During the Hellenistic period, when it was polluted by pagans with their graven images and their desecration of the altar, the people were outraged. The **prophets** spoke of it in increasingly ideal terms, with Ezekiel's grand vision climaxing the image of a city beyond human comprehension, one that would be safe and secure, a home for God's people, the dwelling place of God himself. This Celestial City, which is echoed in Revelation and later repeated by Augustine in his *City of God*, became for Puritans the goal of life, the Pilgrim's progress to the very presence of God. *See also* Stonemasons; War, Warfare: General.

Further Reading

Hirsch, Emil G. and Wilhelm Nowack, "Fortress," http://www.jewishencyclopedia. com (accessed March 4, 2004). Negev, Avraham. *The Archaeological*

Encyclopedia of the Holy Land. New York: Thomas Nelson Publishers, 1986.

Seligsohn, M. "War," http://www.jewishencyclopedia.com (accessed March 5, 2004).

Furnishings, Household

The furnishings for the **tent**-dwellers were simple. There were no large pieces. Everything was portable: straw mats, carpets, skins rather than chairs, tables, and beds. Rugs covered the ground, with the additional bedding at night—mats or carpets. The sleepers covered themselves with the cloaks they wore during the day. The saddle from a **camel** might provide a more elegant seat for the leader, but most of the family sat or lay on mats, kneeled, or squatted to eat, grind meal, cook, or talk.

The tent would be full of **cooking utensils**—pots, kettles, and pans; serving dishes—mats, platters, or larger dishes; cups for drinking; an **olive oil** lamp, a leathern bucket to draw water from the well; sacks of **grain** piled about, the handmill and mortar for pounding the grain; skin bags or bottles for water and other liquids; and an earthen pitcher for carrying the water from the well.

"Furniture is a sign of permanent settlement; nomads have no need for furnishing too cumbersome to carry with them" (Philip J. King and Lawrence E. Stager 2001, 63). Because craftsmen would have made their furniture of wood, few relics have survived to reveal the designs that were common. Some carvings do survive, however, that show the furniture the wealthy used for dining as early as the seventh century B.C. The Hebrew prohibition against graven images, however, limits these discoveries to contemporary pagan cultures, perhaps not typical of the Israelite home.

The usual household would have little more than a bed, a chair, a table, and a lamp. Most might not have even that much furniture, which were the pieces required for a guest of honor (2 Kings 4:10). Bedding, kitchen utensils (storage jars, water jugs, cooking pots, serving bowls), as well as looms for weaving and vessels for grinding and crushing the grain, and other **foods** would be regular furnishings. There were storage boxes and chests, even built-in closets for household goods. Elisha had a bed, a table, a chair, and a lampstand as well (2 Kings 4:10), but these were not common in most homes. They were the pieces required for a guest of honor.

The house might have a raised ledge at one end or around the walls, on which the family placed cushions and mattresses for sitting during the day and sleeping at night. Chairs were seldom used except for "Moses's seat" at the **synagogue** and **thrones** for **kings**. Beds were very rare.

Tables were apparently common for serving **meals**, as well as for functions in official buildings of **government** and religion for such activities as money changing, writing, religious rituals. The Israelite practice was to sit or recline for eating meals, with diners squatting on the floor or stretched out on rugs. Psalm 128 seems to imply that the entire family gathered around a table—like "olive shoots."

As we know, the **houses** were small, the families large, and the one-room cottage of the peasant was likely to house a sheep or two and a goat as well as the family. " A large family often lived, worked, had their meals and slept in a single room. . . . In the dark winter months, it was ill-lit and suffocating" (E.W. Heaton 1956, 71). Under such circumstances, only the most rudimentary furniture would survive.

Foreigners clearly had more elaborate furnishings, which they introduced to the Israelites. The feasts described in Daniel and Esther suggest elaborate banquet halls with tables and couches. In fact, couches were listed among the tribute received from Hezekiah. Amos lamented the indolence of the upper classes who slept on wooden beds adorned with **ivory** (Amos 6:4). In the Roman era, the triclinium, a U shaped couch that fit around a low table, was common. The diners would stretch out on the couches, on their left sides, and reach with the right hand to eat the food furnished. Such was the design probably used for the **Last Supper**. *See also* Cooking, Cooking Utensils; Food; Meals.

Further Reading

Heaton, E.W. *Everyday Life in Old Testament Times*. New York: Charles Scribner's Sons, 1956. King, Philip J. and Lawrence E. Stager, *Life in Biblical Israel*. Louisville, Ky.: Westminster John Knox Press, 2001.

G

Gardens

(Gen.1–3; Song of Sol. 4–6; Isa. 58:11, 61:11; Jer. 31:12; Ezek. 31:8–9; Luke 11:42, 13:9) Eden was the first and only perfect garden. In Scripture, the term for *garden* seems to cover orchards, **vineyards**, and kitchen gardens, as well as royal parks (Emil G. Hirsch and Immanuel Low 2004). Generally a garden in the Bible differs from a cultivated field by its size, the greater diversity of its plants, and its more careful cultivation. Because it was small and usually near the house, it was more carefully tended. When visiting Jesus's burial **cave** in the garden, Mary expected to meet the gardener, indicating that someone was responsible for the garden's constant upkeep. It also suggests that she was free to pass through the garden, but it was protected much of the time (Madeleine S. Miller and J. Lane Miller 1961, 215).

The garden was usually laid out near **water**—a cistern, spring, well, river, or lake. In the dry summers of Israel, irrigation was essential to grow the produce that the owner preferred: fruit **trees**, vines, melon patches, herbs and spices, and flowers. To protect it from **animals** and thieves, it was usually surrounded by a stone, mud, or brick wall or a hedge of brambles and briars. Entrance was provided through a gateway. Apparently ancient peoples learned the values of mulch (using the straw from the fields) and fertilizer (using animal dung, blood, and ashes).

It is generally thought that the delta region in Iraq, which Saddam Hussein drained, was the Garden of Eden, a place with multiple rivers flowing and a great variety of natural flora and fauna, although it is now a desolate, dusty region. From the **Egyptians**, the Israelites apparently learned the methods for irrigating gardens. "The land you are entering to take over is not like the land of Egypt, from which you have come, where you planted your seed and irrigated it by foot as in a vegetable garden," Moses told the Israelites (Deut. 11:10). Even earlier, Abram and Lot had discovered the gardens of Egypt; when Lot looked at the Jordan plain, he noted it was "well watered, like the garden of the Lord," and compared it to the "land of Egypt" (Gen.13:10). Such gardens were still cultivated in Jesus's time: he referred to them in his judgment on the **Pharisees**, who gave God "a tenth of your mint, rue, and all other kinds of garden herbs" (Luke 11:42); and he used the mustard seed for his image of the oversized garden plant (Luke 13:19).

The settlers in the Promised Land apparently learned to cultivate their own gardens. There were **laws** concerning those people who were allowed to enter a garden (a poor person, a potential purchaser). Because gardens were associated with nature religions, particularly the "asherim" or groves sacred to **Asherah**, it is not surprising that the pagan queen Jezebel would have coveted the garden of Naboth, which was near her **palace**. She had her husband, King Ahab, approach Naboth for his vegetable garden and vineyard, but Naboth was unwilling to sell or trade it (1 Kings 21:2). This sturdy landowner consequently lost both his garden and his life to the unscrupulous monarchs.

Because of this pagan connection, **synagogues** were forbidden to have gardens around them. **Graves**, however, were sometimes located in gardens. Because the Jews were forbidden contact with the dead, these tombs were whitewashed so that visitors to the garden would not inadvertently touch a sepulcher. It was in the Garden of Gethsemane, where Joseph of Arimathea arranged for Jesus to be buried, that the women sought Jesus's body and discovered the resurrected Christ.

Solomon had royal gardens, probably as a result of his interest in foreign cultures and his tolerance for foreign gods. The Song of Solomon, which described his beloved in lush garden terminology, was undoubtedly a product of this love of nature and of the fruits of nature. He compared his love to a "garden locked up" (Song of Sol. 4:12) and a "garden fountain" (Song of Sol. 4:15). He referred to the bed of spices (Song of Sol. 6:2), the honeycomb (from the many bees that swarmed through the garden, Song of Sol. 5:1), and its "choice fruits" (Song of Sol. 4:16).

Other **kings** before and after Solomon had royal gardens: Manasseh was buried in his palace garden, "the garden of Uzza" (2 Kings 21:18); there are references to royal gardens or the King's Garden by the Pool of Siloam in the City of David (Neh. 3:15; 2 Kings 25:4). We catch only a hint of Babylon's famous gardens from Esther, who lived in the palace of Ashuerus, where the king's garden was adjacent to her lavish harem quarters. Babylon's Hanging Gardens were considered one of the Seven Wonders of the Ancient World. As a display of wealth, gardens in Egypt, **Assyria**, Persia, and Syria were full of patterned walks, **trees**, and flowers. Sennacherib even built an aqueduct to water the gardens in Nineveh (Madeleine S. Miller and J. Lane Miller 1961, 215).

The **prophets** made lavish use of garden imagery: Isaiah spoke of the garden without water (Isa. 1:30) and of Israel and Judah as the "garden" of God's "delight" (Isa. 5:7). He promised a time when the people would be "like a well-watered garden, like a spring whose waters never fail" (Isa. 58:11); and again "For as the oil makes the sprout come up and a garden causes seeds to grow, so the Sovereign Lord will make righteousness and praise spring up before all nations" (Isa. 61:11). Jeremiah prophesied, using the same imagery of the "well-watered garden" (Jer. 31:12) for that idyllic time when the people would "sorrow no more." In Jeremiah's case, he was painfully aware of the present circumstances; enemy soldiers broke through the city wall near the king's garden (Jer. 52:7). His garden prophecies must have struck the Jews as being especially poignant. Ezekiel's visions were full of a new Eden, "the garden of God": "The cedars in the garden of God could not rival it, nor could the pine trees equal its boughs." This tree had abundant branches, the "envy of all the trees of Eden" (Ezek. 31:8–9). His splendid vision was of the wasteland transformed into the garden of Eden. Joel echoed this same stark archetypal imagery of the wasteland and the garden (Joel 2:3).

Later imagery in art and literature closely followed the biblical examples. Artists painted the lush background of Eden for their portrayals of Adam and Eve, the olive garden for Christ's tormented final time of **prayer**, and carefully tended royal gardens for the stories of Esther and Susanna. The writers of the Middle Ages used the imagery of the Song of Solomon in elaborate symbolism of virginity, especially in the *Romance of the Rose,* which had significant impact on English writers. Milton, Marvell, and others made much the same use of the imagery in their poetry. In American literature, the garden reverted specifically to Eden imagery, making it a place of temptation for lovers, as in *The Scarlet Letter.* See also Agriculture; Animals; Asherah, Ashtoreth, Ashtaroth; Caves; Eden, Garden of; Fall of Man; Graves; Vineyards.

Further Reading

Goldberg, Michael. "*Hortus Conclusus,*" in *A Dictionary of Biblical Tradition in English Literature.* Grand Rapids, Mich.: William B. Eerdmans Publishing Company, 1992. Hirsch, Emil G. and Immanuel Low, "Horticulture," http://www.jewishencyclopedia.com (accessed November 18, 2004). Miller, Madeleine S. and J. Lane Miller, "Garden," in *Harper's Bible Dictionary.* New York: Harper and Row, 1961.

Gates

(Ezek. 40:6–16; Ps. 69:13, 118:19–20; Ezek 48:31–34; Rev. 21:13–15)
In Scripture, the term *gate* often refers to an entrance way, including passageways or groups of buildings that were designed for either ornament or defense. The most famous example was the entrance to the **Temple** court (Ezek. 40:6–16), which had "two thresholds, a number of lodges or guardchambers five cubits apart, and porches and posts, with an open space ten cubits wide, while from the roof of one lodge to the opposite was a breadth of twenty-five cubits; the whole enclosed a court, the walls being broken by windows and the openings spanned by arches" (Emil G. Hirsch 2004).

The gates of cities were usually **stone** or wood, sometimes covered with **metal**. Psalm 107:16 mentions "gates of iron" and other references are to gates of copper or brass with bolts of iron (Ps. 107:16; Deut 33:25). The gates were often double, allowing for the entrance of a horse-drawn **chariot**. Nehemiah discusses the value of having doors in the gates, apparently to allow smaller entrances for individuals (Neh. 6:1).

Excavations at numerous sites in Palestine have revealed from two to six chambers in the gateways. At Dan, there were pillars thought to have supported a **throne**, fitting for a **king** such as David who was reported to be "sitting in the gate; and all the troops came before the king" (2 Sam. 19:9). Six-chambered gates have been found at Megiddo, Hazor, Gezer, Ashdod, Lachish, and Tel 'Ira (Philip J. King and Lawrence E. Stager 2001, 234).

Because the city often had two walls for **fortification**, it would also have two gateways, with space between them. The Temple of Ezekiel's vision had inner and outer gates, with specific directions for each of them—east, west, north, and south (Ezek. 40:6–35). David "was sitting between the inner and outer gates" when he waited for the news of Absalom. He sent the watchman—or gatekeeper—up on the roof of the gateway or the tower of the first gate to watch for runners who would bring the news (2 Sam. 18:24). Levites were designated as the "gatekeepers" of the Temple (Neh. 13:22).

The space in between the gates and around them was often used as a meeting place, most frequently as the assembly area for legal proceedings, where the city elders met (Fred Wight 1953, 239–241). As early as Genesis, the city fathers, including Lot, sat in the gates of the city when judging cases (Gen. 19:1). One of the best scenes at the gates is the one in which Boaz redeems his beloved Ruth from her kinsmen, sealing the contract with a sandal (Ruth 4:1). The **law** of Moses cited the city gates as the place "which the Lord thy God giveth thee, throughout thy tribes, that they shall judge the people with just judgment" (Deut. 16:18).

Proverbs 1:21 notes that the gate was the "chief place of concourse." It was ideal for proclamations, speeches, declarations of war, and for gossip (Ps. 69:12). The prophets found this the perfect place for their sermons: "Go and stand in the gate of the children of the people, whereby the kings of Judah come in, and by which they go out, and in all the gates of Jerusalem" (Jer. 17:19). Metaphorically, this allowed the legal protection for the Levite, the stranger, and the widow "within thy gates" to have specific limits (Deut. 16:14). Lepers, on the other hand, were not allowed in the gates (Lev. 13:46). The heads of slain enemies were exhibited above the gates (1 Sam. 17:51, 54; Emil Hirsch 2004). One particularly gory example notes Jehu's order to pile up heads of 70 slaughtered royal princes near the gate of the city until morning as a signal that Ahab's family no longer ruled the land and would never return to power (2 Kings 10:8).

The gates were also the chief marketplace, thus the "fish-gate" where the fish were bought and sold, or the "sheep-gate." Jerusalem even had gate designated for carrying off the waste from the Temple—the "Dung gate." Some were named for different and obvious reasons: the Water Gate, the Beautiful Gate, the New Gate, etc. Some were named for people. In the New Jerusalem, the gates were to be named after the **Tribes of Israel** (Rev. 21:13–15).

Solomon's "fortified gate" at Megiddo. Note the elaborate protection and multiple defensive positions available for defenders of the fortress.

An inscription was posted over the gate, as over the doorways of Jewish homes. This ceremonial view of the gates, entering into the house of the Lord or the home of the believer, came to refer to more abstract ideas. Thus, we see references to the "gates of death" or the "gates of righteousness" (Ps. 118:19–20). The gates of the Temple were particularly sacred, an entrance way to the sacred space within. One of the loveliest personifications of the gates of Jerusalem is found in Psalm 24: "Lift up your heads, O ye gates."

Jesus used gates in symbolic ways, referring to the narrow gate through which the Christian must enter the Kingdom: "But small is the gate and narrow the road that leads to life, and only a few find it" (Matt. 7:11). He also spoke of himself as the gate to the sheepfold, using the image of the good **shepherd** serving as the doorway that protected the sheep against predators (John 10:1–2).

A broken gate or one burned by enemies was the sign of a destroyed city. A wide open gateway revealed a defenseless town—open to its enemies. The strong gate was the guarantee of the citizens' safety. Ordinarily, the gates would be closed for the night as a security measure. By contrast, those of the New Jerusalem will never close, for there will be no night there (Rev. 21:25).

The gate imagery in Ezekiel and Revelation was to have enormous impact on the architecture of cathedrals. The dramatic—and heavily decorated—entranceways facing different directions, with their beautiful double doors, derived from the gates of sparking jewels in Isaiah (54:12), and of pearl in Revelation (21:21). The glorious imagery of these visions was to fire the imagination of generations of Christian artisans for years to come. *See also* Fortifications, Fortified Cities, Fortresses; Law; Temple.

Further Reading

Hirsch, Emil G. "Gate," http://www.jewishencyclopedia.com (accessed January 11, 2004). King, Philip J. and Lawrence E. Stager. *Life in Biblical Israel.* Louisville, Ky.: Westminster John Knox Press, 2001. Wight, Fred. *Manners and Customs of Bible Lands.* Chicago: Moody Press, 1953.

Gemstones

(Exod. 28:17–20, 39:10–13; Ezek. 28:13) From prehistory to the present, humans have adorned themselves and their possessions with the colorful stones they have found in nature. These stones have been cherished for their rarity and for their brilliant color throughout the ages. Because most of them were not indigenous to Palestine, they were brought from Arabia, India, Egypt, and elsewhere. Ezekiel mentions the merchant caravans (27:22), and Solomon sent forth his ships that sailed to Ophir, bringing back precious cargoes (1 Kings 10:11; 2 Chron. 9:10). Many of the gems listed in Exodus may well have come from **Egypt**, a land rich in ornamentation.

They were in use as ornaments at a comparatively early period in the crown of the Ammonite monarch (2 Sam. 12:30), on robes and canopies (Ezek. 28:13, Esther 14:6), and on golden vessels. Precious jewels "were especially employed for signet-rings and seals, cylinders and cones. David is said to have gathered gems while preparing for the erection of the **Temple**, and Solomon is credited with having studded its interior walls with them" (1 Chron. 29:2, 8; 2 Chron. 2:6; Emil Hirsch 2004).

The modern process of faceting stones so as to produce sparkle was not used by the ancient peoples. Instead, they often rounded, polished, carved, or inscribed them. **Jewelry** made of semi-precious stones and colorful minerals were tributes given to new brides and to monarchs. Scripture has four famous lists of gem stones in addition to numerous references to them:

1. The breastplate of the high **priest** (Exod. 28:17–21, 39:10–13). The breastplate of judgment was to have four rows of stones: on the first, sardius, topaz, and carbuncle; on the second, emerald, sapphire, and diamond; on the third, a ligure, an agate, and amethyst; and on the fourth, a beryl, an onyx, and a jasper. The stones were to be inscribed with the names of the children of Israel—the Twelve **Tribes**.

2. Job's description of the glory of wisdom (28:16–19). Wisdom cannot be valued with "the precious onyx, or the sapphire. The gold and crystal cannot equal it: . . . . No mention shall be made of coral, or of pearls, for the price of wisdom is above rubies. The topaz of Ethiopia shall not equal it." Here we have the expansive vision of gem stones collected from all around the Fertile Crescent, brought from far-flung countries, as well as the highland mines that may have been Job's home region (Madeleine S. Miller and J. Lane Miller 1961, 334).

3. Ezekiel's description of the garments of the merchant-**king** of Tyre (28:13) "Thou hast been in Eden the garden of God; every precious stone was thy covering, the sardius, topaz, and the diamond, the beryl, the onyx, and the jasper, the sapphire, the emerald, and the carbuncle, and gold." None of these embellishments of the perfect man, however, could protect him from iniquity and from condemnation.

4. John's Revelation of the Holy City (21:11, 18–21). The new Jerusalem was to have the glory of God, "and her light was like unto a stone most precious, even like a jasper stone, clear as crystal." The wall was of jasper, the city of pure gold, like glass; the foundations of precious stones: "The first foundation of the wall of it was jasper; the second, sapphire; the third chalcedony; the fourth, an emerald; The fifth, sardonyx; the sixth, sardius; the seventh, chrysolite; the eighth, beryl; the ninth, a topaz; the tenth, a chrysoprasus; the eleventh, a jacinth; the twelfth, an amethyst. And the twelve gates were twelve pearls." In the 12-fold symbolism we see the repetition of the Twelve Tribes symbolized by the breastplate of the high **priest**.

The stones were cherished for their beauty and for their permanence, earthly materials glorified, that mirrored the glory, beauty, and eternal quality of the Holy city (KJV, fn 2016). The listing reveals greater acquaintance with semi-precious than with precious stones.

The actual meaning of the names of these stones has been obscured by time, but numerous scholars have studied the various usages in **Babylonia** and Egypt and have speculated on possible identifications. Translators have struggled to find contemporary equivalents, deciding on the following possibilities:

Agate (Exod. 28:19, Ezek. 28:13) is a type of translucent quartz with layers of different colors. The name may be related to Saba, from whence caravans brought the stone to Palestine. It has bands of various colors and may be highly polished. If the stone is cut so as to show layers of color, it is called *agate*, but if it is cut parallel to the lines of color, it is called *onyx*. This is frequently used for the carving of cameos. The agate stone was thought to alleviate fever, and the eagle was said to place an agate in its nest to guard its young against the bite of venous animals. The red agate was thought to sharpen the vision.

Amethyst was a purple variety of crystalline quartz. There were two forms of amethyst: the oriental amethyst, a form of sapphire that was much like a diamond, and the occidental amethyst, which was a softer stone and could be easily engraved. The amethyst stone had a purple cast, like diluted wine, from deep purple to rose. The Greek name for the amethyst indicates that it was thought to prevent intoxication, and it was often used in beakers for drinking parties. "Inveterate drinkers wore amulets made of it to counteract the action of wine" (Charles Souvay 2005).

Beryl was probably Spanish gold topaz, usually green, sometimes called "emerald." It appears to have differed from the modern emerald in color, being a lighter aquamarine, almost yellowish, sometimes almost white. It was found in upper Egypt.

Carbuncle (Exod. 28:11, Ezek. 28:13) is more mysterious, identified only by its red glittering color. Theophrastus noted that, "Its colour is red and of a kind that when it is held against the sun it resembles a burning coal" (Charles Souvay 2005). This suggests that it may have been the oriental ruby.

Carnelian (Exod. 28:17) has sometimes been translated "sardonyx," an error according to the *Catholic Encyclopedia,* which notes that its name derives from the city of Sardes, where it was first found. "The carnelian is a siliceous stone, flesh colour to a deep blood-red.... Its colour is without clouds or veins; but sometimes delicate veins of extremely light red or white are found arranged much like the rings of an agate. Carnelian is used for rings and seals" (Charles Souvay 2005).

Chadchod (Isa. 54:12, Ezek. 27:16) is thought to be the oriental ruby, although the word is sometimes translated as *jasper.*

Chalcedony may refer to a kind of emerald and jasper. It also appears to have been a siliceous stone, a species of agate, with concentric circles of various colors. The name derives from Chalcedon, where it was found. It was considered excellent as a setting for rings, seals, cups, and beakers.

Chrysolite (Exod. 28:20, Ezek. 1:16, Dan. 10:6) is the ancient word for yellow topaz or yellow quartz. The *Catholic Encyclopedia* identifies it as a topaz, although different in shape in color. Ancient chrysolite was an octangular prism of an orange-yellow color. It came from Ceylon, Arabia, and Egypt and was thought to help drive away devils and cure diseases of the eye.

Chrysophrasus (Exod. 28:20) may have been a kind of green agate, containing mostly silica, with a small percentage of nickel.

Coral (Job 28:18, Prov. 24:7, Ezek. 27:16) may refer to black or red coral or perhaps even to pearl. It was brought by the Syrians to Tyre, where the Phoenicians made beads of coral, forming them into collars and ornaments. They were probably obtained from Babylonian pearl divers in the Red Sea and Indian Ocean. The Hebrews had little understanding of the material and rarely referred to it.

Crystal (Ezek 1:22, Job 28:18) may be gypsum or rock crystal, transparent and colorless—also possibly the meaning of "glass." Job thought it as valuable as gold, onyx, sapphire, and topaz.

Diamonds (Ezek. 3:9, Zach. 7:12, Jer. 17:1), which were unknown in Old Testament times, may have been the name given to a white, opaque stone, possibly a moonstone. On the other hand, the qualities of the diamond, especially its hardness, are noted in the reference of the use of the diamond tip for engraving: "The sin of Judah is written with a pen of iron, with the point of a diamond" (Jer. 17:1), but this may have been referring to another hard substance such as emery, a species of corindon used to polish precious stones rather than the pure carbon diamond.

Emeralds (Exod. 28:17; Rev. 21:19) were green stones, like modern emeralds, or possibly purple almandine garnets. This stone allows a high polish, making its color brilliant and sparkling. In the ancient world, emeralds were thought to preserve the sight or heal the eyes.

Hyacinth (Rev. 21:20) is a mystery to the scholars. It may refer to any one of numerous stones that have the color of the flower from which the name is derived. It appears to be harder than quartz and to be a talisman against tempests. "Ligurus" is probably the same stone.

Jasper (Exod. 28:18; Ezek. 28:13; Rev. 21:19) was a translucent green stone, perhaps *green quartz*. It came from India and Egypt.

Onyx (Exod. 28:20; Ezek. 28:13; Rev. 21:20) was a green stone, or perhaps a translucent agate with layers of black and white. Its layers of color made the stone ideal for the carving of cameos, as with agate. Onyx came from Arabia, Egypt, and India.

Pearls, not really stones, were known to have come from the Red Sea, but the name may not have been meant literally. Some think Revelation may refer to mother-of-pearl. From the time of Solomon, the Hebrews knew pearls, probably from the Phoenicians. Among the ancients, it was considered the most precious of all gems.

Rubies, which were as hard as diamonds, came from Ceylon and India. These may have been either named *carbuncle* or *chodchod.*

Sapphire (Exod. 28:19; Ezek. 28:14) was the ancient name for lapis lazuli, a deep blue stone with golden flecks of iron pyrites. It was imported from India.

Sardius was a red stone, possibly quartz.

Sardonyx was a form of agate with layers of brown and white.

Topaz (Exod. 28:17; Rev. 21:20) was a yellow stone, probably rock crystal or cysolite. It was extremely hard, with a double refraction. It varies in color according to its place of origin (I. A. Marshall 1980, 781–88; Charles Souvay 2005).

The meanings attributed to the various stones have come to conform more to our own terms by the time the great cathedrals of the medieval era were literally embellished with gems in conformity with the descriptions in Revelation. The pearls, for example, became symbols of salvation; carbuncles became symbols of Christ's crucifixion (George Ferguson, *Signs and Symbols in Christian Art,* 41, 43). *See also* Jewelry; Metal: Gold; Metal: Silver.

Further Reading

Ferguson, George. *Signs and Symbols in Christian Art.* New York: Oxford University Press, 1966. Hirsch, Emil G. "Gems," http://www.jewishencyclopedia.com (accessed June 8, 2004). Marshall, I. A. "Jewels," in *The Illustrated Bible Dictionary.* Sydney, Australia: Tyndale House Publishers, 1980. Miller, Madeleine S. and J. Lane Miller. "Jewelry," in *Harper's Bible Dictionary.* New York: Harper and Row, 1961. Souvay, Charles L. "Precious Stones in the Bible," http://www.newadvent.com (accessed January 4, 2005).

Geography

Almost every book of the Bible makes some reference to the geography or the typography of **Israel**. For the original audience, these allusions to their known world was lively and meaningful. The sparseness of Scripture—the lack of description—leaves the sense of place for the reader or hearer to supply. Each narrative had a strong sense of place for the ancients, a kind of genius or spirit of place. Each reference to a "garden," a "waste and desolation," or "Bethlehem" ("the house of bread") had an atmosphere that the Hebrews could understand, either by the name itself or by the location and its association in faith and history (Mary Ellen Chase 1955, 41). After the Diaspora, however, a large number of Jews had little firsthand knowledge of the Holy Land. In the Christian era, this has been an even greater problem, resulting in the loss of an intimate knowledge of biblical geography and a sense of place. This alienation makes visualizing the setting and catching the allusions increasingly difficult for readers. In addition, with the accrual of cultures in Palestine, the destruction and rebuilding of towns, and the renaming of ancient sites, many of the names of biblical places have been lost.

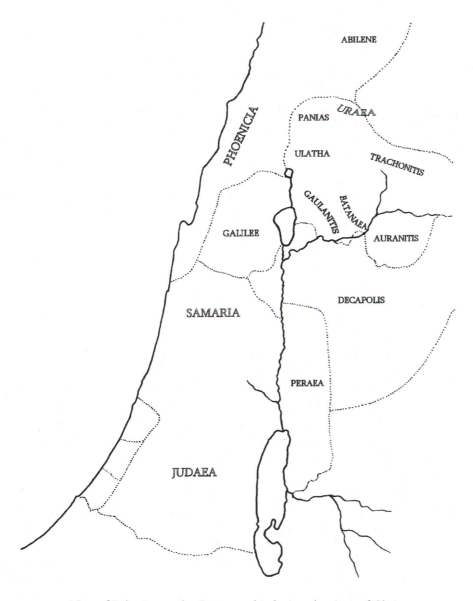

Map of Palestine under Roman rule, during the time of Christ.

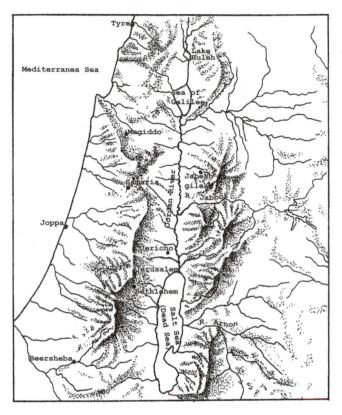

Map of Palestine showing areas of mountains and rivers.

Sources of Evidence

The last few centuries have seen an explosion of research in this area, especially among archaeologists, who have sought to discover the modern names of the biblical places and to understand the plethora of details in Scripture.

Among the most useful Scripture passages in this search have been the ethnographic listing in Genesis 10, which tells of the tribes that derived from Shem, Ham, and Japeth, Noah's sons. The travels of the Hebrews from Egypt is a second rich source (Exodus 13–19). And the tribes, with their locations, in Joshua also help considerably, as do the descriptions of the battles they fought and the land they settled (Joshua 13).

Scholars have undertaken to compare biblical cities and places with those found in the documents of other peoples with considerable success. As the *Catholic Encyclopedia* notes: "Biblical information is in a good many instances paralleled, and not un-frequently supplemented, by the indications gathered from the documents unearthed in **Egypt** and **Assyria**." They cite 119 towns of Palestine in the lists of Thothmes III (about 1600 B.C.) and 70 Canaanite cities in the famous Tell-el Amarna letters (about 1450 B.C.) Additionally, a list of 156 names of places appear on the walls of Karnak, in the boastful records of the conquests of Sheshonk I (Sesac), all in Central and Southern Palestine (935 B.C.). Further, "the inscriptions of the Assyrian kings Tukalti Pal-Esarra III (Teglathphalasar, 745–27), Sarru-kinu (Sargon, 722–05), and Sin-akhi-erba (Sennacherib, 705–681) add a few names. From the comparison of all these lists, it appears that some hundred of the Palestinian cities mentioned in the Bible are also recorded in documents ranging from the sixteenth to the eighth centuries B.C." (Charles Souvay 2005).

Ancient travelers, geographers, and historians have also helped to educate later generations. Especially useful are parts of the works of classical geographers, such as Strabo and Ptolemy; "but they cannot compete with Eusebius's *Onomasticon*." In modern times, many scholars from all over the world have studied the landscape of the Holy Land, sifting through the artifacts in the numerous tells, discovering much of the history and geography of the region. As a result, readers of Scripture are blessed with richly detailed scholarly annotations to help them in their understanding of the world of the biblical places.

The Known World

The earth, as understood by the Hebrews, consisted mainly of the lands within the Fertile Crescent. The **Garden of Eden** was identified as a region between the Tigris and Euphrates Rivers, thought of by modern Iraqis as a fertile section of the country, which has in recent years been drained and rendered sterile. This "parkland" or "paradise" designated as *Eden,* or "delight, enjoyment," may have been not a place but a "state of unbroken fellowship between God and man" (*The King James Study Bible* 1998, 10).

Most of the early stories of Genesis, through the time of Noah and the Great **Flood**, take place in a region "east" of Eden. According to Scripture (Gen. 8:4), Noah and his family and the arkload of **animals** floated onto Mt. Ararat before they were able to disembark. This is usually identified by Jewish, Christian, and Moslem traditions as a mountain range in Armenia. In the narrative following the Flood, other parts of this region are mentioned, including "Babel," a city again located in Mesopotamia, probably one where archaeologists have discovered ancient ziggurats, a brick pyramid tower rising in steplike stages.

Abram (later Abraham) came from Ur of the Chaldees, thought to be an ancient city whose ruins have been uncovered in modern Iraq. Scholars locate this in Sumer, southern Mesopotamia, although this remains open to debate. He later moved to the northern city of Haran, and from there traveled the route of the caravans across **Canaan** into Egypt, returning finally to settle in the "Promised Land" of Canaan. His journey covered the region in which most of Hebrew history occurred, and these lands became the geographical setting for Scripture.

Although time and civilization have wrought fundamental changes in the landscape of the Bible lands, we can still see the major patterns that existed even in the time of Abraham, when he first set foot on this land promised to him by God, a land rich in milk and honey. In his day, it was the major trade route between the great civilizations of Mesopotamia and Egypt. It is a narrow strip of country with the Mediterranean on the west and the desert on the east. From Dan to Beersheba, it was only about 150 miles long. And "from its eastern hills and deserts to the Mediterranean which formed its western border it was but some eighty miles in width at its widest." Chase notes that this smallness along with its natural barriers of sea, mountains, and rivers, "suggested aloofness and might even have defined security had not both been threatened by marauding tribes" on all sides (Mary Ellen Chase 1955, 20).

The ancient name for the region is Canaan, derived from the dye for which the coastal area was famous. The Canaanite people were one of several tribes who lived in the country, now bounded by Syria and Egypt, before the Israelites came. The name *Palestine* was used to designate the territory of the Philistines, and had been used as a geographical description as early as the third millennium B.C. (P. Kyle McCarter, Jr. 1993, 98). After the Roman period, it was "gradually extended to the whole southern portion of Syria. It applies to the country stretching from the Lebanon and Anti-Lebanon to the Sinaitic Desert, and from the Mediterranean to the Arabian Desert" (Charles Souvay 2005).

Within this small area is a great diversity of landscapes: deserts and swamps, hills and plains, both high and low. Only a relief map could explain the complexity of the topography, with the giant fault running the whole length of the country, marked by the waters coming out of the region around Dan to the north, flowing into Lake Huleh, and then down to the Sea of Galilee, running into the Jordan River, and ending in the Dead Sea with the fault carrying further to the Gulf of Aqaba.

Along the Jordan and the Sea of Galilee, where there is abundant water, we see flourishing foliage. Another good agricultural region is the Plain of Esdraelon, where the River Kishon flows, as Deborah's adversaries discovered. Some of the hills, which have heavy dew, are also productive, especially in the springtime.

Most of the region is rocky, with great areas of sandstone under the eastern deserts and hills (the material out of which the rose-red city of Petra was later carved); extensive outcroppings of granite in the south, and basalt (black, hardened lava) in the north (used in building the "long-ruined city of Chorazim"); hard limestone in the Hebron region, softer limestone beyond that. "Between the hills and the sea lie the only recent beds—of sands, alluvium, etc." (George Cansdale 1970, 20).

Each region and each location have their own rock formations, **animals**, history, architecture, and legends. It would take a separate volume to describe these in detail, but the general pattern of imagery in Scripture involves the desert lands, the hill country, the Jordan River, the Dead Sea, and the coastal plain.

Across the Jordan River lay the near neighbors, often mentioned in Scripture: Bashan, Gilead, **Moab**, and **Edom**. To the south were Midian, where Moses lived, and Sheba, from whence the Queen came to visit Solomon. To the West lay Egypt, where Abraham traveled, as did Joseph and his brothers, and where the Israelites lived for hundreds of years before the Exodus. There, too, Mary and Joseph fled with their baby, Jesus.

The warlike **Philistines**, who settled along the coastline, perhaps coming from Crete, surely made the Hebrews aware of a larger world beyond the "Great Sea." But the Hebrews were not a seafaring people. They restricted their travels to the plodding pace of their pack animals. Abraham and Isaac did send servants who returned to their ancestral home, which was called Padan-Aram, apparently in Armenia, for wives of their culture and religion. The time of their slavery in Egypt taught them about the land there, the fertile Nile and the different crops that would grow in swampy land. And their sojourn in the desert taught them about the desert regions to the south and west.

By the time of Solomon, their world had expanded well beyond the Fertile Crescent. This **king** traded with many foreign lands, bringing products from distant places, mentioned nowhere else in Scripture. Unlike any previous monarchs, Solomon sent ships (probably manned by Phoenicians) from the port cities to bring back spices, exotic animals, and lavish fabrics. With the even wider knowledge forced on them by invading armies from Babylon and Assyria, from Greece and Rome, the Jews learned a great deal about geography beyond the Fertile Crescent. By the time of the New Testament, the known world included most of the Mediterranean countries, and disciples were thought to have traveled in missionary journeys during the apostolic times into lands as far away as India and Ethiopia.

The land God promised to Abraham proved remarkably various, with the lush Jordan Valley marking one boundary, the Mediterranean Sea the opposite one. South of the Jordan River, the land falls to the lowest point on earth, the Dead Sea. Between these boundaries were fertile lands, rocky hills, forests, mountains, lakes, and desert lands. Most frequently mentioned are the following regions:

The Jordan Valley

"The River Jordan rises near Mt. Hermon and flows south through Lake Huleh (now largely drained) and into the Sea of Galilee. At the southern end of the Sea it enters a deep valley known as the Ghor" (Pat Alexander 1978, 7) This is sometimes called "the Rift Valley" and "forms a semi-tropical tracts where many plants flourish that are more typical of the upper Nile valley. Papyrus, the bulrush of the Bible, is one such." (George Cansdale 1970, 26).

This famous river became the dividing line for Israel, symbolically the river that Joshua had to cross into the land of Canaan to conquer and settle the Promised Land. It is also the place where Jesus was baptized by John the Baptist. The "plunging of the river bed until it is far below sea level is … a unique geological phenomenon. 'There may be something on the surface of another planet which is similar to the Jordan Valley, but on our planet there certainly is nothing,' wrote George Adam Smith, the Scottish Old

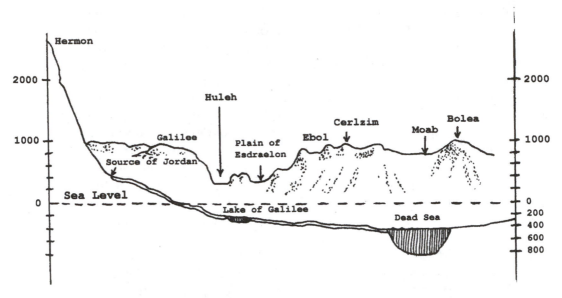

A cross-section view of Palestine from Mt. Hermon to the Dead Sea, revealing the extreme changes in elevation from the high point to the lowest—actually the lowest on earth (north to south).

Testament scholar, in his 'Historical Geography of the Holy Land'" (Werner Keller 1982, 78).

This geological rift, following the faults in the earth's crusts, leads on down to the Dead Sea. It was at Qumran, on the northern shores of the great "Salt Sea," in the numerous limestone caverns and caves that the Dead Sea Scrolls were discovered and the region was excavated, beginning in 1951. It was also in this region that John the Baptist was thought to have spent much of his ministry. The size and shape of this curious lake of salt water have changed over the years, with its coastal cities destroyed. Sodom and Gomorrah were among those lost. As Keller describes this region:

> The nearer one gets to the south end of the Dead Sea the more wild and desolate it becomes. Landscape and mountain grow eerier and more forbidding. The hills stand there silent and everlasting. Their scarred slopes fall sheer and steep down to the sea, their lower reaches are crystal white. The unparalleled disaster which once took place here has left an imperishable and oppressive mark.... To the west of the southern shore and in the direction of the Biblical "Land of the South," the Negev, stretches a ridge of hills about 150 feet high and 10 miles from north to south. Their slopes sparkle and glitter in the sunshine like diamonds.... For the most part this little range of hills consists of pure rock salt.... Many blocks of salt have been worn away by the rain and have crashed downhill. They have odd shapes and

some of them stand on end, looking like statues. It is easy to imagine them suddenly seeming to come to life. (Keller 1982, 80)

This is the legendary location of Sodom and the place where Lot's wife turned to a pillar of salt, as these curious salt shapes would seem to suggest.

The Desert

The great saints of Scripture found the desert an ideal place for meditation. In the wilderness, they were free of interruption as they contemplated their spiritual lives. Elisha, Christ, and Paul all spent preparation time in the bleakest and most sparsely populated regions. This is what Ezekiel appears to refer to as the "Valley of Dry Bones," the land without water. In the springtime, the sections of the desert that are fertile, although too dry to support vegetation, have some rainfall, allowing them to flower suddenly. Such may be the basis of the imagery of the resurrection of the bones.

One author describes Israel's desert regions this way:

Large areas in the south and east consist of desert.... The surface of the desert varies widely.... The wind is often so continuous that the sand is blown away, leaving only rock or gravel in all but protected sites. On the higher ground and steep slopes bare rock is the commonest surface. Nights can be cold for much of the year, but frost is unusual. These rocks are therefore subject to little erosion other than wind, which often carries sharp sand and eats out the softer material, leaving a giant skeleton;... The desert topography includes everything from almost flat plains to steep escarpments...and there is a wealth of colour in the various rocks. Altitudes vary from 1,250 ft. below sea level at the Dead Sea to rather over 2,000 ft. above sea level on the big escarpment. (George Cansdale 1970, 21–22)

The wide fluctuations of temperature make vegetation and animal life sparse. Winter nights may be bitter cold, and only those animals that can survive on minimal water can long survive.

There are some *wadis* (dry river beds), where water may accumulate and shrubs may grow. "Most *wadis* are more or less lined with specialized woody plants, some of which remain green throughout even the hottest weather. Some desert soils are fertile..., and after rain these quickly become covered with grasses and flowering plants, mostly annuals" (George Carsdale 1982, 22). The image of grass, growing quickly and withering, derives from experience such as this (1 Pet. 1:24, Isa. 40:8).

There are also occasional oases of various sizes and types, often with natural springs or wells. Throughout history, these have been the welcome camping grounds for travelers.

Chase notes that the Israelites displayed an "inbred, natural love of barren and desert country" that made Judea a congenial home for the ancient Hebrews from Abraham to David, perhaps because they were "originally a nomadic, shepherd people, wandering with their flocks over the eastern deserts long before they drifted into the land of Canaan." They were accustomed to the violence of winds, the sandstorms, "withering heat by day and cold by night; the scarcity of water; the perils of hunger and thirst; the sheer physical strength and vitality necessary to wrest a livelihood from a forbidding land." This made the high, bare Judean pastures with their rough scrub and thorns, white shelves of stone "jutting out like ribs of prehistoric creatures, their wide transparent skies" a "familiar home" to them. And it was to Judea that they were constantly drawn (Mary Ellen Chase 1955, 23).

The Lowlands and the Plains

The coastal region along the Mediterranean also has sandy areas, but these are mentioned less prominently in Scripture. In Old Testament times, the coastal region was usually under the control of the Philistines. To the Hebrews, these coastlands were not particularly attractive; they consisted of a belt of coastal sand dunes backed by forest, lagoons, and swamp. The Hebrews, not a seafaring people like the Phoenicians, tended to rely on others for their shipping. They had no natural ports on their coastline until the manmade port of Caesarea was built by Herod the Great, about the time of Jesus's birth. This beautiful city served as the first major port on this coast below Mt. Carmel. It was expanded by the Romans and irrigated by great aqueducts, which they built to make the region more favorable for agriculture and habitation. It was the place where Paul was tried and imprisoned, and served as the home of Roman governors, including Pontius Pilate. This coastal plain had various names: south of Mt. Carmel, it was called the Plain of Philistia and the Plain of Sharon; north of Carmel, it was the Plain of Asher.

The central plain is the most famous part of this region: the Plain of Esdraelon, which is some distance from the Mediterranean coast, forming a break in the rock that divides the central highlands from Galilee and the northern mountains. It is shaped in a rough triangle that originally had a marshy floor (Judges 4:15). It is a natural passageway through the mountains and has been strategically important since the earliest caravans traveled between Sumer and Egypt. Called *Via Maris,* "the way of the sea," it was the obvious trade route and the natural path for invaders. Megiddo lies at the western edge, serving as a lasting image of the symbol of the great battle of Armageddon in Revelation 16 (Pat Alexander 1978, 6–7).

The Marshlands, which once existed in areas such as the Plain of Sharon, have long since disappeared, having been drained and filled. At one time there were areas of marsh on the plains and in a few places on the coast, serving as useful barriers against invading armies. Most of these areas were breeding grounds for mosquitoes, as well as frogs and fish, ducks and terns, and herons.

The Hill Country

The central highlands or the hill country was land sloping away from the coast on one side and away from the Jordan Valley on the other. The western slope is gentle and the eastern slope abrupt. Forests at one time covered the land that is now bare limestone and thin, poor soil. This was the home of fortified towns, with strong defenses. Both Judah and Israel, the southern and northern kingdoms, had their capitals in this region—Jerusalem and Samaria, respectively.

On the north of this region is the Plain of Esdraelon, and then the hill country continues toward the jutting promontory of Mt. Carmel (where Elijah had his great conflict with the priests of Baal) on the coast and toward Galilee inland. The vast majority of Bible narratives occur in the hills, from the Galilee in the north, down through Samaria to Jerusalem and Bethlehem. "There is some rainfall (above 24 in.). The nights are cool in summer, cold in winter, when frost and snow are unusual but not unknown" (George Cansdale 1970, 27). The forests that once covered these hills are mentioned in stories of David. His son Absalom was killed in a forest, when his long hair caught on the branches of the trees. At one time, the region was alive with wild animals, which found plenty of grazing land, as well as fruits and nuts from the variety of trees.

The rock formations in the sandstone provide many holes and clefts that have served as homes to humans and beasts throughout the centuries. This was an excellent hiding place for David when he was fleeing Saul, and it was later used to shelter the Zealots and outlaws in Jesus's day.

Galilee, the home of Jesus and his disciples, is north of the Plain of Esdraelon. The upland ranges of the hills here "stretch away northward, gradually rising as they come nearer to the high mountains of Lebanon. They rise in a series of steps, with scarp edges, facing generally south or south-east. The lower steps in the 'staircase' were and are fertile basin lands, separated from each other by barren limestone edges. In the time of Jesus, these basins were known for their **grain**, fruit and **olives**. They formed a prosperous, well-populated area. But the higher steps rise to a bleak and windswept upland. This is isolated and infertile, and lacks the forests of the higher mountain slopes farther north" (Pat Alexander, *Eerdman's Family Encyclopedia of the Bible*, 6–7). This was sometimes divided into the Lower and Upper Galilee, with the northern section often under foreign control.

Galilee was a busy region, crossed by the great trade routes, bringing many strangers with news of the outside world; a mixed community with **fishermen** casting their nets on the Sea of Galilee and farmers tilling the soil of their fertile farmlands. It was full of people who were more racially mixed than in the Jerusalem region, and considered hayseeds by these city-dwellers.

Between this hill country and the coastline was a piedmont region, usually controlled by the Philistines during Old Testament times. Considered hostile territory, it was referred to as the "Shephelah." In the era of the Judges, it was covered with forests of sycamore trees. Samson was a frequent visitor to this region of foothills—with tragic results. It was here that Samson fell in love with Delilah, was captured, and blinded.

Transjordan

East of the Jordan, the region that Lot chose when his uncle Abram gave him his preference, is also hill country, but has broad plateau. This was once the home of those traditional enemies of Israel—**Ammonites**, Moabites and Edomites. These people were the descendants of Lot's incestuous relations with his own daughters after their escape from Sodom.

These uplands are higher than those to the west, well watered, with good pasture for huge flocks of **sheep** and herds of cattle. Scripture notes tributes from the king of Moab to Israel in enormous numbers—100,000 lambs and the wool from 100,000 sheep (2 Kings 3:4). Bashan was noted for its bulls and Gilead for its balm. Ruth came from Moab, a region to which the people of Bethlehem journeyed when they faced famine.

It was in this colorful and variegated land that the great drama of God's battles for and with his chosen people took place. *See also* Ammon, Ammonites; Climate; Egypt, Egyptians; Moab, Moabites; Philistines.

Further Reading

Alexander, Pat, ed. *Eerdmans' Family Encyclopedia of the Bible*. Grand Rapids, Mich.: Wm B. Eerdmans Publishing Co., 1978. Cansdale, George. *All the Animals of the Bible Lands*. Grand Rapids, Mich.: William B. Eerdmans Publishing Co, 1970. Chase, Mary Ellen. *Life and Language in the Old Testament*. New York: W.W. Norton and Company, Inc. 1955. Keller, Werner. *The Bible as History*. New York: Bantam Books, 1982. McCarter, P. Kyle, Jr. "Canaan," in *Oxford Companion to the Bible*. New York: Oxford University Press, 1993. Souvay, Charles L. "Biblical Geography," http://www.newadvent.org (accessed July 8, 2005).

Goad

(Judg. 3:31; 1 Sam. 13:21) The goad itself was a long stick, usually five to seven feet long, but sometimes as much as nine feet long, with a sharp point fixed to one end. The farmer would use it to prick the cattle forward when they grew weary. When **oxen** were yoked and harnessed to the **plow**, the farmer would take the plow in one hand and a goad in the other and spur the oxen to drag the plow through the ground. The goad was also a useful weapon against enemies. Shamgar slew 600 Philistines (Judg. 3:31) using this primitive spear.

In the early days, before Israel had its own **metal** industries, farmers had to rely on the **Philistines** to sharpen their goads, as well as their other metal tools, the plowshares and mattocks, forks, and axes (1 Sam. 13:21).

The image of prodding the reluctant or lazy creature made this a useful metaphor for sharp urging, such as the prick of conscience, the nagging of a mate, or the "words of the wise," which are "firmly embedded nails" in human minds (Eccles. 12:11). When Saul of Tarsus (subsequently Paul) had his encounter with God on the road to Damascus, a voice said to him in Aramaic, "Saul, Saul, why do you persecute me? It is hard for you to kick against the goads" (Acts 26:14 NIV). The image used for the **apostle** here is of a disobedient ox, who is fighting his master. *See also* Agriculture.

Goats

(Gen. 15:9) Goats, which were usually herded along with **sheep**, had many of the same uses and qualities, and some significant differences. They were about the same size and shape, but with a different tail, which stood up. Although "chewers of the cud" like sheep, they preferred the tougher grasses and leaves from young trees. They did not seem to mind the heat of summer and would feed in the hot sun while the sheep sought the shade. Although, like lambs, kids made charming pets, the adults were less cuddly and friendly, with more playful and aggressive traits than sheep. Stronger and more energetic, they were also less vulnerable, able to leap up mountain sides easily, ward off predators, and fight their own battles. When herded with sheep, they tended to lead the flock. During certain times, when herding, breeding, milking, and shearing, the **shepherd** separated the goats from the sheep. Most families had at least one goat for milk.

Goats were among the first of the animals to be domesticated, probably second only to the **dog**. All goats are "hill **animals**, sure-footed and able to live in rugged country. By choice they are browsers rather than grazers" (George Cansdale 1970, 44). They were of various colors, but Scripture mentions only the spotted and specked goats that Jacob bred (Gen. 30). The type of goat preferred in ancient **Canaan** had large hollow horns. The male goat has a strong smell and a bad temper. His horns could be a real danger to his adversary. As one writer who knows goats well explained, "When man domesticated the goat he recruited an assistant second only to

Goat (*Capra hircus mambrica*). Note the goat's similarity to sheep; they are both members of the sheep family—the hollow-horned ruminants, chewers of the cud. They are very different animals in behavior and are referred to in Scripture as "he-goat," "she-goat," "young goat," or "satyr."

himself in destructive powers.... The goat is hardy and well able to fend for itself" (George Cansdale 1970, 46).

Goats were most cherished for their hair, which was (and still is) used for **clothing** and for **tents**. The goathair tent provided more than shelter: it was warm in winter and cool in summer, allowing breezes to come through. Goat's milk, which is plentiful and rich, was the basis for the popular sour milk delicacy called *leben* (Madeleine S. Miller and J. Lane Miller 1961, 229). Some believe that they were first kept as milk producers. Their flesh was less frequently used for feasts than sheep's, but a young kid was considered a great delicacy. Their horns served as vessels for carrying oil.

Their skin was used to make the standard water bottle for travelers. The skin was removed from the body in a single piece (after cutting off the head and legs). The neck then served as the mouth of the container, and the other holes were sewed up, leaving the hair on the outside of the skin to serve as padding. The whole skin was then filled with tanning liquid to cure the skin and set it in the right shape. "These containers were used for milk and also **wine** from early times; wine bottles feature in one of our Lord's parables (Mark 2:22)" (George Cansdale 1970, 45). Because such bottles could not be washed or sterilized, they were better for wine or water than for milk, which would curdle quickly in them. The skin as well as the hair was used for clothing (Heb. 11:37).

The scriptural references differentiate among types: he-goats, goats, and rams refer to the leader of the flock—the chief (Isa.14:9). This tends to be the sacrificial offering or the sin-offering. The kid is the young goat, only a few months old, too young for general sacrifices, but used once as a special burnt offering (Judg.13:19). This is also the creature the Jews were forbidden to cook in his mother's milk, apparently a typical mode of preparation. This seems to be the source of the Hebrew separation of meat products from milk products in cooking. References to "flocks" usually mean both sheep and goats.

Goats were required in some sacrificial offerings, often a young goat, and in smaller numbers than sheep. One of the most distinct religious uses of the goat was as the "scapegoat" on the **Day of Atonement**. A young goat was burdened with the sins of the community and driven into the wilderness— sometimes over a cliff—to die for the sins of the many.

Perhaps because of their nature, perhaps because of their willful ways, they became associated with sin. Isaiah refers to them as "satyrs" (13:21, 34:14) and in other places, they are referred to as "devils" (Lev. 17:7; 2 Chron.11:15). Their traits of ferocity and independence, vigorous sexuality, and strength, especially as they grew mature, made them symbols in mythology of sexual excess—the very image of the satyr, a figure that was half-goat and half-man. Pan is the Greek woodland god who plays the flute and frolics with abandon in the wild country, indulging his senses as does the "Natural Man." Thus, "separating the sheep from the goats" came to mean separating the saved from the damned. *See also* Animals; Cloth; Food; Leather; Sheep; Tents.

Further Reading
Cansdale, George. *All the Animals of the Bible Lands*. Grand Rapids, Mich.: Zondervan Publishing House, 1970. Miller, Madeleine S. and J. Lane Miller. *Harper's Bible Dictionary*. New York: Harper and Row, 1961.

Gospel, Gospels

The term *gospel* derives from the Old English words "god" (good) and "spell" (to tell). It is a translation from the Greek word *euaggelion* or "I bear a message" or "good tidings," as on the occasion when the **angel** told the **shepherd**s, "I bring you good tidings of great joy" (Luke 2:10). The word is used frequently in the New Testament, most notably at the beginning of the Gospel of Mark and throughout the writings of Paul. It refers to the good news of the coming of the **Messiah**.

The four accounts of Jesus's birth, life, death, and resurrection—Matthew, Mark, Luke, and John—are consequently called "Gospels." These first four historical books of the New Testament used the term with the specific meaning "the good news of the kingdom" (Matt. 4:23, Mark 1:15). They themselves came to be referred to as accounts of the gospel, *according to* Matthew, Mark, Luke, or John. Although they have different narrators, purposes, and points of view, they each present a history of the gospel.

In addition to these widely accepted or canonical gospels, other accounts of Christ's words and deeds were also recorded and circulated early in Church history. They include *The Gospel according to the Hebrews, The Gospel of Peter, The Gospel according to the Egyptians, The Gospel of Matthias, The Gospel of Philip, The Gospel of Thomas, The Proto-Evangelium of James, The Gospel of Nicodemus, The Gospel of the Twelve Apostles, The Gospel*

253

of *Basilides, The Gospel of Valentinus, The Gospel of Marcion, The Gospel of Eve, The Gospel of Judas, The Writing of Genna Marias,* and *The Gospel Teleioseos* (J. P. Arendzen 2004).

The early Church rejected these late and spurious texts as apocryphal. The orthodox Fathers considered them false, reserving the privileged position for the four that have been recognized as canonical by most Christian churches and appear in most Scripture (Philip Jenkins 2001, 7). Discoveries at Nag Hammadi in **Egypt** in 1945 uncovered documents that had been concealed since the late fourth century, including *The Gospel of Thomas.* Elaine Pagels, who published *The Gnostic Gospels* in 1979, has done much to bring attention to the fragmentary *Gospel of Mary.* Other fragments have also found attention among the Jesus Seminar, a group of scholars who have studied many of these apocryphal texts in an effort to determine the "actual" words and actions of Jesus. *See also* Epistles.

Further Reading

Arendzen, J. P. "Gnosticism," http://www.newadvent.org (accessed July 14, 2004). Jenkins, Philip. *Hidden Gospels: How the Search for Jesus Lost Its Way.* New York: Oxford University Press, 2001. Miller, Robert J., ed. *The Complete Gospels.* San Francisco: Harper Collins Publisher, 1994.

Government, Civil Authority

"It is not good that man should be alone," God said of his new creature in the **Garden of Eden** (Gen. 2:18). Thus began social relations, and the consequent need for authority, which was given first to Adam, and from thence to various functionaries of God. Government and faith were inextricably intertwined in Hebrew history, with theocracy serving as the primary basis for governance and the family the primary means of organization. At the time of the **Fall**, the authority within the family was assigned to the **husband**. As the families expanded into tribes, the father retained this power, which was thought to be God-given.

Tribal Government from Abraham to the Judges

From the time of Abraham, the family or the tribe was the basic unit of society, the locus for determining matters under dispute and for battling enemies. Like the modern Bedouin nomads of Arabia, the father was the **priest** and **king**, with jurisdiction not only over members of the family, but also those who were employed or enslaved by him. This leader was empowered by God through a **covenant** relationship that included his "seed."

In **Egypt**, the Israelites were totally subject to their Egyptian masters and without rights. By the time Moses led his people to Sinai, the Israelites had multiplied and divided into the **tribes**, a form of extended family. After the **Exodus**, Moses established a theocratic rule. Appointed by God, with **laws** handed down from God, Moses was the chief governor and Aaron was the chief priest. At the advice of his father-in-law, Moses appointed representatives to help in the administration of justice among the tribes, reserving the right to himself to serve as the final authority in irreconcilable disputes.

By the time the Israelites returned to **Canaan** and began to settle the region, the twelve **tribes** had become the basic unit of governance. Their blood relationships gradually expanded to the "blood covenant"—an enlargement of the family to include **slaves**, new members who chose to join the group, and foreign wives as the Israelites intermarried with the indigenous peoples. "Tribes having their fixed pasture districts entertain close relations with neighboring clans and families that share with them the privileges of watering their flocks at certain wells. Moreover, a permanent or accidental community of other interests occasionally unites entire tribes into one body" (Emil G. Hirsch, Immanuel Benzinger, Levi Dembitz 2004). Obviously, attacks by enemies were powerful unifying forces. As seen in the stories of the Judges, most of these men and women of God were also military leaders, usually able to unite only one or two tribes against a common enemy.

In time, **blood** relationships became less significant, and Israel gradually began to lose its kinship ties and developed new local structures based on shared concerns. "The ancient tribal assembly assumed a territorial character and became the assembly of all householders, though often both organizations remained identical" (Ze'ev W. Falk 2001, 36). The local assembly functioned as a **court** of criminal justice, gradually becoming the court of local elders. These elders of the city and villages organized their territories in a pattern parallel to that of the Canaanites, with the surrounding smaller villages becoming in some way dependent on the cities for justice and protection.

The increasingly distinct concerns of local interests divided the country into separate communities, reinforced by geographical separation. Nomadic herdsmen on one side of a river might have very different needs from farmers on the other side. They might join to fight a common enemy under a charismatic leader such as Deborah, but they would then go back to their individual concerns. This localized government system was probably a form of primitive democracy parallel to that discovered in many other societies, including **Babylonia**, Athens, and **Rome**. "The people of the gate" (Gen. 23:10, Ruth 4:2, 11) were the elders of the city who gathered whenever important business was presented for adjudication. The **judges** who were chosen to be leaders were probably charismatic **warriors** such as Deborah and Samson, who served the community as adjudicators of disputes. The Bible speaks of this time as a period when "there was no king in Israel: every man did that which was right in his own eyes" (Judg. 21:25).

Monarchy

In response to this disintegration of the tribal ties and the example of their neighbors, the Israelites begged for a king. They felt the need to unite to fight the much more powerful **Philistines**, who were advancing on them from the west (Hirsch et al. 2005). The first of the kings, Saul, operated much as the judges had done, serving as both judge and as a military leader. David, a much stronger king, brought the tribes together, settled their capital in Jerusalem, and began the practices that his son enlarged. Solomon increased the centralization of power and established a standing army, royal officials, and a pattern of taxation. Samuel had warned the Israelites regarding the powers that the people were ceding to a king when they insisted that they wanted to be like their neighbors. These included the power to conscript their sons, tax their labor, and enslave them.

The king's officials (2 Sam. 20:23 ff) included the general of the army or commander of the royal bodyguard, the chief councilor, the secretary of state, the overseer of labor, and the high priest, not to mention those charged with the administration of the palace, the prefects in charge of the 12 provinces, etc. Under Solomon, the kingdom was divided into 12 districts, with a prefect over each to provide victuals for the king and his house (1 Kings 4:7ff.) The government was not divided into departments. Every official served as a sort of representative of the king in his district, "exercising the latter's prerogatives as military commander, governor, **tax collector**, and **judge**. According to the **Prophets**, it appears that these officials often abused the power placed in their hands; they combined bribery, oppression, and cruelty toward their subordinates with servility toward their superiors" (2 Sam. 11:14ff, 1 Kings 12:10ff, Emil Hirsch et al. 2005). These local officials collected the taxes and recruited for the army and for the extravagant building programs instituted under Solomon. There were even "Crown lands" that the king could give to his servants as fiefs (1 Sam. 8:13). And travelers through the country found that tolls were required by the "King's Law." The king could claim the first fruits of the land or seize the lands of condemned criminals, and he could determine "special need" for taxation. With no constitution to limit his absolute power, the king himself determined the law and the proper stewardship of the silver and gold that he was free to assess his subjects. He was empowered to allow a husband to have only a few wives or hundreds of wives and concubines. Everything depended on his intelligence, ethics, and good will.

There was no principle of hereditary succession to the **throne**, a problem that resulted in the divided kingdom after Solomon. With two capital cities, Samaria and Jerusalem, and two kings, Israel and Judah continued to coexist over centuries, usually leaving the local communities to govern themselves and retaining their judicial functions and their ability to determine local issues. In some cities, such as Succoth, as many as 77 elders sat on the local council (Judg. 8:14). This was determined simply by the number of prominent families in the community.

Persian Rule

During the Exile, the national kingdom perished and the old tribal patterns revived. This marked an interruption in the theocracy and the beginning of the time when Israel was subject to a foreign power. The heads of the families again assumed supreme command in the local communities (Ezra 1:5). The priests and **Levites** did not seem to belong to these bodies, suggesting that the clerical power was now diminished. Ezra tried to reverse this trend, insisting that the local elders forbid mixed **marriages**. The elders probably also policed other local matters (Ezra 10:14). The local population met on market days and on the **Sabbath** in the **synagogue** to discuss common affairs in a kind of primitive democracy portrayed in the apocryphal books of Sirach and Judith.

Over these local structures, the primary authority lay with Persian governors or prefects who resided at Samaria and had a representative in Jerusalem. They, of course, served at the pleasure of Persia. When Cyrus issued the edict that allowed the Jews to return to Jerusalem and rebuild their Temple in 538 B.C., the new settlement around Jerusalem was organized on the basis of self-government under Persian rule. The political power was vested in the governor of Judea, who was sometimes Jewish, but the community of returned exiles was led by the high priest. He was probably chosen by the priests and his election was undoubtedly confirmed by the governor.

Apparently this quasi-democratic form of temple-state was a result of the intervention of Jewish notables in the Persian capital. A royal edict specified the powers of the spiritual head of the community (Ezra 7:12–26; Ze'ev Falk 2001, 38). Ezra was empowered to appoint magistrates and judges, to teach the laws of his God, and to judge the offenders—whether for death, banishment, confiscation of goods, or imprisonment. Apparently Persian emperors generally allowed conquered peoples to retain their own legal systems and their own rulers, applying native law and allowing a fair amount of judicial autonomy. Assemblies of the "officials and the elders" (Ezra 6:7, 10:8) might still be convened as the need arose to promulgate religious regularities.

Hellenistic Period

Apart from the hints found in the words of the prophets, little is known about the governance between the time of Persian rule and the Hellenic period. The Ptolemies and Seleuicids settled on a system of local governance, claiming their right to appoint and dismiss the high priest, but rarely interfering with local governance. The law came into force in 444 B.C. through the efforts of Ezra and Nehemiah, establishing the high priest as the head of the entire community, the president of the ancient aristocratic senate, and the assembly of elders. Occasionally, the local rulers, such as the Hasmoneans, would call themselves "kings," but their actual authority was determined by the Hellenic rulers.

The Temple constitution was abolished by Antiochus IV in 168 B.C., but restored by the Hasmoneans, who combined the civil and military power with the high priesthood in their family's reign. Their secular power was terminated by the conquest of the Romans in 63 B.C. (E. J. Young and F. F. Bruce 1980, 585–587).

Roman Period

Under the Romans, the high priest served also as ethnarch, sharing his functions with the council, now known as the **Sanhedrin**. Locally, the Romans left the Jews a fair amount of freedom in their own affairs, claiming only the usual authority to tax, to adjudicate capital crimes, and to conscript citizens for the army. The Romans appointed and deposed the high priests, who continued to preside over the Sanhedrin. They also appointed a "king" to preside over the people who was limited in his powers by Rome and could be removed from office at their will. This would explain Herod's eagerness to please the Emperor, building cities in honor of Caesar and being careful to avoid his displeasure.

Local administration was handled by the partitioning of a number of republican states in an effort to infiltrate the population and reduce Jewish nationalism. Herodian princes ruled in less tractable areas, while Jerusalem and its neighborhood were under the Sanhedrin. The Caesars used client kings and personal deputies—procurators, along with religious entities to manage the kingdom.

The structure looked like this for the three regions of Palestine:

Herod the Great (40–4 B.C.)		
Idumea/Judaea/Samaria	Galilee/Peraea	Ithuraea Trachonltis
Archaelus (4 B.C.–A.D. 6)	Herod Antipas (4 B.C.–A.D. 39)	Herod Philip (4 B.C.–A.D. 34)
Procurators Coponius (6–9)		

Ambibulus (9–12)

Annius Rufus (12–15)

Valerius Gratus (15–26)

Pntius Pilate (26–36)

Marcellus (36–38)

Marylius (38–44)

Herod Agrippa I
King of Judaea 37–44

Procurators

Cuspius Fodus (44–48)

Tiberius Alexander
(46–48)

Herod Agrippa II
Tetrarch of Chalcis & Northern Territory (48–70)

Ventidius Cumonus (48–52)

Antonius Felix (52–59)

Porcius Festus (59–61)

(Ralph Gower 1987, 281)

This was the environment into which Jesus was born, teaching his followers to "render unto Caesar that which is Caesar's" and finding his main adversaries among the members of the priestly classes. His parents traveled to Bethlehem at the time of his birth to conform to the Roman obligation to be "enrolled" in a census. Among his **disciples** was a tax collector, and he admired the centurion as a man "under orders." The complexities of his trial and crucifixion underscore the complexities of the structure under which he lived and died. At the time of his trial, Pontius Pilate was procurator of Judea and Herod was king of Galilee.

Paul also lived within this structure, being both a Roman citizen and a member of the Temple system, at first assigned by the Sanhedrin the task of

Jewish Nationalist coin of the first century with cup of manna, another with pomegranates, and one with the head of Julius Caesar (which Jesus may have used to demonstrate the need for "rendering unto Caesar the things that are Caesar's and unto God the things that are God's").

259

persecuting the followers of Jesus. Like most of the early Christians, he found himself able to conform to Roman authorities and even encouraged Christians to pray for the people in authority. He found himself in prison during the period when the procurators Felix and Festus were in power. His clever use of the Roman judicial system finally took him all the way to Rome, where he died. At least one of his epistles is addressed to those Christians in Rome.

The structure of Roman governance is apparent all through the New Testament, and the abuses of that system are manifest in the **apocalyptic** vision of Revelation. Under various of the Caesars, whom they refused to worship as gods, the Christians were persecuted and pressured to forswear their faith, especially their allegiance to Christ as the "King of Kings."

The formal destruction of the theocracy was marked by the looting and burning of the Temple in 70 A.D. For Christians, the issue of authority and governance has continued throughout the ages. Claims of the Church and of the State have been settled one way or another for a brief time, only to rise again in another form. *See also* Court Officials; Judges; Kings; Law; Taxes.

Further Reading

DeVaux, Roland. *Ancient Israel: Its Life and Institutions.* Grand Rapids, Mich.: William B. Eerdmans Publishing Company, 1961. Falk, Ze'ev W. *Hebrew Law in Biblical Times.* Provo, Utah: Brigham Young University Press, 2001. Gower, Ralph. *The New Manners and Customs of Bible Times.* Chicago: Moody Press, 1987. Hirsch, Emil G., Immanuel Benzinger, Lewis N. Dembitz. "Government," http://www.jewishencyclopedia.com (accessed October 15, 2004). Young, E. J. and F. F. Bruce, "Government," in *The Illustrated Bible Dictionary.* Sydney, Australia: Tyndale House Publishers, 1980.

Grain

From Cain's time to ours, grain products have been a basic part of daily life, considered a gift of God from the very beginning of human history. Cain, a "tiller of the ground." brought to God an offering of the "fruit of the ground," assumed to be the first "grain offering" (Gen. 4:3). Perhaps because of the manner in which Cain offered his grains, or perhaps because he gave some lesser offering rather than the "first fruits" that God expected of his creatures, his offering was despised by God.

Grain is the most commonly available food for humans and livestock. For the Hebrews, a drought in the region meant a famine because of the grain shortage, sending the Hebrews on travels to more fertile regions, usually **Egypt**, in search of **food**. The imagery of the **prophets**, **Psalms**, and **Gospels** is full of grain references. When Jesus considers the many in need of the word of God, he refers to them as "fields" that are "ripe for the harvest." In Revelation, one mark of the end of time is the hideous horseman signifying drought and hunger. The Israelites were a people heavily dependent on grain, actively involved in growing it and knowledgeable about each step in the process.

The process of planting and harvesting "corn," the term used for various cereals, including rye and millet, but usually barley and wheat, was simple. It began late in October or November, the time of the "former rains." The ground was far too hard to cultivate until some rain has softened it. (Ps. 65:10; Job 29:23.) Using a wooden **plow**, fastening this to the **yoke** holding the **oxen** together, and taking his **goad** in hand, the farmer would begin his task. In the flat fields, he would press down on the plow, goad the oxen forward, and break the ground. Sometimes, concerned with attacks by thieves,

Millstones from the Agricultural Museum in Jerusalem. The millstone was so heavy that it became a symbol for great weight.

Grinding the grain into flour, showing how sticks fit into millstone.

261

a group of farmers might band together, plowing the field close to one another. Elisha was plowing with 11 other farmers, using 24 oxen, when Elijah found him (1 Kings 19:19). When called to minister to Elijah, he slaughtered his yoke of oxen and cooked them, feeding them to the community, thereby signifying that he would not return to his task.

If the land was rocky and mountainous, it was often farmed on terraces, built so that level surfaces, like steps, climbed up the hillside. Sometimes, the fields were too hard to be plowed, forcing the farmer to dig the soil by hand, using a pickaxe or mattock. (Isaiah 7:25 mentions this arduous labor.) It was less common in growing grain than for orchards, where **trees** and vines might grow among the rocks.

When the soil was properly prepared, using grain saved from a previous crop, the farmer would begin sowing his seed. His **donkey** usually carried the seed to the field in a large sack. The farmer would then take some of the seed and put it in a leather bag, which he carried through the field, scattering the seed with his hand as he walked along. The meaning of the Hebrew word "to sow" means "to scatter seed" (Fred H. Wight 1953, 174). Another member of the family would come behind with the plow, covering the seed.

This is the process that Jesus described in the **parable** of the sower. (Matt 13:3–8, Mark 4:3–8, Luke 8:5–8). However, the parable tells accurately the fate of the seeds. Some were eaten by **birds**, which hovered nearby, waiting to devour the grain; some landed on stony places, where they might take root briefly in the mossy covering, only to die when hit by the scorching sun; some fell among thorns, where the thorns choked out the good grain; and some fell on good soil "and brought forth fruit, some an hundredfold, some sixtyfold, some thirtyfold" (Matt. 13:3–8). The enemies to cultivation that Jesus identified here were the most common. In addition there were the tares, locusts, and drought—not to mention enemy armies and thieves who might simply steal any grain they discovered.

The rainy season followed the sowing; heavy rains fell, gushing rains that continued throughout the winter months. Then a third season of rains, lighter spring rains came in March and April before the dry season began. This was called the "latter rain" and was essential for the maturing of the crops: barley in April and May, wheat in May and June. Note that the calendar is also the key to the harvest **festivals** of the Hebrews, with the rains figuring significantly in the cycle of their year.

The harvesting itself was a major task that involved the entire community. The men would chop the grain with sickles, cheap ones made of flint, or bronze and iron ones, common only in later days. A piece of flint might be set in the jawbone of an **animal**, or in a curved piece of wood (Fred Wight 1953, 180). (This might explain Samson's slaughter of the Philistines using the "jawbone of an ass.") The harvesters would gather their grain into bundles, or sheaves, as Joseph mentioned in describing his dream (Gen. 37:7). The harvesters would bind and then tie these onto the donkey's back or the **camel's** packsaddle for transport to the threshing floor.

The harvesters deliberately left grain in the corners of the field and scattered some as they collected the sheaves so that the gleaners could follow along and pick up the leftovers. This custom was part of Mosaic **law**, for the care of the poor (Lev. 23:22) and is portrayed in detail in the book of Ruth (chapter 2). Ruth further discovered that it was dangerous for a woman to glean by herself. The kindly Boaz warned her to stay close by others who could protect her from unwanted advances or violence. Another law connected with grain was the provision that a traveler might walk through the field of ripened grain and eat some of it, although he was not allowed to take a sickle to it. Thus, when Jesus and his **disciples** picked grain to eat as they approached Jerusalem, they were within the law. It was the "harvesting" or working on the **Sabbath** that raised the ire of the **Pharisees**.

After the harvest came the **threshing**, an elaborate process with rules of its own, then the winnowing, sifting, and measuring. The clean grain was then stored in granaries, cisterns, jars, or various other places. Smaller homes would have great earthen jars for grain storage. These were often shaped like barrels and made of wickerwork covered with clay. If enemies or robbers threatened the stock, a dry cistern might suffice to sequester the grain. It could be covered and hidden. The rich man, like the Egyptian rulers, would be bolder, and put his grain in buildings or barns, also known as *garners* (Deut. 28:8, Matt. 3:12, Prov. 3:10). The ones in Egypt must have been massive, containing the accumulated grain of the region for seven fat years. They were apparently usually round, and sometimes below the surface of the ground. Excavations at Gezer and Jericho have revealed ancient granaries (probably public storehouses).

It was such a building that the rich man of Jesus's parable was planning to build, not realizing that "this night thy soul shall be required of thee: then whose shall those things be, which thou has provided?" (Luke 12:18). Christ was clear that laying up treasures on earth is a fruitless endeavor. Using agricultural imagery, he said: "Consider the ravens: for they neither sow nor reap; which neither have storehouses nor barn; and God feedeth them." (Luke 12:24). *See also* Agriculture; Bread; Camel; Donkey, Ass; Goad; Ox, Oxen; Plow.

Further Reading
Wight, Fred H. *Manners and Customs of Bible Lands.* Chicago: Moody Press, 1953.

Sieving grain in preparation for the grinding.

Graves

Scripture is remarkably precise about burial places. For example, the final chapter of Joshua chronicles the burial of Joshua, Joseph, and Eleazar, all with references to their families and their claims to the land:

And they buried [Joshua] in the border of his inheritance in Timnath-serah, which is in mount Ephraim, on the north side of the hill of Gaash.... And the bones of Joseph, which the children of Israel brought up out of Egypt, buried they in Shechem, in a parcel of ground which Jacob bought of the sons of Hamor the father of Shechem for a hundred pieces of silver: and it became the inheritance of the children of Joseph. And Eleazar the son of Aaron died; and they buried him in a hill that pertained to Phineehas his son, which was given him in mount Ephraim. (Josh. 24:30–33)

This passage points to the legal right to the land, the exact location of the tomb, and the inheritance for the children—all important aspects of burial.

A cave tomb with a round stone at doorway that can be rolled away, as in the case of Jesus's burial.

Most of these were apparently **caves** in the hillside, natural tombs that belonged to families. Some scholars suspect that the location of the family tomb and its continued use for succeeding generations helped to codify the ownership of the land. The book of Judges—and the burials of Gideon (Judg. 8:32) and Samson (Judg. 16:31)—testify to this practice of burial in caves near the family home. For Joseph, it was important that his bones be transported from **Egypt** for a second burial to establish his family's claim to the land.

For most of Israel, the preferred grave site was a cave with a small entranceway and a sloping passage, leading to several chambers, each with benches on the sides so that the bodies could be placed in an elevated position until they had decayed. The bones would then be stored in urns or piled in a corner, giving the term "gathered unto his fathers" a literal meaning. There appear to have been no rules for the positioning of the body. In some of these, there are stone headrests shaped like horseshoes.

Although most of these were probably natural caves, some had to be shaped to be useful. Rock-hewn tombs, usually carved into sandstone hillsides, were usually a square or rectangular room with rock-cut benches on three sides of the chamber and a narrow doorway that could be closed with a rock. During the Hellenistic period, a different form of rock-hewn cave appeared, with perpendicular niches cut for the bodies (Roland deVaux 1961, 57). A round stone, which could be rolled away, was the design of Joseph of Arimathea's tomb, which he provided for Jesus's body.

Constructed tombs were more rare than natural caves. Some of the burial sites, apparently used for affluent folk, were nothing more than simple dugout pits for individuals. These "cist graves" were lined with stone slabs or mud brick. And some were stone-built tombs with roofs, which have been unearthed at Megiddo, Dan, and Aphek. Others in the Silwan Village cemetery had either flat or gabled ceilings, some were cube-shaped, some had pyramid-shaped roofs (Philip J. King and Lawrence E. Stager 2001, 371).

Poor people, who could not afford tombs, and criminals were laid to rest in the ground or thrown into common trenches (Roland deVaux 1961, 58). A well-tended tomb was a sign of wealth. It might be marked with a stone or some other funeral monument.

Neighboring peoples used ossuaries, urnlike receptacles, for the bones after the bodies had decayed. By the eighth century, some Assyrians were using "bathtub" coffins, which had rounded edges, squared at one end, with side handles. Several examples of these have been uncovered at Jezreel, Dothan, Megiddo, Shechem, and elsewhere. Some, such as the Phoenicians in the Persian period, used sarcophagi for burial. These stone, clay, or wood coffins were usually inscribed and decorated. These might have contained as many as six bodies (Philip J. King and Lawrence Stager 2001, 366). The Egyptians also used sarcophagi, sometimes carved to look like people. The Egyptians went further than most, with their elaborate pyramids to commemorate the pharaohs and their elaborate techniques for preservation of the bodies. These mummies have allowed archaeologists to understand far more about the Egyptian customs and material culture than most of their contemporaries and neighbors.

The Phoenicians introduced cremation to the Israelites, who considered this an act of desecration. This outrage on the body—burning it—was inflicted only on notorious criminals (Gen. 38:24; Lev. 20:14, 21:9) or on enemies (Amos 2:1). Apparently, they thought the act of destroying the body was a means of annihilation. DeVaux notes that fires were often lit at the death of a king who had died in peace with God, but the body was not burned. Rather, perfumes were burned near the body (Roland deVaux 1961, 57). The Israelites thought it important to preserve the bones, sometimes in urns or jars, sometimes in pits. An exception seems to have been the case of Saul and his sons, who had died and were buried in the wall of Beth-Shean. Later their bodies were taken to Jabesh and burned, and then the bones were buried under a tamarisk tree in Jabesh (1 Sam. 31:12–13). The burial site was important, marked by a stone or a tree at the very least. The Bible is consistent in the concern with the place of burial of the dead, from the time that Abraham bought land at Machpelah to bury his beloved Sarah.

The place for the burial was ordinarily outside the city **gates**, probably because the body was considered unclean. Exceptions were made in the case of David and Solomon, and the high priest Johoiada, who were buried in the City of David (1 Kings 2:10, 11:43; 2 Chron. 24:16). In later days, the whole region surrounding Jerusalem became a necropolis or a city of the dead. Archaeologists have discovered more than a hundred cave and chamber tombs around the city, including various candidates for the burial place of Jesus. Pilgrims still admire the numerous rock-cut tombs in the Kedron valley and the Holy Sepulchre, where Jesus is thought to have been buried. *See also* Caves.

Further Reading

DeVaux, Roland. *Ancient Israel: Its Life and Institutions*. Grand Rapids, Mich.: William B. Eerdmans Publishing Company, 1961. Edersheim, Alfred. *The Life and Times of Jesus the Messiah* Peabody, Mass.: Hendrickson Publishers, Inc., 2004. King, Philip J. and Lawrence E. Stager. *Life in Biblical Israel*. Louisville, Ky.: Westminster John Knox Press, 2001.

Greece, Greek, Hellenists

(Acts 14:11f, 16:1, 18:4, 19:10, 20:21; Rom. 1:16; 1 Cor. 1:24) The Greeks or Hellenes were a people dwelling in the islands of the Aegean and on the isthmus now called *Greece*. The name apparently derives from a mythic son of Thessalos, Graicos, meaning "shaggy haired," "freeman," or "dweller in a valley" (Adrian Fortescue 2004). These were an adventurous, seafaring people, strong and wily **warriors**, who developed extremely advanced systems of government, language, and culture. Their influence over the entire Mediterranean region, through travel, commerce, and conquest, was enormous. Even when conquered by the Romans, the Greeks dominated the culture, making the Romans gods, architecture, and art copies of their own.

The relationships between the Jews and the Greeks date back to ancient times. For about six centuries, Greek (or "the common dialect"—*koine*) was the common language of the Mediterranean region. Certainly, Greek culture had a profound influence on Jewish life during the period of Alexander the Great, the Hellenistic period (333–363 B.C.), and through the Byzantine period (sixth and seventh centuries A.D.) During this time, many of the Jews adopted Greek habits, lived in Greek cities, and became assimilated into Greek life. Long before the birth of Christ, during the third century B.C, as part of the great cultural activities of the scholars of Alexandria, the Old Testament scriptures were translated into the Greek Septuagint. It was this Greek translation that provided the basis of most New Testament quotations from Scripture (Madeleine S. Miller and J. Lane Miller 1961, 662).

In the New Testament, Greeks were in evidence everywhere: as converts to Judaism (called "Hellenes") and later as converts to Christianity. ("Hellenists" were Greek-speaking Jews.) They were the first major group of Gentiles who were welcomed into the early **Christian Church**. Some of the first conflicts among the **apostles** involved this new element, who had their own religious practices and were reluctant to become Jews, hoping instead to be simply Christians. The Council of Jerusalem dealt with this issue directly, reconciling Peter's early insistence on their observance of the **law** with Paul's more open approach.

The New Testament was first written in Greek (some of it based on Aramaic sources); many of the Epistles were addressed to Greek Christians. Paul was knowledgeable in Greek literature, philosophy, and culture. His use of **sports** imagery, for instance, clearly indicates Greek influence. Many scholars have traced his indebtedness to Plato and other Greek philosophers. He even quotes some of the dramatists of that land.

Many of the travels described in Acts deal with the evangelizing of Greek cities, such as Athens and Corinth. The conflicts between the gods of the Greeks, such as Aphrodite and Zeus, and the Christians' God explains much of New Testament discussions. Paul, for instance, was thought to be an enemy of Diana of Ephesus and was attacked for his audacity. On one trip, he and his companion, Barnabas, were mistaken for Jupiter and Mercury, with the more diminutive Paul thought to be the messenger god (Acts 14:12). In Athens, he sought to use the statue of the "Unknown God" as a means of approaching his Greek audience, hoping their openness to new theology would allow the introduction of Christianity.

The Greek influence on Christian architecture, philosophy, and theology is immeasurable. Temples once dedicated to Greek gods became Christian places of worship. The ideas of Plato and Aristotle, which had interested the early Christians, were to return to prominence again in the Renaissance. Christian art of the Renaissance also owed much of its form to ancient Greek and Roman examples. Although incompatible at heart, the traditions of Athens and Jerusalem have enriched and sharpened one another through much of Western history. *See also* Art: Christian; History in the Bible.

Further Reading

Fortescue, Adrian. "Greece," http://www.newadvent.org (accessed July 18, 2004). Gignac, Francis T. "Greek," in *The Oxford Companion to the Bible*. New York: Oxford University Press, 1993. Miller, Madeleine S. and J. Lane Miller. "Greek," "Greeks," "Septuagint," in *Harper's Bible Dictionary*. New York: Harper and Row, 1961.

Hanukkah or Festival of Lights

Hanukkah or *Chanukah* is a **festival** of rededication to the Jewish faith; it falls on the 25th day of Kislev, early in December. Its origins can be traced to 165 B.C., when King Antiochus IV shocked the Jews by trying to force them to assimilate with the **Greek** culture. He massacred many of them, prohibited the rest from the practice of their faith, and desecrated the **altar** of the **Temple** by sacrificing a pig on it. Judas Maccabeus led a revolt that overthrew the Syrian armies. The Jews then rededicated the Temple, but found that little oil that had not been defiled by the Greeks was left for the menorah, the branched candelabra. They lit it anyway and were thrilled by the miraculous replenishment of oil that allowed it to burn for eight days and nights while they prepared new oil to use. Thus Hanukkah is celebrated today by the lighting and burning of the menorah for eight days and nights. The menorah itself has become the symbol of the festival. The story does not appear in the Torah but in the Books of the Maccabees (in the **Apocrypha**).

In modern celebrations, the menorah is displayed in the doorway or window, facing the street in order to be seen by passers by. On the first night of Hanukkah, a candle is placed at the far right of the menorah. The shamas (or *shammus,* the "servant candle" of a different height from the others) is then lit, and three blessings are recited. Then another candle is lighted by the shamas. Each night a candle is added. These candles are to be enjoyed for the pleasure of their presence and are not to serve any productive purpose.

This has become a traditional time for gift giving, especially the "Hanukkah gelt" (real or candy money). The family also plays games and enjoys special **foods** such as potato latkes, pancakes, cheese dishes, and jelly doughnuts. Fried foods are thought to represent the oil of the menorah. Because Hanukkah is not a major holiday of the faith, it is not essential to stay home from work or even to attend worship services. Modern American Jews have found it a holiday that provides a welcome alternative to the Christmas festivities that absorb so many of their neighbors' lives. *See also* Abomination; Festivals; Temple; Time.

Further Reading
Kramer, Amy J. "Hanukah: Origins," http://www.everythingjewish.com (accessed May 10, 2005).

Heaven(s), New Jerusalem, Paradise

(Gen. 1:6–8; Ps. 19:1; Luke 20:38; 1 Cor. 13:12; Revelation 21) The term *heaven* was used in Scripture and continues to be used by moderns as a synonym for God—as in the case where we "thank heaven." The Jewish people came to have such a veneration and respect for the **name of God** that they used "heaven" as a substitute.

In addition, "Heaven" or "the heavens" sometimes described both a literal place in a three-storied universe, and it was sometimes a more abstract concept. The sky was often described as "the heavens" or "the firmament" with the sun and moon and the sun (Gen. 1:6–7). It was additionally conceived as the dwelling place of God and his **angels** (Deut. 26:15; 1 Kings 8:30; John 14:2), thought to be in the northern skies (Job 26:7; Ps. 48:2). It was also the place where God ruled and judged, only occasionally allowing humans a glimpse (as in the vision of Jacob's ladder, when angels came and went between earth and Heaven). In the Old Testament, the term is always plural, even though it is sometimes translated in a singular form (Madeleine S. Miller and J. Lane Miller 1961, 248). Late in Jewish history, the physical Heaven became more precisely visualized, especially with the revelations in the **apocryphal** Book of Enoch. In the prophets and in the New Testament, as the hope of the **afterlife** developed more fully, Heaven became more spiritualized, replaced by the concept of a "better country," the final resting place of the redeemed.

Jesus spoke of it as a place with "many mansions," suggesting that it had plenty of room for the blessed spirits of the saints. He referred to it as "Paradise," when promising another meeting "this day" with one of the robbers on the crosses beside him. He also said that the redeemed will be like angels, with neither marrying nor giving in marriage. These slight hints could not have satisfied his disciples' hunger for a glimpse of the life hereafter about which they were so eager to learn.

The Heavenly City

It was often characterized as a city with **gates**, which was eventually interpreted as the eternal resting place for the blessed, where they live in eternal communion with God. Jesus spoke of there being "many mansions," noting that there would be no marriage or giving in marriage there (Mark 12:18–25). Zechariah and John picture it as the New **Eden** with the **tree** of life and a fountain of pure water issuing from its center from under the **throne** of God (Zech. 14:8; Rev. 21–22; Leland Ryken and U. Milo Kaufmann 1992, 338). It is in Heaven that God sits on his glorious throne, with his son at his right hand, surrounded by bands of angels, judging the just and the unjust (Isa. 66:1, Rev. 19:4–5). Hints of this awesome sight appear in Hebrews, Revelation, and Isaiah: it is a place of glorious light, where we will see "face to face" what we have seen only dimly on earth. The saints of the faith, including those who came before Christ, are gathered there in their transformed bodies, in a sacred harmony that Dante later describes in musical and numerical imagery.

The landscape of Heaven has never been as definite as that of **Hell**. It was assumed to be a place of light, with angels and saints clothed in glorious raiment. It was beautifully pictured as the site of the New Jerusalem in Ezekiel and in Revelation, with its four triple gates and precious **gemstones**, gold, and crystal. Paul spoke of a "third heaven" in 2 Corinthians 12:2; and Dante, relying on the tradition that derived from the apocryphal Book of Enoch, portrayed it as nine circles, each ruled over by a category of angels (e.g., cherubim, seraphim), that had near the center the Rose of the Blessed, where saints looked like bees flying in and out of the glorious petals of the rose. At the still, unmoving and unmoved center was his vision of God as three intertwined circles of light, signifying the interlocking persons of the Trinity. This is a far more abstract and poetic vision than we find in the Scripture itself, which simply portrays Heaven as a place of bliss, joy, and peace. John's great vision (Rev. 21) of the "holy Jerusalem" describes the great city as:

> Having the glory of God: and her light was like unto a stone most precious, even like a jasper stone, clear as crystal; and had a wall great and high, and had twelve gates, and at the gates twelve angels, and names written thereon, which are the names of the twelve tribes of the children of Israel.... And the city lieth four-square, and the length is as large as the breadth.... And the building of the wall of it was of jasper: and the city was pure gold, like unto clear glass. There was no need for a **temple** or for sacrifices, for the Father and Son will be there on their thrones. And the foundations of the wall of the city were garnished with all manner of precious **stones** ... jasper, sapphire, chalcedony, emerald, sardonyx, sardius, crystolite, ... beryl, topaz, chrosophrasus, jacinth, and amethyst.... And the twelve gates were twelve pearls; and every several gate was one pearl: and the street of the city was pure gold, as it were transparent glass.

The great light that suffuses the whole of the New Jerusalem comes from God himself—the Shekinah, God's glory. There is no need for a moon or stars. The gates are never shut, for there is no day or night. Proceeding out of the throne of God and the Lamb is a "pure river of water and life, clear as crystal" (Rev. 22:1).

The image of the New Jerusalem, the Celestial City, had been part of late prophetic thought among the Jews and became a vivid image for Christians. Replacing the older idea that all the dead lived in a gloomy half-life of Hades, this triumphant picture of eschatological hope was very compelling. When Jesus hung on the cross, he turned to the thief who expressed faith in him, saying, "Today shalt thou be with me in Paradise" (Luke 23:43). The term *Paradise* is rarely used in Scripture, generally relating to Eden rather than to the New Eden that is Heaven.

In later literature, Heaven assumed an increasingly complex and picturesque meaning as the final destination of the Christian believer, although not necessarily a physical place. The whole of *The Divine Comedy* moves toward "Paradiso," Dante's glorious portrayal of a place of blinding light, eternal bliss, harmony, and peace. For Calvin it was the ultimate goal of the Christian pilgrimage. Also for Bunyan in *The Pilgrim's Progress*, it was the Pilgrim's goal—the Celestial City, the very antithesis of the City of Destruction, from which he originally escaped. And for Milton, it was the center of angelic voices around the heavenly throne, from which the rebellious Satan had been thrown after a battle of the angels. Moderns have often reduced it to a place of clouds with golden gates guarded by St. Peter, where there are angels playing harps and singing. This surely falls far short of the sense of awe and joy in the scriptural references. In Scripture, the Book of Revelation is the great source of heavenly imagery, presenting Heaven with its full grandeur, including the throne of God, the angelic hosts, the **wedding feast** of the Lamb, and the multitudes from every nation. *See also* Afterlife; Angels; Apocalypse, Apocalyptic Literature; Cosmology; Throne.

Further Reading

Glasson, Thomas Francis. "Heaven," in *The Oxford Companion to the Bible*. New York: Oxford University Press. 1993. Hontheim, Joseph. "Heaven," http://www.newadvent.org (accessed February 5, 2004). Miller, Madeleine S. and S. Lane Miller. "Heaven," in *Harper's Bible Dictionary*. New York: Harper and Row, 1961. Ryken, Leland and U. Milo Kaufmann. "Heaven," in *A Dictionary of the Biblical Tradition in English Literature*. Grand Rapids, Mich.: William B. Eerdmans Publishing, 1992. Segal, Alan F. *Life After Death: A History of the Afterlife in Western Religion*. New York: Doubleday, 2004.

Hell, Sheol

(Num. 6: 31–35; Job 17: 13–15; Isa. 14:9–11; Matt. 5:22, 11:23; Luke 10:15, 16:23; James 3:6) The place where the dead go after death has had numerous names and locations. In modern thought, *Heaven* is the usual destination for all the dead. But among the ancients, it was the underworld—a place that might be the abode of either the faithful or the faithless, the poor or the rich—had numerous designations and characterizations. They included *Sheol, Hades,* and *Hell.*

Sheol

The ancient Hebrews thought Sheol to be a place where the dead congregated. It was deep underneath the earth, at the greatest possible distance from **Heaven**. This horrible, dreary, dark disorderly land (Job 10:21) was approached by way of **gates** somewhere in the far west—"toward the setting of the sun."("Going west" still indicates death in poetic phrasing, and the setting sun is a standard symbol of death.) Sheol was thought to be divided into compartments, where the dead met without distinction of rank and condition (Emil G. Hirsch 2004).

Some believe that the architecture of the more elaborate later tombs that have been discovered among ancient ruins may bear a resemblance to the **houses** that the dead inhabited on earth. They apparently expected to have a parallel home in this hazy residence of the dead (Philip J. King and Lawrence E. Stager 2001, 370). Job speaks twice of Sheol as a house (Job 17:13–15, 30:23). Isaiah, by contrast, speaks of it as "the pit" (Isa. 38:18). Apart from Job, the Old Testament scriptures are silent about an afterlife. Some critics interpret Ezekiel's valley of the dry bones as a promise of the **resurrection** of the dead (Ezek. 37:1–14), but others believe this as a promise of the restoration of Judah after destruction at the hands of the Babylonians (King, 374). Some also interpret Isaiah's promise, "Your dead shall live, their corpses shall rise," (Isa. 26:19) as a promise of resurrection. Another bit of evidence is the statement in Daniel (12:1–4): "Many of those who sleep in the dust of the death shall awake, some to everlasting life, and some to shame and everlasting contempt."

The author of Ecclesiastes hesitates between two views: on the one hand, the speaker hopes that "God shall judge the righteous and the wicked," but on the other believes that "All go unto one place, and are of the dust, and all turn to dust again" (Eccles. 3:17, 20). Later, he asserts that "a living **dog** is better than a dead lion," and that while "the living know that they shall die: but the dead know not any thing, neither have they any more a reward; for the memory of them is forgotten" (Eccles. 9:4–5). In the final chapter of Ecclesiastes, describing death as the loosening of the silver cord and the breaking of the golden bowl, the writer notes that the dust will return to the earth "as it was: but the spirit shall return unto God who gave it" (Eccles. 12:6–7). This sounds like a division between the body and the spirit, with the spirit finding eternal rest in God. Such dualism is not typical of Jewish thought. In Christian tradition as well, the body as well as the soul is thought to be resurrected: Christ walked with his friends, talked with them, and ate with them after he had risen from the dead. He invited Doubting Thomas to touch his wounds.

Like Hades, the pagan abode of the dead, Sheol was thought to be a place of silence, where the deceased continued to live an ethereal existence while their bodies moldered in the family tomb. Some thought it was a "gloomy underworld where the departed spirits descend" (Philip J. King and Lawrence Stager 2001, 374). Isaiah pictured it as a place where shades greeted one another but were too weak to act (Isa. 14:9–11). It apparently was not originally considered a place of **punishment**, but rather a place of separation from God, where the inhabitants could no longer praise or thank him for his mercy (Isa. 38:18).

Although the term *Sheol* is used 66 times in the Bible, it is not clear exactly what the ancient Hebrews meant by the reference. Some believe it originally referred to a pit or garbage dump, some that it was a place of interrogation.

In later Judaism, when Sheol was thought to be a place of punishment, the godless were expected to be taken there to be burned in fire (Num. 16:31–35; Ps. 9:17, 31:17, 55:15; Isa. 5:14, 28:15, 18; 66:24). Clearly this means that there was to be punishment after death. They associated it with the Valley of Hinnom (another name for *Gehenna*), which was a large ravine now called wadi er-rababi, the city garbage dump for Jerusalem, where an idolatrous cult of Moloch worshipers passed their children through the fire in a ritual that shocked the Hebrews. Considered an abomination by the Jews, it was cursed by Jeremiah. "It came to be personified as an insatiable demon with wide open, gaping jaws" (Alan Segal 2004, 135–136; Joseph Hontheim 2004). This imagery had significant impact on later believers who thought of Hell as a fiery pit, a roaring furnace.

Hades

The influence of the **Greeks**, specifically Homer and Plato, led Hellenistic Jews to consider the afterlife in more detail, especially the need for a **Last Judgment** to sort out the saved from the damned. The idea of the resurrection of the dead became an increasingly important idea for **Essenes** and for the **Pharisees**, although it was rejected by the **Sadducees**.

Homer, in the *Odyssey*, had portrayed Hades as the abode of those whose shades continued into the afterlife, but without a sense of judgment for the good or evil they had done on earth. The Roman author Virgil, in the *Aeneid*, later pictured it with more detailed landscape. He also visualized a western entrance, but with a river that the dead had to cross and a churlish boatman who demanded money for the crossing. He also envisioned the Elysian Fields full of shades wandering eternally. He laid particular emphasis on mythic inhabitants such as Tantalus and Sisyphus to give color to the punishments justifiably meted out. Only the aristocrats appeared to inhabit this netherworld, and they would have preferred to live like dogs on earth to being heroes in Hades. For the Greeks, life was too precious to cherish the notion of death.

Hell

The word *Hell* derives from the Old English word *helan* or *behalian*, meaning "to hide," indicating a hole or a hollow. As the *Catholic Encyclopedia* notes: "Thus by derivation hell denotes a dark and hidden place. In ancient Norse mythology Hel is the ill-favoured goddess of the underworld. Only those who fall in battle can enter Valhalla; the rest go down to Hel in the underworld, not all, however, to the place of punishment of criminals" (Joseph Hontheim 2004). In the New Testament the term *Gehenna* is the more frequent word, and *hades* is the pagan version for the place of punishment of the damned.

Although ancient Judaism had only a cursory interest in the afterlife, post-exilic Judaism portrayed Sheol as a place of judgment and punishment. The **Gospels** and James make Hell sound like Gehenna or Sheol (Matt. 5:22, 11:23; Luke 10:15, 16:23; James 3:6), but other writers present it as a place where all the dead are kept until the resurrection (Matt. 16:18; Acts 2:27, 31; Rev. 1:18, 6:8; 20:13; etc.). God was thought to have the power to save the pious from Hell, but he chose not to reign there. He was instead the God of Heaven and earth, leaving Hell to the power of Satan.

In the New Testament, Hell became increasingly explicit. Luke (8:31) and the author of Romans (Rom. 10:7) speak of "the bottomless place," suggesting Isaiah's vision. Hell was thought to be in the lower parts of the world (Ps. 63:10, Eph. 4:9) and sometimes referred to as the "inferno" or the "**abyss**." Located like Sheol in the underworld, it separated the dead from God, who was thought to dwell in Heaven. Revelation refers to the lake of fire in Hell (19:19–21) and notes it as the home of those who are not in the Book of Life (Rev. 20:7–15).

The Harrowing of Hell

The Apostles' Creed asserts of Jesus that "He descended into Hell. The third day he rose again from the dead" before he ascended into Heaven. This belief assumes that Jesus's cry from the cross, "My God, my God, Why has thou forsaken me?" marks the beginning of a time of separation from God the Father. Christ entered Satan's kingdom and remained there three days, when his body lay in the tomb.

Later thought, including the Gospel of Nicodemus, an apocryphal late writing, expanded this to involve the "Harrowing of Hell," a time when Christ was thought to have gathered the righteous souls abiding in Hell like spirits in prison, because they were born too soon. Having no opportunity to know the truth of the Incarnation, they rested on their faith that God would redeem them in his own time. Some believe that Christ broke down the doors of Hell, took Adam by the hand, and conducted the saints to paradise. The catalogue of saints in Hebrews 11 that lists many who had faith, "the substance of things hoped for, the evidence of things not seen" (Heb. 11:1) was thought to support this concept, as were certain other selections of Scripture (Ps. 16:10, 24:7–10; John 5:24; Eph. 4:8–10).

In spite of the rejection of the Gospel of Nicodemus by the Reformation and the Council of Trent, the disputed sentences have remained in the Creed. The image of the Harrowing had impressive impact on the art and literature of the Middle Ages. Bas reliefs and paintings of Christ marching through Hell and choosing the saints while surrounded by the suffering sinners are in many of the cathedrals. Liturgical drama, the cycles of mystery plays, found this a powerful dramatic scene to bring to the stage.

Literary Versions of Hell

The medieval mind was full of images of damnation and salvation. With the Church as the primary patron of the arts, portrayals of Hell and its inhabitants were enormously popular. It was in the Middle Ages that the concept of Hell was married to the classic views of Hades to become a place of numerous compartments, fully inhabited, with elaborate geography—rivers, gorges, and great cliffs.

The medieval Italian poet Dante described Hell as a giant cavern carved out at the time of Satan's fall, with the Great Transgressor at the center, in its deepest circle. His "Inferno" mirrored the psychological landscape of sin, with categories going down into deepest darkness and bitter cold, totally separated from God, where sinners were tormented by living forever with the consequences of their evil choices on earth. The seven circles were based on the seven deadly sins, with pride as the most vicious, as it was the sin of Satan himself. This portrayal had enormous influence on later writers. Milton in *Paradise Lost* portrayed Hell at an earlier period in its evolution, right after Lucifer proclaimed he would not serve God, gathered his angels to fight the forces of Heaven, and led them all into perdition. In their new home, the fiery lake, they gathered together their forces and plotted the fall of man as an act of vengeance against God.

Other writers and artists through the ages have found the concept of Hell fascinating, although it has fallen into disrepute in modern times, when fewer people are inclined to believe in damnation, Hell, or Satan. For many moderns, the idea of Hell is closer to Christopher Marlowe's in *The Tragical History of Dr. Faustus*. When Dr. Faustus sells his soul to the devil in exchange for godlike knowledge, he asks first about Lucifer and Hell. Mephistopheles (a minor devil appointed to be his servant), when asked how he comes to be out of Hell, responds: "Why this is hell, nor am I out of it" (Act I, iii, 80). Hell is life anywhere without God.

Shelley said of it: "Hell is a city much like London...." Eliot picked up on this in the *Waste Land*, portraying the modern city in hellish terms—a kind of "city of dreadful night." Orthodox Christian believers continue to insist—like Jonathan Edwards—on a condition of personal and probably eternal damnation that follows after this life for those who reject God. They are cast into "outer darkness." *See also* Abyss; Afterlife; Heaven(s), New Jerusalem, Paradise; Punishments; Resurrection.

Further Reading

Goldberg, Michael. "Hell," in *Biblical Literature in the English Tradition*. Grand Rapids, Mich.: William B. Eerdmans Publishing Company, 1992. Hirsch, Emil G. "Sheol," http://www.jewishencyclopedia.com (accessed March 11, 2004). Hontheim, Joseph. "Hell," http://www.newadvent.org (accessed March 29, 2004). King, Philip J. and Lawrence E. Stager, *Life in Biblical Israel*. Louisville, Ky.: Westminster John Knox Press, 2001. Scheper, George L. "Harrowing of Hell," in *A Dictionary of Biblical Tradition in English Literature*. Grand Rapids, Mich.: William B. Eerdmans Publishing Company, 1992. Segal, Alan F. *Life after Death: A History of the Afterlife in Western Religion*. New York: Doubleday, 2004.

History in the Bible

Scripture is firmly rooted in human history, which both the Jews and the Christians have seen as the unfolding of God's plan for humanity. Although much of the Pentateuch is prehistory, many of the events of the Old and New Testaments can be dated by reference to events in other cultures. A general listing of major events would include those on the following chart, divided into periods from Creation to the time of persecutions under the Caesars chronicled in Revelation.

Dates	Events, Rulers
Pre-history	**Creation, Great Flood, Tower of Babel**
c. 2000–1700 B.C.	Patriarchs—Abraham, Isaac, Jacob
c. 1700–1290 B.C.	**Egyptian** captivity: from Joseph to Moses
c. 1290 B.C.–1230 B.C.	**Exodus**, 40 years in wilderness
c. 1230–1050 B.C.	Conquest: Joshua, settling **Canaan**, **Judges**, Samuel
c. 1050–922 B.C.	United monarchy, under Saul, David, and Solomon
922–720 B.C.	Divided **king**dom—Jereboam, Reheboam, etc.
722 B.C.	Fall of Samaria, the Northern Kingdom
597 B.C.	The First **Assyrian** Deportation, begin Diaspora
586 B.C.	The Fall of Jerusalem, **Babylonian** Captivity
538–331 B.C.	**Persian** Rule
538 B.C.	Edict of Cyrus, allowing the return to Jerusalem
458–445 B.C.	Rebuilding of the **Temple**, Ezra, Nehemiah
331–320 B.C.	Hellenistic Rule, Alexander the Great
320–198 B.C.	Egyptian Rule, Ptolemies
198–163 B.C.	Seleucid Rulers, Antiochus, etc. Maccabean Revolt

63 B.C.	**Roman** Rulers, Pompey, Julius Caesar, Augustus, etc.
c. 7 B.C.-A.D. 33	Jesus's birth, life, death, and **resurrection**
A.D. 33–64.	**Pentecost**, Peter, Stephen, Paul, and the early **Church**
A.D. 70.	Fall of Jerusalem—persecution under Nero, Vespasian
A.D. 81–96	Persecutions under Domitian

See also Assyria, Assyrians; Babylon, Babylonia; Canaan, Canaanites; Egypt, Egyptians; Greece, Greek, Hellenists; Rome, Romans; Time.

Further Reading

Hirsch, Emil G. and J. Frederic Mc/Curdy, "Israel, People of," http:// jewishencyclopedia.com (accessed December 26, 2004). Keller, Werner. *The Bible as History.* New York: Bantam Books, 1982.

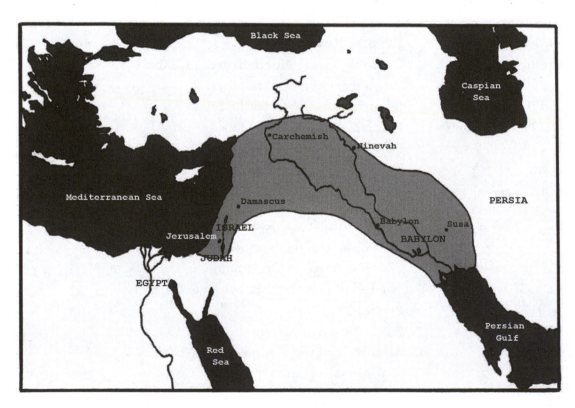

Map of Babylonian Empire.

Hittites

(Gen. 10:15; Josh. 1:4) The Hittites were the invaders who dominated much of the Fertile Crescent from 1700 to 1400 B.C., destroying the **Babylonian** capital of Hammurabi with its **Tower of Babel** (Madeleine S. Miller and J. Lane Miller 1961, 263). The Hebrews also knew them as the "children of Heth," a son of **Canaan** (Gen. 10:15). Later their empire was revived in various city states of Asia Minor, known as Syria or modern Turkey, where they dominated the region from ca.1400 B.C. to 1200 B.C. In 1259 B.C., at the Battle of Qadesh, a treaty set a line across northern Lebanon, the frontier that established the limit for Israel's territory (Josh. 1:4; 2 Sam. 24:6; Alan Millard 1993, 285).

The Hittite Empire collapsed around 1200 B.C., leaving some 24 city-states north of the Taurus range and 7 city-states in Syria to perpetuate the name "Hittite" for several centuries. Many of their battles and treaties involved the **Egyptians**, with whom they developed close relations through marriage. The various invaders, including the **Assyrian** leaders, chronicled their battles with the Hittite cities of Carchemish, Gaza, and Kanulua. In addition, there were constant attacks from various migrant peoples, including the Sea

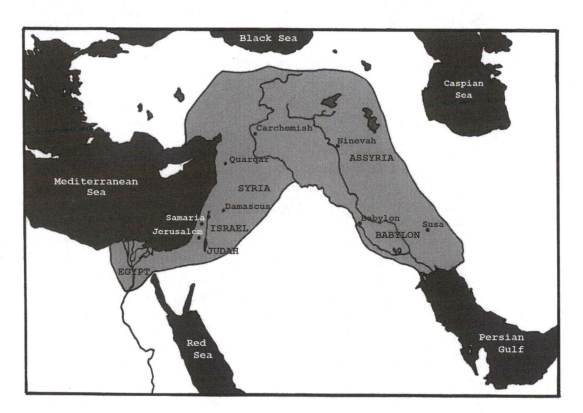

Map of Assyrian Empire.

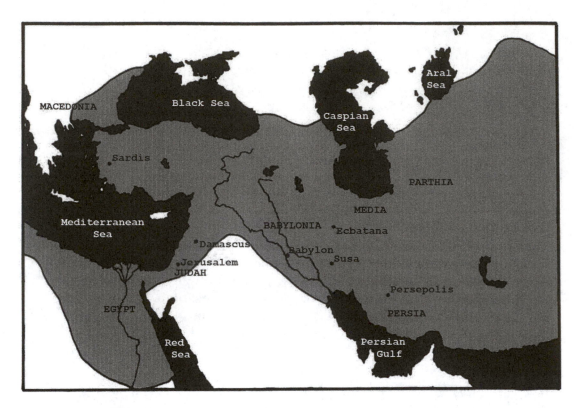

Map of Persian Empire.

Peoples. Eventually Carchemish was conquered and the last Hittite **king**, Pisiris, became an Assyrian captive (Richard Gottheil, Louis H. Gray 2004).

By the time that references of the Hittites are found in the historical records of the Bible, the great nation of the Hittites was reduced to a few locations and a few individuals. Their impact on the Hebrews was certainly stronger than their numbers suggest: Abraham was strongly influenced by their **law** codes and culture. Hebraic and Hittite laws share many rules on purity as well as other items, including the idea of **Cities of Refuge**. Joshua saw them less as a nation than as a tribe, an ethnic group living in Canaan, where they had been since patriarchal times (Josh.1:4).

Today, we know their culture and history only from the Old Testament and from Assyrian, Hittite, and Egyptian inscriptions (Richard Gotteheil and Louis Gray 2004). Contemporary monuments, especially the Egyptian carvings, picture them Mongoloid in type: short and stout, prognathous, with receding foreheads, high cheek-bones, large straight noses, and protruding upper lips. They were yellow-skinned, with black hair and eyes, beardless, with their hair in pigtails. This leads some to speculate that they came from the northeast of Mesopotamia and gradually adapted their language and their names to Semites.

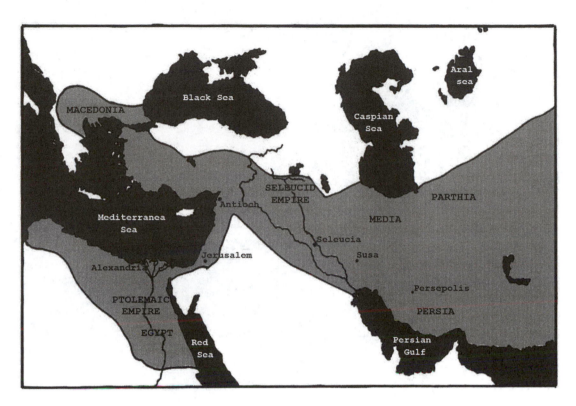

Map of Greek Empire.

Through intermarriage and assimilation, they first transformed their own gods to Babylonian deities—Ishtar and Tar or Tarku (the sun god). Like other pagan cultures, they had sacred prostitution. They were clever silversmiths and skillful lapidaries and carvers on **ivory** who were especially good in portraying **animal** forms. In fact, their gods are frequently pictured as riding on animals. Like many other peoples including the Hebrews, they had the Deluge legend, a version of Noah's story.

Some speculate that the Hittites of Asia Minor were allies of the Trojans and may have been referred to in the *Odyssey* (11:521). The Hittites of Canaan, who may have been a separate people, appear to have inhabited the central ridge of Judah, especially the district of Hebron among whom Abraham lived as "a stranger and a sojourner" and from whom he purchased the field of Machpelah and the **cave** in which he buried Sarah and where he and many of his family were also buried. The record of the purchase follows the pattern of Hittite laws and contracts (F.F. Bruce 1980, 654). Hittites mentioned in Scripture, many of whom have Hebrew names, include two of Esau's wives; Uriah, the husband of Bathsheba; and Abimelech, one of David's companions in his early, outlaw days. Solomon found wives among the Hittites and also bought his **horses** from them.

283

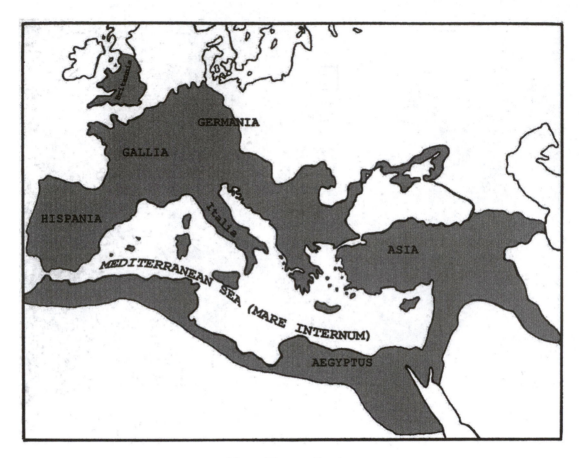

Map of Roman Empire.

Tarsus, Paul the Apostle's home (Acts 9:11), was a Hittite city. By Paul's day, it was the capital of Cilicia, known as a cosmopolitan center, a crossroads where traders of many lands shared their wares and their cultures. A harbor lake made it accessible and safe for Mediterranean shipping and provided this inland city a thriving maritime trade. It had a state-supported university and a citizenry that was enthusiastic about education and philosophy. Some believed it to be the exemplification of the platonic ideal of a state. In Tarsus Paul learned his trade of Cilician cloth-making (Acts 18:3). He also enriched his knowledge of both Judaic and Greek, as well as his skill in oratory. Today Tarsus is the Anatolian Turkish city of Tersoos, no longer a port city, built on the remains of the ancient city. A street of weavers in modern Tersoos provides "a living link with Paul." Artifacts unearthed there—the loom weights, spindle whorls, lamps, coins, and figurines—are also tangible reminders of the world of Paul and the ancient culture of the Hittite descendants who once populated this great city (Madeleine S. Miller and J. Lane Miller 1961, 727–9). *See also* Babylon, Babylonia; Egypt, Egyptians; Law.

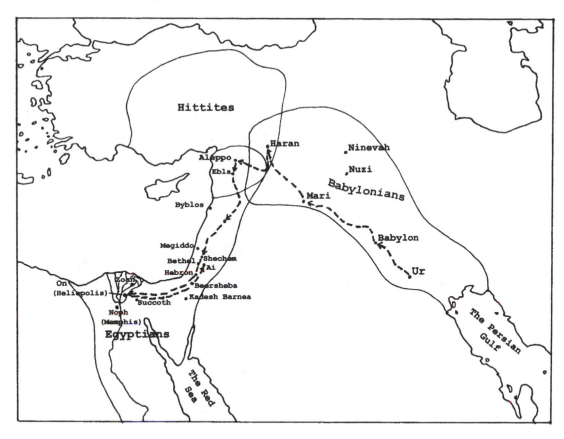

Map showing the Hittite Empire at the time of Abraham.

Further Reading

Bruce, F. F. "Hittites," in *The Illustrated Bible Encyclopedia*. Sydney, Australia: Tyndale House Publishers, 1980. Gottheil, Richard, and Louis H. Gray, "Hittites," http://www.jewishencyclopedia.com (accessed June 23, 2004). Millard, Alan. "Hittites," in *The Oxford Companion to the Bible*. New York: Oxford University Press, 1993. Miller, Madeleine S. and J. Lane Miller, "Hittites," and "Tarsus," in *Harper's Bible Dictionary*. New York: Harper and Row, 1961.

Holy of Holies. *See* Tabernacle; Temple

Holy Spirit, Holy Ghost

(Gen. 1:2, 2:7; Isa. 11:2; Ezek. 2:12, 11:5; Joel 2:28–29; Matt. 1:18, 3:16, 11:32; Mark 1:10; Luke 1:35; Acts 2:2; Cor. 3:3) In the languages of the Bible, there is no term for *spirit,* a word that derives from the Latin word for "breath"—*spiritus.* Numerous mentions of breath or wind, which have been translated as the "Spirit of God," the "Holy Ghost" or the "Holy Spirit," do, however, occur all through Scripture.

The first mention is at the time of **Creation**, when the Spirit of God hovered above the waters (Gen. 1:2), which Christians have taken to mean that the Holy Spirit participated in the Creation. This is reinforced by the opening verses of John's **Gospel**. In Hebrew thought, this spirit was akin to the breath of life that God breathed into Adam, making him a living soul (Gen. 2:7). Breath or wind was frequently used by the writers of Scripture to symbolize the invisible activities of the Spirit. It might even give a hero like Samson the remarkable strength he needed to slay a lion (Judg. 14:6).

This life-giving spirit is also called "Inspiration," becoming the power behind the **prophets** and the great saints. The visions and raptures that are documented in the Bible—ecstatic speech and behavior (1 Sam. 10:6–11)—are said to come from the Spirit of God. When this special spirit of God rests upon man (Isa. 11:1), it may surround him like a garment (Judg. 6:34), providing him insights and inspired words. "The prophet sees and hears by means of the spirit" (Num. 24:2; 1 Sam. 10:6; Zech. 7:12; Joseph Jacobs 2004). Some identify the Holy Spirit with the Shekinah, the glory of God that provides the light in the Holy of Holies. In the Psalms and in Isaiah, this is actually designated as the "holy spirit" (Ps. 51:1; Isa. 63:10–11).

In the later Messianic prophesies, such as Joel, the Holy Spirit was expected to "be poured out on all Israel" and "your sons and daughters will prophesy, your old men will dream dreams and your young men will see visions" (Joel 2: 28). This is the very verse quoted at the time of the **Pentecost**, when the Holy Spirit came like a mighty wind upon the Christians, with tongues of fire (Acts 5:3).

Neither the Jewish Apocrypha nor the Hellenistic Jewish writers referred with any frequency to the Holy Spirit. Especially in the Diaspora, the conception of the Holy Spirit had no prominence in the intellectual life of the Jewish people. It was, however, a prominent concept all through the New Testament, starting with the Virgin birth (Matt.1:18; Luke 1:35). When Jesus was baptized, the Spirit came upon him (Matt. 3:1–17) in the form of a dove, echoing the image of the Spirit at the Creation that hovered over the waters.

It was by the Spirit that Jesus cast out **demons** (Matt. 12:28), but the terminology begins to change at this point, with more frequent references to the "Holy Spirit," anticipating the scene at Pentecost. He promised the coming of the Paraclete, "that he may abide with you forever" (John 14:16, 17). This spirit Christ explained as the Comforter, the Spirit of truth, "who proceedeth from the Father." In anticipation of his death, Jesus commanded his **disciples** to wait for the promise of the Father, the coming of the Spirit (Luke 22:49).

In the New Testament **epistles**, the three Persons of the Trinity become increasingly distinct, with the Holy Spirit distinguishable from the Father and the Son and yet inseparable from them (Edwin Lewis 1961, 266). The Holy Ghost is gradually understood as a Person, referred to by personal pronouns. In addition, Paul refers to his indwelling in the believer: "Know you not, that you are the temple of God, and that the Spirit of God dwelleth in you" (1 Cor. 3:16).

Hendry notes the "five sayings about the Paraclete" in John (14:15–17, 14:25–26, 15:26, 16:4–11, 16:12–15). The term *Paraclete*, he notes, comes from the law courts and refers to a defending counsel or attorney, who presents the case for the accused (George S. Hendry 1993, 288).

Debates over the nature of the Holy Spirit have continued over the centuries, as the doctrine of the Trinity has been discussed. Although most Christians recite in the Apostles' Creed, "I believe in God, Father, Son and Holy Ghost," the variant interpretations of these three Persons of the Trinity have resulted in councils' denouncing heresy, and arguments that left the Church permanently divided. The greatest of these debates resulted in a schism between the Roman and the Greek churches (J. Forget 2004).

Christian writers and preachers often portray the Holy Spirit (as Milton did) as the source of their inspiration. Many students of Scripture note that their reading of the Bible is inspired by the Holy Spirit, who opens the meaning to them. Charismatics celebrate the power of the Spirit that descends on them. Other Christians mention the various gifts of the Spirit (1 Cor. 12:3–11). The Triune blessing that Paul uses at the end of the Second Epistle to the Corinthians (13:14) frequently closes worship services in many Christian churches: "May the grace of the Lord Jesus Christ, and the love of God, and the fellowship of the Holy Spirit be with you all." *See also* Creation; Messiah; Pentecost, or the Day of the First Fruits; Temple.

Further Reading

Forget, J. "Holy Ghost," http://www.newadvent.org (accessed April 7, 2004). Hendry, George S. "Holy Spirit," in *The Oxford Companion to the Bible*. New York: Oxford University Press, 1993. Jacobs, Joseph. "Holy Spirit," http://www.jewishencyclopedia.com (accessed April 11, 2004). Lewis, Edwin. "Holy Spirit," in *Harper's Bible Dictionary*. New York: Harper and Row, 1961.

Horse

(**Deut. 17:16; 1 Kings 10:26–29; 2 Sam. 15:1; Prov. 26:3; Job 39:19; Zech. 10:3; Rev. 6:2–8, 19:11**) The Hebrews preferred **donkeys** to horses as beasts of burden until late in their history. The horse, which was native to grasslands of Europe and Asia, was domesticated as early as 1750 B.C., as documented in a **Babylonian** tablet (George Cansdale 1980, 52–53). They were more suited to flat country than the craggy mountains and hills around

Palestine. As a nomadic and later agrarian people, without a standing army, the **Israelites** had little need for horses, although they did find mules useful. God forbade them to amass horses or to breed mules, rules that they eventually ignored (Deut. 17:16).

Egyptians, on the other hand, had no such God-given **laws**. They were a powerful people who had soldiers and **chariots**, using them for warfare and to ensure domestic tranquility, especially with their enslaved workers. The pharaoh used horses and chariots in pursuit of Moses. The song of Moses, later repeated by Miriam, refers to the fearful horses particularly, "I will sing to the Lord, for he is highly exalted. The horse and its rider he has hurled into the sea" (Exod. 15:1, 21).

When the Hebrews were begging for a king, Samuel warned them that the ban on horses would one day be ignored and that they would suffer (1 Sam. 8:11). Apparently, they obeyed God's command through Saul's reign and most of David's. All this time they watched their enemies' use of units of horses and horsemen (George Cansdale 1970, 77). David was especially concerned about his disadvantage in the face of the Philistines' horse-drawn iron chariots. Before he had decided to use horses himself, he hamstrung the horses he captured in an effort so as to cripple the **Canaanite** army. Eventually David kept enough horses for a hundred chariots (2 Sam. 8:4), becoming a far more fearsome **warrior**. Absalom showed his arrogance by parading around with a chariot and horse (2 Sam. 15:1). Twelve years later, when David was near his deathbed, Adonijah followed Absalom's sad example (1 Kings 1:5). This introduction of the horse into Israel's royal stables signaled the deterioration of the kings' attention to God's law. In their pride, they trusted in military strength rather than in divine protection.

When Solomon came to the **throne**, he emulated the princes of other regions, gathering "chariots and horsemen: and he had a thousand and four hundred chariots, and twelve thousand horsemen, whom he bestowed in the cities for chariots" and "Solomon had horses brought out of Egypt.... And a chariot came up and went out of Egypt for six hundred shekels of silver, and an horse for an hundred and fifty" (1 Kings 10:26–29). In his glory days, when he was demonstrating his power to the peoples of the world, Solomon had stables at Megiddo and at Hazor that provided for his vast collection of horses and chariots. Archaeological digs in these areas have uncovered enough stables for an army. Apparently Solomon also used these **animals** for trade, exporting them to **Hittites** and Arameans.

Most of the Scripture's specific references to horses either suggest foreign influence (as in the story of Esther) or point to the power and willfulness of the animal. The authors of Proverbs note that "A whip for the horse, a halter for the donkey, and a rod for the backs of fools!" as the means for controlling disobedient creatures (Prov. 26:3). God asked the humbled Job, "Do you give the horse his strength or clothe his neck with a flowing mane?" (Job 39:19). The Psalmist noted that the horse and mule "have no understanding but must be controlled by bit and bridle or they will not come to you" (Ps. 32:9). Jeremiah used the horse as a symbol of lust: "They were as fed horses in the morning: every one neighed after his neighbor's wife" (Jer. 5:8).

The Psalmist and the **prophets**—Isaiah, Jeremiah, Zechariah—all looked back to God's demonstrated sovereignty over the horse and chariot, referring to their slaughter in battle. Zechariah spoke of the "proud horse" and also used the image in his **apocalyptic** vision of a red horse "standing among the myrtle trees in a ravine. Behind him were red, brown and white horses" (Zech. 10:3, 1:8). The fearsome image in Revelation of the Four Horsemen draws on the Scriptural sense of dread and the continuing warfaring, echoing Zechariah's vision: "I looked, and there before me was a white horse! Its rider held a bow, and he was given a crown, and he rode out as a conqueror bent on conquest.... Then another horse came out, a fiery red one. Its rider was given power to take peace from the earth and to make men slay each other. To him was given a large sword.... and there before me was a black horse! Its rider was holding a pair of scales in his hand.... I looked, and there before me was a pale horse! Its rider was named Death, and Hades was following close behind him. They were given power over a fourth of the earth to kill by sword, famine and plague, and by the wild beasts of the earth" (Rev. 6:2–8). In a final, redemptive image, John sees **Heaven** "standing open and there before me was a white horse, whose rider was called Faithful and True. With justice he judges and makes war" (Rev. 19:11). This triumphant horseman kills the beast and the kings of the earth—the evil powers.

It is no surprise that Jews and Christians have considered horses images of wars and of foreign power, while the donkey was the gentle creature they associated with peace and domesticity. David, the genuine king, and later his descendant Jesus, the Prince of Peace, both chose the donkey rather than the more regal horse as their mounts

This interpretation of horses as vigorous, uncontrollable creatures led to their use as symbols of lust in Renaissance art (George Ferguson 1966, 20). The Greeks had a kinder view of horses than the Hebrews, making Pegasus the image of poetic inspiration, and picturing horses drawing the chariot of the sun around the earth. Their lustiness, however, is implied in the Centaur, a creature with a man's head and a horse's body. In modern times, heroic sculpture usually involves horses, making military men look larger than life and giving vitality and grandeur to battle scenes. *See also* Animals; Donkey, Ass; Kings; War, Warfare: General.

Further Reading

Carsdale, George. "Animals," in *The Illustrated Bible Dictionary*. Sydney, Australia: Tyndale House Publishers, 1980. Carsdale, George. *All the Animals of the*

Bible Lands. Grand Rapids, Mich.: Zondervan Publishing House, 1970.
Ferguson, George. *Signs and Symbols in Christian Art*. New York: Oxford University Press, 1966.

𝔥ospitality

(Gen.18:1–8; Lev.19:33–34; Deut.10:18; Ps. 23) Hospitality was more than a custom in ancient times. For the Jews, and later for the Christians, it was a religious obligation. "And if a stranger sojourn with thee in your land, ye shall not vex him. But the stranger that dwelleth with you shall be unto you as one born among you, and thou shalt love him as thyself; for ye were strangers in the land of **Egypt**" (Lev. 19:33–34). This commandment regarding the *ger*—strangers, sojourners, or aliens, anyone outside the kin group—set the tone for the treatment of visitors. They were to be welcomed, fed, honored, protected, and sheltered.

The first and most famous example of hospitality is in the story of Abraham greeting his angelic visitors and rushing to feed and honor them (Gen. 18:5). The reference in 3 John 1 also suggests the possibility that the guest at the door might be one of God's **angels**. This was an idea common in the ancient world, which was reinforced by Christ's admonition in Matthew 25.

The first contrary example in Scripture was the treatment of these same guests among the citizens of Sodom, where Lot tried to host them and found his guests threatened by the decadent men of the doomed city. During the time of the **judges**, the trick that Samson's new bride's family played on him at his **wedding** (when they should have honored this new kinsman in their midst) resulted in his brutal reaction. The abuse of hospitality, in one case, caused a civil war in Israel, apparently leading to the extinction of the whole tribe of Benjamites (Judg. 19–20; Emil G. Hirsch, Julius H. Greenstone, Solomon 2004). The only scriptural celebration of a perfidious host is Jael, who invited the Philistine commander

Foot washing ritual for visitor as he enters the home.

Sisera into her tent, offered him milk to drink, encouraged him to sleep, covered him gently, and then drove a tent spike into his temple, clearly a breach of hospitality (Judg. 4:18–21).

Job lists his hospitality among his assets, although his "comforters" insist he was not sufficiently generous (Job 31:31–32, 22:7). Isaiah was to expand on this concept with his description of true religion: "Is it not to deal thy bread to the hungry, and that thou bring the poor that are cast out to thy house? when thou seest the naked, that thou cover him; and that thou hide not thyself from thine own flesh?"(Isa. 58:7). The Twenty-third Psalm beautifully expresses the bountiful manner in which God provides for his guests, preparing a table for them, filling their cups to overflowing.

Jesus was to expand on the Old Testament ideas and customs, not only in the Golden Rule: "Do unto others as you would have them do unto you," but also in his parable of the **king** who rewarded his gracious followers. "For I was an hungered, and ye gave me meat: I was thirsty and ye gave me drink: I was a stranger, and ye took me in: Naked, and ye clothed me: I was sick, and ye visited me: I was in prison, and ye came unto me." He followed this with these words: "Inasmuch as ye have done it unto one of the least of these my brethren, ye have done it unto me" (Matt. 25:35, 40). Jesus loved visiting Peter's family, as well as the home of Mary, Martha, and Lazarus, and numerous others. Like Levi, these friends apparently arranged feasts in his honor, engaged in extended conversations, and provided him and his **disciples** comfortable quarters for the night.

His **apostles** repeatedly admonished members of the **Church** to be hospitable, especially to other Christians (1 Tim. 3:2, 5:10; Titus 1:7–8; Heb. 13:2; 3 John 1:5–8). Paul was on the receiving end of much generosity by Christians all through his missionary travels. He stayed for quite a while with Aquila and Priscilla, for instance (Acts 18:1–2, 18:24–26; Rom. 16:3; 1 Cor. 16:19). It is hardly surprising that he told Timothy that the church officers should be hospitable people.

Generally, whether the guests were friends or strangers, they might expect to be entertained with honor. The guest also had certain obligations to behave in a proper manner, to show gratitude for his treatment, and to leave after a decent interval. A reciprocal bond was established that forced the host to treat the guest as a friend so long as the relationship endured (Fred H. Wight 1953, 70).

This sacred duty required the host to make provision for the guests—a place inside the **tent**, a guest apartment, a guest room, or space in the public guest chamber. Even if the sleeping quarters were not in the tent or home of the host, he was expected to provide **food** and entertainment for the guest. In some cases, guests slept with the family, or they might be provided with a special room, as in the case of the **prophet** (2 Kings 4:10). One reference notes that, as in the story of Lot, the visitors might come to the village gate and wait for an invitation. In the case of Jacob or Moses, travelers found that they could wait at the well to discover a friendly offer of water and an invitation to visit the nearby home.

In the Old Testament, there must have been **inns**, but they seem to have been rare. Rahab was said to be an innkeeper, perhaps another term for prostitute. In New Testament times, when inns were available, these places were usually so squalid and depraved that a decent person would not permit a stranger to stay there. The Good Samaritan deposited the wounded Jew in an inn to be healed, but as a stranger the Samaritan probably had no home or friends in the area where he could provide suitable hospitality.

Certain traditional rituals of hospitality are noted in Scripture: When the visitor was spotted in the distance, the host was expected to wait in the doorway (as Abraham did), bow in a ceremonial greeting, and make a gracious offer of welcome. (This kiss on both cheeks and embrace between men is still typical today. Judas's betrayal of his master with a kiss was a violation of this ritual of friendship.) This was followed by the guest's removal of his shoes so that he might enter the home. (Moses was told to put off his shoes when he touched the holy ground in Exodus 3:5, and Moslems, as well as many other peoples, remove their shoes to step onto the carpets of the host.) The host or a servant would then bring a basin of **water** and wash the feet of the guest, drying them with a towel. (Jesus showed how the good host would do this himself, rather than leaving it to a servant (John 13:4–5). If **olive oil** or spices were available, the host would pour a few drops on the visitor's head. (David famously said, "Thou anointest my head with oil" [Ps. 23:5]). Next came the offer of a drink of water ("My cup runneth over") and a meal of his best food (the "fatted calf").

While the guest was present, the host was expected to protect him, and serve him as if he were the lord of the household. If he stayed overnight, he might sleep with the family, on a rooftop, or in a separate room or compartment. When the visit was concluded, the host would beg the guest to stay, and the guest would graciously protest and take his leave, going on his way. (Fred Wight 1953, 72–79). When the host and guest settled upon a **covenant** (Gen. 26:31), the host would accompany the guest for a distance. The guest was expected to bless the host before taking leave and ask if he had need of anything (2 Kings 4:13). If the guest so wished, he might remain with the clan or in the locale; "he was permitted to select a dwelling place" (Gen. 20:15; Hirsch et al. 2004)

This ritual, which is still common among bedouins today, built a compact between the host and guest that endured after the visit. Even if they were not friends or compatriots, they were responsible for protecting one another. Among Jews and Christians, the tradition survived in the custom of providing meals for poor guests, often itinerant students. Many modern churches have fellowship meals to which any visitors are cordially invited, and many organizations offer hospitality to visitors from foreign lands. *See also* Anointing; Clothing; Washing of Feet; Waters.

Further Reading

Hirsch, Emil G., Julius H. Greenstone, and Solomon Schechter. "Hospitality," http://www.jewishencyclopedia.com (accessed September 20, 2004). King, Philip J. and Lawrence E. Stager. *Life in Biblical Israel.* Louisville, Ky.: Westminster John Knox Press, 2001. Wight, Fred H. *Manners and Customs of Bible Lands.* Chicago: Moody Press, 1953.

Houses

When Abram and his **family** set out for the Promised Land, leaving the settled communities of Mesopotamia, they accepted the nomadic existence, with a life in **tents**. This may have changed to some sort of rude huts during their sojourn in **Egypt**, but we know little of their life there. We do know that they had doorways with lintels, suggesting something more permanent than a tent. Uprooted once again during the **Exodus**, they moved back into tents, spending 40 years wandering in the desert before they finally crossed the Jordan and began to settle in homes in those lands assigned to their **tribes**.

In **Canaan**, the simple house of the Israelite was probably little more than an elaboration of the **goat**-hair tent. It was rectilinear and had separate space for humans and **animals** and for sleeping and cooking that was usually divided into two, three, or four rooms. Using the typical materials available—wood, mud, straw, and stone—builders would often construct these simple homes of sun-dried mud **bricks** with a waterproofing plaster. Such porous walls would be easy for robbers to "break through" and steal belongings (Matt. 6:19–20). The floors were probably flagstones or packed earth covered with a waterproof lime plaster. Later, more elaborate floors, with mosaic designs made of bits of colored tile, indicate a Greco-**Roman** influence.

Such primitive permanent houses are suggested in 1 Sam. 28:24, with the animals housed on the lower level, where they were fed and kept safe for the night. Mangers might be dug out of the floor or constructed of stone or clay (as suggested in Luke 13:15). Straw covered much of the floor on the first level, providing a means of cleaning out the animal and human waste daily. Each morning, the animals would be led out into an open courtyard, and the house might be thoroughly cleaned. The refuse-soaked straw was piled in an area where it was dried and later shaped into cakes and used for fuel.

Ruins of Jericho suggest that the inhabitants the Israelites discovered in Canaan lived in rounded, mud brick huts with leather roofs. Around the outsides of the walled town were grainfields irrigated by spring-fed ditches (Fred Wright 1974, 23).

Many "pillared" homes had a terrace, or second level, which was a living area for the members of the family. Here "food was stored, cooked, and eaten," and the humans slept and lived (Kenneth E. Bailey 1953, 293).

Pillared house showing cooking, storage and working area, animal stalls, with sleeping area upstairs, and flat roof.

Some **cooking**—with open fires or in mud-brick ovens—might be done outside or on the first level. Fire pits have been discovered that reveal that the "hearth" was sometimes simply a hole in the ground. Here a fire was kindled for cooking or warmth (Philip J. King and Lawrence E. Stager 2001,18–19).

The windows were little more than slits, covered with trellises and shutters, some of which were large enough to allow a spy to escape (Josh. 2:15). They were essential to allow some light inside and to provide an escape for smoke fumes. The houses were quite dark inside, lighted only by a single **lamp** (Luke 15:80). The lattices that covered the windows allowed those inside to look out, while those outside could not see in. They might be covered with heavy drapes or shutters, as glass was not available in this era.

The door, usually made of wood, swinging on **leather** hinges, had a tubelike amulet, a "mezuzah," which contained a parchment on which the words of Deut. 6:4–9, 11:13–21 were written. The stone threshold, which protected the home from rain and mud, had a sacred significance. Doorposts on either side supported the lintel, on which the Israelite families sprinkled the symbolic **blood** of **Passover** lamb (Exod. 12:22).

Most of the homes were completely roofed, with wooden steps on the outside of the building or ladders inside. "The most common roof was constructed of thick poles laid flat across the walls" supported by columns or poles if needed. Branches spanned the beams, and these were covered with coarsely woven mats and packed clay. The family used a stone roller on the roof after every rain or snow to keep it from leaking. Eventually, grass might spring up briefly on the roofs. This was the place where crops were dried and stored (Josh. 2:6) or guests entertained (Kenneth E. Bailey 1953, 294). The removable thatched mud-and-clay roof was probably the material of which the roof was made in the house where Jesus was teaching and healing when friends of a paralytic removed it to lower their sick friend and seek Jesus's healing (Mark 2:1–12).

Upper-class home in Palestine, with space for animals next to courtyard for cooking, washing, and so forth; upper floor for sleeping and eating; and roof for other activities.

In summertime, family members might climb onto the roof to sleep under the stars. Peter slept on a rooftop and dreamed about God's meaning of "unclean" animals. Bathsheba bathed on her rooftop and was watched by King David from his loftier **palace** (2 Sam.11:2). The roof was a common place for entertaining guests and was also used for ordinary daily activities: grinding meal and churning butter. It also served as a place for family worship services. Legally, the Israelites were obliged to have a parapet around the roof, to keep people from falling off (Deut. 22:8).

Such homes were clustered inside city walls, often sharing one of these walls, a likely explanation for the story of Rahab's home on the wall of Jericho: "So she let them down by a rope through the window, for the house she lived in was part of the city wall" (Josh. 2:18). The Shunammite woman's home was also built over a casement in the town wall (Philip J. King and Lawrence Stager 2001,19). Archaeologists have found evidence of this custom, which predates the time of Joshua. One explanation might be that Jericho had a hollow wall with chambers partitioned off in it (NIV, fn. 291).

The homes could be expanded as the family grew, allowing additional rooms for the new family members. Wealthier people had larger homes,

Houses crowded in a small town in Palestine.

built higher so that they could look down on the rooftops and courtyards of their neighbors. Such a home is suggested in the "upper room," which was used for the **Last Supper**. Mary and Martha also seem to have had a nice home in Bethany, with several rooms for cooking and living. An affluent **fisherman** like Peter was thought to have had a dwelling with several rooms for various members of his family. Archaeologists have uncovered the ruins of such a dwelling in Capernaum.

By Jesus's day, when cities had grown and the Greco-Roman influence dominated Palestine, whole cities in Israel were built according to classical designs, with stadia, amphitheatres, pagan temples, and marketplaces or agora. In such cities, the homes were more likely to be built around a central courtyard, have stone-slab roofs, and more windows, and more elaborate constructions. *See also* Bricks, Bricklayers; Caves; Fortifications, Fortified Cities, Fortresses; Palaces; Stone.

Further Reading

Bailey, Kenneth E. "Houses," in *Oxford Companion to the Bible*. New York: Oxford University Press, 1953. King, Philip J. and Lawrence E. Stager. *Life in

Biblical Israel. Louisville, Ky.: Westminster John Knox Press, 2001. Wight, Fred H. *Manners and Customs of Bible Lands*. Chicago: Moody Press, 1953. Wright, G. Ernest, ed. *Great People of the Bible and How They Lived*. Pleasantville, N.Y.: The Reader's Digest Association, Inc., 1974.

Hunting

Wild **animals** were abundant in ancient Israel, when there were wooded forests and few humans. Although from the beginning, the Hebrews were **shepherds**, not great hunters of wild game, they were often compelled to kill animals threatening their **sheep**. They knew the techniques for hunting and sometimes ate the animals they killed or even used them as **sacrifice**. When Abraham was prepared to offer his son up to God, a wild ram was provided to take his place. In this case, he was not obliged to trap him, for he was already entangled in a thicket by his horns (Gen. 22:13). Other nationalities indulged in the chase with more enthusiasm than is recorded of the Hebrews, who used traps and nets but did not organize hunting parties or celebrate their prowess as hunters. Wild game must have supplied meat for many families, although our information on this is slight.

The first great hunter named in Scripture was Nimrod, "a mighty hunter before the Lord" (Gen. 10:9) and a descendant of Cush. Ishmael, unlike his brother Isaac, became an archer, probably a hunter of animals (Gen. 21:20). Esau, another "cunning hunter" (Gen. 25:27), also represented a collateral line, not part of the chosen people of God. It was his brother Jacob who became *Israel,* the progenitor of the nation, a **tent**-dweller and a herdsman, not a hunter. For the Israelites, domestic meat was the more regular fare, and dietary regulations forced this pattern still further after the time of Moses.

For most of Israel's history, wild animals were a threat to flocks. It was essential that the sheep be protected against predators such as lions and wolves. Bears and lions were trapped by pitfalls, snares, and nets (Isa. 31:1; Ezek. 19:4, 8; Ps. 91:3) or killed with bows and arrows (Gen. 28:15). Samson was able to tear a lion apart with his bare hands as was David (Judg. 14:6; 1 Sam. 17:34). David proclaimed that he "struck" the lion that was attacking his father's sheep, perhaps with his slingshot. In both cases, these great warriors were engaged in activities provoked by the wild animals, and they responded by defending themselves and their flocks, not killing out of bloodthirsty joy in sport.

Apparently there was a time after the Israelites settled in **Canaan** when the pursuit of wild game became fairly common The **law** protecting the timberlands for the beasts of the field during the Sabbatical years and the listing of **clean** animals—like the hart, the roebuck, the chamois, and the antelope—suggest that these were hunted and eaten (Lev. 17:13, 25:7; Exod. 23:11). Various types of wild deer included fallow deer in wooded places, gazelles in abundance, and "Nubian ibex in the dry hills of Judea, trans-Jordan and the desert" (George Cansdale 1970, 81). The mammals listed as clean (Deut. 14:4, 5) include the wild ox, the gazelle, the Nubian ibex, the Arabian oryx, the mountain sheep, and aurochs (a type of wild **horse**). Different translators have identified these animals in a variety of ways: for example, the deer or gazelle, is often referred to as a "hart," the gazelle as a "roebuck," the Nubian ibex as a "wild goat," the Arabian oryx as a "wild ox" or "antelope," the mountain sheep as a "chamois," and the aurochs as a "wild ox" or "unicorn" (George Cansdale 1970, 82).

Of these, the aurochs are the most interesting, because of the late tradition that a hunter could not capture this small animal by force, but only by a trick. "The hunter was required to lead a virgin to the spot frequented by the unicorn and to leave her there alone. The unicorn, sensing the purity of the maiden, would run to her, lay its head in her lap, and fall asleep" (George Ferguson 1966, 26). From this fanciful story, it is easy to see why the unicorn became a symbol of purity, especially of feminine chastity, and therefore associated with the **Annunciation** and **Incarnation**. The small white creature, with a horn in the middle of its forehead, was usually present in pictures of the Virgin. In actuality, the auroch was probably a wild ox; the last known member of the species died in 1627. Cansdale argues that the passage related to it (Deut. 33:17) speaks clearly of the "horns" of the unicorn, making the one-horned tradition unlikely. Nonetheless, it has become one of the most enduring symbols in Western art and mythology.

The beasts of prey—the bear, the lion, the wolf, the fox, jackal and hyena, weasel, badger, and mongoose—were all enemies to the flocks. They had to be hunted and killed, but could not be eaten. Others, which were pests to gardeners and **farmers**, were sometimes used for **food**, but were usually seen as unclean—the coney, hare, mouse, hedgehog, porcupine, mole-rat, and bat. Some of these are mentioned in Scripture, but without clear identification as animals we still know.

The coney, for example, seems to have been a hyrax—a gray-brown, rabbit-sized mammal with short sturdy legs and feet that can hold to rocks—as is mentioned in Proverbs 30:26: "The conies are but feeble folk, yet they make their houses in the rocks." The hares were larger than wild rabbits, but they lived above ground and could jump farther. This is mentioned as an unclean animal (Lev. 11:6; Deut. 14:7), perhaps because it ate its own droppings rather than chewing the cud. Cansdale suggests that the reason for this prohibition against this creature as food was that rabbits and hares are alternate hosts of the dog tapeworm. If food is not cooked thoroughly, the human can become infected (George Cansdale 1970, 132).

Certain **birds**, such as the partridge, were also considered clean and offered variety for the menu. Birds of passage, such as the pelican, stork, or crane, appeared in their spring migration in large numbers all over Palestine, but it was the tiny quail that fed the Israelites (Exod.16:13). Birds of prey, on the other hand, were strictly forbidden. Thus, eagles and vultures, osprey, buzzards, kits, falcons, hawks, and owls could be snared, but not consumed.

Once settled in Canaan, the Hebrews probably cultivated domestic fowl, especially chickens, partridge, and doves, making hunting unnecessary. In later, more sumptuous times, Solomon enjoyed a great number of more exotic treats. Only in still later times, after the influence of the Greeks and Romans had entered their culture, did the Jews begin to use **horses** in their chase of wild animals. The objections that then rose to hunting were based on the idea that it was cruel and "un-Jewish" or, as one scholar notes: "He who hunts game with **dogs** as Gentiles do will not enjoy the life to come" (Joseph Jacobs 2004).

The **Egyptians** loved to bag falcons, vultures, buzzards, kits, and crows, using greyhounds in their hunting. And the **Assyrian** and **Babylonian** kings engaged in large-scale hunting of lions, standing in their chariots with bows and arrows, prepared to fell their prey. These exploits are commemorated on glazed tiles and in carved reliefs around **palaces**, temples, and on city **gates** (Madeleine S. Miller and J. Lane Miller 1961, 273).

The shedding of **blood** was always a serious and sacrificial act for the Jews, not to be treated lightly, even though they knew the techniques for hunting. Unlike the other peoples of the region, those in Mesopotamia or Egypt, who delighted in the hunt and celebrated these activities in their arts, the Jews would snare birds or club animals only to provide security from danger or food for the table (R. K. Harrison 1980, 673–674). Although the equipment and the habits of the hunters survive in the imagery of Scripture—nets, bows and arrows, slingstones and darts, pits used for trapping and killing a variety of animals—none of these appear with the frequency of the gentle habits of the shepherds. *See also* Animals; Sacrifice, Offerings; Sheep; Shepherds.

Further Reading

Cansdale, George. *All the Animals of the Bible Lands*. Grand Rapids, Mich.: Zondervan Publishing House, 1970. Ferguson, George. *Signs and Symbols in Christian Art*. New York: Oxford University Press, 1966. Harrison, R. K. "Hunting, Hunter," in *The Illustrated Bible Dictionary*. Sydney, Australia: Tyndale House Publishers, 1980. Jacobs, Joseph. "Hunting," http://www.jewishencyclopedia.com (accessed October 21, 2004). Miller, Madeleine S. and J. Lane Miller. "Hunting," in *Harper's Bible Dictionary*. New York: Harper and Row, 1961.

Husband and Wife

(Genesis 2:20–24, 3:14–20; Prov. 31) Created as a social being, man needed a "helpmeet" fit for him. This explanation of the role of woman, the mother of all the living, is clearly portrayed in the **Creation** story, as are the separate obligations and natures of husband and wife. It is clear that they become "one"—a unit separate from the previous families to which they belonged. The authority of the husband is also justified in the words of God at the time of the Expulsion from **Eden**, as is the woman's need for his protection. This sense of mutual obligation is later explained by Paul as being parallel to the love between Christ and his **church** (Col. 3:19). "Husbands, love your wives," he tells the Collosians. And further, "Wives, obey your husbands." Both actions are to be grounded in love and a sense of unity as "one flesh."

From earliest Scripture, a man's selection of a wife was considered one of his most serious decisions. Her faith and culture were of such importance that Isaac and Jacob each went (or sent a servant) back to Paddan-Aram to find an appropriate bride. As the mother of his children and the source of their early acculturation, the woman of faith and virtue was essential. In addition, a quarrelsome wife was considered a great curse (Prov. 21:9, 19; 25:24) and a beautiful woman a great treasure. As seen from Jacob's example and from Isaac's obvious delight in Rebekah, even arranged marriages were often full of love and sexual delight. The marriage tribute in the Song of Solomon is a paen to female physical beauty. The tribute in Proverbs 31, however, celebrates the busy, productive wife, who buys and sells land, keeps busy from sunup until sundown. Such a woman is also the delight of the writer of Ecclesiastes, who speaks—even in old age—of the joys of marriage and their life together (Eccles. 9:9). Rooted deep in the Jewish culture is a sense of the significance of marriage and the balanced roles of husband and wife.

It is clear in the **law** that the wife was regarded as property, but the actual stories of marriages through the Scripture show many instances where the wife was not necessarily treated as such. She was to address her husband as "ba'al" or "lord and master." Even so, from examples such as Sarah and Rebekah, we realize that women had considerable power in the household. Nonetheless, the wife could be set aside or divorced, or she might be replaced by additional wives who were younger, more pleasant, productive, or amenable to her husband's demands. If she proved unfaithful, she could be taken to court and stoned to death.

Men were expected to marry and to produce children who would carry on the family line. In fact, there was no Hebrew word for "bachelor." Although there were **eunuchs** among the Israelites, who were often the administrators of harems, the Hebrews were forbidden to castrate young men.

When the boy children reached a suitable age, the men became their teachers. They taught their children the skills of carpentry or shepherding or farming so that they might assume their proper roles in society. The girls stayed with their mothers, learning the household skills such as spinning, weaving, and cooking. Gender roles were clearly delineated.

Only in Christian times were men and women discouraged from marriage, as interfering with their zeal for the faith, although Paul acknowledged that most people found marriage preferable to "burning" (Matt. 19:11; 1 Cor. 7:32–35). This admonition to remain celibate was, of course, the basis for the vows of chastity taken by **priests** in the Church, and continues in the Roman Catholic Church to modern times. Nuns, who also take vows of chastity, consider themselves married to Christ.

The husband was expected to support his wife in accordance with his status and income. The law required that he must furnish her with meals—at least two a day (Julius H. Greenstone 2004). He was also expected to provide her **clothing** and a home. Her clothes should include "new shoes for each holy day" as well as "bedding" and "kitchen utensils . . . ornaments and perfumes" (Julius H. Greenstone 2004). If his wife should be taken captive, he was expected to ransom her, even if the funds required far exceeded her wedding settlement. He was also expected to love, honor, and nurture her.

The husband was entitled to all of his wife's earnings, to all of her chance gains, and to the fruits of her property. He was also her sole heir at the time of her death. These arrangements continued over many centuries, ending in England only late in the nineteenth century with the Married Women's Property Act, which allowed women to retain the money they earned. Even the children were considered the property of the husband (and still are in some Moslem countries). Throughout most of history, this economic authority of the man made woman totally dependent on his good will for her livelihood.

The wife was expected to do the housework—baking, cooking, washing, tending to children—with or without household help. She was also expected to bear her husband numerous children, particularly sons, to carry on the family line. It was thought to be a curse for a woman was to have a "barren womb."

The greatest tragedy that could befall a woman was to become a widow, bereft of income or protector. We see this lowly status in the story of Ruth, where all three of the women have lost their husbands. In this case, the two younger ones make every effort to remarry. For Ruth, the second marriage provides security for both her and for her mother-in-law as well. In the New Testament Church, the care for orphans and widows was specifically mentioned as a concern of the deacons (Acts 6:1).

Among the Old Testament **prophets**, the unfaithful wife, who "whored" after other men was frequently used as the image of the unfaithful Israel, leaving her God to seek other gods. This particular image worked so effectively, in part, because of the sacred prostitutes of other religions, especially those dedicated to the worship of the Mother Goddess. Ezra made elaborate use of the portrait of the prostitute, in this case, his erring wife. This may well be the basis of the great image of the "whore of Babylon" in Revelation.

Paul encouraged those who were Christians to love one another and to share one another's burdens. Although he saw the man as "head" of the household, he also saw him as a loving leader, no more willing to damage his own wife than he would be to do harm to his own body. The family and its shared love and obligations became the image of the Christian community, and the image of the willing subjection of the wife to the husband the metaphor of the Church's relationship to Christ. *See also* Divorce; Family; Weddings; Work: Men's; Work: Women's.

Further Reading

Achtemeier, Elizabeth. "Women," in *The Oxford Companion to the Bible*. New York: Oxford University Press, 1993. Greenstone, Julius H. "Husband and Wife," http://www.jewishencyclopedia.com (accessed September 30, 2004). King, Philip J. and Lawrence E. Stager. *Life in Biblical Israel*. Louisville, Ky.: Westminster John Knox Press, 2001.

Hypocrite

(Matt 7:5; Luke 6:42) *Hypocrite* is a term used in the Gospels by Jesus, usually referring to the **scribes** and **Pharisees**. It is derived from the Greek word for actor, especially the actors who wore masks in the dramatic presentations.

Idols, Idolatry

(**Exod. 20:4–5, 23–25, 32:1–6; Deut. 4:15–18; Rev. 13:14–15**) The many gods of Israel's neighbors were a continuing source of temptation. **Babylonians**, **Egyptians**, **Canaanites**, **Greeks**, and **Romans** all had statues and wall paintings of their gods. They had temples full of wooden, **gold**-plated, and stone figures, before which they bowed down. Believing that the god dwelt within the figure, they did not necessarily worship the statues themselves, but they nonetheless gave the impression to the Jews of worshipping images of **stone** rather than worshipping the one true God.

An early biblical example of this interest in idols occurs in Genesis. Rachel stole the household gods from Laban, apparently believing that she was taking some mysterious power from him in the act (Gen. 31:19). These "household gods" refer to the popular images that became part of many households all through the Fertile Crescent. Even in Greek and Roman literature, the household gods are mentioned as a part of folk culture. When Aeneas left Troy (in the *Aeneid*), he took his household gods with him. Examples of these small images, often of baked clay, have been found buried in many sites.

While Moses was on the mountain in his amazing sojourn with God, his people gathered down below, melting down their **jewelry** to make the image of a golden calf (Exod. 32:1–6). It is clear that the visible image had a power to tempt a person to forget the invisible God. For this reason, the commandments were essential: "Thou shalt have no other gods before me," and "Thou shalt not make unto thee any graven image" (Exod. 20:3–4).

All through the Old Testament, the Hebrew **prophets** confronted the perils of idolatry, railing against the worship of pagan gods. The Canaanite gods, with their explicitly sexual features, were especially tempting to those who relied on the fertility of the land and the womb (Douglas A. Knight 1993, 297). In the New Testament, the silversmiths who made their living off the manufacture of statues of Artemis were to lead the riot against Paul in Ephesus, realizing his God would put an end to their business. Artemis (or Diana) was noted for the gross sexual portrayals of her and her multiple and ample breasts. Idolatry was a problem among numerous of the **kings**, starting with Solomon, who erected temples for his foreign wives' gods and even worshipped in some of them. **Asherah** was the goddess who caused major concerns.

With the impending fall of Jerusalem and the destruction of the **Temple**, Jeremiah scorned the impotent idols that the Hebrews chose to worship (Jer. 7:20). Other prophets who condemned the worship of idols include

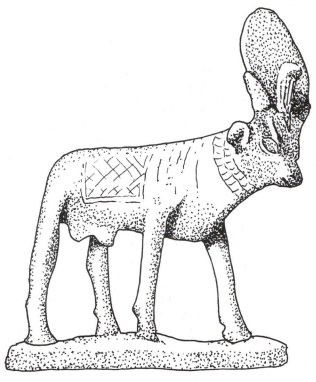

Golden Calf (bull statue discovered at Ashkelon, Israel).

Amos (2:4), Hosea (8:4–6), Isaiah (2:8), Zephaniah, (2:11), and Ezekiel (6:4–6). The Psalmist joined in the condemnation (Ps. 115, 135:15–21).

In the period between the testaments, the Hellenistic leaders tried to introduce images in their cities and even in the Temple in Jerusalem. Many remnants of these statues and paintings have been discovered by archaeologists. The Romans also sought to place portraits of the Caesars and the many gods of Rome in public places and were confronted by angry mobs of Jews who saw this as an abomination. This clash of cultures continued over the centuries, especially as the Romans insisted on emperor worship and the Jews and Christians refused to obey.

Paul made judicial use of pagan idols in his sermon at the Aeropagus, noting the images of many gods, even one to the "unknown god" (Acts 17:23). This gave him an opening to speak to the "itching ears" of the Athenians. He was confronted with problems among the new Greek and Roman Christians, who were concerned about eating meat that had been previously consecrated to pagan idols. Although they had no reason to believe that this altered the food itself, Paul noted that it might be a "stumbling block" to converts, reason enough to avoid eating it (Rom.14:13).

The most frequently mentioned idols in Scripture are of Asherah, whose image was often a sacred wooden post, and **Baal**, who was often cast in metal, pictured as a male standing or striding. **Animals** such as bulls or calves are also common. **Serpents**, as the one that Moses raised, were often cast in **metal** and thought to be connected with fertility. The teraphim, which Rachel stole from her uncle, were small figurines, perhaps connected with ancestor worship and kept in a sacred box (Madeleine S. Miller and J. Lane Miller 1961, 277).

Such clay, metal, or wooden figures were cherished, worshipped, dressed, provided with food, and often kept in shrines. Taking them captive was often a symbol of the defeat of a people—apparently the reason that the

Philistines thought they were victors over God and his people when they captured the **Ark of the Covenant**.

These injunctions kept the Jews from developing much ecclesiastical art apart from the mandated embroideries in the Tabernacle and Temple and a few statues of oxen, cherubim, and seraphim connected with these constructions. They did not develop intricate abstract art for decoration, much like that of Moslem artists in later years. Unlike Baal and the other regional gods, Jehovah could not be portrayed in statues or in painting. This was to change in the Christian era, when artists felt free, after the **Incarnation**, to picture God as King, enthroned among his angelic hosts. Because Christ came as a man, the Christian artists, drawing on the Greek mimetic aesthetic, felt particularly free to paint and sculpt images of him engaged in human activities on earth. Most Jewish **synagogues** continue to avoid images of created things or of God himself, but Christian **church**es are divided on this issue, some using statuary and others rejecting even the images of **angels** or crosses. The Greek Orthodox and the Roman Catholic Churches, among many others, make lavish use of images, but churches in the Calvinist tradition consider images in churches to be "idols." The Lutheran, Methodist, and Episcopal Churches tend to take an intermediate position in this debate.

Just as Paul interpreted idols as anything that people placed between themselves and God, so later Christian authors (including Sir Francis Bacon) spoke of the "Idols of the Marketplace," those practices that the human places before God in his or her life. These can be anything from a lover to a hobby that consumes the human's attention. The scriptural reference behind this is Matthew 6:21: "For where your treasure is, there will your heart be also." *See also* Art: Christian; Art: Jewish; Asherah, Ashtoreth, Ashtaroth; Baal, Baalim; Egypt, Eqyptians; Greece, Greek, Hellenists; Rome, Romans; Synagogue; Tabernacle; Temple.

Baal, a bronze figure found at Ugarit, representing the most popular god-figure in Canaan.

Further Reading

Jeffrey, David L. and John Sandys-Wunsch. "Graven Image," in *The Dictionary of the Biblical Tradition in English Literature*. Grand Rapids, Mich.: William B. Eerdmans Publishing Company, 1992. Knight, Douglas A. "Idols, Idolatry," in *The Oxford Companion to the Bible*. New York: Oxford University Press, 1993. Miller, Madeleine S. and J. Lane Miller. "Idols," in *Harper's Bible Dictionary*. New York: Harper and Row, 1961. Propp, William H.

"Graven Image," in *The Oxford Companion to the Bible*. New York: Oxford University Press, 1993.

Idumaea. *See* Edom

Illness

Much of Hebrew Scripture is designed to promote both spiritual and physical health. The Holiness Code, which requires frequent bathing, and the dietary **laws**, which regulate **food**s, were both crucial. Yet, in spite of these, the Hebrews were faced with a variety of diseases and physical disabilities. Death in childbirth, broken bones, worms, blindness, continual bleeding, leprosy, and madness are mentioned throughout the pages of Scripture. We know that a number of the names of diseases have been changed over the years, so that paralysis may have been poliomyelitis and bloody flux might have been infection of the uterus. The blindness that afflicted Isaac in his old age was probably caused by one of the standard complaints of aging—glaucoma or cataracts. We also know that terms such as *leprosy* have significantly changed over time. The physical manifestations of some of the diseases, such as ulceration, swelling, and hemorrhaging, are sometimes used by moderns to diagnose the original disorder

The cause of most illness was generally thought to be disobedience of God's law. Mental disease, in particular, was thought to be a spiritual disorder. God had promised health if the Israelites followed his law (Exod.15:28; Deut. 28:60–61), leading most of the ancients facing disease or disability to study their behavior to determine how they had sinned. Job's "comforters" echoed this idea as they sought to help him to understand his distress. He in turn argued that this distress was a part of some divine plan, unknowable by humans. Jesus's response to the accusation of sin against a blind man was even more explicit: he told his listeners that neither this man nor his parents had sinned (John 9:2).

Types of illness were various. A "barren womb" was considered a "reproach" or judgment of God, to be remedied by prayer and obedience to God's will (as in the cases of Sarah, Rebekah, and Hannah). Of course, childbirth itself was a risk. Rachel's death when giving birth to Benjamin was probably not an unusual event in the era, although it is the only mention of death in childbirth we find in Scripture; perhaps this was sufficiently common that it was not generally recorded. In fact, most women's deaths are not recorded in the Bible. The wives of the patriarchs are rare examples of females of sufficient prominence that their final days were chronicled.

Numerous **plagues**, probably bubonic, were noted in the Old Testament. The plagues that struck **Egypt** while the Hebrews were seeking to escape captivity were thought to be the result of divine **judgment**. When

Sennacherib planned his attack on Jerusalem, a plague struck in the night, decimating his troops (2 Kings 19:35). Some think this may have been the bubonic plague, some that it was more likely dysentery—"a common ailment with soldiers in the field" (Philip J. King and Lawrence E. Stager 2001, 69).

When Miriam rebelled against her brother Moses, she came down with leprosy and was separated from the people for a time. This "leprosy" was quite different from the modern disease, involving primarily a kind of skin eruption that lasted only briefly and did no permanent damage to her extremities. It was probably more like psoriasis than what we now call *leprosy*.

Job also broke out in boils, or "loathsome sores," which he scraped with potsherds (broken bits of pottery). There were so many regulations in the law regarding the treatment of people with skin eruptions, such as tumors, detailing whether they turn white and have hairs protruding from them that also turn white, that this must have been a common disorder. Boils were the sixth plague to strike Egypt (Exod. 9:9). Wens or other blemishes such as warts rendered a man unclean, but were apparently not considered illnesses.

"Wasting away" (Lev. 26:16, Deut. 28:22) might have been the ancient term for tuberculosis or cancer. Some terms, such as *fever, itch, issue of blood,* and *inflammation,* are not so much diseases as symptoms. The "bloody flux" (Acts 28:8; 2 Chron. 21:15, 18–19) may have been either an infection of the uterus or amebic dysentery.

Kings were as subject to diseases as their subjects: King Saul had a mental disorder, which was soothed by David's **music** on the lyre. Nebuchadnezzar apparently went quite mad, trying to eat grass as he crawled around on all fours. And Herod the Great was thought to have had a combination of worms and venereal diseases toward the end of his nasty life.

Blindness was common during biblical times, often caused by trachoma or gonorrhea in the mother (D. H. Trapnell 1980, 616). The New Testament describes lame and blind beggars and various diseased people who gathered around the Pool of Bethesda, waiting for an **angel** to trouble the waters and cure them (John 5:1–4). Among many others, Jesus cured the blind and the deaf and one man who had a speech impediment (Mark 7:32). Different speech disorders, including dumbness, are mentioned. Even Moses noted that he was unfit to lead because of his speech impediment, which appears to have been slight and certainly not disabling. Some impediments, like Zechariah's, were temporary (Luke 1:20, 22, 64), signs of divine intervention.

Archaeologists have established that there were numerous diseases resulting from the combination of poor hygiene, hot climate, and polluted water. The use of human waste as fertilizer spread many of these diseases. The undercooking of meats encouraged others. And the lack of sewers or clean utensils allowed all kinds of disease to flourish, in spite of the ritual washing of hands before meals. Traces of tapeworm, lice, and flies (which caused tachoma, an eye infection that led to blindness) have been discovered by archaeologists working together with other scientists (Philip J. King and Lawrence E. Stager 2001, 71–75).

One of the major changes in the attitude toward the sick and lame appears in the New Testament with Jesus's healing ministry. His willingness to touch and be touched by such people as the woman who suffered from a "flux" for 12 years, the blind men, or the lepers sets him apart from other good Jews of his time. They would have viewed all of these people as unclean, and they would have fled from their defiling touch. *See also* Birth; Physicians.

Further Reading

King, Philip J. and Lawrence E. Stager. *Life in Biblical Israel.* Louisville, Ky.: Westminster John Knox Press, 2001. Trapnell, D. H. "Health, Disease and Healing, in *The Illustrated Bible Dictionary.* Sydney, Australia: Tyndale House Publishers, 1980.

Incarnation

(John 1:1–14) "The Word became flesh," proclaims the Gospel of John after the magnificent opening section. *Incarnation,* taken from the Latin word *carnis,* or "flesh," literally means "enfleshment" (Madeleine S. Miller and J. Lane Miller 1961, 279). Although the term does not occur in Scripture, the concept is clear in John's presentation of the Son, who was present even at the **Creation**, ("In the Beginning") who became human and "dwelt among us."

The term *Incarnation* was used quite early in **Church** history by the Greek Fathers (180–189 A.D.), reinforced by the Council of Nicaea (325) : "We believe . . . in one Lord Jesus Christ, the Son of God, the Only-begotten, generated of the Father . . . that is, of the substance of the Father, God of God, Light of Light, True God of True God, begotten not made, the same in nature with the Father . . . by Whom all things were made" (Walter Drum 2004).

When John spoke of the "Word becoming Flesh," he appears to have meant "human," God taking on our fleshly human nature, in contrast to the purely spiritual nature of God the Father and God the **Holy Spirit**. "He took upon Himself not only the nature of man, a nature capable of suffering and sickness and death, He became like a man in all save only sin" (Walter Drum 2004). Many of the heresies that have arisen over the centuries have focused on this interpretation of the nature of Christ and have questioned the doctrine of the Trinity.

In the Old Testament, the **Messiah** is described as the perfect **king**, **prophet**, and **priest**, the divine instrument for the redemption of mankind (Ps. 72; Isa. 53, 61:1–3). He was more than the usual prophet, embodying as he did the perfect living Word of God (Heb. 4:12, 13, 24–26). Isaiah 9:6 expresses this messianic prophesy with great beauty: "A child is born, unto us a son is given: and the government shall be upon his shoulders; and his name shall be called Wonderful, Counsellor, The mighty God, the everlasting Father, The Prince of Peace." (Many moderns remember these words from hearing them in Handel's *Messiah*.)

The **Gospels**, especially Matthew's, are filled with evidence of the fulfillment of these prophesies. They thereby reinforce this theological concept, especially in the records of the Virgin **birth** (Luke 1:26–38); the scene of Jesus's **baptism** with the great theophany, revealing the Father, Son, and the Holy Ghost; and in the death and Resurrection of Christ. It was because he was God incarnate that he was able to pay the price for the sins of humankind, thus allowing for reconciliation with God and redemption from sins. *See also* Baptism; Creation; Holy Spirit, Holy Ghost; Resurrection.

Further Reading

Drum, Walter. "The Incarnation," http://www.newadvent.org (accessed December 12, 2004). Miller, Madeleine S. and J. Lane Miller. "Incarnation," in *Harper's Bible Dictionary*. New York: Harper and Row, 1961.

Incense

(**Exod. 30:1–10, 37:29; Lev. 2:1, 16:12–13; Heb. 9:4; Rev. 8:3–4**) Incense is a compound of sweet gums and spices that is burned in a special receptacle, which is often held by the **priest** and swung from side to side. It might also be burned on the **altar**, sending up smoke and fragrance that were thought to veil the presence of the Deity (Madeleine S. Miller and J. Lane Miller 1961, 280).

Inside the Holy Place, near the curtain hiding the Holy of Holies, stood the small golden altar where incense was burned. It was shaped like the great altar in the outer precincts of the **Tabernacle/Temple** design, but was placed on a stand and was much smaller. The Hebrews used it to supplement the **grain** offering (Lev. 2:1) and counteract the stench of burning flesh. The **high priest** used it in censers as he entered the Holy of Holies on the **Day of Atonement** (Lev. 16:12–13). And a priest burned it on the golden altar in the sanctuary twice a day (Exod. 30:1–10; John N. Suggit 1993, 301).

Originally, incense was offered in a pan that the priest carried in his hand—as Aaron and his sons did when offering sacrifice for the sins of their people (Num. 17:11–12; Lev. 10:1), suggesting that each priest had his own censer. The ritual for the Day of Atonement involved the high priest entering the Holy of Holies carrying a pan for the incense in his right hand, filled with live coals, and a spoonlike vessel called a "kaf" in his left hand, which contained the incense. He placed these utensils on the floor, then took the incense from the kaf with the hollow of his hand, heaped it on the pan with the coals, being careful to avoid any spillage (Immanuel Benzinger, Judah David Eisenstein 2004). This "golden censer" is mentioned in Hebrews 9:4 as a furnishing of the Holy of Holies—along with the **Ark of the Covenant**.

Incense is an aromatic substance, made from the gums and resins of certain trees, which, when burned, "exhales" a strong perfume. The two major forms are frankincense (derived from boswellia trees) and galbanum (thought to come from the gum of an umbelliferous plant). Both were foreign to Israel and therefore precious—a source of the wealth of traders who followed the ancient spice trade routes from South Arabia to Gaza and Damascus.

Frankincense, also an ingredient of **anointing** oil (Exod. 30:34), was burned with the grain as a part of the cereal offering. It was placed on the showbread in the Tabernacle (Lev. 24:7) and was burned in the golden altar. The most famous occurrence in Scripture was as the gift of the Wisemen to the newborn Christ child (Matt. 2:11). The galbanum was a strong-smelling spice that was used along with stacte and onycha as a constituent in the sacred incense (F. N. Hepper 1980, 689–690).

The preparation of the incense became increasingly detailed over time—with each element pounded into a fine powder, other spices such as cinnamon-bark, cassia, the flower of nard added, and some ingredients soaked in Cyprus **wine**. Not only would the ideal incense be fragrant, but the smoke would rise to form the stem of the date tree—as opposed to the usual irregular shape of less perfectly prepared incense ingredients. By the time of Herod, the honor of preparing the incense was considered a special privilege of the family of Abtinas (Immanuel Benzinger, Judah David Eisenstein 2004).

Incense is much more widely used in the East than in Europe or America. In the Christian rituals, it has sometimes followed the pattern of the imperial ceremony, with censors carried by servants leading the procession before the entrance of the **king** or emperor. In Revelation 8:3–4, this ritual appears to be the image of worship in heaven: "And another **angel** came and stood at the altar, having a golden censer, and there was given unto him much incense that he should offer it with the prayers of all the saints upon the golden altar which was before the throne. And the smoke of the incense, which came with the **prayers** of the saints, ascended up before God out of the angel's hand. And the angel took the censer, and filled it with fire of the altar, and cast it into the earth" Notice that this image of God emphasizes his majesty, a king sitting on a throne amidst his court of angels.

The censer used for the burning of incense is a portable bowl that usually has three chains and a cover that can be moved by means of a fourth chain. The celebrant uses a spoon to remove some incense from an incense-boat and place it on the burning coals contained in the cassolette. "The smoke is then spread by swaying the censer. The server in charge of this delicate, complex instrument is called a *thurifet*, 'a carrier of incense.'... In Eastern Orthodox churches, incense is very often used in front of icons and is normally highly perfumed (often with roses)" (Dom Robert LeGall 2000, 104). In certain churches, it is regularly used in the celebration of the Eucharist, symbolizing the prayers of God's people (Ps. 141:2). The pervasive odor and the gentle whirls of smoke convey an atmosphere of reverence enhancing the sense of holy space. *See also* Sacrifice; Tabernacle; Temple.

Further Reading

Benzinger, Immanuel, and Judah David Eisenstein, "Incense," http://www.jewishencyclopedia.com (accessed June 7, 2004). Hepper, F. N. "Incense," in *The Illustrated Bible Dictionary*. Sydney, Australia: Tyndale House Publishers, 1980. LeGall, Dom Robert. *Symbols of Catholicism*. New York: Assouline Publishing, 2000. Miller, Madeleine S. and J. Lane Miller. "Incense," in *Harper's Bible Dictionary*. New York: Harper and Row, 1961. Suggit, John N. "Incense," in *The Oxford Companion to the Bible*. New York: Oxford University Press, 1993.

Inheritance

(Num. 27:8–11) Under the ancient patterns of Hebrew custom, the eldest son of the **family** was the heir of the father's property and of his authority as head of the family, a custom known as *primogeniture*. This allowed the estate to remain intact, not divided among a host of children. The wife could not inherit because she was listed among the possessions of the deceased. If no male heirs survived the father's death, a daughter might inherit—as did the daughters of Zelophehad (Num. 27:8–11).

In the case of Abraham, before he had sons, he anticipated willing his estate to his slave Eliezer, even though his nephew Lot was still alive (Gen. 15:3). This followed the legal patterns of his home region in Babylonia. With the birth of two sons, Sarah insisted that Ishmael, the elder, be sent away so that the younger, Isaac, would be named the heir (Gen. 21:10). Apparently, the **birthright** could be assigned to any child the father chose, even if he was not the eldest. Further complications arose when there were concubines who bore children to the *pater familias*—as in the case of Abraham and Hagar, as well as Jacob and his several wives and concubines. If the estate was large enough, the father might choose to divide the property among all of the sons, as Jacob did.

The **rabbis** spent much time interpreting and elaborating on the law of inheritance, concerning themselves with such questions as the maintenance of unmarried daughters of the deceased and the distribution of property when no close relatives survive. The **husband**, it was determined, could inherit from the wife; but the wife could not inherit from her husband, although provision must be made for her if she remained unmarried. Numerous details regarding the disposition of the dowry, which had become a portion of the husband's estate, but which should be returned to the wife at the time of her husband's death. Among the more interesting concerns was the levirate regulation, which obligated the near relative to marry the widow of a brother who died without children, thereby providing heirs for the deceased brother's estate.

As in modern law, certain persons might lay claim to the estate by reason of agreements or contracts (Joseph Jacobs and Julius H. Greenstone 2004). Real estate and personal estate might be bequests made by oral agreement, unlike the modern stipulation that such bequests must be in writing (Marcus Jastrow, David Werner Amram 2004). This was considered a gift and might be challenged in court if the circumstances had changed since the agreement was made. Sons could, of course, be disinherited, and dying men could make deathbed bequests.

The terminology for inheritance was commonly used in Scripture in regard to the bequest of the Promised Land from God in the **covenant** with Abraham. The land became the "inheritance" of the **tribes**, to be passed down in perpetuity from father to son, remaining within the designated tribe, and returning to the proper tribe every Year of the Jubilee (Num. 36:4). Some speculate that this ideal was never really put into practice, that property was bought and sold with only modest effort to retain tribal boundaries (Roland deVaux 1961, 175). In the case of the Levites, who had no real property , their inheritance was a tenth of that tithe given to the Lord (Num.18:26). Joshua noted that "the priestly service of the Lord is their inheritance" (Josh. 18:7).

The Psalms celebrate the "delightful inheritance" of the Lord (Ps. 16:6) and note that those who live a blameless life will see their inheritance endure forever (Ps. 37:18). They use "inheritance" as a sign of God's love and worry that God seems to forsake his people (Ps. 79:1, 94:5, 106) and gives the inheritance to others. Isaiah also notes that the people have desecrated their inheritance from God but will come again to rejoice in it and inherit a double portion in their land "and everlasting joy will be theirs" (Isa. 47:6, 58:14, 61:7).

By this time, the inheritance appears to be God's blessing on Israel, not the physical land in which they live. Jeremiah also speaks of the betrayal of the inheritance. This metaphorical interpretation prevails in the New Testament in **parables**, such as that involving the renters and the murder of the heir to the inheritance (Luke 20:14; Matt. 21:38). The author of Galatians considered the inheritance as the faith, distinguishing between the **slave** and the free, Ishmael and Isaac, as the illegitimate and legitimate heirs to the faith (Gal. 3:18; 4:30). In Ephesians Paul referred to the "inheritance in the kingdom of Christ and of God" (Eph. 5:5). In Collosians he spoke of the "inheritance of the saints in the kingdom of light" (Col. 1:12). Expanding on the theme of the kingdom, the heirs are those who are the legitimate children of Christ the **King**. As the author of Hebrews noted, this is the "eternal inheritance" (Heb. 9:15). Peter spoke memorably of this as "an inheritance that can never perish, spoil or fade—kept in **heaven** for you" (1 Pet. 1:4). *See also* Birthright; Law: Property.

Further Reading

DeVaux, Roland. *Ancient Israel: Its Life and Institutions*. Grand Rapids, Mich.: William B. Eerdmans Publishing Company, 1961. Jastrow, Marcus and David Werner Amram, "Bequest," http://www. jewishencyclopedia.com (accessed August 4, 2004). Jacobs, Joseph, and Julius H. Greenstone, "Inheritance," http://www. jewishencyclopedia.com (accessed August 8, 2004).

Inns

Because of the ancient Hebrew ethic of **hospitality**, inns were not common in Old Testament times. It was the obligation of a family to host a visitor, as Abraham did his angelic guests (Gen. 18:1–8). And it was considered sinful to turn them away or abuse them—as the people of Sodom and Gomorrah did with these same guests. Even settled communities were expected to welcome a stranger, perhaps because such a person might indeed be an **angel** in disguise.

As not all cultures shared the Hebrews' customs of hospitality, some sort of shelter was apparently essential for long-distance travelers. The ancient inn was usually a sordid shelter, which housed both travellers and beasts in "enclosures or caravansaries. A 'lodging-place' accommodated Joseph's bothers on the Egyptian border" (Gen. 42:27). (Madeleine S. Miller and J. Lane Miller 1961, 40). Houses of entertainment for travelers were usually available where caravans or parties of travelers stopped for the night (Gen. 42:7, 43:21; Exod. 4:24), but that does not suggest separate buildings. It is likely that a caravansaries was nothing more than room to pitch a tent and accessibility to a well in primitive settings (Richard Gottheil and Joseph Jacobs 2004).

Scholars debate the character of the female innkeeper, who was often thought to run a house of prostitution, as was the suspicion with Rahab. Men as well as women might serve as innkeepers, also known as "hosts."

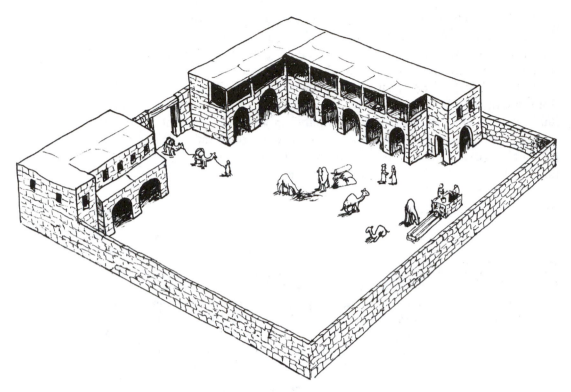

A caravansary, or place for those in a caravan to rest.

This obligations of hospitality continued into New Testament times as "love of strangers" and "to receive as a guest" (Matt .25:35ff). Apparently, when major shifts in population occurred, the usual provisions were not sufficient. Thus, when Caesar Augustus demanded that each family return to its region for the required census, the family of Joseph found there was "no room for them in the inn." M. J. Selman speculates that "Bethlehem's inn (*katalyma*) may have been a fairly simple lodging-place. It was probably not a guestroom in a private house, as no name is given, and may have been the village's common responsibility (M. J. Selman 1980, 667).

The Bethlehem inn is thought to have stood inside the **gate** above the road from Bethlehem to Hebron, its site probably covered today by the Church of the Nativity (Luke 2:7). Jesus referred to an inn to which the Good Samaritan took "a certain man" (Luke 10:34). Its traditional site is shown today on the Wilderness Road descending from Jerusalem to Jericho. "The three taverns" are mentioned by Luke in Acts 28:15 (Madeleine S. Miller and J. Lane Miller 1961, 40).

Elsewhere *katalyma* also describes a room in a private residence borrowed for the **Passover** meal (Mark 14:14; Luke 22:11). The "upper room" in which the **Pentecost** took place might also have been a rented room or perhaps the space provided by a friend.

Some **synagogues** had attached inns for poor strangers. Paul was welcomed at private homes, which also served as house-churches, with no references to staying at inns in spite of his extended travels. *See also* Hospitality.

Further Reading

Gottheil, Richard and Joseph Jacobs. "Inn," http://www.jewishencyclopedia.com (accessed December 14, 2004). Miller, Madeleine S. and J. Lane Miller, *Harper's Bible Dictionary*. New York: Harper and Row, 1961. Selman, M. J. "Hospitality," in *The Illustrated Bible Dictionary*. Sydney, Australia: Tyndale House Publishers, 1980.

Insects

(Exod. 8:16, 10:13–15; Lev.11:22, 41–42; Prov. 6:6, 30:24) Sometimes God uses the smallest creatures in **creation** for his own purposes: to free his people, to feed them, to destroy individual leaders or whole armies, or to do something as trivial as to color the robes of **kings**. Sometimes, they are the same creatures we know today; some are called "creeping things" and appear to be reptiles and tiny quadrupeds. They were labeled as having wings, "breeding abundantly," or "swarming," more by what the Jews noticed about them than by any formal pattern of classification. Insects, creatures without backbones and without prominence in the story of Creation, nevertheless had considerable influence in Scripture.

Insects in Exodus

The most dramatic insect scenes appear in the book of Exodus. Moses, acting as the spokesman for God, threatened a series of **plagues** that would fall on the people of **Egypt** if the pharaoh did not let the Israelites go. Insects were key actors in these disasters: In the second plague, the dust turned to "lice throughout all the land of Egypt" (Exod. 8:16). Lice, or perhaps fleas or sand flies, were very common and not clearly differentiated in Scripture. The Talmud does distinguish between the lice found on the head and those on the body—the former having red blood and the latter white. Both were thought to be a result of uncleanness.

This plague was followed by "swarms of flies ... and the houses of the Egyptians shall be full of swarms of flies and also the ground whereon they are" (v. 21). (Some scholars believe that these were gnats, like the ones mentioned in Matthew 23:24.) Later, after boils and hail, came the most devastating of the insect plagues—the **locusts:** "And the Lord brought an east wind upon the land all that day, and all that night; and when it was morning,

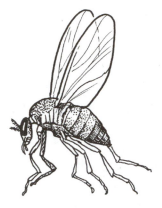

Swarms of different insects, such as gnats (shown here), flies, and locusts, were particular pests in the dry months.

the east wind brought the locusts.... they covered the face of the whole earth, so that the land was darkened; and they did eat every herb of the land, and all the fruit of the **trees** which the hail had left: and there remained not any green thing ... through all the land of Egypt" (Exod. 10:13–15).

The **manna** that God provided for the Israelites' **food** in the wilderness has also been attributed to insects. One theory is that it may be a substance of animal origin. Professor F. S. Bodenheimer believes that the manna was "the exudate of insects related to aphids and therefore analogous to 'honey dew'" (George Cansdale 1970, 237).

Types of Insects

The Hebrews' attitude toward "swarming creatures" was derived from both experience and **law**. Leviticus notes firmly: "All creatures that swarm upon the earth are detestable; they shall not be eaten. Whatever moves on its belly, and whatever moves on all fours, or whatever has many feet" (Lev. 11:41–42). The creature with many feet was probably a millipede. Other creatures mentioned with distaste are the scorpions, which along with snakes, tormented the children of Israel in the wilderness (Deut. 8:15). Like the locusts, the scorpions assume the mythic image of evil in Revelation (9:5), when the plague of locusts has scorpion tails that sting. It is likely that the locust, the cricket, the grasshopper, and the cicada were all used interchangeably, lumped as "locust" because of their destructive habits. Some believe that exception to the legal prohibition was made in the case of locusts, and they were occasionally used for food. Leviticus 11:22 notes that the locust, grasshopper, and beetle may be eaten, although they were clearly not a favorite food.

We know from Scripture that other insects were common: the spider, for instance, which Isaiah notes weaves a web that "cannot be used as **clothing**, they cannot cover themselves with what they make. Their works are works of iniquity, and deeds of violence are in their hands" (Isa. 59:5–6). The Talmud mentions that "Passion is at first like the web of a spider, but afterward it grows as strong as the ropes of a wagon." Another bit of wisdom from the Talmud is "As the cobweb obstructs the light of the sun, so does passion the light of reason" (Emil Hirsch and I. M. Casanowicz 2004).

The moth was known for its destruction of **cloth**: "For the moth will eat them up like a garment, and the worm will eat them like wool; but my deliverance will be forever and my salvation to all generations" (Isa. 51:8). Jesus also mentioned the destructive power of the moth.

The Scripture writers spoke of wasps—or perhaps hornets—as "pestilence" (cf. Deut. 7:20). In Greek and in Latin, the word for *hornet* may be the same one used for *gadfly*—an insect that Socrates used as an image of himself and his irksome words, when describing his effect on the state, which was like a horse being bitten by a gadfly. (See the "Apology" of Socrates.)

Although bees also sting, they were not classified with these other swarming insects. The Israelites, like many other ancient peoples, loved the honey **bee**, or at least the honey that the bees produced.

The flea, which was a real pest in warm countries, was undoubtedly prolific in biblical times (1 Sam. 24:15, 26:20). Its role in carrying plagues was not known but some scholars attribute the defeat of Sennacherib's army to fleas. The army was decimated during the night probably by fleas on the rats that infested the camp. The insects probably bit the soldiers and infected them with the bubonic plague. Scripture simply tells us that "the angel of the Lord went out, and smote in the camp of the Assyrians a hundred fourscore and five thousand; and when they arose early in the morning [sic], behold, they were all dead corpses" (2 Kings 190:35–36). Herodotus, the ancient historian, notes that there was an "army of field mice" that swarmed over their opponents in the night. If he is right, the plague would be a reasonable explanation (Werner Keller 1982, 280–281).

Gnats (Isa. 51:6) were called "tiny creatures" and were thought to have mouths to take in food, but no opening for evacuation. They would appear in swarms that could torture a fettered and defenseless man to death. They could also come in such a cloud that people could not keep them from entering their eyes and noses. One author notes that, although the gnat is insignificant, "it admonishes a man to humility" (Emily G. Hirsch, I. M. Casanowicz 2004).

King Herod Agrippa I died of small creatures doing great work on his body—in his case "worms." Luke tells us that "the angel of the Lord smote him, because he gave not God the glory; and he was eaten of worms, and gave up the ghost" (Acts 12:23). The term *remes* is used in the Talmud for worms that infest the intestines of humans or beasts, but different words appear elsewhere to describe the monarch's terminal illness (Emil. G. Hirsch 2004). Scholars have debated what this might mean, what diseases must have taken over his corrupt old body to bring on his hideous death.

The ant is the single insect that appears to have elicited admiration from the Jews, for its wisdom and hard work. Two Proverbs refer to this hardy creature: "Go to the ant, you lazybones: consider its ways, and be wise" (Prov. 6:6). "Four things on earth are small, yet they are exceedingly wise: the ants are a people without strength, yet they provide their food in the summer" (Prov. 30:24). This observation of the steady work and community spirit of ants led some commentators to see the great difference between the ant and the grasshopper.

The Hebrews were not particularly interested in nature for its own sake, but for the ways it impacted human life. The numerous references to small invertebrates all through Scripture suggest that they realized that even the smallest creature could be useful in the great panorama of creation. *See also* Agriculture; Bees, Honey; Exodus; Locusts.

Further Reading

Cansdale, George. *All the Animals of the Bible Lands.* Grand Rapids, Mich.: Zondervan Publishing House, 1970. Hirsch, Emil G. "Creeping Things," http://www.jewishencyclopedia.com (accessed December 20, 2004). Hirsch, Emil G. and I. M. Casanowicz. "Insects," http://www.jewishencyclopedia.com (accessed December 21, 2004). Keller, Werner. *The Bible as History.* New York: Bantam Books, 1982.

Israel

(Gen. 32:28; Hos. 1–14; Rom. 9–11) The name *Israel* was first given by God to Jacob after he struggled with the **angel**. Thus, the name is often explained as meaning "to strive with." The descendants of Jacob were thereafter called "Israelites," and the land that was promised by God and settled by the 12 families or **Tribes** of Israel was called "Israel." **King** David is usually credited with creating Israel as a political identity. Until the death of his son, Solomon, all 12 tribes were known as the "Children of Israel."

After the division between the southern kingdom of Judah and the northern kingdom of Israel (or Ephraim) in 922 B.C., the name referred only to the 10 northern tribes, which survived for another two centuries before they were taken into captivity. Israel had twice the population and three times the area of Judah and was more productive and wealthier than its southern neighbor. Its location along the strategic caravan routes contributed to its extensive foreign relationships, commercial success, and cultural sophistication and also to its lavish excesses and apostasy. Many of the **prophets** lament the decadence of their northern kinsmen (1 Kings 18:21; Hos. 1–14; Amos 7:1–15).

After Tiglath-pileser III deported numerous of the citizens of Israel to **Assyria** (2 Kings 15:29), the country went through a series of conspiracies, assassinations, and catastrophes. The final fall of Samaria was in 722 B.C. The previous year most of the leading citizens were deported and scattered all over the cities of the Medes (2 Kings 17:6). Subsequently, the king of Assyria shipped people to Samaria to replace the deported Israelites (2 Kings 17:24).

This mixed group was subsequently known as "Samaritans" and heartily despised by the Judeans. (This explains the tenor of some of Jesus's references to travels through Samaria, meetings with Samaritans, and his famous **parable** of the Good Samaritan.) The Israelites were henceforth referred to as the "Ten Lost Tribes" and their scattering as "the Diaspora." In more recent history, various peoples all over the world have laid claim to being the Ten Lost Tribes, including the Church of the Latter Day Saints—the Mormons.

In the New Testament, Israel is replaced by a less physical concept of God's chosen people. Paul speaks of the "elect" and the "saints" as Abraham's spiritual descendants (Rom. 2:28; 4:9). For Christians, Israel was replaced by the Church (Rom. 9–11).

"The Land of Israel" or "the Promised Land" refers to **Canaan**, the country that was later called "Palestine" or "the Holy Land." Ironically, the name *Palestine* derived from the arch enemies of the Israelites—the **Philistines**. Herodotus, the **Greek** historian, used the term in the fifth century when speaking of parts of Syria. The Greeks also used the term. In modern history, Palestine has been divided into the Palestinian territories and Israel, a modern political entity created by a series of treaties, culminating in the 1948 United Nations Declaration, which stated:

> The land of Israel was the birthplace of the Jewish People.
> Here their spiritual, religious, and national identity was formed.
> Here they wrote and gave the Bible to the world.

See also Canaan, Canaanites; History in the Bible; Names: Hebrews'; Philistines; Prophet.

Further Reading

Hirsch, Emil G. and J. Frederic McCurdy. "Israel, People of," http://www. jewishencyclopedia.com (accessed December 3, 2004). Miller, Madeleine S. and J. Lane Miller. "Israel," "Palestine," in *Harper's Bible Dictionary*. New York: Harper and Row, 1961.

Ivory

(2 Chron. 9:21; Ezek. 27:6; Rev.18:12) Ivory, a hard, creamy-white material that comes from the tusk of the elephant, hippopotamus, walrus, and other **animals**, derives from the Hebrew word for "tooth" (Emil G. Hirsch and Immanuel 2004). Although the Hebrews recognized ivory and used it for decoration, they had to import it, largely from Africa. The **Egyptian**s, on the other hand, lived near the elephant hunting grounds and had ready access to large supplies of ivory. Therefore they used it for fan handles, ointment boxes, statuettes of gods, **jewel** boxes, combs, chair legs, dishes, pen cases, headrests, bracelets, game boards, and other everyday items.

Because ivory was scarce and costly for the Israelites, it usually appeared in Scripture as evidence of a lavish lifestyle. Thus, when Solomon, along with his trade ally Hiram of Tyre, sent ships to Ophir in search of ivory, gold, apes, and peacocks (2 Chron. 9:21), he was signaling his great wealth and his love of conspicuous display of that wealth. His "great **throne** of ivory"(2 Kings 10:18) was probably inlaid with pieces of ivory, possibly carved as had been common since early Egyptian times (ca.1490 B.C.) This throne was overlaid with gold and flanked by 12 **lions** on six steps. "This ivory throne was probably one of the sights which dazzled the Queen of Sheba" (2 Chron. 9:1–4; Madeleine S. Miller and J. Lane Miller, 295).

Later, the use of ivory came under considerable criticism as a sign of the decadent tastes of Israel. Amos condemned the luxurious ivory couches (Amos 6:4), and Ahab was said to have built himself an "'ivory **house**,' or **palace**, the halls and chamber of which were enriched with inlaid ivory" (Emil Hirsch and Immanual Benzinger 2004). This is parallel to Homer's description of Menelaus's palace in the *Odyssey*.

Echoing Solomon's far-flung search for elegant merchandise, including ivory, Revelation, also lists "cargoes of gold, silver, precious stones and pearls; fine linen, purple, silk and scarlet cloth; every sort of citron wood, and articles of every kind made of ivory, costly wood, bronze, iron, and marble" (Rev. 18:12).

Archaeologists have uncovered splendid examples of ivories, notably the Samaria ivories, with thousands of fragments, which they have cleaned and pieced together. These may well correspond with the "ivory houses" mentioned by both Amos and Elijah, dating from the ninth or eighth centuries B.C. They appear to have been used for borders, inlay for couches, thrones, and stools, all of which reveal Egyptian influence. Some are inlaid with gold and lapis lazuli. Miller notes that "The Samaria ivories are the most revealing extant record of art created during the Hebrew monarchy. In some instances they are signed with names of craftsmen.... At Megiddo, 400 pieces of ivory were found in a half-underground treasury of three rooms of a palace suddenly abandoned c. 1150 B.C." (Madeleine S. Miller and J. Lane Miller 1961, 296).

In the history of **Christian** art, carved ivory diptychs (two-panel pictures, usually held together with hinges) became popular quite early. The **Church** assimilated the artistic styles of the **Romans** and **Greeks** in working these small ivory pieces that folded together like books. They might also be used for "listing the names of the baptized, bishops, martyrs, saints, and benefactors, and of the living and the dead who were to be prayed for" (Caryl Coleman 2004). Later, the Church used plaques of ivory for book covers, shrines, and other bits of religious paraphernalia. They carved figures of Christ, Paul, Peter, and others. The episcopal chairs were sometimes overlaid with ivory; ivory was also used for crosiers, **altars**, caskets, holy-water buckets, rosary beads, **seals**, and so on. The destruction of many of these became the work of the Reformers, who argued against the affluence of the Church and the use of graven images, which they considered idolatry. *See also* Art: Christian; Art: Hebrew; Furnishings, Household; Idols, Idolatry; Jewelry; Throne.

Further Reading

Coleman, Caryl. "Ivory," http://www.newadvent.org (accessed December 10, 2004). Hirsch, Emil G. and Immanuel Benzinger. "Ivory," http://www.jewishencyclopedia.com (accessed December 15, 2004). Miller, Madeleine S. and J. Lane Miller. "Ivory," in *Harper's Bible Dictionary*. New York: Harper and Row, 1961.

J

Jewelry

(Gen. 24:22; Judg. 8:21–27; Isa. 3:21) Among the most abundant evidences of the past are pieces of jewelry used for personal adornment. **Metals** and **gemstones** are more permanent than the other items of wearing apparel. Jewelry was often buried with the owners, hidden under homes, or stored for safekeeping in sanctuaries. From earliest times, jewelry has been given as presents, taken as spoils in war, counted as wealth before the use of coins, and used as a standard of value. Despite looting and levying by conquerors, some biblical treasures have been excavated and survive. Anklets, bracelets, earrings, necklaces, frontlets, and rings have been found in numerous burial sites, in hoards near larger buildings, and under floors and walls of cultic structures. The Hyksos' golden jewelry, the Phoenician and Egyptian jewelers' work, and the Sumerians' jewelry from the royal tombs are on display in museums in **Egypt**, **Israel**, Lebanon, and the United States. Scholars believe that Palestine had workshops throughout the country for fabricating jewelry and that the Palestinians also imported large quantities of jewelry (Patrick E. McGovern 1993, 367).

Made of gold or silver, encrusted with precious stones, jewelry has been cherished both for its materials and its craftsmanship. Ancient Israel had jewelry made of shell, bone or **ivory**; copper or bronze, glass, faience, and set with semi-precious stones such as quartz, carnelian, agate, and amethyst. In general, the ancients made more use of the abundant semiprecious than of rarer precious stones.

Jewelry in Scripture

From time immemorial, women have enjoyed wearing earrings and other decorations. Abraham's servants had bracelets and nose rings for Rebekah, probably as part of her bride-price (Gen. 24:22). Abraham and Sarah came from a culture that had already developed a sophisticated craft of jewelry-making. The Sumerians' headdresses, earrings, necklaces, and other objects are remarkable for their intricacy and beauty. Leonard Woolley found one funeral site in which the woman buried there had rings on every finger, a golden garter on her knee, and a fluted cup by her hand. Another had an elaborate headdress and several strings of beads, as well as heavy loop earrings. The combination of semi-precious stones with ivory inlay and precious metals made many of these impressive by the standards of any culture.

Scripture includes mentions of various articles of jewelry: anklets, armlets, bracelets, crescent pendants, earrings, frontlets, necklaces, nose rings, and signet rings (cf., listing in Patrick E. McGovern 1993, 367). Although Scripture suggests that only the wealthier of the ancient Israelites would

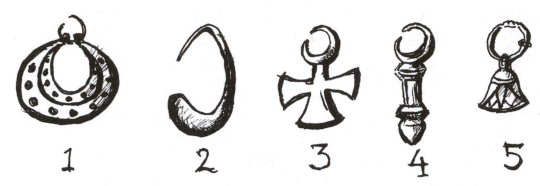

Earrings from 1. Tell el-Ajul, 1600 B.C.; 2. Canaan, 1100 B.C. (gold); 3. Assyria; 4. Assyria; 5. Egypt (with lotus design).

have owned jewels, most families owned gold coins or bracelets that could be used for currency. The most famous list of jewelry in Scripture is in Isaiah. In it he mentions all the "tinkling" accessories worn by the haughty daughters of Zion (Isa. 3:21).

Because the Israelites associated jewelry with royalty and with **marriage,** it appeared most frequently in references to the **king** or brides. Solomon's bride, for example, wears a chain on her neck (Song of Sol. 4:9). Ezekiel speaks of marriage jewelry—rigid bracelets that may have been part of the dowry (Ezek. 16:11–13).

Some of the **prophets** frowned upon jewelry because of the magical powers that it was thought to possess. Amulets and pendants, for example, were often considered good luck charms that men and women wore for protection from evil. The amulets were sometimes concealed on the body and sometimes worn as ornaments. These often had images of **idols** carved on them or were consecrated to idols. It is probably such jewelry as this that the children of Israel took from their delta neighbors and brought with them in their exodus from slavery. When Aaron told the men to break off their wives' sons', and daughters' golden earrings (Exod. 32:2) and then fashioned the Golden Calf from them, he reinforced this link between jewelry and idolatry.

Later, Hosea's adulterous wife adorned herself with earrings and jewels in preparation for her perfidious behavior (Hosea 2:13). The "headbands" or "amulets" that Isaiah mentioned (Isa. 3:18) may have been "little suns," star disc pendants signaling a worship of the stars. Some believe these four-, six-, and eight-rayed varieties of star discs were the kind of jewelry offered to goddess figures in the Near East. Crescent or horn pendants were related to the moon or war god. Others are more directly tied to the Egyptian god figures: flies, frogs, lions, rams, bulls, cats, lotus, mandrake, rosette flowers, etc. The "perfume boxes" (Isa. 3:30) they wore on their foreheads may have been a pagan form of phylactery, with texts written inside.

Among the pieces of jewelry most frequently mentioned in Scripture are the rings. Although the average man avoided lavish jewelry or ornamentation, he might wear a signet ring and carry a carved cane. The gift of the signet ring to Mordecai by Ashuerus (Esther 8:2, 8,10) was an impressive gesture of the honor in which he was held. Kings had their golden **crowns** and rings, marking their superior status. The gem **seals**, which men often wore around their necks, were sometimes beautifully designed.

Jewelers

Most of the Israelite jewelry came from either their Egyptian masters or **Canaanite** conquests. There is little evidence that the Israelites themselves were jewelers or skilled in metal crafts or carving in ancient Palestine, but they seem to have set up workshops over time as the land grew more affluent. Because both Aaron's Golden Calf and Gideon's golden ephod, with its blend of rings, crescents, and pendants (Judg. 8:21–27), proved snares for the people of God, the strictly religious leaders discouraged the cultivation of this craft.

The Tabernacle had some pieces crafted in metal, apparently by an Israelite workman, but only the breastplate of the high priest was decorated with precious gems (Exod. 28:17–20, 39:10–13). The king, of course, had a gold crown (2 Sam.12:30), and Joseph had a gold chain around his neck (Gen. 41:42). It is not clear which pieces of jewelry were made by Israelites and which by foreigners. "Artificers" and engravers of gems (Exod. 28:1) must have learned their craft from neighbors and invaders. The goldsmiths (Neh. 3:8) and silversmiths (Acts 19:24) referred to in Scripture may have been foreigners. (The guild silversmiths in Ephesus carved images of Diana, indicating they were **Greek**.) Nonetheless, the market for products of artificers was sufficiently strong in the latter days of Israel's history for local craftsmen to gather in special quarters of the cities (Wiseman 1980, 123).

In the **Temple**, the gemstones were among the most precious furnishings, a rich target for invading armies. Some of the jewels stolen by the invading armies of Nebuchadnezzar were restored when the Jews returned from the Exile. Ezekiel speaks of them in his vision of the new Temple, and they are part of John's great Revelation as well. It is hard to picture the New Jerusalem without jewels and gold.

Probably as early as the Exile, Jews became increasingly aware of the value of jewelry as portable property for a displaced people. In their relationships with the people of Mesopotamia, they surely found many skilled artisans who worked with gold and silver and precious gems. The Jews had lost their land and their **animals**, but they could carry their jewels along with them into exile. Later, the Diaspora increased this inclination to focus on the crafting and ownership of jewelry, leading to the specialization in gold-work and precious stones among the Jews.

Historians make little mention of Jewish goldsmiths before the flourishing of Jewish artisans in Spain during the Middle Ages. Under Moslem dominance, Spain attracted many of the Jews of the Diaspora. There, along with many Islamic Arabs, they polished their crafts. In various countries since that time, Jews have found that jewelry-making was a craft open to them when other fields were closed. One scholar notes that "For thousands of years Jews and other Semites have been skilled jewelers, fashioning wires of gold and silver into lacy ornaments, often studded with jewels These craftsmen can be seen today sitting with their fining pots (Prov. 17:3) in the shadowy *suks* of old Jerusalem and the jewelry stalls of Damascus" (Madeleine S. Miller and J. Lane Miller 1961 , 333). *See also* Gemstones; Metal: Gold; Metal: Silver; Weddings.

Further Reading

Blau, Ludwig. "Amulet," http://www.jewishencyclopedia.com (accessed May 19, 2005). McGovern, Patrick E. "Jewelry," *The Oxford Companion to the Bible*. New York: Oxford University Press, 1993. Miller, Madeleine S. and J. Lane Miller, "Jewelry," in *Harper's Bible Dictionary*. New York: Harper and Row, 1961. Wiseman, D. J. "Arts and Crafts," in *The Illustrated Bible Dictionary*, 3 volumes. Sydney, Australia: Tyndale House Publishers, 1980.

Judges

(Exod. 18:13–24) Until the time of Moses, Hebrew **families** had managed their own judgments, with the father determining proper conduct among their various wives, children, **slaves**, and servants. Having seen the more sophisticated legal system of **Egypt**, with its courts and judges, Moses, sought to enlarge the role of *paterfamilias,* the father figure. He became the sole judge for the thousands of people in the **tribes** that followed him out of Egypt.

After he brought the **law** down from Mt. Sinai, Moses explained it to the people and administered it, determining all kinds of cases, both large and small. Eventually, his father-in-law, Jethro, advised him to share this task with appointed judges, adjudicating only the most difficult cases himself (Exod.18:13–24). His primary role changed to teacher of the law:

And thou shalt teach them ordinances and laws, and shalt show them the way wherein they must walk, and the work that they must do. Moreover thou shalt provide out of all the people able men, such as fear God, men of truth, hating covetousness.... And let them judge the people at all seasons; and it shall be that every great matter they shall bring into thee, but every small matter they shall judge: so shall it be easier for thyself, and they shall bear the burden with thee (Exod. 18:20–22).

The Judges Listed in Scripture

The following people, not all of them judges, are named in the Book of Judges, and their exploits are described in varying detail:

Othniel (1:11–13, 3:7–11)
Ehud (3:12:30).
Shamgar (3:31)
Deborah (4–5)
Gideon (6:1–8:32)
Abimelech (8:33–9:57)
Tola (10:1–2)
Jair (10:3–5)
Jephthah (10:6–12:7)
Ibzan (12:8–10)
Elon (12:11–12)
Abdon (12:13–15) (Buckner B. Trawick 1968, 87)

The Role of Judges

Because the law was God-given, justice was administered in the name of God, who was thought to supervise the judges as well as the **priests,** serving as judges in religious cases (2 Chron. 19:6–7; Ps. 82). In fact, the court sessions were often convened in a sanctuary at a time of religious ceremony (Exod.15:25; Josh. 24:25; Ps.122:5). In the days of the monarchy, the **king** might have assumed the role of supreme judge, but it was not within his power to change the law or to circumvent it. Certain crimes—murder and adultery—were tried in public because of their impact on the purity of the community.

By the time of Joshua, judges became local leaders, sometimes even **warriors,** who were charismatic personalities, chosen by the community. Such figures as Deborah, Gideon, and Samson present a colorful indication of the various judges selected to help the people decide cases and battle their perennial enemies, the **Philistines.** In the case of Samuel, the judge was also a priest and a prophet, and the one who selected (with God's guidance) both of Israel's first two kings.

As the monarchy matured, the judges acted at different levels: local leaders, elders who judged in the city **gates,** priests who judged in the local **synagogue,** and the king who judged the cases in Jerusalem. There were also professional secular judges, probably appointed by the king.

The Deuteronomic Code, the collection of laws instituted by Moses, commanded that judges, registrars, or **scribes** be appointed in every town (Deut.16:18–20). There was no appeal from their judgment. They conducted the inquiry, heard the case, determined the verdict, and oversaw the **punishment,** which was administered in their presence (Roland deVaux 1961, 153). At the next level was the court of priests, or Levites, and the heads of Israelite families who served as the court of "first instance" for those living in Jerusalem and as a court of appeal for those from other towns. The high priest presided over this court when it dealt with sacred matters, the chief of the house of Judah for secular ones. Levites served as notaries and scribes (deVaux, 153–154). Actually, in Israel's law, there was little distinction between the sacred and secular, as all of life and law was under the guidance of Jehovah. This implies that the priests had roles in most trials, even those handled by elders or professional judges. Priests, after all, were the scholars who studied the Torah and knew the various interpretations of the law; and scribes were even called "lawyers."

Foreign dominance and captivity by **Babylon, Assyria, Persia, Greece,** and **Rome** presented new structures and new laws, leaving the Hebrews to restrict their judgments to their own law within the boundaries of the ruling regime. This sometimes resulted in baroque structures with multiple layers of judges and courts.

Much of this complexity of structure is revealed in the complex situation of Jesus's **trial** and **crucifixion.** He was arrested by a religious body, the Sanhedrin, and tried for **blasphemy** by that court. He was then handed over to the **Roman** authority, Pontius Pilate, because his was deemed a capital offense, which could be punished only by the Romans. Pilate determined that his residence in Galilee rendered him a subject of the Jewish King Herod, serving as a regent for Caesar, but Herod turned Jesus back, asserting that this was an issue for the Roman authority, which eventually and reluctantly sentenced Jesus to death by crucifixion, a punishment allotted to offenders against Rome. *See also* Government, Civil Authority; Law; Punishments.

Further Reading

DeVaux, Roland. *Ancient Israel: Its Life and Institutions*, trans by John McHugh. Grand Rapids, Mich.: William B. Eerdmans Publishing Company, 1961. Falk, Ze'ev W. *Hebrew Law in Biblical Times*. Provo, Utah: Brigham Young University Press, 2001. Trawick, Buckner B. *The Bible as Literature*. New York: Harper and Row, 1968.

R

Kenites

(Gen.15:19, Judg.1:16) The Kenites, supposedly descendants of Cain through Tubal-Cain, were one of the **tribes** of Palestine that the Hebrews met on their wanderings. Abraham noted that they possessed a part of the promised land (Gen. 15:19). At the time of the **Exodus**, the tribe inhabited the vicinity of Sinai and Horeb where Moses sought refuge (Judg. 1:16). Some believe that Jethro, who became Moses's father-in-law and good friend, was part of this tribe, although he lived in Midian; some conclude that the terms *Kenites* and *Midianites* refer to the same people, but their stories seem to differ. Another mysterious group, the Rekabites, to whom Jeremiah referred (Jer. 35), may have been connected with the Kenites as well.

This nomadic group became examples of good behavior—refusing to drink **wine**, to build **houses**, to sow seed, to plant vines, or to own property. Rather, they lived in **tents** all their lives because of an admonition handed down from their ancestors. In as much as the knowledge of the Kekabites begins with Jehu and ends with Jeremiah, it is impossible to know their exact origin or location (Roland deVaux 1961, 15).

They apparently were a tribe of prosperous "travelling tinkers" who learned **metalsmithing** long before the Israelites, and may have taught the Israelites their skills. (Their name means "belonging to the coppersmith." They traveled up and down the Wadi Arabah, supporting themselves by their work, probably using copper and iron from the Jordan Valley (Madeleine S. Miller and J. Lane Miller 1961, 364).

The Kenites befriended the Israelites, journeying with them to Palestine (Judg. 1:16), perhaps because their ancestors came from this region. Later they moved to northern Palestine (Judg. 4:11), where they still lived in the time of Saul. He rewarded them for the kindness they had shown Israel in the wilderness, sparing them from the wars he was waging. Later, David shared the spoils he took from the Amelekites with them (1 Sam. 15:6, 30:29; Emil G. Hirsch, Bernhard Pick, and George A. Barton 2004). David later incorporated them into the tribe of Judah.

A marginal group that never fully assimilated into Israelite society, the Kennites were usually seen as fierce supporters of Yahwism (2 Kings 10:15–28). Some scholars suggest that Jethro, who is identified as a Kenite (Judg.1:16; 4:11), introduced Moses to Yahweh. Moses, of course, might as easily have learned of God through the Israelites who nurtured him in his youth. Only in Numbers 24:21–22 is there an unfavorable reference to the tribe. Here it is foretold that they will perish (Paula M. McNutt 1993, 407). *See also* Canaan, Canaanites; Metal: Copper and Bronze; Tribes of Israel.

Further Reading

DeVaux, Roland. *Ancient Israel: Its Life and Institution*. Grand Rapids, Mich.: William B. Eerdmans Publishing Company, 1961. Hirsch, Emil G., Bernhard Pick, and George A. Barton. "Kenites," http://www. jewishencyclopedia. com (accessed December 10, 2004). McNutt, Paula M. "Kenites," in *The Oxford Companion to the Bible*. New York: Oxford University Press, 1993. Miller, Madeleine S. and J. Lane Miller. "Kenites," in *Harper's Bible Dictionary*. New York: Harper and Row, 1961.

Kingdom of God

(Isa. 9:2–7; Matt. 5:3–12; Mark 10:14) Derived from the concept of God as King of Kings, the idea of "kingdom of God" or the "kingdom of **Heaven**" means an ideal condition on earth in which God's will is done, "on earth as it is in Heaven." This kingdom is bound together by love, more like a devoted **family** than a traditional kingdom, filled with love that motivates people to acts of service and generosity. In this kingdom, the "first shall be last and the last shall be first," and those who enter must be like little children (Mark 10:14).

The idea traces back to God's promise to Abraham in the **covenant** relationship (Gen. 22:17, 18). The Israelites believed that God was their **king**, and that he ruled his people, provided them **laws**, and ultimately would judge them. The demands for an earthly king, in defiance of God's rule, did not eliminate the theological view that the nation of **Israel** was God's kingdom. This vision of a theocracy was reinforced by the role of the **prophets** in the selection and **anointing** of the kings and by the kings' roles in **sacrifices** and worship.

The prophets idealized the Kingdom of David as a Messianic kingdom stretching over the whole earth, with its king being "King of Kings and Lord of Lords" (Isa. 9:2–7, 16:5). This future orientation—or **apocalyptic** concept—envisioned a time to come when the Lord will reign over the whole earth, bringing a universal peace, when "he shall judge among the nations, and shall rebuke many people: and they shall beat their swords into plowshares, and their spears into pruning hooks: nation shall not lift up sword against nation, neither shall they learn war any more"(Isa. 2:4). It is envisioned as a time when all of nature will finally be at peace: "The wolf and the lamb shall feed together, and the lion shall eat straw like the bullock: and dust shall be the serpent's meat. They shall not hurt, nor destroy in all my holy mountain, saith the Lord" (Isa. 65:25). This vision of a return of God's kingdom proved a means to comfort God's people at a time of deep distress. Jeremiah presented this ideal as a spiritual fellowship, a "new covenant" that was "written on the heart" and available to all (Jer. 31:31–34).

In the **Gospels**, Jesus spoke often of the Kingdom and of the King, often using the phrasing of the prophets. He explicitly rejected the power and authority of earthly, political kingship, even when acclaimed by the crowds. Although he accepted some of the trappings of a king for his Triumphal Entry into Jerusalem, he clearly taught of a spiritual kingdom, into which one entered by being born again—as he told the Rich Young Ruler. The **Zealots**, among whom Judas Iscariot may have been numbered, were relentlessly determined to bring the kingdom to pass on earth through any means necessary. This is the reason that Pilate posed the political question to Jesus: "Art thou King of the Jews?"

Jesus responded quite clearly: "My kingdom is not of this world; if my kingdom were of this world, then would my servants fight" (John 18:36). Presenting himself as the "suffering servant" pictured in Isaiah, he was no **warrior** king, but the "Prince of Peace." The **Beatitudes** (Matt. 5:3–12) outline the characteristics of the citizens of this kingdom. Although Christ noted that the kingdom is within (Luke 17:21), and is not of this world, yet the citizens are expected to function in the sphere of this world (Matt. 6:10; Madeleine S. Miller and J. Lane Miller 1961, 368).

Much of Christ's preaching was the "good news" of the kingdom of God and its "secrets" (Luke 4:43). "By speaking of the kingdom, Jesus adopted the language of sacred Scripture (as used in **synagogues**) and of **prayer** and made that language his own. The kingdom in his preaching was not merely promised but announced as a divine activity that demanded repentance and that could be entered by participating in its divine force" (Bruce D. Chilton 1993, 408). In this dual use of the term, he proclaimed it as both the "once and future" kingdom.

Idealistic writers and artists have repeatedly found this dream of the universal peaceable kingdom attractive. Tolstoy used it for his criticism of Christians' mistaken materialization in *The Kingdom of God Is within You;* Francis Thompson wrote a poem entitled "The Kingdom of God"; and the French painter of the nineteenth century, Henri Rousseau, painted a famous forest scene with the animals all living in harmony, entitled "The Peaceable Kingdom." *See also* Day of Judgment, Day of the Lord; Kings; Messiah; Zealots.

Further Reading

Chilton, Bruce D. "Kingdom of God," in *The Oxford Companion to the Bible*. New York: Oxford University Press, 1993. Jeffrey, David Lyle. "Kingdom of God," in *A Dictionary of the Biblical Tradition in English Literature*. Grand Rapids, Mich.: William B. Eerdmans Publishing Company, 1992. Miller Madeleine S. and J. Lane Miller, "Kingdom of God," in *Harper's Bible Dictionary*. New York: Harper and Row, 1961.

Kings

(1 Sam. 6: 4–22; 2 Sam., 1 and 2 Kings, Chronicles) A richly robed man, with a **crown** on his head, a **scepter** in one hand and a spear in the other, sitting on a **throne**, surrounded by his royal court in his lavishly furnished **palace**, with his **chariots** and **warriors** outside—this is the romantic image of the king. Throughout history, it has in fact been the image of God himself, in all his power and glory. A human king, however, is simply a ruler—whether over a town, a **tribe**, or a nation. He might be no more impressive than the mayor of a small town, or he might be the conqueror of multitudes.

Early Rulers of Israel

Early usage of the word *king* in Genesis tends to refer to the leader of a city, as in the case of Melchizadek, "king of Salem." On the other hand, the "king" of **Egypt** apparently had a much larger authority. The five kings that Abraham fought, after their attack on Lot, may have been leaders of tribes on the eastern coast of the Dead Sea. The term, however, was never used for the tribe of Abraham, Isaac, or Jacob, whose leader was the father or patriarch. Only after the sojourn in Egypt did the hunger for an Israelite king begin to gnaw at the Israelites. Once settled in the Promised Land, they were for a time content to be ruled by **judges**, **priests**, and **prophets**—chosen by God and by the people. Gideon, a warrior-judge with a great popular following, refused the offer to be made king. A later judge, Abimelech, wanted with all his heart to be king of Sechem. The prophet Samuel tried to discourage the increasing demands from the people for a king to lead them.

During the time of Samuel, the people ratcheted up their clamoring for a king: The elders gathered and approached Samuel, complaining that he was old and his sons were not likely to be good successors, and they now wanted to be "like all the nations" with their own king to judge them. Samuel, concerned that they were seeking the wrong thing, prayed to the *Lord*, who told him: "Listen to all that the people are saying to you; it is not you they have rejected, but they have rejected me as their king."

Obeying God's command that he warn the elders, he explained: "This is what the king who will reign over you will do: He will take your sons and make them serve with his chariots and **horses**, and they will run in front of his chariots." He prophesied wisely that future generations would be the king's servants: his warriors, his farmers, and their daughters would be his confectioneries and cooks and bakers. The king would levy **taxes;** take their fields, **vineyards**, and **olive** gardens; and give them to his own servants. He would demand a tenth of their seed and vineyards for his officers and enslave their servants and put them to his work. He would take their **animals**, their servants, and the fruits of their labor for himself. "When that day comes, you will cry out for relief from the king you have chosen, and the Lord will not answer you in that day."

God responded to their unwise prayer: "Listen to them and give them a king."

Then, in obedience to God and the people, Samuel anointed Saul, a Benjamite, to be the new king, and the people acclaimed him with the cry that has become a tradition in many countries: "Long live the king!" Samuel **anointed** their king and then began to withdraw from his role as their leader, distressed at their decision, insisting that he was "old and gray" (1 Sam. 12:2).

As the chronicle of the kings of Israel unfurled, Samuel proved to be prescient. Even the first of the kings, Saul, turned out to be a disappointment to Israel and to God. Each of the following kings proved a disappointment in some ways, and some were total disasters.

The Selection Process

In Deuteronomy 17, the selection process for kingship had been sketched for the people: they were to appoint a man chosen by God, from among their "brothers," not a foreigner (v. 15). One curious stipulation was that he was not to acquire "a great number of horses for himself nor make the people return to Egypt to get more of them" (v. 16).

In fact, Hebrew kingship was based on two **covenants** that defined the duties of the crown toward God and toward the people: his relationship to God was "conceived as that of a vassal toward his overlord. He was installed in the office by divine election, on condition that he remain loyal to God and keep his laws (2 Sam. 23:5; Ps. 132:12). Whenever the king transgressed the terms of this covenant, he could be criticized by priests and prophets." Should he pay no heed to the warning, God might instruct the prophet to choose another, more suitable king. God would then be assumed to have rejected the unworthy ruler and to have selected a better one in his place.

His covenant with the nation functioned like a modern constitution (2 Sam. 3:21, 5:3; 2 Chron. 23:3). "The various conditions were probably recited at the accession to the throne" (Judg. 9:15; 1 Sam.10:25 referring to 8:11). His responsibilities, which were proclaimed at the time of his installation, are mirrored in Psalms 72 and 101 (Ze'ev W. Falk 2001, 31–32). The pattern for selecting and installing the kings subsequently became a tradition: the appointment by God, through a prophet, of a man who could function as a military leader, a religious leader, and a judge.

The Investiture Ceremony

The king, once chosen, was anointed by a prophet or a priest, signaling his divine selection and placing his life in a special category. David, for example, was fearful of harming "the Lord's anointed" even when Saul was seeking David's death. At Solomon's coronation, "Zadok the priest took the horn of oil from the sacred **tent** and anointed Solomon." (From this selection and installation process comes the concept of the "divine right of kings"—the king serving as God's authority on earth.)

Next came the investiture of the monarch with authority from God. The priests "sounded the trumpet and all the people shouted, 'Long live King Solomon!'" (1 Kings 1:39). In some cases, a crown was placed on his head and a scepter in his hand as signs of his authority. In the case of David's coronation (2 Sam. 12:30), he was crowned with a heavy gold crown, set with precious **stones**, pointing to the kings' temptation to be corrupted by power. He then took his seat on the throne, elevated above the others in the community.

The ceremony was followed by the proclamation to the people, who affirmed their approval by shouting, "Long live the king" (1 Sam. 10:24; 2 Sam. 16:16; 1 Kings 1:25, 34; 2 Kings 11:12), thus providing a form of democratic affirmation of his leadership.

Music apparently was often a part of the ceremony of investiture, particularly the blowing of trumpets. The king was then presented with a copy of the covenant to remind those present of their part in the covenant relationship (2 Kings 11:12).

The Role of the King

As a natural descendent of the judges, the kings functioned as the court of final appeal. For example, when Solomon had judged the two women's case for the child they both claimed, **Israel** was delighted: "they held the king in awe, because they saw that he had wisdom from God to administer justice" (1 Kings 3:28). The kings sat on "thrones of judgment" from which they responded to complaints and rendered judgments. Reference is also made to kings sitting "in the gateway" or "by the pillars," suggesting that special places were designated for the king to sit in judgment (2 Sam.19:8).

The kings also had significant roles in worship. David had brought the **Ark of the Covenant** to Zion, leading the gala parade, singing and **dancing**. He also wrote and sang many of the **Psalms**, clearly intended for use in worship. Chronicles notes that he also supervised the music, the cymbals, lyres, and harps (1 Chron. 25:6). In David's case, this role was probably a recognition of his musical abilities rather than his kingship.

Solomon built the **Temple** and then gathered the "whole assembly of Israel" and blessed them, offered **sacrifices** (including 22,000 cattle and 120,000 sheep and goats), and consecrated the courtyard in front of the Temple, offering burnt offerings, grain offerings, and the fat of the fellowship offerings" before sending the people away. "They blessed the king and then went home, joyful and glad in heart for all the good things the Lord had done for ... his people Israel" (1 Kings 8:14–66).

In performing this function, King Solomon spent a fortune, enslaved his own people, and added to his own palace "the supporting terraces, the wall of Jerusalem, and Hazor, Megiddo and Gezer"(1 Kings 9:15), thereby fulfilling the prophesy of Samuel. With power and glory for the king came taxation and servitude for the people.

In building his army and outfitting his men, King Solomon displayed his taste for opulence. His shields of hammered gold (1 Kings 10:16), his chariots and horses, his fleet of trading ships "carrying gold, silver and ivory, and apes and baboons" led the **scribe** to observe: "King Solomon was greater in riches and wisdom than all the other kings of the earth" (1 Kings 10:22–23). His main strategy for maintaining international power was less by force than by marriage. He "loved many foreign women" starting with the Pharaoh's daughter, leading eventually to **"Moabites, Ammonites, Edomites**, Sidonians, and **Hittites"** (1 Kings 10:27).

Although kings of Israel usually served for life, Saul was replaced before he died. Others were murdered or killed in battle. David survived only by suppressing his son's rebellion. The kings were usually succeeded to the throne by their sons (although at least one was succeeded by his mother). The son who assumed the throne was not necessarily the firstborn. Solomon, for example, was selected by David as his heir to the throne and provided his blessing, even though he had older brothers by David's previous wives. The rebellions and arguments among David's sons signal a confusion regarding the succession process. The division of the kingdom after Solomon's death was a further result of confusion regarding the proper pattern of accession to the throne.

The most powerful days of the united monarchy were during David's and Solomon's reigns. In a few years the king of Israel had transformed his court from Saul's **caves** and tents to Solomon's royal palaces. The bands of fellow tribesmen who defended and fought for Saul and David became Solomon's lavish retinues with warriors and architects, workmen and scholars, horsemen, counselors, and a host of others who captained his ships, selected his wardrobe, and tended his many wives and concubines.

The opulence and power of Solomon's court led to a divided kingdom. At his death, the united monarchy split into the Northern Kingdom of Israel and the Southern Kingdom of Judah. Some of the kings in those days were just and decent men, like Josiah, and many were vicious and arbitrary rulers like Ahab. They were under constant pressure from within and without The great powers of the Near East threatened them and their own prophets corrected and warned them.

Eventually, God punished the corrupt kings and the disobedient people, allowing the march of history, and foreign invaders to put an end to Israel and to Judah. When they returned from their long Exile, they had only puppet kings who served at the pleasure of foreign sovereigns.

The Kings of the Southern Kingdom (Judah)

After the death of Solomon, the kingdom was divided, with Solomon's son Rehoboam assuming the throne. This is the listing of the kings of Judah, the Scripture that notes their reigns, and the approximate dates of their time on the throne:

Zedekiah, the last of the kings of Judah, rebelled against Nebuchadnezzar, leading to the capture and destruction of Jerusalem. Zedekiah's sons were killed, the king's eyes put out, and a governor appointed to rule the land. When the Jews returned after the Exile, they no longer had their own king.

Rehoboam (922–915 B.C.)	1 Kings 12; 14:21–31.
Abijam (915–913 B.C.)	1 Kings 15:1–8.
Asa (913–873 B.C.)	1 Kings 15:9–24.
Jehoshaphat (873–849 B.C.)	1 Kings 22.
Jehoram (Joram) (849–842 B.C.)	2 Kings 8:16–24.
Ahaziah (842 B.C.)	2 Kings 8:25–29; 9:16–28.
Athaliah (842–837 B.C.) (actually a queen)	2 Kings 11.
Joash (Jehoash) (837–800 B.C.)	2 Kings 12.
Amaziah (800–783 B.C.)	2 Kings 14:1–20.
Azariah (Uzziah) (783–742 B.C.)	2 Kings 14:21–22; 15:1–7.
Jotham (750–735 B.C.)	2 Kings 15:32–38.
Ahaz (735–715 B.C.)	2 Kings 16.
Hezekiah (715–687 B.C.)	2 Kings 18–20.
Manesseh (687–642 B.C.)	2 Kings 21:1–18.
Amon (642–640 B.C.)	2 Kings 21:19–26.
Josiah (640–609 B.C.)	2 Kings 22:1–23:30.
Jehoahaz (609 B.C.)	2 Kings 23:31–34.
Jehoiakim (Eliakim) (609–598 B.C.)	2 Kings 23:34–24:5.
Jehoiachin (598 B.C.)	2 Kings 24:6–16, 25; 27:30.
Zedekiah (Mattaniah) (598–586 B.C.)	2 Kings 24:17–25:22.

The Kings of the Northern Kingdom (Israel)

When the 10 northern tribes revolted against Rehoboam, they selected Jereboam I as their leader, a bad king who set up golden calves for worship in Dan and Bethel and appointed a priesthood not descended from Levi. He made Shechem his capital. Shown here is a list of the kings of the Northern Kingdom until it came to an end. The people were taken captive and dispersed all over the **Assyrian** Empire, never to return as a group to Israel.

Jereboam I (922–901 B.C.)	1 Kings 12:12–14:20.
Nabab (901–900 B.C.)	1 Kings 14:20, 15:25–31.
Baasha (900–877 B.C.)	1 Kings 15:27–16:7.
Elah (877–876 B.C.)	1 Kings 16:8–10.
Zimri (876 B.C.)	1 Kings 16:9–20.
Omri (876–869 B.C.)	1 Kings 16:16–28.
Ahab (and Jezebel, his queen) (869–850 B.C.)	1 Kings 16:29–22:40.
Ahaziah (850–849 B.C.)	1 Kings 22:40; 2 Kings 1:1–18.
Joram (Jehoram) (849–842 B.C.)	2 Kings 1:17–9:26.
Jehu (842–815 B.C.)	2 Kings 9–10.
Jehoahaz (815–801 B.C.)	2 Kings 13:1–9.
Joash (Jehoash) (801–786 B.C.)	2 Kings 13:9–14:16.
Jeroboam II (786–746 B.C.)	2 Kings 14:23–29.
Zachariah (746–745 B.C.)	2 Kings 15:8–12.
Shallum (745 B.C.)	2 Kings 15:13–15.
Menahem (745–738 B.C.)	2 Kings 15:14–22.
Pekahiah (738–736 B.C.)	2 Kings 15:22–26.
Pekah (736–732 B.C.)	2 Kings 15:27–31.
Hoshea (732–724 B.C.)	2 Kings 17.
End of the Northern Kingdom (722 B.C.)	

(Buckner B. Trawick 1968, 117–120).

Foreign Kings

During the periods of Exile, the Israelites learned the absolute power of foreign kings. They had seen the power of the Pharaoh to enslave a people in his quest for immortality. They watched as vicious conquerors beheaded their captives and blinded the conquered king of Judah. Daniel, a courtier under various Babylonian and Median potentates, saw the inner workings of the court, and knew the perils of crossing the authorities.

The Book of Esther has one of the fullest portrayals of an oriental court, revealing the despotic nature of Xerxes's reign. In his world, the uninvited guest might be summarily put to death (Esther 4:11). The Jewish maiden, Esther, was a member of his harem, who addressed her master only when discreetly appearing before him in her royal robes, approaching the great hall by way of the inner court of the palace, while the king sat on his royal throne in the hall, facing the entrance (Esther 5:1).

Daniel discovered the same sort of power and the same level of opulence in the courts of Nebuchadnezzar. The lavish food and rich lifestyle suggested the great wealth that came to the leaders of powerful nations, who could throw slaves into fiery furnaces or make them counselors in his court—all on a whim.

The Jews finally witnessed the king's ability to do great good when Cyrus simply signed a paper that allowed them to return to Jerusalem.

The Messianic Ideal of the King

Even as the Jews discovered the warped nature of sovereign power, they retained a dream of what the true king should be. The idealistic vision of the king appears most clearly in the Psalms, where David, who was fully aware that the earthly king is but a flawed copy of the real King of Kings, proclaimed: "The Lord is King for ever and ever" (Ps. 10:16). For David, the real coronation ceremony was not for the King of Israel, but for "the Lord strong and mighty, the Lord mighty in battle"—the "King of Glory" (Ps. 24:8). He "sits enthroned over the flood; the Lord is enthroned as King forever" (Ps. 29:10). This "great King above all gods" (95:3) owns Israel's shields (89:18), and is the ultimate judge—the very source of justice (Ps. 72:1).

Isaiah continued these exalted ideas, noting that "the Lord is our judge ... our lawgiver, the Lord is our king," and our salvation (Isa. 33:22). In an increasingly powerful message, Isaiah proclaims: "This is what the Lord says— Israel's King and Redeemer, the Lord Almighty: I am the first and I am the last; apart from me there is no God" (Isa. 44:6). Jeremiah also uses royal language to reveal the awesome power of God: "But the Lord is the true God; he is the living God, the eternal King. When he is angry, the earth trembles; the nations cannot endure his wrath" (Jer. 10:10). By comparison, this king over the whole earth reduces the monarchs in their splendor to strutting puppets.

The Tradition in the Christian Era

This messianic vision of the King of Kings provides a key to understanding the **Gospels**. From the moment that the corrupt King Herod found himself threatened by "the one who has been born king of the Jews" (Matt. 2:2), through the day when Jesus entered Jerusalem like a king "gentle and riding on a **donkey**, on a colt, the foal of a donkey" (Matt 21:5), with crowds shouting, "Hosanna!" "Blessed is he who comes in the name of the Lord!" "Blessed is the King of Israel!" (John 12:13) to the final scene on the cross, with its message "This is Jesus, the King of the Jews" (Matt. 27:11, 29, 37; John 19:19); through all of his life, Jesus clearly was the Christ, the long-awaited Messiah, the King of the Jews.

Although Jesus was from the line of David, the proper heritage to be an earthly king (Matt. 1:1–16), it is clear from his preaching that he was more concerned about the Kingdom of Heaven. At the time of his Temptation, he explicitly rejected the kingdoms of this earth (Luke 4:5–7). Pilate, the Roman procurator, was worried only about any challenge to earthly kings, asking him whether he was indeed King of the Jews. To this Jesus responded, "Yes, it is as you say" (Matt. 27:11; Mark 15:2, 18, 26; Luke 23:3, 38; John 18:38, 19:3). It was for this reason that the Romans mocked him by placing on his head a crown of thorns, putting a staff in his right hand, and pretended to hail him, bowing down before him, and writing the inscription on the board above his head.

The message of the Gospels continued in the Pauline letters. As he concluded his **epistle** to Timothy, Paul said, "Now to the King eternal, immortal, invisible, the only God, be honor and glory for every and ever. Amen" (1 Tim. 1:17). In his great Revelation, John remembered the song of Moses and merged it with the "song of the Lamb": "Great and marvellous are your deeds, Lord God Almighty. Just and true are your ways, King of the ages" (Rev. 15:3). This is the Lamb that will overcome the adversaries—the warrior king—who is "Lord of lords and king of kings" (Rev. 17:14, 19:16). Thus the Scripture returns to the original message that God is the only king of his people—forever and ever.

For centuries the accepted doctrine of most Christian countries was that earthly kings were endowed with God's just authority and consequently required the obedience of their subjects (Rom. 13:1). This theory was called "the divine right of kings." This became an effective tool in maintaining authority, even when the man or woman on the throne was a heartless despot. When kings were deposed, revolutionaries were considered enemies of God's regent on earth. The real and final kingship, however, lives now and forever in God himself.

This powerful concept of a God-ordained representative on earth resonates in much religious art. The early **Church** artists portrayed God enthroned with Christ at his right hand. The kingship of God also inspired much of medieval, Renaissance, and later art and music. Among the most famous was the music of Handel's *Messiah*—"King of Kings, Lord of Lords." Moderns also resonate to the concept of God as our king. The enthusiasm for such stories and films as *Lord of the Rings* testifies to the hunger for such a blessed and benevolent authority. *See also* Court Officials; Crown; Crucifixion, Cross; History in the Bible; Kingdom of God; Messiah; Scepter; Throne.

Further Reading

DeVaux, Roland. *Ancient Israel: Its Life and Institutions.* Grand Rapids, Mich.: William B. Eerdmans Publishing Company, 1961. Falk, Ze'ev W. *Hebrew*

Law in Biblical Times. Provo, Utah: Brigham Young University Press, 2001. Trawick, Buckner B. *The Bible as Literature*. New York: Harper and Row, 1968.

King's Household

The **palace** of the king had its **court officials**, its armed guard, its treasury, etc. It would also have included the various members of the "household," those people connected to the king by **blood**, bondage, or **marriage**.

The Royal Children

The dozens, if not hundreds, of the king's children would have been a significant part of the king's household. The princesses apparently lived in the palace until they were married. They were constantly under the care of women, who dressed them in distinctive clothing (Ronald deVaux 1961, 119). There are no references in Scripture as to their tasks, although in the early days of the monarchy, they probably had tasks much like the other women. By the time of Solomon, they were probably political pawns, to be married off to monarchs as warrants of peaceful intentions. Solomon himself married a number of princesses to guarantee treaties.

The young men often had major staff requirements for their clothing, feeding, education, and preparation for adult life. The story of Absalom suggests the luxury that many of them may have known, with their own **horses** and **chariots**, concubines, and followers. They were encouraged to marry young and live independent lives, either within the palace or in their own palaces, supervising their own herds and lands. They might serve the king by performing various duties as **warriors**, governors, or in other official roles.

Preparation for their adult lives as leaders required a large staff of nurses, cooks, cleaning women, tutors, and other servants. Because they were numerous and wealthy and because the throne could be the prize inherited by only one of them, they were a constant source of intrigue, plotting against one another and the king.

The Queen, "The Great Lady," and the Harem

The term *queen* appears only once in the Old Testament, and then not for an individual. A variant does appear in referring to foreign rulers: the queen of Sheba (1 Kings 10) or the queen of Persia (Esther 2:17). The terms *mistress* or *great lady*, especially if she was the mother of the heir to the throne, do appear numerous times.

The primary wife of the king, although without power in her own right, had considerable influence over the king. If we consider Abraham to be a "king," Sarah was the first of the queens of Israel. Sarah, for example, faced all the perils of her husband, Abraham, as well as others. She was so beautiful, even in her old age, that she was taken into the pharaoh's harem and was later solicited for a minor king. Without protection from her husband, she relied entirely on God to keep her chaste. Abraham accepted Hagar, an Egyptian princess, as a tribute from the pharaoh. She became the mother of his first child, Ishmael, before being cast out of his presence at the insistence of his wife. Later patriarchs, **judges**, and kings also indulged in some form of polygamy, in spite of monogamy being the Hebrew ideal.

Scripture does not use the term *harem* in reference to the large number of wives and concubines of kings such as David or Solomon. It is clear nonetheless that their women, whether simple handmaidens or regal daughters of foreign allies, must have lived in some sort of community. For kings, the large number of beautiful and fecund bed partners "was a mark of wealth and power. It was also a luxury which few could afford, and it became the privilege of kings" (deVaux 1961, 115). Thus, Saul had at least one concubine (2 Sam. 3:7) and numerous wives; David had at least six wives, including the illicitly acquired Bathsheba, in addition to at least 10 concubines (2 Sam.11:27, 15:16, 16: 21–22, 20:3). Solomon topped them all with 700 wives and 300 concubines (Deut. 17:17). Later kings continued the practice, but with smaller numbers.

Some of these wives were married for political reasons, but some were acquired for their beauty. Their number suggests that most had little power over the king and could be forced to live "as widows" if the king were displeased with their behavior. Bathsheba was a rare figure, inciting David to kill her husband in order to marry her, then forcing him to honor his promise and make her son, Solomon, the king. After David's death, she continued to wield power with her son, who placed her on a throne beside him.

The foreign queen Jezebel also demonstrated considerable authority in the reign of her husband, Ahab. He turned a blind eye as she brought large numbers of pagan priests to her table, and meekly acquiesced when she demanded that he appropriate the vineyard of a neighbor. Her brutal death was much celebrated by the prophets.

Ataliah, the wife of Jereboam, was another such powerful queen, who seized power after her son had been killed. She put to death all the "royal seed" except for the young prince Joash (2 Kings 11:2). When the rightful heir to the throne came to power, she was summarily slain.

The harem was clearly a regular part of the Hebrew royal household. The king apparently lived separate from the women, sometimes even allotting them another palace. These women, some of whom became mothers of young princes, were honored and coveted by power-hungry courtiers. In the early days of the monarchy, the harem apparently passed on to the king's successor (2 Sam.12:8). Because David assumed Saul's harem, Absalom in turn tried to take David's concubines as an act of rebellion against his father (2 Sam.16:21–22). Solomon suspected his half-brother of a similar act of perfidy in his efforts to acquire Abishag, a member of David's harem, and had the young man killed (1 Kings 2:13–22).

The most vivid portrayal of the oriental harem appears in Esther, a narrative of the Exile. This beautiful young Jewish girl was taken to the king's palace, prepared for him through a long series of beauty treatments, and finally presented to him as queen, replacing his previous mate. Her obsequiousness in his presence and her use of feminine wiles to appeal to him on behalf of her people suggest that a queen served at the pleasure of the monarch and could be summarily cast aside or executed. The same kind of treatment is implied in the stories of the wives of the Herods. The brutal King Herod the Great repudiated most of his 10 queens and probably executed some, along with children and courtiers. The later Herods brought scandal to the countryside by their wife-trading. Herodias (the niece and wife of Herod's brother Philip) was furious with John the Baptist for taking note of her harlotry. She used her daughter Salome to charm King Herod Antipas, and then demanded John's head on a platter.

Although there are good and powerful women in Scripture, the queens do not appear to be in their number. *See also* Court Officials; History in the Bible; Kings; Palaces; Warriors.

Further Reading

DeVaux, Roland. *Ancient Israel: Its Life and Institutions.* Grand Rapids, Mich.: William B. Eerdmans Publishing Company, 1961. Jacobs, Joseph and Israel Abrahams. "Kings," http://www.jewishencyclopedia.com (accessed December 10, 2004).

L

Lamentations

(Jer. 9:16–17; Book of Lamentations) Lament for the dead formed a chief part of the funeral ceremony for Israelites. The **prophet** Jeremiah said, "Thus says Yahweh of hosts: Consider, and call for the mourning women to come; send for the skilled women to come; let them quickly raise a dirge over us" (Jer. 9:16–17). "In its simplest form it was a sharp, repeated cry, compared in Micah 1:8 to the call of the jackal or the ostrich. They cried 'Alas, alas!'" (Roland deVaux 1961, 60). Added to this might be a reference to the relationship—"my brother," or "my sister." David calls his son by name, using the customary repetition: "O my son Absalom, my son, my son Absalom! would God I had died for thee, O Absalom, my son, my son!" (2 Sam. 18:33). Earlier, David's famous lament for King Saul and his son Jonathan set the form for many of the great lamentations: "How the mighty have fallen" (2 Sam. 1:10–27). He also wrote a lament for Abner (2 Sam. 3:33–34).

It was more customary for professional men or women to compose and sing the lamentations. The trade of professional mourner was taught by women to their daughters. They used stock themes in fixed forms, which they then applied to the individual. Like our funeral sermons, they praised the dead, mourned their fate, and expressed the sorrow of the community. DeVaux notes that the scriptural laments never have religious content: they are human expressions of sympathy and regret.

The prophets' use of the form, especially the book of Lamentations, follows the pattern of the individual's lament, with Israel, her kings and enemies, presented in very human terms. Lamentations consists of five poems dealing with the siege and fall of Jerusalem (587/586 B.C.). Jerusalem is personified as a despised woman, "Her filthiness is in her skirts" (1:9). She is abandoned by her lovers, who deceived her, her **priests** and her elders, who betrayed her (1:19).

Originally the book was named for the repeated first word—"How." Several chapters begin with this exclamation of loss, echoing David's cry over Saul and Jonathan: "How doth the city sit solitary, that was full of people! How is she become as a widow!" (1:1); "How hath the Lord covered the daughter of Zion with a cloud of his anger" (2:1), or "How is the gold become dim!" The very personal, self-pitying tone of chapter 3 could have been ripped out of the book of Job—"I am a man that hath seen affliction by the rod of his wrath" (3:1).

The chapters are unusual in their structure, which is dominated by the demand they be alphabetical acrostics, perhaps for ease in memorization, perhaps as a demonstration of skill. Some (chapters 1 and 2) are made up of three-line stanzas, others (chapter 4) have two-line stanzas but are dominated by the order of the alphabet rather than by the meaning of the lament. Scholars have noted a "lament meter" or a "limping meter" in which the second of two parallel lines is shorter than the first (Delbert R. Hillers 1993, 420). This creates a sense of loss.

The form was known at least as far back as the Babylonian civilization from which the tribe of Abraham came. The Sumerians "cultivated a genre of composition known as 'lament over the ruined city and temple.' " In their songs, copied by the **scribes**, as in the later Hebrew versions, "a holy city is destroyed by a god of that city" much as Jeremiah weeps over Jerusalem (Delbert R. Hillers 1993, 420).

The author of the Book of Lamentations is usually thought to have been the prophet Jeremiah. 2 Chronicles 35:25 says: "And Jeremiah lamented for Josiah; and all the singing men and the singing women spake of Josiah in their lamentations to this day, and made them an ordinance in Israel: and, behold, they are written in the lamentations." Josephus (Antiquities x. 5, 1) has also transmitted this tradition: "But all the people mourned greatly for him [Josiah], lamenting and grieving on his account for many days: and Jeremiah the prophet composed an elegy to lament him, which is extant till this time also." In later times, the book was read on the Ninth of Ab, in memory of the destruction of the Solomonic and Herodian Temples, a custom that may have originated even during the time of Zerubbabel's Temple (Solomon Schechter and Julius Greenstone 2004).

Christian churches have sometimes used Lamentations for generalized sorrow on Good Friday, along with pleas for divine mercy. In the modern world, Mideastern funerals continue to have formal lamentation, but most of the West is more subdued and often very informal in expressions of sorrow, with mourners speaking at funerals in personal terms.

The change in the view of the **afterlife** may have had some effect on the intensity of the mourning, as Christians assume that they will meet their fellow believers in **Heaven**. Nonetheless, threnodies, or songs for the dead, have been written for a number of English poets. Milton's "Lycidas" and Shelley's "Adonais" are famous examples of a formal dirge or lament. John Donne, a cleric as well as a poet, adapted "The Lamentations of Jeremy" but dropped the acrostic typology, allowing a free translation of this cry over a captive and desolate Jerusalem, bereft of her people" (R. K. Harrison 1992, 433). The term *lamentation* or *lament* was reduced in Medieval literature to *complaint* as the concept was also trivialized so that the songs or poems focused on the lover's anguish for a lost love (C. Hugh Holman 1972, 115). In literature, the classical elegy also served as a lament for the dead, but is longer and far more contrived. *See also* Afterlife; Mourning.

Further Reading

DeVaux, Roland. *Ancient Israel: Its Life and Institutions.* Grand Rapids, Mich.: William B. Eerdmans Publishing Company, 1961. Gaster, Theodor H. *Myth* and *Legend and Custom in the Old Testament.* New York: Harper & Row, Publishers, 1918. Harrison, R. K. "Lamentations," in *A Dictionary of the Biblical Tradition in English Literature.* Grand Rapids, Mich.: William B. Eerdmans Publishing Company, 1992. Hillers, Delbert R. "Lamentations of Jeremiah, The," in *The Oxford Companion to the Bible.* New York: Oxford University Press, 1993. Hirsch, Emil G, Max Löhr, and Solomon Schechter. "Lamentations," http://www. jewishencyclopedia.com/images/spacer.gif (accessed November 20, 2004). Holman, C. Hugh. *A Handbook to Literature,* 3rd ed. New York: The Odyssey Press, 1972. Schechter, Solomon and Julius H. Greenstone. "Funeral Rites," http://www. jewishencyclopedia. com/images/spacer.gif (accessed November 20, 2004).

Lamp

(Exod. 25:3ff.; 1 Kings 7:49; 1 Sam. 3:3; 2 Kings 4:10; Dan. 5:5; Matt. 5:15; Rev. 1:13, 20) Images of light and dark run all through Scripture, most remarkably in the opening verses of Genesis and of the Gospel of John. For ancient people, who spent much of their time in darkness where even their homes were dark, the light brought by a torch, a lamp, or a candle was essential. Torches, the most primitive form of lighting, were safer and more effective out of doors. Firebrands were probably the method that Gideon and his men used to light up their pitchers and confuse the enemy (Judg. 7:16, 20). Lanterns and torches were used into Roman times and beyond.

Homes, however, called for a steadier, longer lasting, and safer form of lighting. Lamps made of clay became common in Palestinian homes. The usual Palestinian lamp was shaped like a saucer, with a pinched edge in at least one spot to hold the wick, which was made of flax (Isa. 49:3) or hemp. The saucer was filled with **olive** oil, with the wick touching the oil and hanging over the lip so that it provided a steady flame. It had to be "trimmed" regularly if it was to burn properly. Archaeologists have also uncovered ceramic lamps with multiple lips that must have been used to provide brighter light. Once the Israelites had access to **metal**, they made their lamps of bronze, copper, or gold, using the same shapes as with the ceramic lamps. They often had handles and were sometimes made into symbolic or fanciful shapes such as a lady's foot, a duck, or a hedgehog. In Hellenistic and Roman times, lamps were mass produced.

Houses and **tents** had wall niches for the lamps, sometimes on a small shelf on a stone pillar or on the supporting wood beam. Often they burned all day and all night as a protection against thieves and evil spirits (Madeleine S. Miller and J. Lane Miller 1961, 379). Sometimes they were placed on a lampstand (2 Kings 4:10), but lampstands were more common for religious uses than domestic ones. The **Tabernacle** and the **Temple**, for example, both called for lampstands and for candlesticks and candelabra.

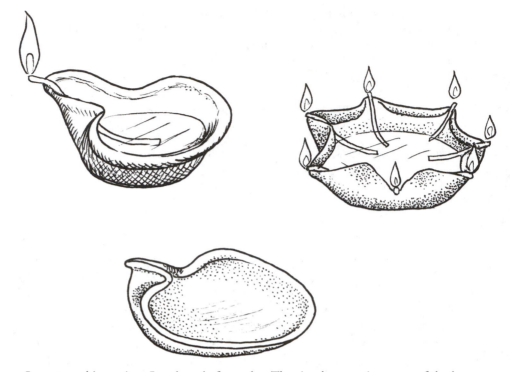

Lamps used in ancient Israel made from clay. The simplest one is a copy of the lamps found in tombs at Jericho, dating to ca. 1900 B.C., and the later versions, with a longer spout or multiple lips come from Hellenistic and later periods. The bowl of the lamp was filled with crude olive oil or other fat, and the wick (which extended out of the lip to be lighted) was made of flax or other fiber (Isa. 42:3).

The small Palestinian hand lamps were only three or four inches long, and could be carried in the palm of the hand, as the virgins did in Christ's **parable** (Matt. 25:1–13). These hand-held lamps were usually flat-bottomed, but might be rounded if designed to hang from a stick for use along dark pathways, as in the case of the Psalmist's image: "Thy word is a lamp unto my feet, and light unto my path" (Ps. 119:105).

Lamps were regularly part of worship from at least the time of the Tabernacle (Exod. 27:20). The successors of Aaron were tasked with keeping the Temple lamps trimmed and glowing for the worshipers (Num. 4:9). Cleaning and polishing the lamps were a regular part of worship preparation until Herod's Temple was destroyed (70 A.D.), when the lamps were finally carried off by the Roman conquerors. The Arch of Titus in **Rome** testifies to this final looting of the Temple treasures.

From early Pharisaic times, the lighting of the **Sabbath** lamp in Jewish homes was considered an obligation of the housewife. She waited for the sound of the trumpet, marking sundown, the beginning of the Sabbath. As she lit it, she was to say, "Blessed art Thou . . . who hast sanctified us with

Thy commandments and enjoined us to light the Sabbath lamp" (Kohler and Greenstone 2004), After this act, the housewife was to do no further work until the conclusion of the Sabbath rest the next day. Should she neglect this duty, she was open to "heavenly punishment."

The early **Christians** needed lamps to light their subterranean chambers, the catacombs, where they gathered to worship, but there is no evidence that these lamps were used for symbolic purposes until somewhat later. The discoveries of lamps from these sites indicate that they had the same designs as the Jewish lamps, although sometimes they were decorated with Christian symbols. "During all the Middle Ages the burning of lamps, or sometimes candles, before relics , shrines, statues, and other objects of devotion was considered a form of piety which greatly appealed to the alms of the faithful" (Herbert Thurston 2004).

The use of candles for liturgical purposes continues in many modern churches, where services often begin with the lighting of the candles at the **altar**. The Roman Catholic **Church** "prescribes that at least one lamp should continually burn before the tabernacle ... not only as an ornament of the altar, but for the purpose of worship. It is also a mark of honour. It is to remind the faithful of the presence of Christ, and is a profession of their love and affection. Mystically it signifies Christ, for by this material light He is represented who is the 'true light which enlighteneth every man' " (John 1:9, A. J. Schulte 2004). Christ himself spoke of his followers as the "light of the world" and warned them not to hide their light under a basket (Matt. 5:14–15).

The burning lamp was considered a symbol of life, snuffing it a symbol of death (Prov. 13:9). Some speculate that the placement of lamps in tombs may have been expressions of this. They were also a symbol of joy and prosperity as well as of God's guidance. Lamps also became a regular part of **apocalyptic** visions (Ezek. 1:13; Dan. 10:6; Zech. 4:2; Rev. 4:5). God's light shining forth in the darkness of this world has remained a powerful symbol throughout the ages. In John's great vision, Christ walks among the lampstands—the seven churches. The lamps have become a symbol of God's light as expressed through his people on earth. *See also* Hanukkah or Festival of Lights; Houses; Tabernacle; Temple.

Further Reading

Adler, Cyrus and I. M. Casanowicz. "Lamp, Perpetual," http://www.jewishencyclopedia.com (accessed December 30, 2004). Hassett, Maurice, "Early Christian Lamps," http://www.newadvent.org (accessed December 30, 2004). Kohler, Kaufumann and Julius H. Greenstone. "Lamp, Sabbath," http://www.jewishencyclopedia.com (accessed December 30, 2004). Miller, Madeleine S. and J. Lane Miller. "Lamp," in *Harper's Bible Dictionary*. New York: Harper and Row, 1961. Nixon, R. E. "Lamp, Lampstand, Lantern," in *The Illustrated Bible Dictionary.* Sydney, Australia: Tyndale House Publishers, 1980. Schulte, A. J. "Altar Lamp," http://www.newadvent.org (accessed December 30, 2004). Thurston, Herbert. "Lamp and Lampadarii," http://www.newadvent.org (accessed December 30, 2004).

Last Supper

(Matt. 26:26–29; Mark 14:22–25; Luke 22:15–20; 1 Cor. 11:17–34) The final meal that Christ ate with his **disciples**, on the eve of his arrest, trial, and **crucifixion**, is usually referred to as the "Last Supper." It is clear from the various narratives that the **meal** was eaten on a Thursday, although there is some controversy regarding the actual date of the meal. It was his celebration of the Jewish ritual of the **Passover**—the Feast of Unleavened Bread. In memory of God's redemption of his people from bondage in **Egypt**, the Jews ate unleavened **bread** and killed the paschal lamb for this ceremonial feast. The traditional opening of the Jewish meal was the breaking and distribution of bread, accompanied with a prayer of thanksgiving and the drinking of wine (I. Howard Marshall 1993, 466).

It was at this dinner in the "Upper Room" that Jesus explained the significance of the loaf and the cup, the loaf serving as a symbol of his body, the cup a symbol of his **blood**. He also told the Disciples that this was the last meal he would share with them. In his words, he referred to his "coming again," a foretaste of the Second Coming, when the **Messiah** would return to celebrate the new age with his disciples (Matt. 8:11). And he announced that one of his disciples would betray him, clearly accusing Judas, who left quickly. The Gospel writers differ slightly, but not substantially, in their telling of the event. It is a clear establishment of the New **Covenant**, replacing the Old Covenant with Moses and the **Israelites**.

Christian Beliefs and Practices

In Christianity, the Last Supper became the basis for the sacrament of the Lord's Supper, also known in various churches as Mass, Communion, and Eucharist. (The Greek term *eucharistia* means "gratefulness." The term *mass* probably derives from *missa*, a shortened form of a **blessing** and sending out into the world at the conclusion of the liturgy.) In Paul's **Epistle** to the Corinthians (1 Cor. 11:17–34), the **apostle** noted that he had "received of the Lord" the command that his followers should also partake of the bread and the wine, signifying Christ's body broken for us and his blood shed for the redemption of our sins. Paul makes it clear that this is to be a regular communal activity, not a feast but a "remembrance." He corrected the Corinthian Church, where the people apparently treated the meal as an opportunity for overeating and excessive drinking, with the richer members refusing to share their bounty with their poorer brethren.

This has led to various interpretations through the years, with the Roman Catholic **Church** holding to the idea of *transubstantiation,* the belief that the bread and wine are changed into the real body and blood of Christ—the concept of the "Real Presence." (This is based, in part, on the transformation of the water into wine at the marriage feast at Cana.) This doctrine was fully developed by the twelfth century, defined finally by Thomas Aquinas in the thirteenth century. For Lutherans and others, a somewhat different concept of *consubstantiation* describes the mystery of Christ's presence as a miraculous, but not physical, change in the elements. (Luther compared this to the **Incarnation**.) Calvin, like Luther, believed that Christ is "truly given and received" in the sacrament, stressing the relationship to the Incarnation, but he did not accept the idea of the miraculous change in the elements.

For most Protestants, the sacrament is a symbolic action, representing but not replacing the sacrifice. It is an act of remembrance and an occasion for **prayer** and soul-searching. In all cases, this is perceived as a sacrament of the Church Universal that unites the Body of Christ, the Church, with other communicants and with Christ himself.

The liturgical practices also vary from one denomination to another. It may occur at different places within the service, at different intervals, some churches having weekly communion, some restricting it to several times a year. In addition, some churches practice "closed communion" and some "open communion," depending on whether only members are invited to commune, or if it is open to any who profess belief.

The Lord's Supper in the Arts

The Lord's Supper was so significant an event in the life of Christ and so powerful a scene in his final days on earth that it has inspired numerous Christian artists. Medieval cathedrals often had portrayals of the scene in their stained glass windows. The sinister image of Judas next to the gracious figure of Jesus invited viewers to consider the lurking threat of the betrayal. The other **Disciples** were presented in groupings or rigidly in frontal positions, sometimes laughing and talking with one another, sometimes properly solemn. Various frescoes (painting in wet plaster) often decorated the walls or ceilings of the grand churches. Leonardo da Vinci's painting in Milan is the most famous of these. Numerous of the Renaissance masters portrayed the Disciples gathered around the table, with Christ at the center. Moderns have continued the tradition. Curiously, the more famous paintings depict a standard banquet table rather than the historically correct triclineum—the three-sided table where the reclining guests would have leaned on one elbow and reached for their food with the other hand.

The subject was also a standard part of medieval mystery plays, those cycles of plays that told the story of the Bible from the **Creation** to the Second Coming. In England, the Corpus Christi plays of the fourteenth and fifteenth centuries portrayed the Last Supper in dramatic form (e.g., Coventry and York).

Much of English poetry touches on the mystery of the Eucharist as practiced in the Church of England. The poems and hymns of Isaac Watts frequently refer to the sacred elements (e.g., "When I Survey the Wondrous Cross"). One of the most dramatic presentations of the doctrines appears in the Graham Greene novel *The Power and the Glory*. Greene, a twentieth-century Roman Catholic novelist, demonstrates the efficacy of the sacrament, even when performed by a degenerate "whiskey priest."

In **music**, the Lord's Supper has inspired numerous requiems—by Bach, Andrew Lloyd Weber, Handel, etc. (David Jeffrey and I. Howard Marshall 1992, 249).

In its rich symbolism, bringing together the long history of the preservation of God's people, the communal fellowship, the hunger and thirst after union with God, Jesus's last supper with his friends has become one of the most powerful sacraments of the Christian Church. *See also* Covenant; Disciples; Festivals; Meals.

Further Reading

Jeffrey, David L. and I. Howard Marshall. "Eucharist," in *A Dictionary of the Biblical Tradition in English Literature*. Grand Rapids, Mich.: William B. Eerdmans Publishing Company, 1992. Marshall, I. Howard. "Lord's Supper," in *The Oxford Companion to the Bible*. New York: Oxford University Press, 1993. Mershman, Francis. "The Last Supper," http://www.newadvent.org (accessed January 2, 2005).

Law

(**Exod. 20ff.; The Book of Deuteronomy; The Book of Leviticus**) The law of Moses, laid out in **Exodus**, Leviticus, and Deuteronomy, has proven one of the great glories of Judaism. Over the centuries, it has been studied, explained, elaborated, and shaped by thousands of **scribes** and **rabbis**, forming a vast body of learning. One of the most sacred moments in the Jewish worship ceremony is the opening of the Torah, the five books of Moses; taking it from its sanctuary; carrying it through the congregation; and reading it to the worshippers.

The Hebrew Idea of the Law

The traditional coming-of-age ritual for Jewish males is the *bar mitzvah*. Jewish boys become men when they can read the Scripture in Hebrew and discuss the law found in it, an achievement celebrated by the entire community. Although some believe that *torah* means "law," it really means "words," or "instruction," or "teaching." There are specific Hebrew words for statutes and rules. A *mitzvah*, for instance, is a commandment. The Torah does not so much present a complete code of law; rather it is "selective, illustrative, and paradigmatic" (Edward L. Greenstein 1992, 84). It deals with those rules relevant to the life of the Hebrews, assuming a great number of things about the kingship of God, the **covenant** relationship with Israel, and God's presence in the midst of his people. It gives details regarding some features of life, but it is entirely silent on others.

Unlike most other civilizations, **Israel** believed her law came directly from God. On Mt. Sinai, God gave Moses a series of laws, which he transcribed and read to the people. In their covenant becoming God's people, the Hebrews accepted the obligation to follow his law. From time to time, various Hebrew leaders repeated this ritual of reading the law to the people, thereby reaffirming their covenant relationship with God. The regular reading and studying of the Torah with the local rabbi firmly imprinted the law on the minds and hearts of the Hebrew people. When the people forgot the law or neglected it, doing "what was right in their own eyes," (Judg. 21:25) as during the time of the Judges, chaos resulted. Faithfulness to the law held the people together; forgetfulness resulted in sin and destruction.

For the devout Hebrews, the law was to be loved and cherished. The **Psalms** celebrated the law, insisting that it must be written on the hearts of God's people (Ps. 40:8). The Psalmist noted that the good man finds "delight is in the law of the Lord; and in his law he doth he meditate day and night" (Ps. 1:2). More than a dozen of the Psalms focus on the power and beauty of the law, the longest and most detailed being Psalm 119. The **Proverbs** also point to the blessedness and wisdom of studying and following the law (28:7–9; 29:9, 18; 31:5). The Hebrews were not just to obey the law, God wanted them to love it.

The **prophets** admonished the people to cherish the law, pointing to the essential role of the law in Hebrew life: Jeremiah noted that the people had failed to follow God's law and his stipulations, and "this disaster has come upon you" (Jer. 44:23). Ezekiel complained that even the **priests** "do violence to my law and profane my holy things; they do not distinguish between the holy and the common; they teach that there is no difference between the unclean and the **clean**; and they shut their eyes to the keeping of my **Sabbaths**, so that I am profaned among them" (Ezek. 22:26). The distress that they came to know, as a result of this neglect of God and his laws is manifest in **Lamentations**, where the prophet mourns the fall of Zion: "Her **gates** are sunk into the ground; he hath destroyed and broken her bars: her **king** and princes are among the

Gentiles: the law is no more; her prophets also find no vision from the Lord" (Lam. 2:9). It is clear throughout that the love of the law serves as the force that holds this people together, reflecting the love of the Lord, the giver of the law.

The Law as Presented in Scripture

This law actually consists of several parts.

The Ten Commandments

Also known as the Decalogue and found in Exodus 20, the Ten Commandments is the most famous and condensed statement of the "Ten Words" of Yahweh—the essentials of morality:

And God spake all these words, saying,
  I am the Lord thy God, which have brought thee out of the land of Egypt, out of the house of bondage.
  Thou shalt have no other gods before me.
  Thou shalt not make unto thee any graven image, or any likeness of any thing that is in heaven above, or that is in the earth beneath, or that is in the water under the earth:
  Thou shalt not bow down thyself to them, nor serve them: for I the Lord thy God am a jealous God, visiting the iniquity of the fathers upon the children unto the third and fourth generation of them that hate me;
  And showing mercy unto thousands of them that love me, and keep my commandments.
  Thou shalt not take the name of the Lord thy God in vain: for the Lord will not hold him guiltless that taketh his name in vain.
  Remember the sabbath day, to keep it holy.
  Six days shalt thou labor, and do all thy work:
  But the seventh day is the sabbath of the Lord thy God: in it thou shalt not do any work, thou, nor thy son, nor thy daughter, thy manservant, nor thy maidservant, nor thy cattle, nor thy stranger that is within thy gates.
  For in six days the Lord made heaven and earth, the sea, and all that in them is, and rested the seventh day: wherefore the Lord blessed the sabbath day, and hallowed it.
  Honor thy father and thy mother that thy days may be long upon the land which the Lord thy God giveth thee.
  Thou shalt not kill.
  Thou shalt not commit adultery.
  Thou shalt not steal.
  Thou shalt not bear false witness against thy neighbor.

Thou shalt not covet thy neighbor's house, thou shalt not covet thy
neighbor's wife, nor his manservant, nor his maidservant, nor his ox,
nor his ass, nor any thing that is thy neighbor's (Exodus 20:1–17).

Notice that these verses are divided into different commandments by different groups of Christians. Some cluster them in such a manner that the
forbidding of graven images is simply a part of the first commandment.
Some consider it a second commandment. The manner in which they are
separated and clustered makes the emphasis somewhat different, leading to
different interpretations.

Within these few verses are the underpinnings of Western jurisprudence,
the laws of property, of trial procedures, along with the theological justification for the covenant promises. They also include the foundations of
proper relationships with God and other men, which Jesus summarized for
the lawyers who asked what he considered the "chief" of the commandments. In his response, Jesus noted that two rules underlay all the law,
"Thou shalt love the Lord thy God with all thy heart, and with all thy soul
and with all thy mind. This is the first and great commandment. And the
second is like unto it, Thou shalt love thy neighbor as thyself" (Matt.
22:36–40). This summary, dividing the Ten Commandments into two
groups: four honoring God and six loving mankind. It takes the form of the
original Decalogue and rephrases it in the positive, succinct condensation
of the essential teachings of the Torah.

The Code of the Covenant

This "code"(Exod. 20:22, 23:33) brings together the main civil and
criminal laws. This section is expanded and repeated in the legislative section of Deuteronomy (Deut. 12–26), pointing to a more complex culture.
It is this section that is thought to have been discovered in the **Temple** in
the reign of Josiah (2 Kings 22:8f). When read aloud to the people, the
rediscovered law triggered a great religious revival.

The Law of Holiness

This set of regulations (Lev. 17–26) involves the rules of **sacrifices**, rituals, and the priesthood, ending with **blessings** and **curses**.

The Priestly Code

Found in the rest of Leviticus, the rules for the priesthood continue the
regulations for sacrifices, installation of priests, laws regarding purity, and
other matters.

The form in which most of the laws are recorded is "apoditic"—rules or
orders, shaped as the famous "Thou shalt" or "Thou shalt not" Occasionally, as in other legal systems, the cause or rationale may also be included,
so that the law may read, "If . . . then" These were not negotiable and could

not be changed. They came from God, who might choose to be gracious and forgive the transgressor, but a violation of the law was also seen as a sin against God. There was no wall of separation between private morality and public behavior, between sin and crime. Both were enforceable by the courts. Thus, the admonition to love parents was not simply a pious plea, but a regulation, the breach of which could be punished by death.

The History of the Law

The Hebrews were not unique among ancient peoples in their documentation of the laws that governed their community. In Babylonia, for example, Abram probably knew Hammurabi's Code long before he started his perilous journey to the Promised Land. The Hebrews, however, were unique in their blending of theological and civic matters, their belief that the law came from God, not from legislative concurrence or the command of kings. Even kings were subject to the Mosaic law, which was interpreted by the scribes and the priests in councils and **trials**.

The **family** was expected to teach the law to the children, and the rabbis or scribes undertook to complete the **education** for full manhood or citizenship in the community. The ability to read the law and discuss it resulted in an unusually high level of literacy among the Jews. It also marked them as a very distinct people, separate and apart from all others—God's Chosen People.

Over time, because of specific circumstances and questions, the scribes and others added to the law, interpreting and expanding on the biblical regulations. This "Oral Torah" was transmitted from generation to generation and later transcribed as the Mishnah, the core document of the Talmudic tradition (Robert Goldenberg 1992, 131). The Pharisees aimed at a state of levitical purity, extending the laws so that they related to every aspect of daily life. Rather than concerning themselves with special events, they sought to put routine activities under the regulation of laws, even the washing of hands before meals. By the time of Jesus, for example, the regulations involved in "keeping the Sabbath" had expanded to hundreds of specific rules about what constituted "work." The scribes, men who devoted their entire lives to the study and teaching of Scripture and to the interpretation of it, were considered a source of infinite wisdom. Unfortunately, this scrupulous concern for sanctification of all of life turned into detailed ritual and sanctimonious attitudes (Robert Goldenberg 1992, 130).

The Christian View of the Law

Jesus complained that the experts in the law "load the people down with burdens they can hardly carry, and you yourselves will not lift one finger to help them" (Luke 11:46). Although Jesus insisted that he came to fulfill the law, not to abolish it (Matt. 5:17), he sought to force a radical reconsideration of many of these additional rules that had accumulated around the law. When confronted by the scribes and **Pharisees** for plucking grain and eating it on the Sabbath, he compared the action to pulling an **ox** out of a ditch, a necessity that is a rare occurrence. He insisted that, "the Sabbath was made for man, not man for the Sabbath" (Matt. 12:1–12), calling himself "Lord of the Sabbath."

In the New Testament mentions of the law, Jesus and his followers apparently refer to the entire body of legalistic interpretations, not just the Torah. At other times, the word "law" seems to refer to all of Hebrew Scripture (cf., Rom. 3:19). Sometimes, the phrase is instead "the law and the prophets" (Matt. 5:17, 7:12, 11:13, etc.) Paul seems to have used the word to indicate both the Mosaic law given to the Hebrews at Sinai (Rom. 5:13; Gal. 3:17) and the legalistic religion, which led to reliance on good works rather than on faith (Rom 4:14; Gal 3:18; Phil 3:9).

Such reliance on careful adherence to the law—to outward obedience—was the target of much of New Testament criticism. The New Covenant was based on faith, not works. As John notes (1:17), "For the law was given through Moses; grace and truth came through Jesus Christ." This distinction between being "under law" (Rom. 6:14) and enjoying the grace of God in the **Gospel** occupies much of New Testament discussion. Nevertheless, as a student of the law himself, Paul and others saw the law as a good teacher, leading the faithful to righteousness, even though it was only a dim foreshadowing of the good things that are coming (Heb. 10:1). He noted in Romans, "Do we then overthrow the law by this faith? By no means! On the contrary, we uphold the law" (Rom. 3:31). James noted that the Christian has the "perfect law of liberty" (James 1:25), that "faith without works is dead" (2:17).

The Christians' decision at the Council of Jerusalem (Acts 15) to allow gentiles to become Christians without submission to Jewish law was a watershed moment in the history of the Church. The emphasis of most of the **epistles** became the grace of God and salvation through faith, not works. The assertion by the author of the book of Hebrews that the law had become a subject of veneration rather than a tool for redemption led many Christians to turn against Jewish legalism. Some, in fact, argued that no law at all was necessary for Christians who were "free men in Christ."

This argument found its way into Luther's 95 theses and into much of the Protestant Reformation. In *The Pilgrim's Progress,* Moses is portrayed as a villain, holding the Christian back from the path to salvation until the Pilgrim is dissuaded by Jesus. Others, such as the twentieth-century American writer Thornton Wilder, have also pictured him as a stern judge, incapable of mercy. Calvin, on the other hand, was an admirer of Moses, noting that the **miracles** certified that the law delivered by him was taught by God. Milton agreed with this view, noting that Moses was "the only lawgiver that we can believe to have been visibly taught of God" (Preface to *The Reason of Church Government*). Milton, a public figure at a crucial time in English history, wrote extensively on the issue of Christian liberty and the perils of falling into license.

In spite of this perennial debate regarding the law of Moses, it has formed the basis of most Western legal systems. Recent arguments about placing the Ten Commandments in public places, especially in court houses, have grown from this general acknowledgment of the privileged place that Hebrew law has in modern civilization. In American contemporary thought, it is its God-given basis that disturbs the adversaries, who insist that the nation's law should be separate from religion. Rooting out all Hebrew law from American jurisprudence, however, would be a Herculean task at best. *See also* Birthright; Blasphemy; Covenant; Inheritance.

Further Reading

Falk, Ze'ev W. *Hebrew Law in Biblical Times.* Provo, Utah: Brigham Young University Press, 2001. Goldenberg, Robert. "Talmud," in *Back to the Sources: Reading the Classic Jewish Texts.* New York: Simon and Schuster, Inc., 1992. Greenstein, Edward L. "Biblical Law," in *Back to the Sources: Reading the Classic Jewish Texts.* New York: Simon and Schuster, Inc., 1992. Jeffrey, David L. and John V. Fleming. "Moses," in *A Dictionary of the Biblical Tradition in English Literature.* Grand Rapids, Mich.: William B. Eerdmans Publishing Company, 1992. Slater, T. "Moral Aspects of Divine Law," http://www.newadvent.org (accessed December 29, 2004)

Law, Civil and Criminal

(Exod. 20:22–23:33; Deut. 12–26) The Code of the **Covenant** (Exod. 20:22, 23:33) brings together the main civil and criminal laws of Israel, providing specific laws for "a community of **shepherds** and peasants" (Roland deVaux 1961, 143) formed into **tribes** wandering in the wilderness under the leadership of Moses. These laws enumerated in Exodus 20 are expanded and explained in the following chapters to include the concerns of the more settled life the Israelites were to know in the Promised Land, with regulations regarding cattle, fields, **slaves, houses,** and **vineyards**. This section was then further expanded and repeated in the legislative section of Deuteronomy (Deut.12–26), pointing to an even later and more complex culture. It is this section that is thought to have been discovered in the **Temple** in the reign of Josiah (2 Kings 22:8f). When read aloud to the people, the rediscovered law triggered a great religious revival.

The major social concerns addressed in the covenant are humanitarian. The code addressed the issue of personhood, noting that everyone has a right to be secure, not only against violence or rape, but also against false accusations. Each Israelite has the dignity and right to be God's freeman and servant, rights to be safeguarded over time. He also has the right to enjoy the fruits of his own labor, to be secure in the ownership of his own property. No one, not even the king, is above the law. And no one has the right to exploit the poor, disabled, or powerless. Everyone has a place in God's social order and is to be respected for that role. Everyone, down to the humblest servant and the resident alien, including even most of the **animals**, is to have rest on God's **Sabbath**.

When charged with a crime, every citizen has free access to the **courts** and the right to a fair trial (Exod. 23:6, 8; Lev. 19:15; Deut. 1:17). The trial must conform to the **covenant** law, with appropriate procedures and limited **punishments** (Deut. 25:1–5). Those found guilty of false charges and false testimony must themselves stand trial (Exod. 20:16).

Those who could not care for themselves including **women**, slaves, the poor, and the infirm, are especially noted. Sexual laws were specifically designed for the protection of women, **marriage** laws to protect the family and the children, and many of the laws regarding **agriculture** were intended for the protection of the poor.

Jesus, like most Jews of his time, knew the law and respected it. His great concern was that the **scribes** and the **Pharisees** had become so concerned with details of tithing the last of their spices—mint, dill and cumin, that they "neglected the more important matters of the law—justice, mercy and faithfulness" (Matt. 23:23). He noted that God's people needed the law in his day as they had needed it in Moses's time: "It was because your hearts were hard that Moses wrote you this law" (Mark 10:5). At the time, he was speaking specifically of the law regarding divorce, but the reference suggests a more general criticism. As he said on another occasion, the "experts" in the law had taken away the key to knowledge. They loaded "people down with burdens they can hardly carry, and you yourselves will not lift one finger to help them" (Luke 11:46, 52). Rather than helping their weaker brethren, the leaders hindered them from entering the Kingdom of Heaven. According to Jesus, these "teachers of the law. . . . like to walk around in flowing robes and love to be greeted in the marketplaces and have the important seats in the **synagogues** and the places of honor at banquets" (Luke 20:46). With such condemnation, it is no wonder that Jesus found these same teachers to be his fiercest adversaries.

Later John continued the same theme of legalism versus good works growing out of faith, asserting that "the law was given through Moses" but "grace and truth came through Jesus Christ" (John 1:17). The code of the covenant had become so elaborate that no one could possibly keep every jot and tittle of it. The followers of Christ used this circumstance to insist on a radical reassessment of the law, and a faith in the grace and mercy of God rather than his rules and regulations. *See also* Agriculture; Covenant; Divorce; Marriage; Punishments; Women.

Further Reading

DeVaux, Roland. *Ancient Israel: Its Life and Institutions.* Grand Rapids, Mich.: William B. Eerdmans Publishing Company, 1961. Falk, Ze'ev W. *Hebrew Law in Biblical Times.* Provo, Utah: Brigham Young University Press, 2001.

Law, Dietary

Most of the day-to-day diet of the Hebrews consisted of vegetables or fruit. This law allowed snacking on **olives** or dried figs, dining on dishes of stewed beans, or eating the various **breads** and dried **grain** (Gen. 1:29). Of course, the "first fruits" belonged to God, and the poor had rights as gleaners at the end of the harvest. The fruit of a tree was forbidden for three years after its planting (Lev. 19:23–25), and there was to be celebration in Jerusalem when the harvest of the fourth year emerged, at which time the fruit was to be offered there—or the money if the distance from the orchard made the journey too difficult (Solomon Schechter, Julius H. Greenstone et al. 2004). These rules were based on the law stated in Exodus: "The first of the first-fruits of thy land thou shalt bring into the house of the Lord thy God" (Exod. 23:19). Nonetheless, in general the preparing and eating of grain or fruit were unregulated.

The products of the animal kingdom were a different story. Because **animals** had **blood**, the very stuff of life, they were seen as more significant. Animals were divided into "**clean**" and "unclean" categories, with the unclean, such as pigs or **camels**, expressly forbidden. Even the products, including the milk, that came from or were made of unclean animals were forbidden.

Only those clean animals that had been killed in the prescribed ritual manner, with the blood entirely drained and given to God, might be used for food, and only specified portions of the carcass. The meat was not to be eaten if the animal had been slaughtered and used for an idolatrous purpose, such as being consecrated to an **idol**. Nor was it to be eaten if it was designated for complete burning on the **altar**, or if it was the **priests'** portion.

If the animal should be discovered to have disease, it was forbidden, along with any milk or cheese from it. If an animal died a natural death or was killed or torn apart by beasts, it was considered impure (Exod. 22:30; Deut.13:21). Some of the neighboring peoples would cut off the limb of a still-living beast to use for food, a practice the Jews looked on "with horror" (Solomon Schechter et al. 2004). Nor could the Hebrews eat fat of oxen, sheep, or goats, although they might eat the fat of **birds** or wild animals (Lev. 7:23–25).

Birds might be eaten, but only clean birds—those that did not prey on carrion. Their eggs were also permitted, although not if there was a drop of blood in the yoke of the egg (an indication that life had begun).

Milk products were especially regulated. Three times the law noted the prohibition against seething (or simmering) a kid in its mother's milk (Exod. 23:19, 34:26; Deut. 14:21), leading the **rabbis** to believe that milk and meat products might not be cooked or eaten in any mixture. This has been expanded over the years into rules for keeping a kosher kitchen in which there are different sets of dishes for milk and meat products and a separation of the dishes so that a **meal** might include one or the other, but never both.

As the Hebrews assimilated with other peoples, the **scribes** and rabbis multiplied the prohibitions in an effort to keep their people pure. It was forbidden, for instance to eat the bread of a non-Jew or a dish cooked by a non-Jew, although bakers and servants who were not Jews might cook for the family if they were in the household and assisted by members of the family (Solomon Schechter et al. 2004).

For the Christians, who were conscientiously seeking to convert Gentiles to their faith, these Judaic regulations proved a stumbling block. Paul, in his first letter to the Corinthians, addressed the problem of eating meat that had been offered to foreign gods, suggesting that this was no longer forbidden, but the practice might still be unwise if it proved a problem for the new Christians (1 Cor. 8:13). He saw it as a matter of compassion for weaker brothers and a choice that demonstrated Christian liberty. Peter, who was deeply concerned about the weakening of the dietary laws, had a vision in which he was confronted by a host of unclean things and ordered by God to eat. When he rejected this direction, God said, "What God hath cleansed, that call not thou common" (Acts 11:9). This revelation led him to lead the party who favored relaxing the old law for the new converts. At the Council of Jerusalem, he told the gathering that God no longer put a "difference between us and them, purifying their hearts by faith. Now therefore why tempt ye God, to put a **yoke** upon the neck of the disciples, which neither our fathers nor we were able to bear?" (Acts 15:9–10).

For the Hebrews, the rituals of preparing, serving, and eating meals were closely associated with their ancient faith and culture. At some of the **feasts**, the individual foods, the lamb, the unleavened bread, the bitter herbs, etc., were symbols of the **Passover** experience. **Prayers** at the beginning and end of meals, toasts, and **songs** were all part of making the meal a sacred event. Rationalists point out that the Hebrew dietary laws have proven good for both body and soul. "Indeed many statisticians have declared that the observance of the dietary laws has greatly contributed to the longevity and physical as well as moral power of the Jewish race" (Solomon Schechter et al. 2004). Preserving the purity of the nation's diet also testified to their reverence for God. *See also* Animals; Cooking, Cooking Utensils; Food; Law; Punishments.

Further Reading

Falk, Ze'ev W. *Hebrew Law in Biblical Times*. Provo, Utah: Brigham Young University Press, 2001. Schechter, Solomon, Julius H. Greenstone, Emil G. Hirsch, and Kaufmann Kohler, "Dietary Laws," http://www.jewishencyclopedia.com (accessed November 10, 2004).

Law, Property

(Gen.1:28; Exod. 20:17, 15) Ancient Hebrew laws regarding property grew out of the **Creation** story: the earth and everything in it belongs to God; he put man in the **garden** as a caretaker, not an owner. Therefore the land is the Lord's to promise to any person or **tribes** he chooses, including Abraham and his descendants. They held it in trust from him. It was not the actual possession of individuals, even after the **Israelites** settled **Canaan** and divided the country among the tribes. Although they might transfer it, they held it in common, and it returned to its rightful steward every Sabbatical year or every Year of the Jubilee. So also were all of the personal possessions held in trust by the individual for the Lord. The owner of them nonetheless had rights under the law of Moses and the understanding of the community.

Abraham and his itinerant family had little interest in real estate. His only transaction was the purchase of the Cave of Machpelah for his family's burial place (Gen. 23). Grazing rights and water rights for wandering tribes apparently were undisputed among these **tent**-dwellers, although Abraham and Lot decided to separate their herds and their lives by a mutual agreement rather than risk quarrels. Concerned with his **animals** and servants, however, Abraham kept count of "**oxen** and asses, flocks and manservants and maidservants" (Gen. 32:6). When Lot and others were robbed and taken captive by the five **kings**, Abraham led his **warriors** to Dan to retrieve the people and their property. Unlike most conquerors of the time, he was not interested in taking booty, only in recovering for Lot what was rightly his. Abraham demonstrates through these behaviors that he brought the ideas of Mesopotamia with him, including the famous Code of Hammurabi. He understood property rights, that his flocks should be free from thieves, and that he had the right to retaliate if someone stole his or his family's goods.

Although Abraham is thought to have been an affluent trader, accustomed to traveling the caravan route from Sumer to **Egypt**, he probably relied on barter rather than coinage for his commercial dealings. In the purchase of property, he did pay in silver, a rare occurrence in ancient times. It is not clear that the contract for the land was written; the parties probably relied on the testimony of witnesses who oversaw the transaction. Contracts were clearly understood, agreed on, and honored. For generations, his family had the right to return to this land he had purchased and use it for the purposes he had originally intended. If he had accepted it as a gift, he may have relinquished this right of return.

Few items of portable property are mentioned in the early stories of Genesis, and those usually in connection with unlawful taking. Rebekah's theft of Laban's "gods" was part of a whole scene of mutual double-dealing and clever outwitting between the parsimonious Laban and the wily Jacob. The earlier argument between Jacob and Esau over the **birthright** also involved property that the firstborn would inherit. Later, Jacob's gift of a many-colored coat to his favorite son led to anger and crime. Joseph in turn pretended that Benjamin had stolen his precious cup, yet another indication that possessions were becoming increasingly important. There was also the money, which the brothers received for selling Joseph into **slavery**, which they later planned to use as payment for the **grain** they were purchasing. When dealing with foreigners, silver was apparently the standard for purchases. When the Israelites left Egypt, they took with them the **jewelry** of the Egyptians, as well as their herds—again portable property.

The increasing references to possessions, whether money, animals, or jewelry, points to the need for laws dealing with likely abuses. The commandment against theft and the numerous stipulations against damaging animals, family, servants, and other "property" were clearly aimed at people who needed to understand the obligations of holding personal property and respecting the property of others.

The relevant commandments were the prohibition against coveting **houses**, wives, servants, oxen, asses or "anything that is thy neighbor's," and "Thou shalt not steal" (Exod. 20:17, 15). In addition, a number of the regulations in the Sinai **covenant** deal with property: damaging possessions, hurting animals, stealing crops, etc. Among the more unusual and considerate are the regulations regarding allowing animals to rest on the **Sabbath** and the prohibition against sexual contact with them.

Some of the commands included in the Sinai covenant appear to be related to the life the Israelites were to lead in the land of **Canaan**, where for the first time they were established inhabitants rather than nomadic tribesmen. They took over real estate, either by conquest, purchase (Gen. 23, 33:19), or by colonization (Josh. 17:18). Much of the land was open while the cities were held by the Canaanites. Taking seriously Joshua's instruction to "settle" the land, not just conquer it, the Israelites eventually "owned" most of the country.

In anticipation of this activity, Joshua had divided the land among the tribes, assuming that the land would be preserved within families, who would live as simple farmers. The shared vision was later expressed as "every man under his vine and under his fig-tree" (1 Kings 5:5). They were reminded that the land was God's inheritance: "The land shall not be sold in perpetuity, for the land is mine, and you are strangers and sojourners with me" (Lev. 25:23). Falk notes that the "rules of Jubilee and redemption

369

were, in fact, intended to preserve the ideas of divine ownership and of the common tenancy of the family with regard to any single plot of land" (Ze'ev W. Falk 2001, 84).

The system of common property assumed that brothers would live together (Deut. 25:5) in a single household, perhaps dividing their lands by lot (Ps. 16:5–6; Prov. 1:14; Mic. 2:5). The custom of levirate **marriage**, which we see in the book of Ruth, indicates that this practice continued into the days of the **Judges**. In the famous scene at the **gate**, when Boaz confronted his kinsman to determine which of them would become the redeemer of Ruth's deceased husband's claim to the land, we have a picture of the negotiations and contract arrangements under the law. The land belonged to the family. Rather than having women in line to inherit the ownership, the law stipulated that a relative of the husband would take the widow as his wife, keeping the land within the same bloodline. This arrangement, in Boaz's case, was sealed with the exchange of a sandal, apparently an accepted means of guaranteeing the payment of the price or performing the act required. A note within the text of Ruth explains: "Now this was the manner in former time in Israel concerning redeeming and concerning changing, for to confirm all things; a man plucked off his shoe, and gave it to his neighbor: and this was a testimony in Israel" (Ruth 4:7).

The kinsman who was negotiating with Boaz was interested in redeeming the field, but not the widow. He did not want to "mar mine own inheritance" (Ruth 4:6). He was acknowledging that, if Ruth should bear him a son, that child (rather than any children of an earlier marriage) would inherit the land.

The cities were different from the small towns, with city-dwellers often taking over the property previously owned by Canaanites. "Except for the Levitical cities, which upheld the tribal tradition, the rules of Jubilee and of redemption did not apply to the cities. Instead, there existed only a limited right of redemption exercisable within one year of the date of sale" (Lev. 25:29; Ze'ev Falk 2001, 84). These breaches in the older customs gradually moved into the countryside, where land was transferred without limitations. The theft of Naboth's orchard by the king (1 Kings 21:2) is an extreme example of this violation of the law.

After the fall of both the Northern and Southern kingdoms, there was probably a more equitable distribution of wealth within Canaan. This trend was interrupted by the reintroduction of Mosaic law by Ezra, but the dispersion of the Jews shifted their focus to commercial interests rather than real estate. Generation after generation lived in an urban culture, where they rarely owned land. Rather than lament their lost heritage, the **prophets** encouraged them to learn to deal in other properties. Ezekiel saw in Nebuchadnezzar's country a vast array of opportunity to find treasures, of buying and selling, a virtual Vanity Fair. He listed in lavish detail the luxuries of this vast kingdom. For an exiled people, portable properties, not real estate, proved the key to wealth.

Christ, a man from Nazareth, a modest sized town, not from his family's traditional home, which was Bethlehem, apparently had little property and abandoned that which he had. He encouraged his **disciples** to leave even their plows or **fishing** boats and follow him. He told them he had no home—no place to lay his head. During the three years of his ministry, he depended on the **hospitality** of friends and strangers. He encouraged his followers to "take no thought what ye shall eat or what ye shall drink or wherewithal ye shall be fed" They were not to worry about thieves breaking in and stealing their possessions. Rather, they were to focus on the message of the **Kingdom of God** and the treasures that they could lay up for themselves in **Heaven**. When facing the rich young ruler, he lamented the difficulties faced by the wealthy in finding salvation. Ironically, Jesus was crucified between two thieves and buried in the tomb of a rich member of the **Sanhedrin**.

It is not surprising that Jesus's followers continued to discourage the obsession with earthly possessions. Paul even noted that the love of money was the root of all evil. For a time, the followers of Jesus held all things in common. They frequently gave generously to their neighbors. Some abandoned possessions entirely and wandered as beggars; others, like Paul, had "tent-making ministries" in which they combined work with preaching. Ownership of vast wealth was discouraged because it led invariably to covetousness and theft.

Some Christians saw vast wealth as a burden that they must divest themselves of before becoming pilgrims on their way to the City Beautiful (as in Bunyan's *Pilgrim's Progress*). Others thought that wealth was the reward God provides his faithful and a clear sign of his favor. A few came to believe that wealth was evidence of the blessings bestowed on God's elect. The arguments regarding wealth and faith have continued throughout **Church** history, some Christians taking vows of poverty and living as hermits, and others believing that the church buildings should be splendid and the clergy richly rewarded. In the conflicts of the Protestant Reformation, the debate has continued: some believing wealth to be a trap; others believing it to be a reward to the faithful and a means of benevolent deeds.

The ancient view of the Lord's ownership of the land has been replaced by elaborate systems of deeds and contracts, careful surveys of claims, and thorough searches of records. America's uncharted West and open ranges were replaced by settler's claims, and finally by strong sense of personal ownership of a house or a plot of land. Only among such groups as the Amish do we see clans still holding onto land from one generation to another, living side by side as families who see themselves as stewards of the land in the Old Testament tradition. Needless to say, the few square miles of real estate that constitute the Holy Land have been a matter of dispute and a cause of bloodshed for thousands of years. *See also* Punishments.

Further Reading

Falk, Ze'ev W. *Hebrew Law in Biblical Times*. Provo, Utah: Brigham Young University Press, 2001. Murray, J. "Law," in *The Illustrated Bible Dictionary*. Sydney, Australia: Tyndale House Publishers, 1980.

Leather

(Gen. 3:21, 25:25; 1 Kings 19:13; 2 Kings 1:8, 2:8, 13ff; Zech. 13:4; Matt. 3:4, 7:15; Acts 9:43; 10:6, 32) Leather is the skin of such animals as **sheep**, **goats**, cattle, **horses**, **camels**, or even dolphins, usually scraped clean of fur, fat, and **blood**. It is tanned and then used for a variety of purposes.

When Adam and Eve realized they were naked, they covered themselves with fig leaves, which God replaced with **animal** skins. The "coat of skins" was soon replaced with the lighter materials for **clothing**, but the mantle of skins continued to serve as the garb of the **prophets**. As late as John the Baptist, the girdle of skin was the mark of his prophetic role.

Leather had numerous uses in Old and New Testament times. It was used for the curtain of the **Tabernacle** (Exod. 26:14), for clothing (2 Kings 1:8), helmets, shields, straps, ropes, sleeping mats, containers for liquid (Gen. 21:14), sandals, and scrolls. Utensils for the daily use of a nomadic people were often made of leather, which does not break like clay or ceramic. Thus, buckets, table tops, pails, and flasks might be made of the skins of goats or sheep. Asses were hobbled with leather straps, and cows were led by means of straps tied to their horns. "Women used to tie their hair with leathern straps; and by similar means shoes and sandals were fastened to the feet, and the tefillin to the head and arm. Flagellation was performed by means of three straps—one of calfskin and two of ass' skin; straps are frequently mentioned as instruments of punishment, especially of children" (Cyrus Adler et al. 2004).

The tanning process is very ancient, dating at least to the fourth millennium B.C. The Hebrews often mentioned the red skins, apparently because the skins were reddened by the tanning process. As early as the third millennium B.C. in **Egypt**, tanned skins had been used for vellum, a flat surface for **writing**. It could be rolled into scrolls or flattened and bound like a book. Most of the manuscripts in the collection of the Dead Sea Scrolls are inscribed on leather (King and Stager 2001, 164).

The tanning process for animal skins involves cleaning and soaking the skin to remove "dirt, blood, hair, fat, and flesh. Solutions from plant extracts, lime, and tree bark facilitate the process, and the removal of hair from the hide can be accomplished by steeping it in water with salt or urine" (Philip J. King and Lawrence E. Stager 2001, 162). The process itself is not mentioned in Scripture.

There are only a few references to tanners in Scripture: Peter stayed in the house of Simon the tanner at Joppa (Acts 9:43). As a "tent-maker," Paul may have handled leather products, although some believe he worked with cloth. Because tanners handled bloody skins of dead animals and their craft involved an unpleasant odor, they were relegated to the outskirts of towns. They would have been characterized as "unclean." *See also* Animals; Clothing; Tents.

Further Reading

Adler, Cyrus, Immanuel Benzinger, and M. Seligsohn. "Leather," http://www.jewishencyclopedia.com (accessed December 31, 2004). King, Philip J. and Lawrence E. Stager. *Life in Biblical Israel.* Louisville, Ky.: Westminster John Knox Press, 2001.

Locusts

(Exod. 10; Judg. 6:5, 7:12; Isa. 33:4; Amos 4:9, 7:1; Rev. 9:3–8) The locust is an insect related to the grasshopper. It swarms through many regions of the world, destroying vegetation as it goes. Even as recently as 2004, hoards of locusts descended on **Egypt** like a great sandstorm. The chomping and crunching continued relentlessly until the once-green countryside looked like the landscape of the moon. When their devastation is complete, the whirring of their wings marks their migration to another field and another feast. The Near East knows this blight only too well, as do many other parts of the world. The Egyptians in biblical times also watched as the **plague** of the locusts when their pharaoh refused Moses's plea to let his people go (Exod. 10). The creatures destroyed their fertile fields, which were already flattened by the plague of hail.

Once the Israelites had settled in Canaan, they themselves periodically faced this same plague. This dreaded enemy of the **grain** farmer would darken the sky, invading in vast multitudes (Judg. 6:5, 7:12), occupying land 10 or 12 miles long, and four or five miles wide (Wight 1953, 176–177).

Their strength was so great that the Israelites compared them to an army: "Locusts have no **king**, but they march in ranks" (Prov. 30:27). Their vast numbers became a metaphor for multitudes: "Your plunder, O nations, is harvested as by young locusts; like a swarm

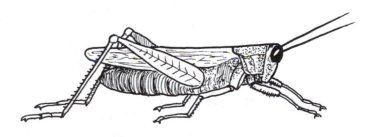

Locusts, the perennial scourge of the Middle East.

of locusts men pounce on it" (Isa. 33:4). Their mysterious appearance and disappearance, without warning, made them even more fearful. Nahum, for example, notes that some officials and guards are "like swarms of locusts that settle in the walls on a cold day—but when the sun appears they fly away, and no one knows where"(Nah. 3:17).

The **prophets** knew the entire lifecycle of the locusts, having been forced to study them for protection. Joel mentions the swarms of the locusts that come and go. Then the young locusts follow: "what the great locusts have left the young locusts have eaten; what the young locusts have left other locusts have eaten" (Joel 1:4). The King James Version of Scripture translates these stages as the "palmerworm" and "cankerworm" and "caterpillar"—apparently stages of development of the locust, which one school translates as "the gnawer," "the multiplier," "the licker," and "the devourer" (Ernest Wight 1953, 177). The manner in which the locust stripped the trees, leaving them without bark, clean and bare, "the branches thereof are made white" (Joel 1:7) led the prophet to assume that the locust's teeth were the "teeth of a lion." Amos, a herdsman and tender of trees, was especially concerned that a swarms of locusts (or grasshoppers) could totally destroy the crops of fig and olive **trees**, as well as the **vineyards** (Amos 4:9; 7:1).

Levitical **law** permitted the eating of locusts (Lev. 11:22). **Assyrians** arranged them on skewers for serving at feasts, but we do not know how the Hebrews served them (E. W. Heaton 1956, 86). We do know that John the Baptist, while he was in the wilderness, limited his diet to locusts and honey (Mark 1:6).

Their heads, which are shaped like horses' heads (Joel 2:4), led John to portray them in these dramatic words in his description of the "bottomless pit": "And there came out of the smoke locusts upon the earth: and unto them was given power, as the scorpions of the earth have power. And it was commanded them that they should not hurt the grass of the earth, neither any green thing, neither any tree; but only those men which have not the seal of God in their foreheads ... The shapes of the locusts were like unto **horses** prepared unto battle; and on their heads were as it were **crowns** like gold, and their faces were as the faces of men. And they had hair as the hair of women, and their teeth were as the teeth of lions" (Rev. 9:3–8). The description continues, making it clear that these apocalyptic locusts are the minions of Apollyon. *See also* Agriculture; Insects.

Further Reading

Heaton, E. W. *Everyday Life in Old Testament Times*. New York: Charles Scribner's Sons, 1956. Wight, Fred Hartley. *Manners and Customs of Bible Lands*. Chicago: Moody Press, 1953.

Lord's Prayer

(Matt. 6:9–13, Luke 11:2–4) Also known as the *pater noster* or "Our Father" because of the opening words, the Lord's Prayer is the model **prayer** provided for the followers of Christ. He said to them:

After this manner therefore pray ye:

Our Father which art in **heaven**, Hallowed by thy name.
Thy kingdom come. Thy will be done in earth, as it is in heaven.
Give us this day our daily **bread**.
And forgive us our debts, as we forgive our debtors.
And lead us not into temptation, but deliver us from evil: For thine is the kingdom, and the power, and the glory, for ever. Amen. (Matt. 6:9–13).

The prayer draws heavily on older Jewish prayers, using many of the same phrases common at the time (Cyrus Adler and M. H. Harris 2005). There are a number of variant translations and differences. For example, the final doxology does not appear in some manuscripts, but the powerful words (similar to 1 Chronicles 29:11) have been generally accepted for liturgical purposes.

The shorter form of the prayer, which is found in Luke, was given in response to the plea, "Lord, teach us to pray." In both Matthew's and Luke's **Gospels**, Jesus used the familiar "Abba" or "Father" for his opening, in contrast to the much more formal Old Testament addresses to God. Scholars also debate "daily" as a modifier for "bread." The Revised Version continues to use it, while suggesting "our bread for the coming day." The American Committee prefers to add "our needful bread." Different translations use "transgressions" rather than "debts." Both words are drawn from the Aramaic word for "sin"—the clear meaning of the plea for forgiveness. Some debate regarding "deliver us from evil" has led to a change in some forms to "deliver us from the evil one," suggesting Jesus is referring to Satan in this phrase.

The prayer as reported by Matthew has been used since apostolic times as a regular portion of **Church** liturgy, the most important common prayer throughout most of Christendom. It has formed a model for the seven things for which the **Christian** should pray. Augustine associated the seven gifts of the **Holy Ghost** with these petitions, and later authors related them to the seven deadly sins in Roman Catholic theology.

After the Reformation, it was referred to as the "Lord's Prayer" rather than the *pater noster* because it was recited in English. The form that most Protestants use is based on the translation in Tyndale's New Testament and was "imposed upon England" by Henry VIII in the 1549 and 1552 editions of *The Book of Common Prayer* so that congregations could learn and recite the prayer in unison (Herbert Thurston 2005). *See also* Prayer; Sermon on the Mount.

Further Reading

Adler, Cyrus and M.H. Harris. "Prayer," http://www.jewishencyclopedia.com (accessed January 20, 2005). Coggan, Donald. "Lord's Prayer," in *The Oxford Companion to the Bible*. New York: Oxford University Press, 1993. Murphy, Michael. "*Pater Noster,*" in *A Dictionary of the Biblical Tradition in English Literature*. Grand Rapids, Mich.: William B. Eerdmans Publishing Company, 1992. Thurston, Herbert. "The Lord's Prayer," http://www. newadvent.org (accessed January 2, 2005).